MERCURY READER  a custom publication

Susan Holdren, Professor
Hu Huth, Assistant Professor
Pam Kirst, Instructor
Senti Longkumer, Instructor
Freshman Composition

Pearson Custom Publishing

New York   Boston   San Francisco
London   Toronto   Sydney   Tokyo   Singapore   Madrid
Mexico City   Munich   Paris   Cape Town   Hong Kong   Montreal

Senior Vice President, Editorial and Marketing: Patrick F. Boles
Senior Sponsoring Editor: Natalie Danner
Development Editors: Mary Kate Paris and Katherine R. Gehan
Editorial Assistant: Jill Johnson
Operations Manager: Eric M. Kenney
Database Product Manager: Jennifer Berry
Rights Manager: Katie Huha
Art Director: Renée Sartell
Cover Designers: Renée Sartell and Sharon Treacy

Cover Art: "Gigantia Mountains & Sea of Cortes," by R.G.K. Photography, Copyright © Tony Stone Images; "Dime," courtesy of the Shaw Collection.

Please visit our websites at *www.pearsoncustom.com* and *www.mercuryreader.com*.

Attention bookstores: For permission to return any unsold stock, contact us at *pe-uscustomreturns@pearson.com*.

**Pearson
Custom Publishing**
is a division of

www.pearsonhighered.com

ISBN 10: 0-536-36928-3
ISBN 13: 978-0-536-36928-4

Contents

What Is Intelligence, Anyway?

Isaac Asimov

Isaac Asimov (1920–1992) was born in Russia but grew up in America. He received his Ph.D. in chemistry from Columbia University and thereafter taught biochemistry. He is better known as a science and science fiction writer. His three Foundation *novels were published in the 1950s, followed by the* Robot *novels and literally dozens of additional novels, collections of short stories, popular science books, and essays. Although educated as a scientific specialist and academician, Asimov always made it his goal to write for nonspecialized readers. He is perhaps best known for his writing—both nonfiction and fiction—that explains scientific concepts and realities for the general public. You will see that quality in this essay, which addresses the question of what intelligence really is. The essay is obviously written for a general reader and avoids technical or scientific discussion of intelligence. This approach has both strengths and weaknesses as Asimov seeks to increase our understanding of the quality of intelligence.*

1   What is intelligence, anyway? When I was in the Army, I received a kind of aptitude test that all soldiers took and, against a normal of 100, scored 160. No one at the base had ever seen a figure like that, and for two hours they made a big fuss over me. (It didn't mean anything. The next day I was still a buck private with KP as my highest duty.)

All my life I've been registering scores like that, so that I have the complacent feeling that I'm highly intelligent, and I expect other people to think so, too. Actually, though, don't such scores simply mean

Reprinted with the permission of the Estate of Isaac Asimov, c/o Ralph M. Vicinanza, Ltd.

that I am very good at answering the type of academic questions that are considered worthy of answers by the people who make up the intelligence tests—people with intellectual bents similar to mine?

For instance, I had an auto repairman once, who, on these intelligence tests, could not possibly have scored more than 80, by my estimate. I always took it for granted that I was far more intelligent than he was. Yet, when anything went wrong with my car, I hastened to him with it, watched him anxiously as he explored its vitals, and listened to his pronouncements as though they were divine oracles—and he always fixed my car.

Well then, suppose my auto repairman devised questions for an intelligence test. Or suppose a carpenter did, or a farmer, or, indeed, almost anyone but an academician. By every one of those tests, I'd prove myself a moron. And I'd *be* a moron, too. In a world where I could not use my academic training and my verbal talents but had to do something intricate or hard, working with my hands, I would do poorly. My intelligence, then, is not absolute but is a function of the society I live in and of the fact that a small subsection of that society has managed to foist itself on the rest as an arbiter of such matters.

5 Consider my auto repairman, again. He had a habit of telling me 5
jokes whenever he saw me. One time he raised his head from under the automobile hood to say, "Doc, a deaf-and-dumb guy went into a hardware store to ask for some nails. He put two fingers together on the counter and made hammering motions with the other hand. The clerk brought him a hammer. He shook his head and pointed to the two fingers he was hammering. The clerk brought him nails. He picked out the sizes he wanted, and left. Well, doc, the next guy who came in was a blind man. He wanted scissors. How do you suppose he asked for them?"

Indulgently, I lifted my right hand and made scissoring motions with my first two fingers. Whereupon my auto repairman laughed raucously and said, "Why, you dumb jerk, he used his *voice* and asked for them." Then he said, smugly, "I've been trying that on all my customers today." "Did you catch many?" I asked. "Quite a few," he said, "but I knew for sure I'd catch *you*." "Why is that?" I asked. "Because you're so goddamned educated, doc, I *knew* you couldn't be very smart."

And I have an uneasy feeling he had something there.

Questions on Meaning

1. Asimov mentions both intelligence and intelligence tests, and he seems to imply that what people generally call "intelligence" is just the ability to score well on a certain kind of test. How do you respond to his statement that such tests could also be created by a carpenter or a farmer?
2. What is the difference, according to most people's thinking, between intelligence and manual dexterity? What does Asimov here imply about such a distinction?
3. Is it important to distinguish between intelligence (ability) and knowledge (learned)? Why or why not?

Questions on Rhetorical Strategy and Style

1. The repairman gives an example of what he means by "smart." See if you can find a concrete example Asimov gives of "intelligence," and comment on the significance of your finding for the success of the essay.
2. When Asimov misses the repairman's joke and gives the wrong answer, the repairman says, apparently only half-jokingly, that Asimov isn't very smart. What is the implied difference between being intelligent and being smart? Is Asimov truly saying that he isn't smart, or how else do you explain the ending line?

Writing Assignments

1. Asimov would seem to argue that there is not an absolute quality or set of abilities we can call intelligence. Do you agree with Asimov about this? Write an essay in which you define what you mean by intelligence.
2. In this essay Asimov uses the rhetorical strategy of definition to discuss intelligence. Write an essay in which you use the strategy of definition to discuss a similar abstract trait of your own choice.

Growing Up

Russell Baker

Russell Baker (1925–) was born in a rural town in Virginia and grew up in New Jersey and Maryland. He received his B. A. in English from Johns Hopkins University in 1947 and worked as a reporter for the Baltimore Sun *and then the* New York Times. *In 1962 he began writing his "Observer" column for the* Times, *which was syndicated in over 400 newspapers for more than two decades. His topics range from the mundane everyday annoyances to serious social problems, and his style is generally casual but thoughtful. In 1979 he received the Pulitzer Prize for distinguished commentary; he received the Prize again for his autobiography* Growing Up *(1982), from which the following selection is excerpted. His collections of columns and essays include* All Things Considered *(1965),* Poor Russell's Almanac *(1972),* So This Is Depravity *(1980)* The Rescue of Miss Yaskell and Other Pipe Dreams *(1983), and* There's a Country in My Cellar *(1990). The following excerpt from his autobiography describes, with humor and insight, the moment when he decides he wants to become a writer.*

1   I began working in journalism when I was eight years old. It was my mother's idea. She wanted me to "make something" of myself and, after a levelheaded appraisal of my strengths, decided I had better start young if I was to have any chance of keeping up with the competition.

The flaw in my character which she had already spotted was lack of "gumption." My idea of a perfect afternoon was lying in front of the radio rereading my favorite Big Little Book, *Dick Tracy Meets*

Stooge Viller. My mother despised inactivity. Seeing me having a good time in repose, she was powerless to hide her disgust. "You've got no more gumption than a bump on a log," she said. "Get out in the kitchen and help Doris do those dirty dishes."

My sister Doris, though two years younger than I, had enough gumption for a dozen people. She positively enjoyed washing dishes, making beds, and cleaning the house. When she was only seven she could carry a piece of short-weighted cheese back to the A&P, threaten the manager with legal action, and come back triumphantly with the full quarter-pound we'd paid for and a few ounces extra thrown in for forgiveness. Doris could have made something of herself if she hadn't been a girl. Because of this defect, however, the best she could hope for was a career as a nurse or schoolteacher, the only work that capable females were considered up to. in those days.

This must have saddened my mother, this twist of fate that had allocated all the gumption to the daughter and left her with a son who was content with Dick Tracy and Stooge Viller. If disappointed, though, she wasted no energy on self-pity. She would make me make something of myself whether I wanted to or not. "The Lord helps those who help themselves," she said. That was the way her mind worked.

She was realistic about the difficulty. Having sized up the material the Lord had given her to mold, she didn't overestimate what she could do with it. She didn't insist that I grow up to be President of the United States.

Fifty years ago parents still asked boys if they wanted to grow up to be President, and asked it not jokingly but seriously. Many parents who were hardly more than paupers still believed their sons could do it. Abraham Lincoln had done it. We were only sixty-five years from Lincoln. Many a grandfather who walked among us could remember Lincoln's time. Men of grandfatherly age were the worst for asking if you wanted to grow up to be President. A surprising number of little boys said yes and meant it.

I was asked many times myself. No, I would say, I didn't want to grow up to be President. My mother was present during one of these interrogations. An elderly uncle, having posed the usual question and exposed my lack of interest in the Presidency, asked, "Well, what *do* you want to be when you grow up?"

I loved to pick through trash piles and collect empty bottles, tin cans with pretty labels, and discarded magazines. The most desirable job on earth sprang instantly to mind. "I want to be a garbage man," I said.

My uncle smiled, but my mother had seen the first distressing evidence of a bump budding on a log. "Have a little gumption, Russell," she said. Her calling me Russell was a signal of unhappiness. When she approved of me I was always "Buddy."

When I turned eight years old she decided that the job of starting me on the road toward making something of myself could no longer be safely delayed. "Buddy," she said one day, "I want you to come home right after school this afternoon. Somebody's coming and I want you to meet him."

When I burst in that afternoon she was in conference in the parlor with an executive of the Curtis Publishing Company. She introduced me. He bent low from the waist and shook my hand. Was it true as my mother had told him, he asked, that I longed for the opportunity to conquer the world of business?

My mother replied that I was blessed with a rare determination to make something of myself.

"That's right," I whispered.

"But have you got the grit, the character, the never-say-quit spirit it takes to succeed in business?"

My mother said I certainly did.

"That's right," I said.

He eyed me silently for a long pause, as though weighing whether I could be trusted to keep his confidence, then spoke man-to-man. Before taking a crucial step, he said, he wanted to advise me that working for the Curtis Publishing Company placed enormous responsibility on a young man. It was one of the great companies of America. Perhaps the greatest publishing house in the world. I had heard, no doubt, of the *Saturday Evening Post?*

Heard of it? My mother said that everyone in our house had heard of the *Saturday Post* and that I, in fact, read it with religious devotion.

Then doubtless he said, we were also familiar with those two monthly pillars of the magazine world, the *Ladies Home Journal* and the *Country Gentleman.*

Indeed we were familiar with them, said my mother.

Representing the *Saturday Evening Post* was one of the weightiest honors that could be bestowed in the world of business, he said. He was personally proud of being a part of that great corporation.

My mother said he had every right to be.

Again he studied me as though debating whether I was worthy of a knighthood. Finally: "Are you trustworthy?"

My mother said I was the soul of honesty.

"That's right," I said.

The caller smiled for the first time. He told me I was a lucky young man. He admired my spunk. Too many young men thought life was all play. Those young men would not go far in this world. Only a young man willing to work and save and keep his face washed and his hair neatly combed could hope to come out on top in a world such as ours. Did I truly and sincerely believe that I was such a young man?

"He certainly does," said my mother.

"That's right," I said.

He said he had been so impressed by what he had seen of me that he was going to make me a representative of the Curtis Publishing Company. On the following Tuesday, he said, thirty freshly printed copies of the *Saturday Evening Post* would be delivered at our door. I would place these magazines, still damp with the ink of the presses, in a handsome canvas bag, sling it over my shoulder, and set forth through the streets to bring the best in journalism, fiction, and cartoons to the American public.

He had brought the canvas bag with him. He presented it with reverence fit for a chasuble. He showed me how to drape the sling over my left shoulder and across the chest so that the pouch lay easily accessible to my right hand, allowing the best in journalism, fiction, and cartoons to be swiftly extracted and sold to a citizenry whose happiness and security depended upon us soldiers of the free press.

The following Tuesday I raced home from school, put the canvas bag over my shoulder, dumped the magazines in, and, tilting to the left to balance their weight on my right hip, embarked on the highway of journalism.

We lived in Belleville, New Jersey, a commuter town at the northern fringe of Newark. It was 1932, the bleakest year of the Depression. My father had died two years before, leaving us with a few pieces of Sears, Roebuck furniture and not much else, and my mother had taken Doris and me to live with one of her younger brothers. This was my Uncle Allen. Uncle Allen had made something of himself by 1932.

As salesman for a soft-drink bottler in Newark, he had an income of $30 a week; wore pearl-gray spats, detachable collars, and a three-piece suit; was happily married; and took in threadbare relatives.

With my load of magazines I headed toward Belleville Avenue. That's where the people were. There were two filling stations at the intersection with Union Avenue, as well as an A&P, a fruit stand, a bakery, a barber shop, Zuccarelli's drugstore, and a diner shaped like a railroad car. For several hours I made myself highly visible, shifting position now and then from corner to corner, from shop window to shop window, to make sure everyone could see the heavy black lettering on the canvas bag that said THE SATURDAY EVENING POST. When the angle of the light indicated it was suppertime, I walked back to the house.

"How many did you sell, Buddy?" my mother asked.

35 "None."

"Where did you go?"

"The corner of Belleville and Union Avenues."

"What did you do?"

"Stood on the corner waiting for somebody to buy a *Saturday Evening Post*."

40 "You just stood there?"

"Didn't sell a single one."

"For God's sake, Russell!"

Uncle Allen intervened. "I've been thinking about it for some time," he said, "and I've about decided to take the *Post* regularly. Put me down as a regular customer." I handed him a magazine and he paid me a nickel. It was the first nickel I earned.

Afterwards my mother instructed me in salesmanship. I would have to ring doorbells, address adults with charming self-confidence, and break down resistance with a sales talk pointing out that no one, no matter how poor, could afford to be without the *Saturday Evening Post* in the home.

45 I told my mother I'd changed my mind about wanting to succeed in the magazine business.

"If you think I'm going to raise a good-for-nothing," she replied, "you've got another think coming." She told me to hit the streets with the canvas bag and start ringing doorbells the instant school was out next day. When I objected that I didn't feel any aptitude for salesmanship, she asked how I'd like to lend her my leather belt so she could whack some sense into me, I bowed to superior will and entered journalism with a heavy heart.

My mother and I had fought this battle almost as long as I could remember. It probably started even before memory began, when I was a country child in northern Virginia and my mother, dissatisfied with my father's plain workman's life, determined that I would not grow up like him and his people, with calluses on their hands, overalls on their backs, and fourth-grade educations in their heads. She had fancier ideas of life's possibilities. Introducing me to the *Saturday Evening Post,* she was trying to wean me as early as possible from my father's world where men left with their lunch pails at sunup, worked with their hands until the grime ate into the pores, and died with a few sticks of mail-order furniture as their legacy. In my mother's vision of the better life there were desks and white collars, well-pressed suits, evenings of reading and lively talk, and perhaps—if a man were very, very lucky and hit the jackpot, really made something important of himself—perhaps there might be a fantastic salary of $5,000 a year to support a big house and a Buick with a rumble seat and a vacation in Atlantic City.

And so I set forth with my sack of magazines. I was afraid of the dogs that snarled behind the doors of potential buyers. I was timid about ringing the doorbells of strangers, relieved when no one came to the door, and scared when someone did. Despite my mother's instructions, I could not deliver an engaging sales pitch. When a door opened I simply asked, "Want to buy a *Saturday Evening Post?*" In Belleville few persons did. It was a town of 30,000 people, and most weeks I rang a fair majority of its doorbells. But I rarely sold my thirty copies. Some weeks I canvassed the entire town for six days and still had four or five unsold magazines on Monday evening; then I dreaded the coming of Tuesday morning, when a batch of thirty fresh *Saturday Evening Post*s was due at the front door.

"Better get out there and sell the rest of those magazines tonight," My mother would say.

I usually posted myself then at a busy intersection where a traffic light controlled commuter flow from Newark. When the light turned red I stood on the curb and shouted my sales pitch at the motorists.

"Want to buy a *Saturday Evening Post?*"

One rainy night when car windows were sealed against me I came back soaked and with not a single sale to report. My mother beckoned to Doris.

"Go back down there with Buddy and show him how to sell these magazines," she said.

Brimming with zest, Doris, who was then seven years old, returned with me to the corner. She took a magazine from the bag, and when the light turned red she strode to the nearest car and banged her small fist against the closed window. The driver, probably startled at what he took to be a midget assaulting his car, lowered the window to stare, and Doris thrust a *Saturday Evening Post* at him.

55 "You need this magazine," she piped, "and it only costs a nickel." 55

Her salesmanship was irresistible. Before the light changed half a dozen times she disposed of the entire batch. I didn't feel humiliated. To the contrary, I was so happy I decided to give her a treat. Leading her to the vegetable store on Belleville Avenue, I bought three apples, which cost a nickel, and gave her one.

"You shouldn't waste money," she said.

"Eat your apple." I bit into mine.

"You shouldn't eat before supper," she said. "It'll spoil your appetite."

60 Back at the house that evening, she dutifully reported me for 60 wasting a nickel. Instead of a scolding, I was rewarded with a pat on the back for having the good sense to buy fruit instead of candy. My mother reached into her bottomless supply of maxims and told Doris, "An apple a day keeps the doctor away."

By the time I was ten I had learned all my mother's maxims by heart. Asking to stay up past normal bedtime, I knew that a refusal would be explained with, "Early to bed and early to rise, makes a man healthy, wealthy, and wise." If I whimpered about having to get up early in the morning, I could depend on her to say, "The early bird gets the worm."

The one I most despised was, "If at first you don't succeed, try, try again." This was the battle cry with which she constantly sent me back into the hopeless struggle whenever I moaned that I had rung every doorbell in town and knew there wasn't a single potential buyer left in Belleville that week. After listening to my explanation, she handed me the canvas bag and said, "If at first you don't succeed . . . "

Three years in that job, which I would gladly have quit after the first day except for her insistence, produced at least one valuable result. My mother finally concluded that I would never make something of myself by pursuing a life in business and started considering careers that demanded less competitive zeal.

One evening when I was eleven I brought home a short "composition" on my summer vacation which the teacher had graded with an A. Reading it with her own schoolteacher's eye, my mother agreed that it was top-drawer seventh grade prose and complimented me. Nothing more was said about it immediately, but a new idea had taken life in her mind. Halfway through supper she suddenly interrupted the conversation.

65 "Buddy," she said, "maybe you could be a writer." 65

I clasped the idea to my heart. I had never met a writer, had shown no previous urge to write, and hadn't a notion how to become a writer, but I loved stories and thought that making up stories must surely be almost as much fun as reading them. Best of all, though, and what really gladdened my heart, was the ease of the writer's life. Writers did not have to trudge through the town peddling from canvas bags, defending themselves against angry dogs, being rejected by surly strangers. Writers did not have to ring doorbells. So far as I could make out, what writers did couldn't even be classified as work.

I was enchanted. Writers didn't have to have any gumption at all. I did not dare tell anybody for fear of being laughed at in the schoolyard, but secretly I decided that what I'd like to be when I grew up was a writer.

Questions on Meaning

1. What does Baker mean by "gumption"? How does he use that word throughout this story to classify activities he doesn't like, just as he wants to be a writer because it does not require having gumption?
2. How would you characterize Baker's relationship with his mother? His sister? What descriptions in the narrative give you that impression?
3. Do you agree with Baker's assessment of writing: "what writers did couldn't even be classified as work"? In what sense, to him at least, is it *not* work?

Questions on Rhetorical Strategy and Style

1. Describe the tone of this story. Identify some of the language Baker uses that reveals his attitude toward his subject.
2. This section of Baker's autobiography is mostly written as narration. What specific writing techniques does Baker use to keep us interested?
3. What is the effect of Baker's sense of humor? For example, when he seems to make fun of his mother for having a maxim for every occasion, what is he really satirizing—his mother as a person, or an attitude toward life? What gives you that impression?

Writing Assignments

1. Can you recall when you first decided what you wanted to be when you grew up? What led you to that decision—family members, friends, observations, personal interests? Can you remember the specifics of your thinking at that time—what made you so sure of your decision? Compare that state of mind with your present thoughts about that particular occupation. What is different about how adults think about "work" than how children think of it?
2. Baker's essay supports the truism that one's occupation should ideally fit one's personality. Consider your own plans for a career or profession after you complete your education. Why have you chosen your field of interest? Beyond the concept of finding a certain career "interesting," what personality characteristics do you imagine are most important for someone working day to day in that area? Do you have these characteristics? Write a personal essay exploring and explaining your choice of career in terms of these questions.

Just Say No to Rugs

Dave Barry

Dave Barry (1947–) was born in Armonk, New York. A graduate of Haverford College (B.A. 1969), he joined The Miami Herald *in 1983 and has written a syndicated column for that paper for many years. A noted satirist, Barry received the Pulitzer Prize for commentary in 1988. Barry's books include* Stay Fit and Healthy Until You're Dead *(1985),* Dave Barry Turns 40 *(1990),* Dave Barry Does Japan *(1994),* Dave Barry's Complete Guide to Guys *(1996),* My Teenage Son's Goal in Life is to Make Me Feel 3500 Years Old and Other Thoughts on Parenting *(2001),* Dave Barry's Money Secrets *(2006), and* The Greatest Invention in the History of Mankind Is Beer *(2006). In the following essay, from* Dave Barry Talks Back *(1991), Barry confronts the realities of pet ownership.*

1 Everybody should have a pet. And I'm not saying this just because the American Pet Council gave me a helicopter. I'm also saying it because my family has always owned pets, and without them, our lives would not be nearly so rich in—call me sentimental, but this is how I feel—dirt.

Pets are nature's way of reminding us that, in the incredibly complex ecological chain of life, there is no room for furniture. For example, the only really nice furnishing we own is an Oriental rug that we bought, with the help of a decorator, in a failed attempt to become tasteful. This rug is way too nice for an onion-dip-intensive household like ours, and we seriously thought about keeping it in a large safe-deposit box, but we finally decided, in a moment of abandon, to put it on the floor. We then conducted a comprehensive rug-behavior training seminar for our main dog, Earnest, and our small auxiliary dog, Zippy.

From *Dave Barry Talks Back*. Published by Crown Publishers, Inc. Copyright © 1991 by Dave Barry.

"NO!!" we told them approximately 75 times while looking very stern and pointing at the rug. This proven training technique caused them to slink around the way dogs do when they feel tremendously guilty but have no idea why. Satisfied, we went out to dinner.

I later figured out, using an electronic calculator, that this rug covers approximately 2 percent of the total square footage of our house, which means that if you (not you *personally*) were to have a random diarrhea attack in our home, the odds are approximately 49 to 1 against your having it on our Oriental rug. The odds against your having *four* random attacks on this rug are more than *five million to one.* So we had to conclude that it was done on purpose. The rug appeared to have been visited by a group of specially bred, highly trained Doberman Poopers, but we determined, by interrogating both dogs, that the entire massive output was the work of Zippy. Probably he was trying to do the right thing. Probably, somewhere in the Coco Puff–sized nodule of nerve tissue that serves as his brain, he dimly remembered that The Masters had told him *something about the rug,* Yes! That's it! *To the rug!*

At least Zippy had the decency to feel bad about what he did, which is more than you can say for Mousse, a dog that belonged to a couple named Mike and Sandy. Mousse was a Labrador retriever, which is a large enthusiastic bulletproof species of dog made entirely from synthetic materials. This is the kind of dog that, if it takes an interest in your personal regions (which of course it does) you cannot fend it off with a blowtorch.

So anyway, Mike and Sandy had two visitors who wore expensive, brand-new down-filled parkas, which somehow got left for several hours in a closed room with Mousse. When the door was finally opened, the visibility in the room had been drastically reduced by a raging down storm, at the center of which was a large quivering down clot, looking like a huge mutant duckling, except that it had Mousse's radiantly happy eyes.

For several moments Mike and Sandy and their guests stared at this apparition, then Mike, a big, strong, highly authoritative guy, strode angrily into the room and slammed the door. He was in there for several minutes, then emerged, looking very serious. The down clot stood behind him, wagging its tail cheerfully.

"I talked to Mousse," Mike said, "and he says he didn't do it."

People often become deranged by pets. Derangement is the only possible explanation for owning a cat, an animal whose preferred mode of communication is to sink its claws three-quarters of an inch into your flesh. God help the cat owner who runs out of food. It's not uncommon to see an elderly woman sprinting through the supermarket with one or more cats clinging, leech-like, to her leg as she tries desperately to reach the pet-food section before collapsing from blood loss.

10   Of course for sheer hostility in a pet, you can't beat a parrot. I base   10 this statement on a parrot I knew named Charles who belonged to a couple named Ed and Ginny. Charles had an IQ of 260 and figured out early in life that if he talked to people, they'd get close enough so he could bite them. He especially liked to bite Ed, whom Charles wanted to drive out of the marriage so he could have Ginny, the house, the American Express card, etc. So in an effort to improve their relationship, Ginny hatched (ha ha!) this plan wherein Ed took Charles to—I am not making this up—Parrot Obedience School. Every Saturday morning, Ed and Charles would head off to receive expert training, and every Saturday afternoon Ed would come home with chunks missing from his arm. Eventually Ginny realized that it was never going to work, so she got rid of Ed.

I'm just kidding, of course. Nobody would take Ed. Ginny got rid of Charles, who now works as a public-relations adviser to Miss Zsa Zsa Gabor. So we see that there are many "pluses" to having an "animal friend," which is why you should definitely buy a pet. If you act right now, we'll also give you a heck of a deal on a rug.

Questions on Meaning

1. What are the purposes of pets, according to Barry? Do you agree?
2. Why does Barry believe that "derangement" is the only logical explanation for owning a cat? Does his contention apply to cat owners you know?
3. Why did Charles, the parrot, talk to people?

Questions on Rhetorical Strategy and Style

1. Read the essay aloud, preferably to a group of friends. Mark the passages that you find the most humorous, in particular any places in which you laugh aloud. What makes Barry's writing so humorous?
2. Barry uses classification and division in his descriptions of the various pets. How would you classify Earnest, Zippy, Mousse, all cats, and Charles. How would you classify any pets you have known intimately?

Writing Assignments

1. What experiences have you had with pets that parallel Barry's commentary? Why do you think the pets seem to get the upper hand? What *human* characteristics is Barry spoofing?
2. Satire such as Barry's—short and simple—can be a lot more difficult to write than it seems. Write a humorous essay about some human foible, such as compulsive car washing or intractable daily habits. Use witty phrases, as Barry does, but keep the essay brief and unencumbered.

Naïveté

Robert Bly

Minnesota poet Robert Bly (1926–) has written poetry on archetypal themes drawn from the writings of the Swiss psychologist C. G. Jung and from mythological sources. His books of poetry were known to a small, primarily academic, audience until the publication of his prose book Iron John: A Book About Men *(1990). The book entered a market prepared by feminist examinations of the role of woman in society, by a newly energized men's movement, and by a general culture of interest in self-help and popularized psychology. In the excerpt from* Iron John *reprinted here, Bly examines the problematic mindset of the man who idolizes women. His description personifies the trait, naïveté, as a man whose character is ruled by this motivation. As you read the essay, note the tone of intimacy, self-assurance, and wisdom created by Bly's short, simple statements.*

1   We see more and more passivity in men, but also more and more naïveté. The naïve man feels a pride in being attacked. If his wife or girlfriend, furious, shouts that he is "chauvinist," a "sexist," a "man," he doesn't fight back, but just takes it. He opens his shirt so that she can see more clearly where to put the lances. He ends with three or four javelins sticking out of his body, and blood running all over the floor. If he were a bullfighter, he would remain where he was when the bull charges, would not even wave his shirt or turn his body, and the horn would go directly in. After each fight friends have to carry him on their shoulders to the hospital.

He feels, as he absorbs attacks, that he is doing the brave and advanced thing; he will surely be able to recover somewhere in isolation.

From *Iron John: A Book About Men*. Published by Addison-Wesley Publishing Company, Inc. Copyright © 1990 by Robert Bly.

A woman, so mysterious and superior, has given him some attention. To be attacked by someone you love—what could be more wonderful? Perhaps the wounds may pay for some chauvinistic act, and so allow him to remain special still longer.

The naïve man will also be proud that he can pick up the pain of others. He particularly picks up women's pain. When at five years old he sat at the kitchen table, his mother may have confided her suffering to him, and he felt flattered to be told of such things by a grown-up, even if it showed his father up poorly. He becomes attracted later to women who "share their pain." His specialness makes him, in his own eyes, something of a doctor. He is often more in touch with women's pain than with his own, and he will offer to carry a woman's pain before he checks with his own heart to see if this labor is proper in the situation. In general, I think each gender drops its own pain when it tries to carry the pain of the other gender. I don't mean that men shouldn't listen. But hearing a woman's pain and carrying it are two different things. Women have tried for centuries to carry men's pain, and it hasn't worked well.

The word special is important to the naïve man, and he has special relationships with certain people. We all have some special relationships, but he surrounds the special person with a cloying kind of goodwill. The relationship is so special that he never examines the dark side of the person, which could be a son, a daughter, a wife, a male friend, a girlfriend. He accepts responses that are way off, conspires somehow with their dark side. "Some people are special," he says.

5   We might say that if he doesn't investigate his son's or daughter's   5 dark side, perhaps they will not investigate his. He may also have a secret and special relationship with a wounded little boy inside himself. If so, he won't challenge the little boy, nor will he point out his self-pity, nor actually listen to the boy either. He will simply let the boy run his life.

Sincerity is a big thing with him. He assumes that the person, stranger, or lover he talks with is straightforward, goodwilled, and speaking from the heart. He agrees with Rousseau and Whitman that each person is basically noble by nature, and only twisted a little by institutions. He puts a lot of stock in his own sincerity. He believes in it, as if it were a horse or a city wall. He assumes that it will, and should, protect him from consequences that fall to less open people. He may say, "It's true that I betrayed you with your best friend while you were away, and even after you were back, but I was frank with you and told about it. So why should you be angry with me?"

A naïve man acts out strange plays of self-isolation. For example, when an angry woman is criticizing him, he may say, quite sensibly, "You're right. I had no right to do that." If her anger turns to rage, he bends his head and says, "I've always been this way." In the third act, he may implicate his father. "He was never there; he never gave me any support." Her rage continues and he bends over still farther. He is losing ground rapidly, and in the fourth act he may say: "All men are shits." He is now many more times isolated than he was a few minutes ago. He feels rejected by the woman and he is now isolated from all other men as well. One man I knew went through this play every time he had a serious fight with a woman, about once a week.

The naïve man will lose what is most precious to him because of a lack of boundaries. This is particularly true of the New Age man, or the man seeking "higher consciousness." Thieves walk in and out of his house, carrying large bags, and he doesn't seem to notice them. He tells his "white light" experiences at parties; he confides the contents of last night's dream to a total stranger. Mythologically, when he meets the giant he tells him all his plans. He rarely fights for what is his; he gives away his eggs, and other people raise the chicks. We could say that, unaware of boundaries, he does not develop a good container for his soul, nor a good container for two people. There's a leak in it somewhere. He may break the container himself when he sees an attractive face. As an artist he improvises; as a poet his work lacks meter and shape. Improvisation is not all wrong, but he tends to be proud of his lack of form because he feels suspicious of boundaries. The lack of boundaries will eventually damage him.

The naïve man tends to have an inappropriate relation to ecstasy. He longs for ecstasy at the wrong time or in the wrong place, and ignores all masculine sources of it. He wants ecstasy through the feminine, through the Great Mother, through the goddess, even though what may be grounding for the woman ungrounds him. He uses ecstasy to be separated from grounding or discipline.

The naïve man will sink into a mood as if into a big hole. Some women, we notice, are able to get around a mood. If a woman has a bad mood before a party, for example, she may walk around the mood, detach it, and get rid of it, at least for a time. But the naïve man's mood seems attached as if to a mountain. He can't separate it. If he

19

feels hurt, or in a low mood, he identifies with the mood, and every-one around him has to go down into the hole. In his mood-trance, he is not present to wife, children, friends.

The man without limitations may also specialize in not telling. If, for example, he and others decide that some chairs should be arranged before a performance, and he is assigned to do that, he will probably not tell anyone that he has decided to leave the chairs as they are. The people involved, usually older, immediately get mad and shout. Basi-cally he has tricked them into carrying the anger, and its heaviness. He is clean and light, and wonders why other people get angry so often.

The naïve man often doesn't know that there is a being in him that wants to remain sick. Inside each man or woman there is a sick person and a well person: and one needs to know which one is talk-ing at any moment. But awareness of the sick being, and knowledge of how strong he is, is not part of the naïve man's field of perceptions.

The naïve man often lacks what James Hillman has called "nat-ural brutality." The mother hawk pushes the younglings out of the nest one day; we notice the father fox drives the cubs away in early October. But the ascender lets things go on too long. At the start of a relationship, a few harsh words of truth would have been helpful. In-stead he waits and waits, and then a major wounding happens farther down the line.

His timing is off. We notice that there will often be a missing beat a second or so after he takes a blow, verbal or physical. He will go di-rectly from the pain of receiving the blow to an empathetic grasp of the reason why it came, skipping over the anger entirely. Misusing Jesus' remark, he turns the missing cheek.

15 As a final remark about naïveté, we might mention that there is 15 something in naïveté that demands betrayal. The naïve man will have a curious link to betrayal, deceit, and lies. Not only will he betray oth-ers easily, being convinced his motives are always good, but when a woman lives with a truly naïve man for a while, she feels impersonally impelled to betray him. When there is too much naïveté around, the universe has no choice but to crystallize out some betrayal.

Questions on Meaning

1. Look up the word *naïveté* in the dictionary and copy out the definition.
2. Why would a man feel pride in being attacked by a woman? Why is the bullfighter analogy appropriate? Is Bly making an ironic comment with the bullfighter analogy? Explain.
3. Which of the qualities of the naïve man seem most true of men you know? Which seem unfamiliar or false?

Questions on Rhetorical Strategy and Style

1. Summarize Bly's definition of the naïve man. Contrast the definition you compose with the definition of naïveté from the dictionary.
2. Explain the logical problems with the sincerity defense that the naïve man uses ("He assumes that it will, and should, protect him from consequences that fall to less open people.")

Writing Assignments

1. Bly refers to a "lack of boundaries" as characteristic of the naïve man, meaning that the naïve man does not have a clear idea of appropriate and inappropriate limitations between himself and another person, so that he sometimes permits a person too much access to him and sometimes too little. Using a personal situation in which you feel that someone takes too many liberties with your time, money, space, or good will, define appropriate boundaries between yourself and the person.
2. Tell the story of a relationship you have experienced or observed that would have profited from "natural brutality," telling a difficult truth at the very beginning of the relationship. Alternatively, analyze a situation you find in current politics or in a work of literature in which telling hard truths would resolve the situation. Envision the consequences for good and ill as a result of the truth-telling.

There Will Come Soft Rains

Ray Bradbury

Ray Douglas Bradbury (1920–) was born in Waukegan, Illinois. A storywriter and novelist, a playwright, a screenwriter, and a poet, Bradbury is one of the most distinguished and beloved science fiction writers. In 1934, Bradbury moved to Los Angeles, California where he met such famous people as the great comedian, George Burns, who paid Bradbury for his very first work—a joke for Burns's comedy show. In 1947 Bradbury published his first collection of short stories, Dark Carnival. The Martian Chronicles *(1950), in which he imagined humans colonizing Mars, made him famous. In 1953* Fahrenheit 451 *struck a darker note as it imagined a world where books were burned and ideas suppressed. Bradbury has won the O. Henry Memorial Award; the Benjamin Franklin Award (1954); the Aviation-Space Writer's Association Award for Best Space Article in an American Magazine (1967); and the World Fantasy Award for Lifetime Achievement. His work was included in the* Best American Short Stories *collections for 1946, 1948, and 1952. Bradbury's most unusual honor came when an Apollo astronaut named Dandelion Crater on the moon after Bradbury's novel,* Dandelion Wine.*

"There Will Come Soft Rains" was first published in* Colliers *magazine on May 6, 1950. The story revolves around a house that was built to withstand nuclear blasts and to run itself for human convenience. In the story the*

Reprinted from *The Martian Chronicles* by permission of Don Congdon Associates. Copyright © 1977 by Ray Bradbury.

house stands, but the family is burned into the outer wall by a blast. The tale ends with the house reading Sara Teasedale's poem about the world without humans.

1   In the living room the voice-clock sang, *Tick-tock, seven o'clock, time to get up, time to get up, seven o'clock!* as if it were afraid that nobody would. The morning house lay empty. The clock ticked on, repeating and repeating its sounds into the emptiness. *Seven-nine, breakfast time, seven-nine!*

In the kitchen the breakfast stove gave a hissing sigh and ejected from its warm interior eight pieces of perfectly browned toast, eight eggs sunnyside up, sixteen slices of bacon, two coffees, and two cool glasses of milk.

"Today is August 4, 2026," said a second voice from the kitchen ceiling, "in the city of Allendale, California." It repeated the date three times for memory's sake. "Today is Mr. Featherstone's birthday. Today is the anniversary of Tilita's marriage. Insurance is payable, as are the water, gas, and light bills."

Somewhere in the walls, relays clicked, memory tapes glided under electric eyes.

5   *Eight-one, tick-tock, eight-one o'clock, off to school, off to work, run, run, eight-one!* But no doors slammed, no carpets took the soft tread of rubber heels. It was raining outside. The weather box on the front door sang quietly: "Rain, rain, go away; rubbers, raincoats for today . . ." And the rain tapped on the empty house, echoing.

Outside, the garage chimed and lifted its door to reveal the waiting car. After a long wait the door swung down again.

At eight-thirty the eggs were shriveled and the toast was like stone. An aluminum wedge scraped them into the sink, where hot water whirled them down a metal throat which digested and flushed them away to the distant sea. The dirty dishes were dropped into a hot washer and emerged twinkling dry.

Nine-fifteen, sang the clock, *time to clean.*

Out of warrens in the wall, tiny robot mice darted. The rooms were acrawl with the small cleaning animals, all rubber and metal. They thudded against chairs, whirling their mustached runners, kneading the rug nap, sucking gently at hidden dust. Then, like mysterious invaders, they popped into their burrows. Their pink electric eyes faded. The house was clean.

10   *Ten o'clock.* The sun came out from behind the rain. The house 10 stood alone in a city of rubble and ashes. This was the one house left standing. At night the ruined city gave off a radioactive glow which could be seen for miles.

    Ten-fifteen. The garden sprinklers whirled up in golden founts, filling the soft morning air with scatterings of brightness. The water pelted windowpanes, running down the charred west side where the house had been burned evenly free of its white paint. The entire west face of the house was black, save for five places. Here the silhouette in paint of a man mowing a lawn. Here, as in a photograph, a woman bent to pick flowers. Still farther over, their images burned on wood in one titanic instant, a small boy, hands flung into the air; higher up, the image of a thrown ball, and opposite him a girl, hands raised to catch a ball which never came down.

    The five spots of paint—the man, the woman, the children, the ball—remained. The rest was a thin charcoaled layer.

    The gentle sprinkler rain filled the garden with falling light.

    Until this day, how well the house had kept its peace. How carefully it had inquired, "Who goes there? What's the password?" and, getting no answer from lonely foxes and whining cats, it had shut up its windows and drawn shades in an old- maidenly preoccupation with self-protection which bordered on a mechanical paranoia.

15   It quivered at each sound, the house did. If a sparrow brushed a 15 window, the shade shapped up. The bird, startled, flew off! No, not even a bird must touch the house!

    The house was an altar with ten thousand attendants, big, small, servicing, attending, in choirs. But the gods had gone away, and the ritual of the religion continued senselessly, uselessly.

    Twelve noon.

    A dog whined, shivering, on the front porch.

    The front door recognized the dog voice and opened. The dog, once huge and fleshy, but now gone to bone and covered with sores, moved in and through the house, tracking mud. Behind it whirred angry mice, angry at having to pick up mud, angry at inconvenience.

20   For not a leaf fragment blew under the door but what the wall 20 panels flipped open and the copper scrap rats flashed swiftly out. The

offending dust, hair, or paper, seized in miniature steel jaws, was raced back to the burrows. There, down tubes which fed into the cellar, it was dropped into the sighing vent of an incinerator which sat like evil Baal in a dark corner.

The dog ran upstairs, hysterically yelping to each door, at last realizing, as the house realized, that only silence was here.

It sniffed the air and scratched the kitchen door. Behind the door, the stove was making pancakes which filled the house with a rich baked odor and the scent of maple syrup.

The dog frothed at the mouth, lying at the door, sniffing, its eyes turned to fire. It ran wildly in circles, biting at its tail, spun in a frenzy, and died. It lay in the parlor for an hour.

Two o'clock, sang a voice.

25 Delicately sensing decay at last, the regiments of mice hummed out as softly as blown gray leaves in an electrical wind.

Two-fifteen.

The dog was gone.

In the cellar, the incinerator glowed suddenly and a whirl of sparks leaped up the chimney.

Two thirty-five.

30 Bridge tables sprouted from patio walls. Playing cards fluttered onto pads in a shower of pips. Martinis manifested on an oaken bench with egg-salad sandwiches. Music played.

But the tables were silent and the cards untouched.

At four o'clock the tables folded like great butterflies back through the paneled walls.

Four-thirty.

The nursery walls glowed.

35 Animals took shape: yellow giraffes, blue lions, pink antelopes, lilac panthers cavorting in crystal substance. The walls were glass. They looked out upon color and fantasy. Hidden films clocked through well-oiled sprockets, and the walls lived. The nursery floor was woven to resemble a crisp, cereal meadow. Over this ran aluminum roaches and iron crickets, and in the hot still air butterflies of delicate red tissue wavered among the sharp aroma of animal spoors! There was the sound like a great matted yellow hive of bees within a dark bellows, the lazy bumble of a purring lion. And there was the patter of okapi feet and the murmur of a fresh jungle rain, like other

hoofs, falling upon the summer-starched grass. Now the walls dissolved into distances of parched weed, mile on mile, and warm endless sky. The animals drew away into thorn brakes and water holes.

It was the children's hour.

Five o'clock. The bath filled with clear hot water.

Six, seven, eight o'clock. The dinner dishes manipulated like magic tricks, and in the study a *click*. In the metal stand opposite the hearth where a fire now blazed up warmly, a cigar popped out, half an inch of soft gray ash on it, smoking, waiting.

Nine o'clock. The beds warmed their hidden circuits, for nights were cool here.

Nine-five. A voice spoke from the study ceiling:

"Mrs. McClellan, which poem would you like this evening?"

The house was silent.

The voice said at last, "Since you express no preference, I shall select a poem at random." Quiet music rose to back the voice. "Sara Teasdale. As I recall, your favorite. . . .

"There will come soft rains and the smell of the ground,
And swallows circling with their shimmering sound;

And frogs in the pools singing at night,
And wild plum trees in tremulous white;

Robins will wear their feathery fire,
Whistling their whims on a low fence-wire;

And not one will know of the war, not one
Will care at last when it is done.

Not one would mind, neither bird nor tree,
If mankind perished utterly;

And Spring herself, when she woke at dawn
Would scarcely know that we were gone."

The fire burned on the stone hearth and the cigar fell away into a mound of quiet ash on its tray. The empty chairs faced each other between the silent walls, and the music played.

At ten o'clock the house began to die.

The wind blew. A falling tree bough crashed through the kitchen window. Cleaning solvent, bottled, shattered over the stove. The room was ablaze in an instant!

"Fire!" screamed a voice. The house lights flashed, water pumps shot water from the ceilings. But the solvent spread on the linoleum, licking, eating, under the kitchen door, while the voices took it up in chorus: "Fire, fire, fire!"

The house tried to save itself. Doors sprang tightly shut, but the windows were broken by the heat and the wind blew and sucked upon the fire.

The house gave ground as the fire in ten billion angry sparks moved with flaming ease from room to room and then up the stairs. While scurrying water rats squeaked from the walls, pistoled their water, and ran for more. And the wall sprays let down showers of mechanical rain.

But too late. Somewhere, sighing, a pump shrugged to a stop. The quenching rain ceased. The reserve water supply which had filled baths and washed dishes for many quiet days was gone.

The fire crackled up the stairs. It fed upon Picassos and Matisses in the upper halls, like delicacies, baking off the oily flesh, tenderly crisping the canvases into black shavings.

Now the fire lay in beds, stood in windows, changed the colors of drapes!

And then, reinforcements.

From attic trapdoors, blind robot faces peered down with faucet mouths gushing green chemical.

The fire backed off, as even an elephant must at the sight of a dead snake. Now there were twenty snakes whipping over the floor, killing the fire with a clear cold venom of green froth.

But the fire was clever. It had sent flames outside the house, up through the attic to the pumps there. An explosion! The attic brain which directed the pumps was shattered into bronze shrapnel on the beams.

The fire rushed back into every closet and felt of the clothes hung there.

The house shuddered, oak bone on bone, its bared skeleton cringing from the heat, its wire, its nerves revealed as if a surgeon had torn the skin off to let the red veins and capillaries quiver in the scalded air. Help, help! Fire! Run, run! Heat snapped mirrors like the brittle winter ice. And the voices wailed Fire, fire, run, run, like a tragic nursery rhyme, a dozen voices, high, low, like children dying in a forest, alone, alone. And the voices fading as the wires popped their sheathings like hot chestnuts. One, two, three, four, five voices died.

In the nursery the jungle burned. Blue lions roared, purple giraffes bounded off. The panthers ran in circles, changing color, and ten million animals, running before the fire, vanished off toward a distant steaming river. . . .

60   Ten more voices died. In the last instant under the fire avalanche,   60 other choruses, oblivious, could be heard announcing the time, playing music, cutting the lawn by remote-control mower, or setting an umbrella frantically out and in the slamming and opening front door, a thousand things happening, like a clock shop when each clock strikes the hour insanely before or after the other, a scene of maniac confusion, yet unity; singing, screaming, a few last cleaning mice darting bravely out to carry the horrid ashes away! And one voice, with sublime disregard for the situation, read poetry aloud in the fiery study, until all the film spools burned, until all the wires withered and the circuits cracked.

The fire burst the house and let it slam flat down, puffing out skirts of spark and smoke.

In the kitchen, an instant before the rain of fire and timber, the stove could be seen making breakfasts at a psychopathic rate, ten dozen eggs, six loaves of toast, twenty dozen bacon strips, which, eaten by fire, started the stove working again, hysterically hissing!

The crash. The attic smashing into kitchen and parlor. The parlor into cellar, cellar into sub-cellar. Deep freeze, armchair, film tapes, circuits, beds, and all like skeletons thrown in a cluttered mound deep under.

Smoke and silence. A great quantity of smoke.

65   Dawn showed faintly in the east. Among the ruins, one wall   65 stood alone. Within the wall, a last voice said, over and over again and again, even as the sun rose to shine upon the heaped rubble and steam:

"Today is August 5, 2026, today is August 5, 2026, today is . . ."

Questions on Meaning

1. What is the significance of a house that can withstand destruction and humans who cannot? Why does the house survive? What does the death of the dog mean?
2. What kind of people lived in a house that did all the housework and even planned the days? What is the story saying about our tendency to rely on technology? Are we able to take care of ourselves without that technology?
3. Why is the poem so poignant? What does it say about the ability of nature to come back even if all the brilliant humans have disappeared? Is the poem hopeful or negative or both? Why?

Questions on Rhetorical Strategy and Style

1. The story plays on human fears by introducing the worst of those fears being fulfilled at the beginning of the tale. Why does the image of the dying dog seem to end all human hope?
2. The house reads the poem as the center of the story. Why does the poem work as the centerpiece of the tale? How does it work as the turning point for both humanity and for the house?
3. At the end of the story the house begins to self-destruct, just as the human race has done. What are the stages of the destruction? How do these stages show the breakdown of society?

Writing Assignments

1. Bradbury wrote this story just after the first atomic bombs were dropped on Japan. Find images of the destruction of the Japanese cities, and write about the images of them.
2. Many people think that terrorism is the worst that the human race has faced. Read about the Cuban missile crisis. How close did the world come to atomic destruction? Write about the Cold War and its fear factors, and compare those factors to the world today.
3. Consider the images in the poem that centers the story. Write about the world of nature and the human effects on nature. Would nature be better off without the destructive species that humans have proved to be? What could we do better?

A Fable for Tomorrow

Rachel Carson

Rachel Carson (1907–1964), a pioneer of the environmental movement, was born in Pennsylvania. A naturalist by training, she specialized in marine biology and developed a particular affection for the rocky coast of Maine. Her seminal book Silent Spring *(1962) resulted from her work as an aquatic biologist for the U.S. Fish and Wildlife Service, during which she became acutely aware of the ecological hazards of herbicides and insecticides. She also wrote* The Sea Around Us *(1951), for which she received the National Book Award,* Under the Sea Wind *(1952), and* The Edge of the Sea *(1955). Although Carson's writing was not without controversy, and for many years she was criticized as being an alarmist, she is now credited with being one of America's most important environmentalists. The fable that follows, from* Silent Spring, *illustrates the ecological damage that can result when pesticides enter the ecosystem.*

1 There was once a town in the heart of America where all life seemed to live in harmony with its surroundings. The town lay in the midst of a checkerboard of prosperous farms, with fields of grain and hillsides of orchards where, in spring, white clouds of bloom drifted above the green fields. In autumn, oak and maple and birch set up a blaze of color that flamed and flickered across a backdrop of pines. Then foxes barked in the hills and deer silently crossed the fields, half hidden in the mists of the fall mornings.

Along the roads, laurel, viburnum and alder, great ferns and wild-flowers delighted the traveler's eye through much of the year. Even in winter the roadsides were places of beauty, where countless birds came to feed on the berries and on the seed heads of the dried weeds rising above the snow. The countryside was, in fact, famous for the abundance and variety of its bird life, and when the flood of migrants was pouring through in spring and fall people traveled from great distances to observe them. Others came to fish the streams, which flowed clear and cold out of the hills and contained shady pools where trout lay. So it had been from the days many years ago when the first settlers raised their houses, sank their wells, and built their barns.

Then a strange blight crept over the area and everything began to change. Some evil spell had settled on the community: mysterious maladies swept the flocks of chickens; the cattle and sheep sickened and died. Everywhere was a shadow of death. The farmers spoke of much illness among their families. In the town the doctors had become more and more puzzled by new kinds of sickness appearing among their patients. There had been several sudden and unexplained deaths, not only among adults but even among children, who would be stricken suddenly while at play and die within a few hours.

There was a strange stillness. The birds, for example—where had they gone? Many people spoke of them, puzzled and disturbed. The feeding stations in the backyards were deserted. The few birds seen anywhere were moribund; they trembled violently and could not fly. It was a spring without voices. On the mornings that had once throbbed with the dawn chorus of robins, catbirds, doves, jays, wrens, and scores of other bird voices there was now no sound; only silence lay over the fields and woods and marsh.

On the farms the hens brooded, but no chicks hatched. The farmers complained that they were unable to raise any pigs—the litters were small and the young survived only a few days. The apple trees were coming into bloom but no bees droned among the blossoms, so there was no pollination and there would be no fruit.

The roadsides, once so attractive, were now lined with browned and withered vegetation as though swept by fire. These, too, were silent, deserted by all living things. Even the streams were now lifeless. Anglers no longer visited them, for all the fish had died.

In the gutters under the eaves and between the shingles of the roofs, a white granular powder still showed a few patches; some weeks before it had fallen like snow upon the roofs and the lawns, the fields and streams.

No witchcraft, no enemy action had silenced the rebirth of new life in this stricken world. The people had done it themselves.

This town does not actually exist, but it might easily have a thousand counterparts in America or elsewhere in the world. I know of no community that has experienced all the misfortunes I describe. Yet every one of these disasters has actually happened somewhere, and many real communities have already suffered a substantial number of them. A grim specter has crept upon us almost unnoticed, and this imagined tragedy may easily become a stark reality we all shall know.

Questions on Meaning

1. What happened to Carson's fictional town? What is the "white granular powder" she mentions?
2. Many people accused Carson of being alarmist when she published *Silent Spring*. Reread the last sentence of the third paragraph. How would you respond if you read that statement in a report? Find other statements that might feed charges of being an alarmist. Why do you think she chose to include such dramatic examples in narrative?
3. Explain the namesake for the title of the book that is the source of this fable, *Silent Spring*.

Questions on Rhetorical Strategy and Style

1. Find the single sentence that summarizes Carson's thesis. Restate it in your own words.
2. Carson uses descriptive imagery to let us see, hear, and smell her representational town before and after the disaster. What are the most dramatic differences?
3. Notice the sound and rhythm of Carson's writing: "There once was a town," "so it had been," and "only silence lay over the fields and woods and marsh." Why did she choose this smooth, almost biblical-sounding pattern for much of the fable? Where does this writing style abruptly end?

Writing Assignments

1. At the time Carson wrote this fable, "ecology" was not a household word; few people considered the interrelationship of plants and animals. Do some research to trace the impact of an insecticide on apples. Why should a fruit grower be concerned about chemical sprays used at a neighboring farm to kill bugs?
2. Write an essay about the annual Earth Day celebrations held across America. What is their purpose? Do you believe they are an effective way to teach environmental awareness, or are they simply a bunch of "tree huggers"—environmental radicals warning of doom and gloom? What would you talk about if you were asked to speak at an Earth Day rally?

Grant and Lee: A Study in Contrasts

Bruce Catton

Bruce Catton (1899–1978) is best known for his popular histories of the American Civil War. He wrote a dozen books and many articles about the War, including A Stillness at Appomattox, *which won the Pulitzer Prize and the National Book Award in 1954. Having first worked as a newspaper journalist, Catton was interested in writing for the popular press rather than scholarly historians, and his writing always sought to make history real and living. "Grant and Lee: A Study in Contrasts" was published in 1956 in a book of essays by various historians called* The American Story. *As you read it, notice how Catton takes us far beyond just the story of these two Civil War generals meeting at the end of the War—he is indeed writing a chapter in an American story. As you read this focused exploration of the character of these two men and the times they embody, you will also be learning something about the Civil War itself and the nature of great men.*

1   When Ulysses S. Grant and Robert E. Lee met in the parlor of a modest house at Appomattox Court House, Virginia, on April 9, 1865, to work out the terms for the surrender of Lee's Army of Northern Virginia, a great chapter in American life came to a close, and a great new chapter began.

These men were bringing the Civil War to its virtual finish. To be sure, other armies had yet to surrender, and for a few days the fugitive Confederate government would struggle desperately and vainly, trying to find some way to go on living now that its chief support was gone.

From *The American Story,* edited by Earl Schenck Miers. Published by the U.S. Capitol Historical Society.

But in effect it was all over when Grant and Lee signed the papers. And the little room where they wrote out the terms was the scene of one of the poignant, dramatic contrasts in American history.

They were two strong men, these oddly different generals, and they represented the strengths of two conflicting currents that, through them, had come into final collision.

Back of Robert E. Lee was the notion that the old aristocratic concept might somehow survive and be dominant in American life.

5   Lee was tidewater Virginia, and in his background were family, culture, and tradition . . . the age of chivalry transplanted to a New World which was making its own legends and its own myths. He embodied a way of life that had come down through the age of knighthood and the English country squire. America was a land that was beginning all over again, dedicated to nothing much more complicated than the rather hazy belief that all men had equal rights and should have an equal chance in the world. In such a land Lee stood for the feeling that it was somehow of advantage to human society to have a pronounced inequality in the social structure. There should be a leisure class, backed by ownership of land; in turn, society itself should be keyed to the land as the chief source of wealth and influence. It would bring forth (according to this ideal) a class of men with a strong sense of obligation to the community; men who lived not to gain advantage for themselves, but to meet the solemn obligations which had been laid on them by the very fact that they were privileged. From them the country would get its leadership; to them it could look for the higher values—of thought, of conduct, of personal deportment—to give it strength and virtue.

Lee embodied the noblest elements of this aristocratic ideal. Through him, the landed nobility justified itself. For four years, the Southern states had fought a desperate war to uphold the ideals for which Lee stood. In the end, it almost seemed as if the Confederacy fought for Lee; as if he himself was the Confederacy . . . the best thing that the way of life for which the Confederacy stood could ever have to offer. He had passed into legend before Appomattox. Thousands of tired, underfed, poorly clothed Confederate soldiers, long since past the simple enthusiasm of the early days of the struggle, somehow considered Lee the symbol of everything for which they had been willing to die. But they could not quite put this feeling into words. If the Lost Cause, sanctified by so much heroism and so many deaths, had a living justification, its justification was General Lee.

Grant, the son of a tanner on the Western frontier, was everything Lee was not. He had come up the hard way and embodied nothing in particular except the eternal toughness and sinewy fiber of the men who grew up beyond the mountains. He was one of a body of men who owed reverence and obeisance to no one, who were self-reliant to a fault, who cared hardly anything for the past but who had a sharp eye for the future.

These frontier men were the precise opposites of the tidewater aristocrats. Back of them, in the great surge that had taken people over the Alleghenies and into the opening Western country, there was a deep, implicit dissatisfaction with a past that had settled into grooves. They stood for democracy, not from any reasoned conclusion about the proper ordering of human society, but simply because they had grown up in the middle of democracy and knew how it worked. Their society might have privileges, but they would be privileges each man had won for himself. Forms and patterns meant nothing. No man was born to anything, except perhaps to a chance to show how far he could rise. Life was competition.

Yet along with this feeling had come a deep sense of belonging to a national community. The Westerner who developed a farm, opened a shop, or set up in business as a trader, could hope to prosper only as his own community prospered—and his community ran from the Atlantic to the Pacific and from Canada down to Mexico. If the land was settled, with towns and highways and accessible markets, he could better himself. He saw his fate in terms of the nation's own destiny. As its horizons expanded, so did his. He had, in other words, an acute dollars-and-cents stake in the continued growth and development of his country.

10   And that, perhaps, is where the contrast between Grant and Lee   10
becomes most striking. The Virginia aristocrat, inevitably, saw himself in relation to his own region. He lived in a static society which could endure almost anything except change. Instinctively, his first loyalty would go to the locality in which that society existed. He would fight to the limit of endurance to defend it, because in defending it he was defending everything that gave his own life its deepest meaning.

The Westerner, on the other hand, would fight with an equal tenacity for the broader concept of society. He fought so because everything he lived by was tied to growth, expansion, and a constantly widening horizon. What he lived by would survive or fall with the nation itself. He could not possibly stand by unmoved in the face of an attempt to destroy the Union. He would combat it with everything he had, because he could only see it as an effort to cut the ground out from under his feet.

So Grant and Lee were in complete contrast, representing two diametrically opposed elements in American life. Grant was the modern man emerging; beyond him, ready to come on the stage, was the great age of steel and machinery, of crowded cities and a restless burgeoning vitality. Lee might have ridden down from the old age of chivalry, lance in hand, silken banner fluttering over his head. Each man was the perfect champion of his cause, drawing both his strengths and his weaknesses from the people he led.

Yet it was not all contrast, after all. Different as they were—in background, in personality, in underlying aspiration—these two great soldiers had much in common. Under everything else, they were marvelous fighters. Furthermore, their fighting qualities were really very much alike.

Each man had, to begin with, the great virtue of utter tenacity and fidelity. Grant fought his way down the Mississippi Valley in spite of acute personal discouragement and profound military handicaps. Lee hung on in the trenches at Petersburg after hope itself had died. In each man there was an indomitable quality . . . the born fighter's refusal to give up as long as he can still remain on his feet and lift his two fists.

15 Daring and resourcefulness they had, too; the ability to think 15 faster and move faster than the enemy. These were the qualities which gave Lee the dazzling campaigns of Second Manassas and Chancellorsville and won Vicksburg for Grant.

Lastly, and perhaps greatest of all, there was the ability, at the end, to turn quickly from war to peace once the fighting was over. Out of the way these two men behaved at Appomattox came the possibility of a peace of reconciliation. It was a possibility not wholly realized, in the years to come, but which did, in the end, help the two sections to become one nation again . . . after a war whose bitterness might have seemed to make such a reunion wholly impossible. No part of either man's life became him more than the part he played in this brief meeting in the McLean house at Appomattox. Their behavior there put all succeeding generations of Americans in their debt. Two great Americans, Grant and Lee—very different, yet under everything very much alike. Their encounter at Appomattox was one of the great moments of American history.

Questions on Meaning

1. As you read the essay, did you sense that Catton respected either Grant or Lee more than the other? If so, go back through the essay and underline phrases and sentences that give this impression. If not, explain how he manages to maintain such even-handedness while describing contrasting figures.
2. How has your understanding of these men, or the Civil War in general, been changed after reading this essay?
3. Catton speaks of Grant and Lee as "representing two diametrically opposed elements in American life." Without looking back to the essay, summarize these two aspects of America. Do you see any parallels to these two aspects in contemporary America?

Questions on Rhetorical Strategy and Style

1. Catton obviously uses the rhetorical strategies of comparison and contrast to shape the essay and develop its themes. Examining one paragraph at a time, make a brief outline of the essay that shows how Catton balances and finally integrates his exploration of the two men.
2. Like most effective writers arguing his ideas, Catton supports and develops his generalizations with examples—even in this brief, general essay. Reread the essay and take note of how specifics are used to demonstrate the abstract character traits Catton describes, such as these generals' "utter tenacity."
3. The essay's title emphasizes differences between Grant and Lee, as does the opening statement about "one of the poignant, dramatic contrasts in American history." Other phrases throughout the essay, such as "precise opposites," further this contrast. Yet by the end of the essay we see Grant and Lee have become "very much alike." How has the war brought about these changes in the two generals' characters?

Writing Assignments

1. As a historian, Catton is interested in broad sweeping changes in a society or culture as well as the individual stories of individual people. When he ends this essay with the statement about "one of the great moments in American history," we see again that the essay is about a much larger change in America. Choose a

different "moment" in U.S. or world history that you think represents a significant change from one time to another. Write an essay explaining that change.

2. Choose two people you admire: one a public figure, the other someone you have known personally. Write an essay in which you explore the admirable characteristics of both, looking for both similarities and differences.

The Myth of the Latin Woman: I Just Met a Girl Named María

Judith Ortiz Cofer

Judith Ortiz Cofer (1952–) was born in Hormigueros, Puerto Rico, and emigrated to the United States when she was four. Cofer attended Augusta College and Florida Atlantic University; she was also a Scholar of the English Speaking Union at Oxford University. She has worked as a bilingual teacher in the Florida public schools, and as a visiting writer at Vanderbilt University and the University of Michigan, Ann Arbor. Cofer is currently the Franklin Professor of English and Creative Writing at The University of Georgia. An award-winning poet, Cofer has received grants from the Witter Bynner Foundation and the National Endowment for the Arts. Her books include The Line of the Sun *(1989),* Silent Dancing *(1990),* The Latin Deli *(1993),* Reaching for the Mainland and Selected New Poems *(1995),* The Year of Our Revolution *(1998),* Woman In Front of the Sun: On Becoming a Writer *(2000),* A Love Story Beginning in Spanish: Poems *(2005), as well as a children's book,* Call Me Maria *(2004). Cofer, who has also written for* Glamour *and* The Kenyon Review, *often combines her love of language with her interest in the lives and traditions of Puerto Ricans. In this essay, from* The Latin Deli, *Cofer describes how her Latino ancestry attracts unpleasant stereotyping.*

1   On a bus trip to London from Oxford University where I was earning some graduate credits one summer, a young man, obviously fresh from a pub, spotted me and as if struck by

From *The Latin Deli: Prose and Poetry* by Judith Ortiz Cofer. Published by the University of Georgia Press.

inspiration went down on his knees in the aisle. With both hands over his heart he broke into an Irish tenor's rendition of "Maria" from *West Side Story.* My politely amused fellow passengers gave his lovely voice the round of gentle applause it deserved. Though I was not quite as amused, I managed my version of an English smile: no show of teeth, no extreme contortions of the facial muscles—I was at this time of my life practicing reserve and cool. Oh, that British control, how I coveted it. But "Maria" had followed me to London, reminding me of a prime fact of my life: you can leave the island, master the English language, and travel as far as you can, but if you are a Latina, especially one like me who so obviously belongs to Rita Moreno's gene pool, the island travels with you.

This is sometimes a very good thing—it may win you that extra minute of someone's attention. But with some people, the same things can make *you* an island—not a tropical paradise but an Alcatraz, a place nobody wants to visit. As a Puerto Rican girl living in the United States and wanting like most children to "belong," I resented the stereotype that my Hispanic appearance called forth from many people I met.

Growing up in a large urban center in New Jersey during the 1960s, I suffered from what I think of as "cultural schizophrenia." Our life was designed by my parents as a microcosm of their *casas* on the island. We spoke in Spanish, ate Puerto Rican food bought at the *bodega,* and practiced strict Catholicism at a church that allotted us a one-hour slot each week for mass, performed in Spanish by a Chinese priest trained as a missionary for Latin America.

As a girl I was kept under strict surveillance by my parents, since my virtue and modesty were, by their cultural equation, the same as their honor. As a teenager I was lectured constantly on how to behave as a proper *senorita.* But it was a conflicting message I received, since the Puerto Rican mothers also encouraged their daughters to look and act like women and to dress in clothes our Anglo friends and their mothers found too "mature" and flashy. The difference was, and is, cultural; yet I often felt humiliated when I appeared at an American friend's party wearing a dress more suitable to a semi-formal than to a playroom birthday celebration. At Puerto Rican festivities, neither the music nor the colors we wore could be too loud.

5   I remember Career Day in our high school, when teachers told us   5
to come dressed as if for a job interview. It quickly became obvious that to the Puerto Rican girls "dressing up" meant wearing their mother's

ornate jewelry and clothing, more appropriate (by mainstream standards) for the company Christmas party than as daily office attire. That morning I had agonized in front of my closet, trying to figure out what a "career girl" would wear. I knew how to dress for school (at the Catholic school I attended, we all wore uniforms), I knew how to dress for Sunday mass, and I knew what dresses to wear for parties at my relatives' homes. Though I do not recall the precise details of my Career Day outfit, it must have been a composite of these choices. But I remember a comment my friend (an Italian American) made in later years that coalesced my impressions of that day. She said that at the business school she was attending, the Puerto Rican girls always stood out for wearing "everything at once." She meant, of course, too much jewelry, too many accessories. On that day at school we were simply made the negative models by the nuns, who were themselves not credible fashion experts to any of us. But it was painfully obvious to me that to the others, in their tailored skirts and silk blouses, we must have seemed "hopeless" and "vulgar." Though I now know that most adolescents feel out of step much of the time, I also know that for the Puerto Rican girls of my generation that sense was intensified. The way our teachers and classmates looked at us that day in school was just a taste of the cultural clash that awaited us in the real world, where prospective employers and men on the street would often misinterpret our tight skirts and jingling bracelets as a "come-on."

Mixed cultural signals have perpetuated certain stereotypes—for example, that of the Hispanic woman as the "hot tamale" or sexual firebrand. It is a one-dimensional view that the media have found easy to promote. In their special vocabulary, advertisers have designated "sizzling" and "smoldering" as the adjectives of choice for describing not only the foods but also the women of Latin America. From conversations in my house I recall hearing about the harassment that Puerto Rican women endured in factories where the "boss-men" talked to them as if sexual innuendo was all they understood, and worse, often gave them the choice of submitting to their advances or being fired.

It is custom, however, not chromosomes, that leads us to choose scarlet over pale pink. As young girls, it was our mothers who influenced our decisions about clothes and colors—mothers who had grown up on a tropical island where the natural environment was a riot of primary colors, where showing your skin was one way to keep cool as well as to look sexy. Most important of all, on the island, women perhaps felt freer to dress and move more provocatively since, in most cases, they were protected by the traditions, mores, and laws of a Spanish/Catholic system of morality and machismo whose main rule was: *You may look at my sister, but if you touch her I will kill you.* The extended family and church structure could provide a young woman with a circle of safety in her small pueblo on the island; if a man "wronged" a girl, everyone would close in to save her family honor.

My mother has told me about dressing in her best party clothes on Saturday nights and going to the town's plaza to promenade with her girl-friends in front of the boys they liked. The males were thus given an opportunity to admire the women and to express their admiration in the form of *piropos:* erotically charged street poems they composed on the spot. (I have myself been subjected to a few *piropos* while visiting the island, and they can be outrageous, although custom dictates that they must never cross into obscenity.) This ritual, as I understand it, also entails a show of studied indifference on the woman's part; if she is "decent," she must not acknowledge the man's impassioned words. So I do understand how things can be lost in translation. When a Puerto Rican girl dressed in her idea of what is attractive meets a man from the mainstream culture who has been trained to react to certain types of clothing as a sexual signal, a clash is likely to take place. I remember the boy who took me to my first formal dance leaning over to plant a sloppy, over-eager kiss painfully on my mouth; when I didn't respond with sufficient passion, he remarked resentfully: "I thought you Latin girls were supposed to mature early," as if I were expected to *ripen* like a fruit or vegetable, not just grow into womanhood like other girls.

It is surprising to my professional friends that even today some people, including those who should know better, still put others "in their place." It happened to me most recently during a stay at a classy metropolitan hotel favored by young professional couples for weddings. Late one evening after the theater, as I walked toward my room with a colleague (a woman with whom I was coordinating an arts program), a middle-aged man in a tuxedo, with a young girl in satin and lace on his arm, stepped directly into our path. With his champagne glass extended toward me, he exclaimed "Evita!"

10   Our way blocked, my companion and I listened as the man half-   10
recited, half-bellowed "Don't Cry for Me, Argentina." When he

finished, the young girl said: "How about a round of applause for my daddy?" We complied, hoping this would bring the silly spectacle to a close. I was becoming aware that our little group was attracting the attention of the other guests. "Daddy" must have perceived this too, and he once more barred the way as we tried to walk past him. He began to shout-sing a ditty to the tune of "La Bamba"—except the lyrics were about a girl named Maria whose exploits rhymed with her name and gonorrhea. The girl kept saying "Oh, Daddy" and looking at me with pleading eyes. She wanted me to laugh along with the others. My companion and I stood silently waiting for the man to end his offensive song. When he finished, I looked not at him but at his daughter. I advised her calmly never to ask her father what he had done in the army. Then I walked between them and to my room. My friend complimented me on my cool handling of the situation, but I confessed that I had really wanted to push the jerk into the swimming pool. This same man—probably a corporate executive, well-educated, even worldly by most standards—would not have been likely to regale an Anglo woman with a dirty song in public. He might have checked his impulse by assuming that she could be somebody's wife or mother, or at least *somebody* who might take offense. But, to him, I was just an Evita or a Maria: merely a character in his cartoon-populated universe.

Another facet of the myth of the Latin woman in the United States is the menial, the domestic—Maria the housemaid or counter-girl. It's true that work as domestics, as waitresses, and in factories is all that's available to women with little English and few skills. But the myth of the Hispanic menial—the funny maid, mispronouncing words and cooking up a spicy storm in a shiny California kitchen—has been perpetuated by the media in the same way that "Mammy" from *Gone with the Wind* became America's idea of the black woman for generations. Since I do not wear my diplomas around my neck for all to see, I have on occasion been sent to that "kitchen" where some think I obviously belong.

One incident has stayed with me, though I recognize it as a minor offense. My first public poetry reading took place in Miami, at a restaurant where a luncheon was being held before the event. I was nervous and excited as I walked in with notebook in hand. An older woman motioned me to her table, and thinking (foolish me) that she wanted me to autograph a copy of my newly published slender volume of verse, I went over. She ordered a cup of coffee from me, assuming that I was the waitress. (Easy enough to mistake my poems for menus, I suppose.) I know it wasn't an intentional act of cruelty. Yet of all the good things that happened later, I remember that scene most clearly, because it reminded me of what I had to overcome before anyone would take me seriously. In retrospect I understand that my anger gave my reading fire. In fact, I have almost always taken any doubt in my abilities as a challenge, the result most often being the satisfaction of winning a convert, of seeing the cold, appraising eyes warm to my words, the body language change, the smile that indicates I have opened some avenue for communication. So that day as I read, I looked directly at that woman. Her lowered eyes told me she was embarrassed at her faux pas, and when I willed her to look up at me, she graciously allowed me to punish her with my full attention. We shook hands at the end of the reading and I never saw her again. She has probably forgotten the entire incident, but maybe not.

Yet I am one of the lucky ones. There are thousands of Latinas without the privilege of an education or the entrees into society that I have. For them life is a constant struggle against the misconceptions perpetuated by the myth of the Latina. My goal is to try to replace the old stereotypes with a much more interesting set of realities. Every time I give a reading, I hope the stories I tell, the dreams and fears I examine in my work, can achieve some universal truth that will get my audience past the particulars of my skin color, my accent, or my clothes.

I once wrote a poem in which I called all Latinas "God's brown daughters." This poem is really a prayer of sorts, offered upward, but also, through the human-to-human channel of art, outward. It is a prayer for communication and for respect. In it, Latin women pray "in Spanish to an Anglo God/with a Jewish heritage," and they are "fervently hoping/that if not omnipotent,/at least He be bilingual."

Questions on Meaning

1. How were women "protected" when they dressed provocatively in Puerto Rico? How did that change when they were in an Anglo environment?
2. What does Cofer mean by the "cartoon-populated" universe when dismissing the man who serenaded her with "Don't Cry for Me, Argentina"?
3. What are the *piropos* kept in check by their composition and by the response of the women to whom they are directed?

Questions on Rhetorical Strategy and Style

1. How does Cofer compare and contrast the dress styles of Puerto Rican girls and Anglo girls? How did her mother give her a "conflicting message"?
2. What examples does Cofer use to illustrate cultural differences between Puerto Rican women and Anglo women that result in dramatic differences in how they present themselves? How does she explain that "customs not chromosomes" lead Puerto Rican women to wear scarlet rather than pale pink? Why were flashy, attention-grabbing colors quite normal on Puerto Rico? How do many Anglos misinterpret the dress of Puerto Rican women?
3. Find where Cofer uses cause and effect to explain why adjectives such as "hot" and "sizzling" are often used to describe Latino women, as well as Latin American food.

Writing Assignments

1. Most ethnic groups carry some stereotype baggage that results in their being "put in their place." Think of the associations often attached to American Indians, African-Americans, Asians, Europeans, and Middle Easterners. Why do you think some ethnic groups are seen more positively, others more negatively? What would be a general rule of thumb for dealing respectfully and intelligently with people from a background different from yours?
2. "I have almost always taken any doubt in my abilities as a challenge," Cofer states. Write an essay describing a time when a challenge to your abilities inspired you to prove yourself. It might have been a test at school, an athletic contest, a building project, or preparing a fancy meal. Who doubted your ability and why? How did that make you feel? What was the outcome?

The Chase

Annie Dillard

Annie Dillard (1945–) was born in Pittsburgh, Pennsylvania. She received a B. A. (1967) and an M. A. (1968) from Hollins College and then embarked on a career as a writer and teacher. Dillard has worked as a columnist for The Living Wilderness *and a contributing editor for* Harper's *and taught at Western Washington University and Wesleyan University in Connecticut. Fascinated with the intricacies of the natural world and blessed with an introspective, poetic mind, Dillard has developed a reputation for exploring the relationships between humans and nature, physically and spiritually. She has been compared to Henry David Thoreau, and her work has been compared to his* Walden. *An accomplished writer, Dillard has published nonfiction, poetry, literary criticism, essays, autobiographies, and a novel. Her published work includes* Pilgrim at Tinker Creek *(1974), observations about nature for which she received the Pulitzer Prize;* Tickets for a Prayer Wheel *(1974), a volume of poetry;* Living By Fiction *(1982), a collection of literary criticism;* Teaching a Stone to Talk *(1982), a collection of essays;* An American Childhood *(1987), an account of her youth in Pittsburgh;* The Writing Life, *(1989), reflections on the process of writing; and* The Living, *(1992), a novel. Although usually associated with nature writing, Dillard turns her descriptive talents to humans in this snowball-throwing essay on coming of age.*

1   Some boys taught me to play football. This was fine sport. You thought up a new strategy for every play and whispered it to the others. You went out for a pass, fooling everyone. Best, you got to throw yourself mightily at someone's running legs. Either you

From *An American Childhood.* Published by HarperCollins Publishers, Inc. Copyright © 1987 by Annie Dillard.

brought him down or you hit the ground flat out on your chin, with your arms empty before you. It was all or nothing. If you hesitated in fear, you would miss and get hurt: you would take a hard fall while the kid got away, or you would get kicked in the face while the kid got away. But if you flung yourself wholeheartedly at the back of his knees—if you gathered and joined body and soul and pointed them diving fearlessly—then you likely wouldn't get hurt, and you'd stop the ball. Your fate, and your team's score, depended on your concentration and courage. Nothing girls did could compare with it.

Boys welcomed me at baseball, too, for I had, through enthusiastic practice, what was weirdly known as a boy's arm. In winter, in the snow, there was neither baseball nor football, so the boys and I threw snowballs at passing cars. I got in trouble throwing snowballs, and have seldom been happier since.

On one weekday morning after Christmas, six inches of new snow had just fallen. We were standing up to our boot tops in snow on a front yard on trafficked Reynolds Street, waiting for cars. The cars traveled Reynolds Street slowly and evenly; they were targets all but wrapped in red ribbons, cream puffs. We couldn't miss.

I was seven; the boys were eight, nine, and ten. The oldest two Fahey boys were there—Mikey and Peter—polite blond boys who lived near me on Lloyd Street, and who already had four brothers and sisters. My parents approved Mikey and Peter Fahey. Chickie McBride was there, a tough kid, and Billy Paul and Mackie Kean too, from across Reynolds, where the boys grew up dark and furious, grew up skinny, knowing, and skilled. We had all drifted from our houses that morning looking for action, and had found it here on Reynolds Street.

5

It was cloudy but cold. The cars' tires laid behind them on the snowy street a complex trail of beige chunks like crenellated castle walls. I had stepped on some earlier; they squeaked. We could have wished for more traffic. When a car came, we all popped it one. In the intervals between cars we reverted to the natural solitude of children.

I started making an iceball—a perfect iceball, from perfectly white snow, perfectly spherical, and squeezed perfectly translucent so no snow remained all the way through. (The Fahey boys and I considered it unfair actually to throw an iceball at somebody, but it had been known to happen.)

I had just embarked on the iceball project when we heard tire chains come clanking from afar. A black Buick was moving toward us

48

down the street. We all spread out, banged together some regular snowballs, took aim, and, when the Buick drew nigh, fired.

A soft snowball hit the driver's windshield right before the driver's face. It made a smashed star with a hump in the middle.

Often, of course, we hit our target, but this time, the only time in all of life, the car pulled over and stopped. Its wide black door opened; a man got out of it, running. He didn't even close the car door.

He ran after us, and we ran away from him, up the snowy Reynolds sidewalk. At the corner, I looked back; incredibly, he was still after us. He was in city clothes: a suit and tie, street shoes. Any normal adult would have quit, having sprung us into flight and made his point. This man was gaining on us. He was a thin man, all action. All of a sudden, we were running for our lives.

Wordless, we split up. We were on our turf; we could lose ourselves in the neighborhood backyards, everyone for himself. I paused and considered. Everyone had vanished except Mikey Fahey, who was just rounding the corner of a yellow brick house. Poor Mikey, I trailed him. The driver of the Buick sensibly picked the two of us to follow. The man apparently had all day.

He chased Mikey and me around the yellow house and up a backyard path we knew by heart: under a low tree, up a bank, through a hedge, down some snowy steps, and across the grocery store's delivery driveway. We smashed through a gap in another hedge, entered a scruffy backyard and ran around its back porch and tight between houses to Edgerton Avenue; we ran across Edgerton to an alley and up our own sliding woodpile to the Halls' front yard; he kept coming. We ran up Lloyd Street and wound through mazy backyards toward the steep hilltop at Willard and Lang.

He chased us silently, block after block. He chased us silently over picket fences, through thorny hedges, between houses, around garbage cans, and across streets. Every time I glanced back, choking for breath, I expected he would have quit. He must have been as breathless as we were. His jacket strained over his body. It was an immense discovery, pounding into my hot head with every sliding, joyous step, that this ordinary adult evidently knew what I thought only children who trained at football knew: that you have to fling yourself at what you're doing, you have to point yourself, forget yourself, aim, dive.

Mikey and I had nowhere to go, in our own neighborhood or out of it, but away from this man who was chasing us. He impelled us forward; we compelled him to follow our route. The air was cold; every breath tore my throat. We kept running, block after block; we kept improvising, backyard after backyard, running a frantic course and choosing it simultaneously, failing always to find small places or hard places to slow him down, and discovering always, exhilarated, dismayed, that only bare speed could save us—for he would never give up, this man—and we were losing speed.

15   He chased us through the backyard labyrinths of ten blocks before he caught us by our jackets. He caught us and we all stopped.

We three stood staggering, half blinded, coughing, in an obscure hilltop backyard: a man in his twenties, a boy, a girl. He had released our jackets, our pursuer, our captor, our hero: he knew we weren't going anywhere. We all played by the rules. Mikey and I unzipped our jackets. I pulled off my sopping mittens. Our tracks multiplied in the backyard's new snow. We had been breaking new snow all morning. We didn't look at each other. I was cherishing my excitement. The man's lower pants legs were wet; his cuffs were full of snow, and there was a prow of snow beneath them on his shoes and socks. Some trees bordered the little flat backyard, some messy winter trees. There was no one around: a clearing in a grove, and we the only players.

It was a long time before he could speak. I had some difficulty at first recalling why we were there. My lips felt swollen; I couldn't see out of the sides of my eyes; I kept coughing.

"You stupid kids," he began perfunctorily.

We listened perfunctorily indeed, if we listened at all, for the chewing out was redundant, a mere formality, and beside the point. The point was that he had chased us passionately without giving up, and so he had caught us. Now he came down to earth. I wanted the glory to last forever.

20   But how could the glory have lasted forever? We could have run through every backyard in North America until we got to Panama. But when he trapped us at the lip of the Panama Canal, what precisely could he have done to prolong the drama of the chase and cap its glory? I brooded about this for the next few years. He could only have fried Mikey Fahey and me in boiling oil, say, or dismembered us piecemeal, or staked us to anthills. None of which I really wanted, and none of which any adult was likely to do, even in the spirit of fun. He could only chew us out there in the Panamanian jungle, after months or years of exalting pursuit. He could only begin, "You stupid kids," and

continue in his ordinary Pittsburgh accent with his normal righteous anger and the usual common sense.

If in that snowy backyard the driver of the black Buick had cut off our heads, Mikey's and mine, I would have died happy, for nothing has required so much of me since as being chased all over Pittsburgh in the middle of winter—running terrified, exhausted—by this sainted, skinny, furious redheaded man who wished to have a word with us. I don't know how he found his way back to his car.

Questions on Meaning

1. What is Dillard's thesis in this essay? What does her run through the backyards of Pittsburgh tell her about how one must live life?
2. What were Dillard's feelings about her pursuer as the chase unfolded? How did this feeling change once she and Mikey were caught?
3. Why does Dillard use words such as "joyous" and "exhilarated" to describe her attempt to escape? Why does she comment that she "would have died happy" if the Buick driver had cut off their heads?

Questions on Rhetorical Strategy and Style

1. What is the basic rhetorical strategy of this essay? Where does Dillard alter this strategy? What different rhetorical strategies does she use to begin and end the essay?
2. Dillard creates vivid images throughout her essay, such as describing car tracks on the snowy road as "beige chunks like crenellated castle walls." Without rereading the essay, describe the imagery Dillard creates of the Buick and the driver. How does this add to the essay's impact?
3. What is the effect of Dillard's final sentence? Reread the last paragraph without that sentence. How does it affect the conclusion?

Writing Assignments

1. Observe a group of children playing. Imagine yourself doing exactly what they are doing—whether it is chasing each other around a playground or sitting in a sandbox, endlessly digging holes and filling buckets. Could you spend a day doing what they do? Could you apply their intensity to a simple task? Why or why not?
2. Write an essay about something you "fling yourself at." Why is it important to you? Why are you able to lose yourself in it? Define how it is different from activities that do not attract such enthusiasm from you.

On Dumpster Diving

Lars Eighner

Lars Eighner (1948–) became homeless in the 1980s after losing a job and being unable to find another immediately. He had been a student at the University of Texas at Austin before this, at which time he had been thrown out of his mother's house for being gay. While homeless he wrote stories and articles for magazines when he was able to find a typewriter to use and stay in one place long enough to write. He remained homeless for about three years, caring for and traveling with his dog, Lizbeth. In 1993 he published Travels with Lizbeth: Three Years on the Road and on the Streets, *an autobiographical account of that period which is in turns humorous, philosophical, and a good narrative. The following essay is an excerpted chapter from that book. Eighner's writing is successful because of the unabashedly honest and self-aware way he takes on his subject and opens his reader to a new world—here, the contents of trash dumpsters.*

This chapter was composed while the author was homeless. The present tense has been preserved.

1 Long before I began Dumpster diving I was impressed with Dumpsters, enough so that I wrote the Merriam-Webster research service to discover what I could about the word *Dumpster.* I learned from them that it is a proprietary word belonging to the Dempsey Dumpster company. Since then I have dutifully capitalized the word, although it was lowercased in almost all the citations Merriam-Webster photocopied for me. Dempsey's word is too apt. I have never heard these things called anything but Dumpsters. I do not

know anyone who knows the generic name for these objects. From time to time I have heard a wino or hobo give some corrupted credit to the original and call them Dipsy Dumpsters.

I began Dumpster diving about a year before I became homeless.

I prefer the word *scavenging* and use the word *scrounging* when I mean to be obscure. I have heard people, evidently meaning to be polite, use the word *foraging*, but I prefer to reserve that word for gathering nuts and berries and such which I do also according to the season and the opportunity. *Dumpster diving* seems to me to be a little too cute and, in my case, inaccurate because I lack the athletic ability to lower myself into the Dumpsters as the true divers do, much as their increased profit.

I like the frankness of the word *scavenging,* which I can hardly think of without picturing a big black snail on an aquarium wall. I live from the refuse of others. I am a scavenger. I think it a sound and honorable niche, although if I could I would naturally prefer to live the comfortable consumer life, perhaps—and only perhaps—as a slightly less wasteful consumer, owing to what I have learned as a scavenger.

5   While Lizbeth and I were still living in the shack on Avenue B as my   5
savings ran out, I put almost all my sporadic income into rent. The necessities of daily life I began to extract from Dumpsters. Yes, we ate from them. Except for jeans, all my clothes came from Dumpsters. Boom boxes, candles, bedding, toilet paper, a virgin male love doll, medicine, books, a typewriter, dishes, furnishings, and change, sometimes amounting to many dollars—I acquired many things from the Dumpsters.

I have learned much as a scavenger. I mean to put some of what I have learned down here, beginning with the practical art of Dumpster diving and proceeding to the abstract.

What is safe to eat?

After all, the finding of objects is becoming something of an urban art. Even respectable employed people will sometimes find something tempting sticking out of a Dumpster or standing beside one. Quite a number of people, not all of them of the bohemian type, are willing to brag that they found this or that piece in the trash. But eating from Dumpsters is what separates the dilettanti from the professionals. Eating safely from the Dumpsters involves three principles: using the senses and common sense to evaluate the conditions of the found materials, knowing the Dumpsters of a given area and checking them regularly, and seeking always to answer the question "Why was this discarded?"

Perhaps everyone who has a kitchen and a regular supply of groceries has, at one time or another, made a sandwich and eaten half of it before discovering mold on the bread or got a mouthful of milk before realizing the milk had turned. Nothing of the sort is likely to happen to a Dumpster diver because he is constantly reminded that most food is discarded for a reason. Yet a lot of perfectly good food can be found in Dumpsters.

10   Canned goods, for example, turn up fairly often in the Dumpsters   10
I frequent. All except the most phobic people would be willing to eat from a can, even if it came from a Dumpster. Canned goods are among the safest of foods to be found in Dumpsters but are not utterly foolproof.

Although very rare with modern canning methods, botulism is a possibility. Most other forms of food poisoning seldom do lasting harm to a healthy person, but botulism is most certainly fatal and often the first symptom is death. Except for carbonated beverages, all canned goods should contain a slight vacuum and suck air when first punctured. Bulging, rusty, and dented cans and cans that spew when punctured should be avoided, especially when the contents are not very acidic or syrupy.

Heat can break down the botulin, but this requires much more cooking than most people do to canned goods. To the extent that botulism occurs at all, of course, it can occur in cans on pantry shelves as well as in cans from Dumpsters. Need I say that home-canned goods are simply too risky to be recommended

From time to time one of my companions, aware of the source of my provisions, will ask, "Do you think these crackers are really safe to eat?" For some reason it is most often the crackers they ask about.

This question has always made me angry. Of course I would not offer my companion anything I had doubts about. But more than that, I wonder why he cannot evaluate the condition of the crackers for himself. I have no special knowledge and I have been wrong before. Since he knows where the food comes from, it seems to me he ought to assume some of the responsibility for deciding what he will put in his mouth. For myself I have few qualms about dry foods such as crackers, cookies, cereal, chips, and pasta if they are free of visible contaminates and still dry and crisp. Most often such things are found in the original packaging, which is not so much a positive sign as it is the absence of a negative one.

15   Raw fruits and vegetables with intact skins seem perfectly safe to 15 me, excluding of course the obviously rotten. Many are discarded for minor imperfections that can be pared away. Leafy vegetables, grapes, cauliflower, broccoli, and similar things may be contaminated by liquids and may be impractical to wash.

Candy, especially hard candy, is usually safe if it has not drawn ants. Chocolate is often discarded only because it has become discolored as the cocoa butter de-emulsified. Candying, after all, is one method of food preservation because pathogens do not like very sugary substances.

All of these foods might be found in any Dumpster and can be evaluated with some confidence largely on the basis of appearance. Beyond these are foods that cannot be correctly evaluated without additional information.

I began scavenging by pulling pizzas out of the Dumpster behind a pizza delivery shop. In general, prepared food requires caution, but in this case I knew when the shop closed and went to the Dumpster as soon as the last of the help left.

Such shops often get prank orders; both the orders and the products made to fill them are called *bogus.* Because help seldom stays long at these places, pizzas are often made with the wrong topping, refused on delivery for being cold, or baked incorrectly. The products to be discarded are boxed up because inventory is kept by counting boxes: A boxed pizza can be written off; an unboxed pizza does not exist.

20   I never placed a bogus order to increase the supply of pizzas and 20 I believe no one else was scavenging in this Dumpster. But the people in the shop became suspicious and began to retain their garbage in the shop overnight. While it lasted I had a steady supply of fresh, sometimes warm pizza. Because I knew the Dumpster I knew the source of the pizza, and because I visited the Dumpster regularly I knew what was fresh and what was yesterday's.

The area I frequent is inhabited by many affluent college students. I am not here by chance; the Dumpsters in this area are very rich. Students throw out many good things, including food. In particular they tend to throw everything out when they move at the end of a semester, before and after breaks, and around midterm, when many of them despair of college. So I find it advantageous to keep an eye on the academic calendar.

Students throw food away around breaks because they do not know whether it has spoiled or will spoil before they return. A typical discard is a half jar of peanut butter. In fact, nonorganic peanut butter does not require refrigeration and is unlikely to spoil in any reasonable time. The student does not know that, and since it is Daddy's money, the student decides not to take a chance. Opened containers require caution and some attention to the question. "Why was this discarded?" But in the case of discards from student apartments, the answer may be that the item was thrown out through carelessness, ignorance, or wastefulness. This can sometimes be deduced when the item is found with many others, including some that are obviously perfectly good.

Some students, and others, approach defrosting a freezer by chucking out the whole lot. Not only do the circumstances of such a find tell the story, but also the mass of frozen goods stays cold for a long time and items may be found still frozen or freshly thawed.

Yogurt, cheese, and sour cream are items that are often thrown out while they are still good. Occasionally I find a cheese with a spot of mold, which of course I just pare off, and because it is obvious why such a cheese was discarded, I treat it with less suspicion than an apparently perfect cheese found in similar circumstances. Yogurt is often discarded, still sealed, only because the expiration date on the carton had passed. This is one of my favorite finds because yogurt will keep for several days, even in warm weather.

25   Students throw out canned goods and staples at the end of se-   25 mesters and when they give up college at midterm. Drugs, pornography, spirits, and the like are often discarded when parents are expected—Dad's day, for example. And spirits also turn up after big party weekends, presumably discarded by the newly reformed. Wine and spirits, of course, keep perfectly well even once opened, but the same cannot be said of beer.

My test for carbonated soft drinks is whether they still fizz vigorously. Many juices or other beverages are too acidic or too syrupy to cause much concern, provided they are not visibly contaminated. I have discovered nasty molds in vegetable juices, even when the product was found under its original seal; I recommend that such products be decanted slowly into a clear glass. Liquids always require some care. One hot day I found a large jug of Pat O'Brien's Hurricane mix. The jug had been opened, but it was still ice cold. I drank three large glasses before it became apparent to me that someone had added the rum to the mix, and not a little rum. I never tasted the rum, and by the time I began to feel the effects I had already ingested a very large quantity of the beverage. Some divers would have considered this a boon, but being suddenly intoxicated in a public place in the early afternoon is not my idea of a good time.

I have heard of people maliciously contaminating discarded food and even handouts, but mostly I have heard of this from people with vivid imaginations who have had no experience with the Dumpsters themselves. Just before the pizza shop stopped discarding its garbage at night, jalapeños began showing up on most of the discarded pizzas. If indeed this was meant to discourage me it was a wasted effort because I am native Texan.

For myself, I avoid game, poultry, pork, and egg-based foods, whether I find them raw or cooked. I seldom have the means to cook what I find, but when I do I avail myself of plentiful supplies of beef, which is often in very good condition. I suppose fish becomes disagreeable before it becomes dangerous. Lizbeth is happy to have any such thing that is past its prime and, in fact, does not recognize fish as food until it is quite strong.

Home leftovers, as opposed to surpluses from restaurants, are very often bad. Evidently, especially among students, there is a common type of personality that carefully wraps up even the smallest leftover and shoves it into the back of the refrigerator for six months or so before discarding it. Characteristic of this type are the reused jars and margarine tubs to which the remains are committed. I avoid ethnic foods I am unfamiliar with. If I do not know what it is supposed to look like when it is good, I cannot be certain I will be able to tell if it is bad.

30 No matter how careful I am I still get dysentery at least once a 30 month, oftener in warm weather. I do not want to paint too romantic a picture. Dumpster diving has serious drawbacks as a way of life.

I learned to scavenge gradually, on my own. Since then I have initiated several companions into the trade. I have learned that there is a predictable series of stages a person goes through in learning to scavenge.

At first the new scavenger is filled with disgust and self-loathing. He is ashamed of being seen and may lurk around, trying to duck behind things, or he may try to dive at night. (In fact, most people instinctively look away from a scavenger. By skulking around, the novice calls attention to himself and arouses suspicion. Diving at night is ineffective and needlessly messy.)

Every grain of rice seems to be a maggot. Everything seems to stink. He can wipe the egg yolk off the found can, but he cannot erase from his mind the stigma of eating garbage.

That stage passes with experience. The scavenger finds a pair of running shoes that fit and look and smell brand-new. He finds a pocket calculator in perfect working order. He finds pristine ice cream, still frozen, more than he can eat or keep. He begins to understand: People throw away perfectly good stuff, a lot of perfectly good stuff.

35   At this stage, Dumpster shyness begins to dissipate. The diver, 35 after all, has the last laugh. He is finding all manner of good things that are his for the taking. Those who disparage his profession are the fools, not he.

He may begin to hang on to some perfectly good things for which he has neither a use nor a market. Then he begins to take note of the things that are not perfectly good but are nearly so. He mates a Walkman with broken earphones and one that is missing a battery cover. He picks up things that he can repair.

At this stage he may become lost and never recover. Dumpsters are full of things of some potential value to someone and also of things that never have much intrinsic value but are interesting. All the Dumpster divers I have known come to the point of trying to acquire everything they touch. Why not take it, they reason, since it is all free? This is, of course, hopeless. Most divers come to realize that they must restrict themselves to items of relatively immediate utility. But in some cases the diver simply cannot control himself. I have met several of these pack-rat types. Their ideas of the values of various pieces of junk verge on the psychotic. Every bit of glass may be a diamond, they think, and all that glisters, gold.

I tend to gain weight when I am scavenging. Partly this is because I always find far more pizza and doughnuts than water-packed tuna, nonfat yogurt, and fresh vegetables. Also I have not developed much faith in the reliability of Dumpsters as a food source, although it has been proven to me many times. I tend to eat as if I have no idea where my next meal is coming from. But mostly I just hate to see food go to waste and so I eat much more than I should. Something like this drives the obsession to collect junk.

As for collecting objects, I usually restrict myself to collecting one kind of small object at a time, such as pocket calculators, sunglasses, or campaign buttons. To live on the street I must anticipate my needs to a certain extent: I must pick up and save warm bedding I find in August because it will not be found in Dumpsters in November. As I have no access to health care, I often hoard essential drugs, such as antibiotics and antihistamines. (This course can be recommended only to those with some grounding in pharmacology. Antibiotics, for example, even when indicated are worse than useless if taken in insufficient amounts.) But even if I had a home with extensive storage space, I could not save everything that might be valuable in some contingency.

40   I have proprietary feelings about my Dumpsters. As I have mentioned, it is no accident that I scavenge from ones where good finds are common. But my limited experience with Dumpsters in other areas suggests to me that even in poorer areas, Dumpsters, if attended with sufficient diligence, can be made to yield a livelihood. The rich students discard perfectly good kiwifruit; poorer people discard perfectly good apples. Slacks and Polo shirts are found in the one place; jeans and T-shirts in the other. The population of competitors rather than the affluence of the dumpers most affects the feasibility of survival by scavenging. The large number of competitors is what puts me off the idea of trying to scavenge in places like Los Angeles.

Curiously, I do not mind my direct competition, other scavengers, so much as I hate the can scroungers.

People scrounge cans because they have to have a little cash. I have tried scrounging cans with an able-bodied companion. Afoot a can scrounger simply cannot make more than a few dollars a day. One can extract the necessities of life from the Dumpsters directly with far less effort than would be required to accumulate the equivalent value in cans. (These observations may not hold in places with container redemption laws.)

Can scroungers, then, are people who must have small amounts of cash. These are drug addicts and winos, mostly the latter because the amounts of cash are so small. Spirits and drugs do, like all other commodities, turn up in Dumpsters and the scavenger will from time to time have a half bottle of a rather good wine with his dinner. But the wino cannot survive on these occasional finds; he must have his daily dose to stave off the DTs. All the cans he can carry will buy about three bottles of Wild Irish Rose.

I do not begrudge them the cans, but can scroungers tend to tear up the Dumpsters, mixing the contents and littering the area. They become so specialized that they can see only cans. They earn my contempt by passing up change, canned goods, and readily hockable items.

45   There are precious few courtesies among scavengers. But it is   45 common practice to set aside surplus items: pairs of shoes, clothing, canned goods, and such. A true scavenger hates to see good stuff go to waste, and what he cannot use he leaves in good condition in plain sight.

Can scroungers lay waste to everything in their path and will stir one of a pair of good shoes to the bottom of a Dumpster, to be lost or ruined in the muck. Can scroungers will even go through individual garbage cans, something I have never seen a scavenger do.

Individual garbage cans are set out on the public easement only on garbage days. On other days going through them requires trespassing close to a dwelling. Going through individual garbage cans without scattering litter is almost impossible. Litter is likely to reduce the public's tolerance of scavenging. Individual cans are simply not as productive as Dumpsters; people in houses and duplexes do not move so often and for some reason do not tend to discard as much useful material. Moreover, the time required to go through one garbage can that serves one household is not much less than the time required to go through a Dumpster that contains the refuse of twenty apartments.

But my strongest reservation about going through individual garbage cans is that this seems to me a very personal kind of invasion to which I would object if I were a householder. Although many things in Dumpsters are obviously meant never to come to light, a Dumpster is somehow less personal.

I avoid trying to draw conclusions about the people who dump in the Dumpsters I frequent. I think it would be unethical to do so, although I know many people will find the idea of scavenger ethics too funny for words.

50   Dumpsters contain bank statements, correspondence, and other   50 documents, just as anyone might expect. But there are also less

obvious sources of information. Pill bottles, for example. The labels bear the name of the patient, the name of the doctor, and the name of the drug. AIDS drugs and antipsychotic medicines, to name but two groups, are specific and are seldom prescribed for any other disorders. The plastic compacts for birth-control pills usually have complete label information.

Despite all of this sensitive information, I have had only one apartment resident object to my going through the Dumpster. In that case it turned out the resident was a university athlete who was taking bets and who was afraid I would turn up his wager slips.

Occasionally a find tells a story. I once found a small paper bag containing some unused condoms, several partial tubes of flavored sexual lubricants, a partially used compact of birth-control pills, and the torn pieces of a picture of a young man. Clearly she was through with him and planning to give up sex altogether.

Dumpster things are often sad—abandoned teddy bears, shredded wedding books, despaired-of sales kits. I find many pets lying in state in Dumpsters. Although I hope to get off the streets so that Lizbeth can have a long and comfortable old age, I know this hope is not very realistic. So I suppose when her time comes she too will go into a Dumpster. I will have no better place for her. And after all, it is fitting, since for most of her life her livelihood has come from the Dumpster. When she finds something I think is safe that has been spilled from a Dumpster, I let her have it. She already knows the route around the best ones. I like to think that if she survives me she will have a chance of evading the dog catcher and of finding her sustenance on the route.

Silly vanities also come to rest in the Dumpsters. I am a rather accomplished needleworker. I get a lot of material from the Dumpsters. Evidently sorority girls, hoping to impress someone, perhaps themselves, with their mastery of a womanly art, buy a lot of embroider-by-number kits, work a few stitches horribly, and eventually discard the whole mess. I pull out their stitches, turn the canvas over, and work an original design. Do not think I refrain from chuckling as I make gifts from these kits.

55 I find diaries and journals. I have often thought of compiling a 55 book of literary found objects. And perhaps I will one day. But what I find is hopelessly commonplace and bad without being, even unconsciously, camp. College students also discard their papers. I am

horrified to discover the kind of paper that now merits an A in an undergraduate course. I am grateful, however, for the number of good books and magazines the students throw out.

In the area I know best I have never discovered vermin in the Dumpsters, but there are two kinds of kitty surprise. One is alley cats whom I meet as they leap, claws first, out of Dumpsters. This is especially thrilling when I have Lizbeth in tow. The other kind of kitty surprise is a plastic garbage bag filled with some ponderous, amorphous mass. This always proves to be used cat litter.

City bees harvest doughnut glaze and this makes the Dumpster at the doughnut shop more interesting. My faith in the instinctive wisdom of animals is always shaken whenever I see Lizbeth attempt to catch a bee in her mouth, which she does whenever bees are present. Evidently some birds find Dumpsters profitable, for birdie surprise is almost as common as kitty surprise of the first kind. In hunting season all kinds of small game turn up in Dumpsters, some of it, sadly, not entirely dead. Curiously, summer and winter, maggots are uncommon.

The worst of the living and near-living hazards of the Dumpsters are the fire ants. The food they claim is not much of a loss, but they are vicious and aggressive. It is very easy to brush against some surface of the Dumpster and pick up half a dozen or more fire ants, usually in some sensitive area such as the underarm. One advantage of bringing Lizbeth along as I make Dumpster rounds is that, for obvious reasons, she is very alert to ground-based fire ants. When Lizbeth recognizes a fire-ant infestation around our feet, she does the Dance of the Zillion Fire Ants. I have learned not to ignore this warning from Lizbeth, whether I perceive the tiny ants or not, but to remove ourselves at Lizbeth's first pas de bourrée. All the more so because the ants are the worst in the summer months when I wear flip-flops if I have them. (Perhaps someone will misunderstand this. Lizbeth does the Dance of the Zillion Fire Ants when she recognizes more fire ants than she cares to eat, not when she is being bitten. Since I have learned to react promptly, she does not get bitten at all. It is the isolated patrol of fire ants that falls in Lizbeth's range that deserves pity. She finds them quite tasty.)

By far the best way to go through a Dumpster is to lower yourself into it. Most of the good stuff tends to settle at the bottom because it is usually weightier than the rubbish. My more athletic companions have often demonstrated to me that they can extract much good material from a Dumpster I have already been over.

60 To those psychologically or physically unprepared to enter a 60 Dumpster, I recommend a stout stick, preferably with some barb or hook at one end. The hook can be used to grab plastic garbage bags. When I find canned goods or other objects loose at the bottom of a Dumpster, I lower a bag into it, roll the desired object into the bag, and then hoist the bag out—a procedure more easily described than executed. Much Dumpster diving is a matter of experience for which nothing will do except practice.

Dumpster diving is outdoor work, often surprisingly pleasant. It is not entirely predictable; things of interest turn up every day and some days there are finds of great value. I am always very pleased when I can turn up exactly the thing I most wanted to find. Yet in spite of the element of chance, scavenging more than most other pursuits tends to yield returns in some proportion to the effort and intelligence brought to bear. It is very sweet to turn up a few dollars in change from a Dumpster that has just been gone over by a wino.

The land is now covered with cities. The cities are full of Dumpsters. If a member of the canine race is ever able to know what it is doing, then Lizbeth knows that when we go around to the Dumpsters, we are hunting. I think of scavenging as a modern form of self-reliance. In any event, after having survived nearly ten years of government service, where everything is geared to the lowest common denominator, I find it refreshing to have work that rewards initiative and effort. Certainly I would be happy to have a sinecure again, but I am no longer heartbroken that I left one.

I find from the experience of scavenging two rather deep lessons. The first is to take what you can use and let the rest go by. I have come to think that there is no value in the abstract. A thing I cannot use or make useful, perhaps by trading, has no value however rare or fine it may be. I mean useful in a broad sense—some art I would find useful and some otherwise.

I was shocked to realize that some things are not worth acquiring, but now I think it is so. Some material things are white elephants that eat up the possessor's substance. The second lesson is the transience of material being. This has not quite converted me to a dualist, but it has made some headway in that direction. I do not suppose that ideas are immortal, but certainly mental things are longer lived than other material things.

65 Once I was the sort of person who invests objects with sentimen- 65 tal value. Now I no longer have those objects, but I have the sentiments yet.

Many times in our travels I have lost everything but the clothes I was wearing and Lizbeth. The things I find in Dumpsters, the love letters and rag dolls of so many lives, remind me of this lesson. Now I hardly pick up a thing without envisioning the time I will cast it aside. This I think is a healthy state of mind. Almost everything I have now has already been cast out at least once, proving that what I own is valueless to someone.

Anyway, I find my desire to grab for the gaudy bauble has been largely sated. I think this is an attitude I share with the very wealthy—we both know there is plenty more where what we have came from. Between us are the rat-race millions who nightly scavenge the cable channels looking for they know not what.

I am sorry for them.

Questions on Meaning

1. Describe your initial reaction to this essay, and explain what about the essay caused this reaction. For example if you were surprised, what specifically did you find surprising?
2. As Eighner analyzes the contents of the dumpsters, he also analyzes the motives of the people who threw these things away. How do these two levels of analysis shape the essay and contribute to its theme?
3. By the end of this essay Eighner has moved to reflective comments on society at large, including the "rat-race millions." What ultimately is he saying about our society? Discuss how consistent this ending is with the development of the essay overall.

Questions on Rhetorical Strategy and Style

1. Eighner's polished use of language and his vocabulary are sophisticated, giving the impression of an educated and intelligent person. To what extent is this consistent with your previous image of what most homeless people are like? Explain the effects of Eighner's very careful definition and explanation of his subject.
2. In addition to analyzing types of food and types of motives for throwing things away, the essay analyzes many other aspects of the "dumpster diving" experience, such as his analysis and classification of different sorts of scavengers. How many different types does he identify? Describe how they are different and what they have in common.
3. This essay is powerful in part because of Eighner's vivid use of detail. Choose any part of the essay describing in detail the contents of dumpsters, and identify in his description the words that most successfully evoke a physical image of the dumpster.

Writing Assignments

1. How do you react to Eighner's comments about wasteful, affluent students? Ask some other students about what things they throw away, and consider your own habits. Do Eighner's descriptions apply to you and other students you know? Why or why not? If so, how does that make you feel? Organize your findings into an essay about possessions.

2. What are your own favorite possessions? Think about your feelings for them, and reflect on what these feelings reveal about what makes you happy. Write an essay in which you explore the relationship between "things" and happiness, using yourself and others as examples.

The Brown Wasps

Loren Eiseley

Loren Eiseley (1907–1977) was born in Lincoln, Ne-braska. A noted anthropologist, educator, poet, and author, Eiseley was lauded for his beautiful prose and his ability to make science interesting and entertaining to lay readers. Eiseley taught at the University of Kansas at Lawrence, Oberlin College, and the University of Pennsylvania. His books include The Immense Journey *(1957)*, Darwin's Century *(1958)*, The Firmament of Time *(rev. ed. 1960), and* Night Country *(1971). In this essay, Eise-ley notes the ability of humans as well as other animals to hold an image in the mind—the homing instinct—despite the proof of reality.*

1   There is a corner in the waiting room of one of the great Eastern stations where women never sit. It is always in the shadow and overhung by rows of lockers. It is, however, always frequented—not so much by genuine travelers as by the dying. It is here that a certain element of the abandoned poor seeks a refuge out of the weather, clinging for a few hours longer to the city that has fathered them. In a precisely similar manner I have seen, on a sunny day in midwinter, a few old brown wasps creep slowly over an abandoned wasp nest in a thicket. Numbed and forgetful and frost-blackened, the hum of the spring hive still resounded faintly in their sodden tissues. Then the temperature would fall and they would drop away into the white oblivion of the snow. Here in the station it is in no way different save that the city is busy in its snows. But the old ones cling to their seats as though these were symbolic and could not be given up. Now and then they sleep, their gray old heads resting with painful awkwardness on the backs of the benches.

From *The Night Country* by Loren Eiseley. Published by Scribner, a Division of Simon & Schuster. Copyright © 1971 by Loren Eiseley.

Also they are not at rest. For an hour they may sleep in the gasping exhaustion of the ill-nourished and aged who have to walk in the night. Then a policeman comes by on his round and nudges them upright.

"You can't sleep here," he growls.

A strange ritual then begins. An old man is difficult to waken. After a muttered conversation the policeman presses a coin into his hand and passes fiercely along the benches prodding and gesturing toward the door. In his wake, like birds rising and settling behind the passage of a farmer through a cornfield, the men totter up, move a few paces and subside once more upon the benches.

One man, after a slight, apologetic lurch, does not move at all. Tubercularly thin, he sleeps on steadily. The policeman does not look back. To him, too, this has become a ritual. He will not have to notice it again officially for another hour.

Once in a while one of the sleepers will not awake. Like the brown wasps, he will have had his wish to die in the great droning center of the hive rather than in some lonely room. It is not so bad here with the shuffle of footsteps and the knowledge that there are others who share the bad luck of the world. There are also the whistles and the sounds of everyone, everyone in the world, starting on journeys. Amidst so many journeys somebody is bound to come out all right. Somebody.

Maybe it was on a like thought that the brown wasps fell away from the old paper nest in the thicket. You hold till the last, even if it is only to a public seat in a railroad station. You want your place in the hive more than you want a room or a place where the aged can be eased gently out of the way. It is the place that matters, the place at the heart of things. It is life that you want, that bruises your gray old head with the hard chairs; a man has a right to his place.

But sometimes the place is lost in the years behind us. Or sometimes it is a thing of air, a kind of vaporous distortion above a heap of rubble. We cling to a time and place because without them man is lost, not only man but life. This is why the voices, real or unreal, which speak from the floating trumpets at spiritualist seances are so unnerving. They are voices out of nowhere whose only reality lies in their ability to stir the memory of a living person with some fragment of the past. Before the medium's cabinet both the dead and the living revolve endlessly about an episode, a place, an event that has already been engulfed by time.

This feeling runs deep in life; it brings stray cats running over endless miles, and birds homing from the ends of the earth. It is as though all living creatures, and particularly the more intelligent, can survive only by fixing or transforming a bit of time into space or by securing a bit of space with its objects immortalized and made permanent in time. For example, I once saw, on a flower pot in my own living room, the efforts of a field mouse to build a remembered field. I have lived to see this episode repeated in a thousand guises, and since I have spent a large portion of my life in the shade of a nonexistent tree, I think I am entitled to speak for the field mouse.

10   One day as I cut across the field which at the time extended on   10
one side of our suburban shopping center, I found a giant slug feeding from a runnel of pink ice cream in an abandoned Dixie cup. I could see his eyes telescope and protrude in a kind of dim, uncertain ecstasy as his dark body bunched and elongated in the curve of the cup. Then, as I stood there at the edge of the concrete, contemplating the slug, I began to realize it was like standing on a shore where a different type of life creeps up and fumbles tentatively among the rocks and sea wrack. It knows its place and will only creep so far until something changes. Little by little as I stood there I began to see more of this shore that surrounds the place of man. I looked with sudden care and attention at things I had been running over thoughtlessly for years. I even waded out a short way into the grass and the wild-rose thickets to see more. A huge black-belted bee went droning by and there were some indistinct scurrying in the underbrush.

Then I came to a sign which informed me that this field was to be the site of a new Wanamaker suburban store. Thousands of obscure lives were about to perish, the spores of puffballs would go smoking off to new fields, and the bodies of little white-footed mice would be crunched under the inexorable wheels of the bulldozers. Life disappears or modifies its appearances so fast that everything takes on an aspect of illusion—a momentary fizzing and boiling with smoke rings, like pouring dissident chemicals into a retort. Here man was advancing, but in a few years his plaster and bricks would be disappearing once more into the insatiable maw of the clover. Being of an archaeological cast of mind, I thought of this fact with an obscure sense of satisfaction and waded back through the rose thickets to the concrete parking lot. As I did so, a mouse scurried ahead of me, frightened of my steps if not of that ominous Wanamaker sign. I saw him vanish in the general direction of my apartment house, his little body quivering with fear in the great open sun on the blazing concrete. Blinded and confused, he was running straight away from his field. In another week scores would follow him.

I forgot the episode then and went home to the quiet of my living room. It was not until a week later, letting myself into the apartment, that I realized I had a visitor. I am fond of plants and had several ferns standing on the floor in pots to avoid the noon glare by the south window.

As I snapped on the light and glanced carelessly around the room, I saw a little heap of earth on the carpet and a scrabble of pebbles that had been kicked merrily over the edge of one of the flower pots. To my astonishment I discovered a full-fledged burrow delving downward among the fern roots. I waited silently. The creature who had made the burrow did not appear. I remembered the wild field then, and the flight of the mice. No house mouse, no *Mus domesticus,* had kicked up this little heap of earth or sought refuge under a fern root in a flower pot. I thought of the desperate little creature I had seen fleeing from the wild-rose thicket. Through intricacies of pipes and attics, he, or one of his fellows, had climbed to this high green solitary room. I could visualize what had occurred. He had an image in his head, a world of seed pods and quiet, of green sheltering leaves in the dim light among the weed stems. It was the only world he knew and it was gone.

Somehow in his flight he had found his way to this room with drawn shades where no one would come till nightfall. And here he had smelled garden leaves and run quickly up the flower pot to dabble his paws in common earth. He had even struggled half the afternoon to carry his burrow deeper and had failed. I examined the hole, but no whiskered twitching face appeared. He was gone. I gathered up the earth and refilled the burrow. I did not expect to find traces of him again.

15   Yet for three nights thereafter I came home to the darkened room 15 and my ferns to find the dirt kicked gaily about the rug and the burrow reopened, though I was never able to catch the field mouse within it. I dropped a little food about the mouth of the burrow, but it was never touched. I looked under beds or sat reading with one ear cocked for rustlings in the ferns. It was all in vain; I never saw him. Probably he ended in a trap in some other tenant's room.

But before he disappeared I had come to look hopefully for his evening burrow. About my ferns there had begun to linger the insubstantial vapor of an autumn field, the distilled essence, as it were, of a mouse brain in exile from its home. It was a small dream, like our dreams, carried a long and weary journey along pipes and through spider webs, past holes over which loomed the shadows of waiting cats, and finally, desperately, into this room where he had played in the shuttered daylight for an hour among the green ferns on the floor. Every day these invisible dreams pass us on the street, or rise from beneath our feet, or look out upon us from beneath a bush.

Some years ago the old elevated railway in Philadelphia was torn down and replaced by a subway system. This ancient El with its barnlike stations containing nut-vending machines and scattered food scraps had, for generations, been the favorite feeding ground of flocks of pigeons, generally one flock to a station along the route of the El. Hundreds of pigeons were dependent upon the system. They flapped in and out of its stanchions and steel work or gathered in watchful little audiences about the feet of anyone who rattled the peanut-vending machines. They even watched people who jingled change in their hands, and prospected for food under the feet of the crowds who gathered between trains. Probably very few among the waiting people who tossed a crumb to an eager pigeon realized that this El was like a food-bearing river, and that the life which haunted its banks was dependent upon the running of the trains with their human freight.

I saw the river stop.

The time came when the underground tubes were ready; the traffic was transferred to a realm unreachable by pigeons. It was like a great river subsiding suddenly into desert sands. For a day, for two days, pigeons continued to circle over the El or stand close to the red vending machines. They were patient birds, and surely this great river which had flowed through the lives of unnumbered generations were merely suffering from some momentary drought.

They listened for the familiar vibrations that had always heralded an approaching train; they flapped hopefully about the head of an occasional workman walking along the steel runways. They passed from one empty station to another, all the while growing hungrier. Finally they flew away.

I thought I had seen the last of them about the El, but there was a revival and it provided a curious instance of the memory of living things for a way of life or a locality that has long been cherished. Some weeks after the El was abandoned workmen began to tear it down. I went to work every morning by one particular station, and the time came when the demolition crews reached this spot. Acetylene torches showered passersby with sparks, pneumatic drills hammered at the base of the structure, and a blind man who, like the pigeons, had clung with his cup to a stairway leading to the change booth, was forced to give up his place.

It was then, strangely, momentarily, one morning that I witnessed the return of a little band of the familiar pigeons. I even recognized one or two members of the flock that had lived around this particular station before they were dispersed into the streets. They flew bravely in and out among the sparks and the hammers and the shouting workmen. They had returned—and they had returned because the hubbub of the wreckers had convinced them that the river was about to flow once more. For several hours they flapped in and out through the empty windows, nodding their heads and watching the fall of girders with attentive little eyes. By the following morning the station was reduced to some burned-off stanchions in the street. My bird friends had gone. It was plain, however, that they retained a memory for an insubstantial structure now compounded of air and time. Even the blind man clung to it. Someone had provided him with a chair, and he sat at the same corner staring sightlessly at an invisible stairway where, so far as he was concerned, the crowds were still ascending to the trains.

I have said my life has been passed in the shade of a nonexistent tree, so that such sights do not offend me. Prematurely I am one of the brown wasps and I often sit with them in the great droning hive of the station, dreaming sometimes of a certain tree. It was planted sixty years ago by a boy with a bucket and a toy spade in a little Nebraska town. That boy was myself. It was a cottonwood sapling and the boy remembered it because of some words spoken by his father and because everyone died or moved away who was supposed to wait and grow old under its shade. The boy was passed from hand to hand, but the tree for some intangible reason had taken root in his mind. It was under its branches that he sheltered; it was from this tree that his memories, which are my memories, led away into the world.

After sixty years the mood of the brown wasps grows heavier upon one. During a long inward struggle I thought it would do me good to go and look upon that actual tree. I found a rational excuse in which to clothe this madness. I purchased a ticket and at the end of two thousand miles I walked another mile to an address that was still the same. The house had not been altered.

25   I came close to the white picket fence and reluctantly, with great effort, looked down the long vista of the yard. There was nothing there to see. For sixty years that cottonwood had been growing in my mind. Season by season its seeds had been floating farther on the hot prairie winds. We had planted it lovingly there, my father and I, because he had a great hunger for soil and live things growing, and because none of these things had long been ours to protect. We had planted the little sapling and watered it faithfully, and I remembered that I had run out with my small bucket to drench its roots the day we moved away. And all the years since it had been growing in my mind, a huge tree that somehow stood for my father and the love I bore him. I took a grasp on the picket fence and forced myself to look again.

A boy with the hard bird eye of youth pedaled a tricycle slowly up beside me.

"What'cha lookin' at?" he asked curiously.

"A tree," I said.

"What for?" he said.

30   "It isn't there," I said, to myself mostly, and began to walk away at a pace just slow enough not to seem to be running.

"What isn't there?" the boy asked. I didn't answer. It was obvious I was attached by a thread to a thing that had never been there, or certainly not for long. Something that had to be held in the air, or sustained in the mind, because it was part of my orientation in the universe and I could not survive without it. There was more than an animal's attachment to a place. There was something else, the attachment of the spirit to a grouping of events in time; it was part of our morality.

So I had come home at last, driven by a memory in the brain as surely as the field mouse who had delved long ago into my flower pot or the pigeons flying forever amidst the rattle of nut-vending machines. These, the burrow under the greenery in my living room and the red-bellied bowls of peanuts now hovering in midair in the minds of pigeons, were all part of an elusive world that existed nowhere and yet everywhere. I looked once at the real world about me while the persistent boy pedaled at my heels.

It was without meaning, though my feet took a remembered path. In sixty years the house and street had rotted out of my mind. But the tree, the tree that no longer was, that had perished in its first season, bloomed on in my individual mind, unblemished as my father's words. "We'll plant a tree here, son, and we're not going to move any more. And when you're an old, old man you can sit under it and think how we planted it here, you and me, together."

I began to outpace the boy on the tricycle.

35   "Do you live here, Mister?" he shouted after me suspiciously I   35 took a firm grasp on airy nothing—to be precise, on the bole of a great tree. "I do," I said. I spoke for myself, one field mouse, and several pigeons. We were all out of touch but somehow permanent. It was the world that had changed.

Questions on Meaning

1. "A man has a right to his place," Eiseley writes. Why does he feel it is important that humans—and other animals—have a place they can return to, even if only in their minds? What does the essay say about how and where he would choose to die?
2. What does Eiseley find when he returns to find his cottonwood tree? Why does he write that it "had perished in its first season"?
3. What does the boy on the tricycle symbolize to Eiseley? How would it have affected his closing if he had omitted that anecdote from the story?

Questions on Rhetorical Strategy and Style

1. How does Eiseley compare and contrast the "home" of the wasps, field mouse, the pigeons, the homeless persons, the blind man, and himself? What did each find when they tried to find their "home"? How do you react to his juxtaposing the "instincts" of humans with other animals?
2. Eiseley uses a number of descriptive narrative passages in this essay. Reread and outline the essay. Find and mark his transitions between these narratives.
3. List the stages in which Eiseley analyzes the process by which the pigeons left and then returned to their home.

Writing Assignments

1. Do you have a special place that lingers in your memory, such as a place you lived when you were young, a grandparent's home, an elementary school you attended, or a special hideaway in which you played one summer? Describe the place and what it has symbolized for you. If you have ever returned, describe how it had changed and how returning affected your memories. Did you wish you had not returned?
2. Development projects are often opposed because of the destruction of animal habitats. Write an essay about the changes on local animal life caused by a development project you are familiar with. If the development site formerly was a forest, for example, research the types of birds, ground animals, and insects that were killed or displaced; if an open field, determine the animals who would have lived in that habitat. Consider the time of year in your

analysis: fall construction would destroy winter burrows and nests, while spring construction could displace or kill newly born or hatched animals. What options are available to developers to minimize the impact on animals?

Trust Me. In These Parts, Hot Dogs Actually Repel Bears

Ian Frazier

Ian Frazier was born in Cleveland, Ohio in 1951. He wrote for the Harvard Lampoon *while a student at Harvard University, where he graduated in 1973. He has been a staff writer for* The New Yorker *for many years. Frazier's most recent work is* On the Rez *(2000), a first-person narrative of Frazier's trip to Pine Ridge Indian Reservation in South Dakota. He is known especially for his comic essays on rural America. In this selection, from* Outside *magazine, Frazier takes a humorous and ironic look at our tendency to accept bad advice while traveling through the back roads of the United States.*

Let us now celebrate one of our most bountiful outdoor resources: bad advice. And if you listen carefully and act right away, it's absolutely free!

1   Some years ago, on a camping trip in the pine woods of northern Michigan, my friend Don brought along a copy of an outdoor cookbook that appeared on the best-seller lists at the time. This book contained many ingenious and easy-sounding recipes; one that Don especially wanted to try was called "Breakfast in a Paper Bag." According to this recipe, you could take a small paper lunch sack, put strips of bacon in the bottom, break an egg into the sack on top of the

"Trust Me. In These Parts, Hot Dogs Actually Repel Bears" by Ian Frazier, published in *Outside* magazine, December 1999.

bacon, fold down the top of the sack, push a stick through the fold, hold the sack over hot coals, and cook the bacon and egg in the sack in about ten minutes.

I watched as Don followed the directions exactly. Both he and I remarked that we would naturally have thought the sack would burn; the recipe, however, declared, "grease will coat the bottom of the bag as it cooks." Somehow we both took this to mean that the grease, counterintuitively, actually made the bag less likely to burn. Marveling at the "who would have guessed" magic of it, we picked a good spot in the hot coals of our campfire, and Don held the sack above them. We watched. In a second and a half, the bag burst into leaping flames. Don was yelling for help, waving the bag around trying to extinguish it, scattering egg yolk and smoldering strips of bacon and flaming paper into the combustible pines while people at adjoining campfires stared in horror and wondered what they should do.

The wild figures that the burning breakfast described in midair as Don waved the stick, the look of outraged, imbecile shock reflected on our faces—those are images that stay with me. I replay the incident often in my mind. It is like a parable. Because a book told us to, we attempted to use greased paper as a frying pan on an open fire. For all I know, the trick is possible if you do it just so; we never repeated the experiment. But to me the incident illustrates a larger truth about our species when it ventures out of doors. We go forth in abundant ignorance, near-blind with fantasy, witlessly trusting words on a page or a tip a guy we'd never met before gave us at a sporting-goods counter in a giant discount store. About half of the time, the faith that leads us into the outdoors is based in advice that is half-baked, made-up, hypothetical, uninformed, spurious, or deliberately, heedlessly bad.

Greenland, for example, did not turn out to be very green, Viking hype to the contrary. Despite what a Pawnee or Wichita Indian told the Spanish explorer Francisco Vásquez de Coronado, there were no cities of gold in western Kansas, no canoes with oarlocks made of gold, no tree branches hung with little gold bells that soothed the king (also nonexistent) during his afternoon nap; a summer's march on the Great Plains in piping-hot armor presumably bore these truths upon the would-be conquistador in an unforgettable way. Lewis and Clark found no elephants on their journey, though President Jefferson, believing reports from the frontier, had said they should be on the lookout for them. And then there was Lansford W. Hastings, the adventurer and promoter of Sacramento, purveyor of some of the worst advice of all time. He told the prospective wagon-train emigrants to California that he had discovered a shortcut (modestly named the Hastings Cutoff) that reduced travel time by many days. Yes, it did cross a few extra deserts and some unusually high mountain ranges; the unfortunate Donner Party read Hastings's book, followed his route, and famously came to its grisly end below the narrow Sierra pass that now bears its name. According to local legend, the air in the Utah foothills is still blue from the curses that emigrants heaped on Lansford W. Hastings along the way.

People will tell you just any damn thing. I have found this to be especially so in establishments called Pappy's, Cappy's, Pop's, or Dad's. The wizened, senior quality of the names seems to give the people who work in such places a license to browbeat customers and pass on whatever opinionated misinformation they please. When I go through the door of a Pappy's or Cappy's—usually it's a fishing tackle shop, a general store, or a bar—usually there's a fat older guy sitting behind the counter with his T-shirt up over his stomach and his navel peeking out. That will be Pappy, or Cappy. Sometimes it's both. Pappy looks at me without looking at me and remarks to Cappy that the gear I've got on is too light for the country at this time of year, and Cappy agrees, crustily; then I ask a touristy, greenhorn question, and we're off. Cappy, backed by Pappy, says the rig I'm driving won't make it up that forest service road, and I'm headed in the wrong direction anyhow, and the best place to camp isn't where I'm going but far in the other direction, up top of Corkscrew Butte, which is closed now, as is well known.

The saddest part is that I crumble in this situation, every time. I have taken more wrong advice, have bought more unnecessary maps, trout flies, water filtration devices, and assorted paraphernalia from Pappys and Cappys with their navels showing than I like to think about. Some essential element left out of my psychic immune system causes me always to defer to these guys and believe what they say. And while the Lansford W. Hastings type of bad advice tells people they can do things they really can't, the Cappy-Pappy type of advice is generally the opposite. Cappy and Pappy have been sitting around their failing store for so long that they are now convinced you're a fool for trying to do anything at all.

Complicating matters still further is Happy. She used to be married to Cappy but is now married to Pappy, or vice-versa. Happy has missing teeth and a freestyle hairdo, and she hangs out in the back of the store listening in and irritatedly yelling statements that contradict most of what Pappy and Cappy say. The effect is to send you out the door as confused as it is possible to be. What's different about Happy, however, is that eventually she will tell you the truth. When you return your rented bicycle or rowboat in the evening, Pappy and Cappy are packed away in glycolene somewhere and Happy is waiting for you in the twilight, swatting mosquitoes and snapping the elastic band of her trousers against her side. You have found no berries, seen no birds, caught no fish; and Happy will tell you that the birds were right in front of the house all afternoon, the best berry bushes are behind the snow-machine shed, and she herself just caught 50 fish right off the dock. She will even show you her full stringer, cackling, "You gotta know the right place to go!"

Of course, people usually keep their best advice to themselves. They'd be crazy not to, what with all the crowds tramping around outdoors nowadays. I can understand such caution, in principle; but I consider it stingy and mean when it is applied to me. There's a certain facial expression people often have when they are withholding the one key piece of information I really need. They smile broadly with lips shut tight as a mason jar, and a cheery blankness fills their eyes. This expression irks me to no end. Misleading blather I can put up with, and even enjoy if it's preposterous enough; but smug, determined silence is a posted sign, a locked gate, an unlisted phone. Also, I think it's the real message behind today's deluge of information-age outdoor advice, most of which seems to be about crampons, rebreathers, and synthetic sleeping bag fill. What you wanted to know does not appear. Somehow, especially in the more desirable destinations outdoors, withheld advice is the most common kind.

I craved good advice one summer when I fished a little-known midwestern river full of brown trout. Every few days I went to the local fly-fishing store and asked the guys who worked there where in the river the really big fish I had heard about might be. The guys were friendly, and more than willing to sell me stuff, but when I asked that question I met the mason-jar expression I've described. I tried being winsome; I portrayed myself as fishless and pitiable, told jokes, drank coffee, hung around. On the subject of vital interest, nobody offered word one.

10   I halfway gave up and began driving the back roads aimlessly. 10 Then just at sunset one evening I suddenly came upon a dozen or more cars and pickups parked in the high grass along a road I'd never been on before. I pulled over, got out, and crashed through the brush to investigate. There in a marshy lowland was a section of river I had never tried, with insects popping on its surface and monster brown trout slurping them down and fly rods swishing like scythes in the summer air. Among the intent anglers along the bank I recognized the fishing-store owner's son, one of the mason-jar-smiling regulars. The experience taught me an important outdoor fact: Regardless of what the people who know tell you or don't tell you, an off-road gathering of parked cars doesn't lie.

In case you're wondering, this particular good fishing spot was on the Pigeon River near the town of Vanderbilt, Michigan, upstream from the dam. It's been years since I fished there, so I can't vouch for the up-to-dateness of my information. But unlike smarter outdoorsmen, I am happy to pass along whatever I can because I myself am now gabby and free with advice to an embarrassing degree. I noticed the change as I got older; I hit my midforties, and from nowhere endless, windy sentences of questionable advice began coming out of me. An old-guy voice takes on its own momentum, and I seem unable to stop it even when I have no idea what I'm talking about. Sometimes when strangers ask me for directions on a hiking trail or just around town, I give detailed wrong answers off the top of my head rather than admit I don't know. When my hearers are out of sight my reason returns and I realize what I've done. Then I make myself scarce, for fear that they will discover my ridiculousness and come back in a rage looking for me.

Outdoor magazines I read as a child featured authoritative fellows in plaid shirts and fedoras who offered sensible tips about how to find water in the desert by cutting open cacti, how to make bread from cattail roots, or how to predict the weather by the thickness of the walls of muskrat dens. I wish I had down-to-earth wisdom like that to impart, but when I search my knowledge all that comes to mind is advice that would cause me to run and hide after I gave it. The one piece of real advice that I do have is not outdoor advice, strictly speaking; I think, however, that its soundness makes up for that drawback. It is true virtually every time, in all lands and cultures. I offer it as the one completely trustworthy piece of advice I know, and it is this: Never marry a man whose nickname is "The Killer."

Other than that, you're on your own.

Questions on Meaning

1. Have you ever received or given the kind of advice Frazier recounts in this article? Why or why not? What social trends or conditions exist today that make this piece particularly relevant and funny?
2. Why do people give bad advice? What makes it so difficult for us to admit that we don't know something?

Questions Rhetorical Strategy and Style

1. One storytelling tradition centers on creating the "tall tale" or lore. How is the Frazier essay written in that manner? In what ways does it draw on exaggeration for its effect?
2. What other sources of humor does the writer draw on? How is he able to poke fun at people and still get his readers laughing? How would you describe his relationship with his readers?
3. Why does Frazier begin the piece with the account of the paper bag? Why does he take such pains to describe every step in the process?

Writing Assignments

1. Research a current trend in U.S. society. The trend can be amusing or serious. Describe that trend in detail so that your readers can fully understand it. In your essay, speculate as to "the larger truth about our species" revealed through this behavior or activity.
2. Write an essay in which you discuss how life in the Information Age and changed our relationship to the outdoors, for better or for worse. Either way, try to use humor to appeal to your readers.

The Median Isn't the Message

Stephen Jay Gould

Stephen Jay Gould (1941–2002) was born in New York City. A graduate of Antioch College (1963) and Columbia University (Ph.D., 1967) Gould joined the faculty of Harvard University in 1973, where he taught geology, biology, and the history of science. An evolutionist who enjoyed explaining complex scientific theories to lay audiences, Gould wrote extensively (often on the theory of evolution), including a monthly column for Natural History, *"This View of Life." Gould's books include* Ontogeny and Phylogeny *(1977),* The Mismeasure of Man *(1981),* Time's Arrow, Time's Cycle *(1987), and* Wonderful Life *(1989). His essay collections include* Ever Since Darwin *(1977),* The Panda's Thumb *(1980),* Hen's Teeth and Horse's Toes *(1983),* The Flamingo's Smile *(1985),* Urchin in the Storm: Essays About Books and Ideas *(1987),* Bully for Brontosaurus *(1991), and* Eight Little Piggies *(1993). Gould received a National Book Award and was named a MacArthur Prize Fellow. In this typically enlightening essay from* Bully for Brontosaurus, *Gould uses his 1982 diagnosis of cancer to expose common misinterpretations of statistics.*

My life has recently intersected, in a most personal way, two of Mark Twain's famous quips. One I shall defer to the end of this essay. The other (sometimes attributed to Disraeli identified three species of mendacity, each worse than the one before—lies, damned lies, and statistics.

Consider the standard example of stretching truth with numbers— a case quite relevant to my story. Statistics recognizes different measures of an "average," or central tendency. The *mean* represents our usual concept of an overall average—add up the items and divide them by the number of sharers (100 candy bars collected for five kids next Halloween will yield 20 for each in a fair world). The *median,* a different measure of central tendency, is the halfway point. If I line up five kids by height, the median child is shorter than two and taller than the other two (who might have trouble getting their mean share of the candy). A politician in power might say with pride, "The mean income of our citizens is $15,000 per year." The leader of the opposition might retort, "But half our citizens make less than $10,000 per year." Both are right, but neither cites a statistic with impassive objectivity. The first invokes a mean, the second a median. (Means are higher than medians in such cases because one millionaire may outweigh hundreds of poor people in setting a mean, but can balance only one mendicant in calculating a median.)

The larger issue that creates a common distrust or contempt for statistics is more troubling. Many people make an unfortunate and invalid separation between heart and mind, or feeling and intellect. In some contemporary traditions, abetted by attitudes stereotypically centered upon Southern California, feelings are exalted as more "real" and the only proper basis for action, while intellect gets short shrift as a hang-up of outmoded elitism. Statistics, in this absurd dichotomy, often becomes the symbol of the enemy. As Hilaire Belloc wrote, "Statistics are the triumph of the quantitative method, and the quantitative method is the victory of sterility and death."

This is a personal story of statistics, properly interpreted, as profoundly nurturant and life-giving. It declares holy war on the downgrading of intellect by telling a small story to illustrate the utility of dry, academic knowledge about science. Heart and head are focal points of one body, one personality.

5   In July 1982, I learned that I was suffering from abdominal mesothelioma, a rare and serious cancer usually associated with exposure to asbestos. When I revived after surgery, I asked my first question of my doctor and chemotherapist: "What is the best technical literature about mesothelioma?" She replied, with a touch of diplomacy (the

only departure she has ever made from direct frankness), that the medical literature contained nothing really worth reading.

Of course, trying to keep an intellectual away from literature works about as well as recommending chastity to *Homo sapiens,* the sexiest primate of all. As soon as I could walk, I made a beeline for Harvard's Countway medical library and punched mesothelioma into the computer's bibliographic search program. An hour later, surrounded by the latest literature on abdominal mesothelioma, I realized with a gulp why my doctor had offered that humane advice. The literature couldn't have been more brutally clear: Mesothelioma is incurable, with a median mortality of only eight months after discovery. I sat stunned for about fifteen minutes, then smiled and said to myself: So that's why they didn't give me anything to read. Then my mind started to work again, thank goodness.

If a little learning could ever be a dangerous thing, I had encountered a classic example. Attitude clearly matters in fighting cancer. We don't know why (from my old-style materialistic perspective, I suspect that mental states feed back upon the immune system). But match people with the same cancer for age, class, health, and socioeconomic status, and, in general, those with positive attitudes, with a strong will and purpose for living, with commitment to struggle, and with an active response to aiding their own treatment and not just a passive acceptance of anything doctors say, tend to live longer. A few months later I asked Sir Peter Medawar, my personal scientific guru and a Nobelist in immunology, what the best prescription for success against cancer might be. "A sanguine personality," he replied. Fortunately (since one can't reconstruct oneself at short notice and for a definite purpose), I am, if anything, even-tempered and confident in just this manner.

Hence the dilemma for humane doctors: Since attitude matters so critically, should such a somber conclusion be advertised, especially since few people have sufficient understanding of statistics to evaluate what the statements really mean? From years of experience with the small-scale evolution of Bahamian land snails treated quantitatively, I have developed this technical knowledge—and I am convinced that it played a major role in saving my life. Knowledge is indeed power, as Francis Bacon proclaimed.

The problem may be briefly stated: What does "median mortality of eight months" signify in our vernacular? I suspect that most people, without training in statistics, would read such a statement as "I will probably be dead in eight months"—the very conclusion that must be avoided, both because this formulation is false, and because attitude matters so much.

I was not, of course, overjoyed, but I didn't read the statement in this vernacular way either. My technical training enjoined a different perspective on "eight months median mortality." The point may seem subtle, but the consequences can be profound. Moreover, this perspective embodies the distinctive way of thinking in my own field of evolutionary biology and natural history.

We still carry the historical baggage of a Platonic heritage that seeks sharp essences and definite boundaries. (Thus we hope to find an unambiguous "beginning of life" or "definition of death," although nature often comes to us as irreducible continua.) This Platonic heritage, with its emphasis on clear distinctions and separated immutable entities, leads us to view statistical measures of central tendency wrongly, indeed opposite to the appropriate interpretation in our actual world of variation, shadings, and continua. In short, we view means and medians as hard "realities," and the variation that permits their calculation as a set of transient and imperfect measurements of this hidden essence. If the median is the reality and variation around the median just a device for calculation, then "I will probably be dead in eight months" may pass as a reasonable interpretation.

But all evolutionary biologists know that variation itself is nature's only irreducible essence. Variation is the hard reality, not a set of imperfect measures for a central tendency. Means and medians are the abstractions. Therefore, I looked at the mesothelioma statistics quite differently—and not only because I am an optimist who tends to see the doughnut instead of the hole, but primarily because I know that variation itself is the reality. I had to place myself amidst the variation.

When I learned about the eight-month median, my first intellectual reaction was: Fine, half the people will live longer; now what are my chances of being in that half. I read for a furious and nervous hour and concluded, with relief: damned good. I possessed every one of the characteristics conferring a probability of longer life: I was young; my disease had been recognized in a relatively early state; I would receive the nation's best medical treatment; I had the world to live for; I knew how to read the data properly and not despair.

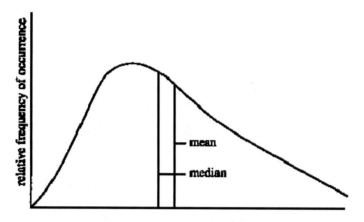

A right-skewed distribution showing that means must be higher than medians, and that the right side of the distribution extends out into a long tail.

Another technical point then added ever more solace. I immediately recognized that the distribution of variation about the eight-month median would almost surely be what statisticians call "right skewed." (In a symmetrical distribution, the profile of variation to the left of the central tendency is a mirror image of variation to the right. Skewed distributions are asymmetrical, with variation stretching out more in one direction than the other—left skewed if extended to the left, right skewed if stretched out to the right.) The distribution of variation had to be right skewed, I reasoned. After all, the left of the distribution contains an irrevocable lower boundary of zero (since mesothelioma can only be identified at death or before). Thus, little space exists for the distribution's lower (or left) half—it must be scrunched up between zero and eight months. But the upper (or right) half can extend out for years and years, even if nobody ultimately survives. The distribution must be right skewed, and I needed to know how long the extended tail ran—for I had already concluded that my favorable profile made me a good candidate for the right half of the curve.

The distribution was, indeed, strongly right skewed, with a long tail (however small) that extended for several years above the eight-month median. I saw no reason why I shouldn't be in that small tail, and I breathed a very long sigh of relief. My technical knowledge had helped. I had read the graph correctly. I had asked the right question and found the answers. I had obtained, in all probability, that most precious of all possible gifts in the circumstances—substantial time. I didn't have to stop and immediately follow Isaiah's injunction to Hezekiah—set thine house in order: for thou shalt die, and not live. I would have time to think, to plan, and to fight.

One final point about statistical distributions. They apply only to a prescribed set of circumstances—in this case to survival with mesothelioma under conventional modes of treatment. If circumstances change, the distribution may alter. I was placed on an experimental protocol of treatment and, if fortune holds, will be in the first cohort of a new distribution with a high median and a right tail extending to death by natural causes at advanced old age.*

It has become, in my view, a bit too trendy to regard the acceptance of death as something tantamount to intrinsic dignity. Of course I agree with the preacher of Ecclesiastes that there is a time to love and a time to die—and when my skein runs out I hope to face the end calmly and in my own way. For most situations, however, I prefer the more martial view that death is the ultimate enemy—and I find nothing reproachable in those who rage mightily against the dying of the light.

The swords of battle are numerous, and none more effective than humor. My death was announced at a meeting of my colleagues in Scotland, and I almost experienced the delicious pleasure of reading my obituary penned by one of my best friends (the so-and-so got suspicious and checked; he too is a statistician, and didn't expect to find me so far out on the left tail). Still, the incident provided my first good laugh after the diagnosis. Just think, I almost got to repeat Mark Twain's most famous line of all: The reports of my death are greatly exaggerated.**

---

*So far so good.

**Since writing this, my death has actually been reported in two European magazines, five years apart. *Fama volat* (and lasts a long time). I squawked very loudly both times and demanded a retraction; guess I just don't have Mr. Clemens's *savoir faire*.

Questions on Meaning

1. Define mean, average, and median.
2. How do statistics become the "symbol of the enemy"? What is the significance of that label? Who or what is the "enemy"?
3. What does Gould mean by "means and medians are the abstractions"? What is reality?

Questions on Rhetorical Strategy and Style

1. How does Gould use a writing strategy of cause and effect to argue that he will survive the abdominal mesothelioma? What personal characteristics does he bring to the battle? Explain how he puts statistics on his side (e.g., the right-skewed median). What could cause the statistical odds of his survival to rise or fall?
2. How does Gould compare and contrast "Platonic heritage" with the "actual world"? Why does he consider "Platonic heritage" to be "historical baggage" with regard to disease mortality?
3. In his opening paragraph, Gould notes that he will be mentioning two Mark Twain quotations, one of which he will save for the conclusion. Why do you think Gould announced this to the reader? Do you think he wanted (or expected) the reader to turn to it before beginning the essay? Did you immediately flip to the end of the essay to find the second Twain quotation? How would it have affected the essay to place both quotations at the beginning?
4. Mind over matter is an intriguing proposition, particularly applied to healing. What information can you find that supports Gould's statement (he was diagnosed in 1982, remember) that "attitude clearly matters in fighting cancer"? Explain why or why not this information is statistically relevant.

Writing Assignments

1. Weather reports often rely heavily on statistics—historical highs and lows, average precipitation, seasonal temperature variations, etc. Read a comprehensive weather report for a week. Do the statistics simply give data, or are they used to dramatize? Explain how a reader's understanding of statistics might affect his or her perception of this weather information.
2. Death to Gould is "the ultimate enemy." Write an essay about how you would react if you were diagnosed with a terminal disease, as

Gould was. Would you "rage mightily," ignore it, deny it, be overcome by it, or accept it stoically? How do you define the "dignity" associated with death?

Women's Brains

Stephen Jay Gould

Stephen Jay Gould (1941–2002) was born in New York City. A graduate of Antioch College (1963) and Columbia University (Ph.D., 1967) Gould joined the faculty of Harvard University in 1973, where he taught geology, biology, and the history of science. An evolutionist who enjoyed explaining complex scientific theories to lay audiences, Gould wrote extensively (often on the theory of evolution), including a monthly column for Natural History, *"This View of Life." Gould's books include* Ontogeny and Phylogeny *(1977),* The Mismeasure of Man *(1981),* Time's Arrow, Time's Cycle *(1987), and* Wonderful Life *(1989). His essay collections include* Ever Since Darwin *(1977),* The Panda's Thumb *(1980),* Hen's Teeth and Horse's Toes *(1983),* The Flamingo's Smile *(1985),* Urchin in the Storm: Essays About Books and Ideas *(1987),* Bully for Brontosaurus *(1991), and* Eight Little Piggies *(1993). Gould received a National Book Award and was named a MacArthur Prize Fellow. Gould reveals in this essay how scientists have used theories about brain size to argue the "inferiority" of women.*

1   In the prelude to *Middlemarch,* George Eliot lamented the unfulfilled   1
lives of talented women:

> *Some have felt that these blundering lives are due to the inconvenient indefiniteness with which the Supreme Power has fashioned the natures of women: if there were one level of feminine incompetence as strict as the ability to count three and no more, the social lot of women might be treated with scientific certitude.*

Eliot goes on to discount the idea of innate limitation, but while she wrote in 1872, the leaders of European anthropometry were trying to measure "with scientific certitude" the inferiority of women. Anthropometry, or measurement of the human body, is not so fashionable a field these days, but it dominated the human sciences for much of the nineteenth century and remained popular until intelligence testing replaced skull measurement as a favored device for making invidious comparisons among races, classes, and sexes. Craniometry, or measurement of the skull, commanded the most attention and respect. Its unquestioned leader, Paul Broca (1824–80), professor of clinical surgery at the Faculty of Medicine in Paris, gathered a school of disciples and imitators around himself. Their work, so meticulous and apparently irrefutable, exerted great influence and won high esteem as a jewel of nineteenth-century science.

Broca's work seemed particularly invulnerable to refutation. Had he not measured with the most scrupulous care and accuracy? (Indeed, he had. I have the greatest respect for Broca's meticulous procedure. His numbers are sound. But science is an inferential exercise, not a catalog of facts. Numbers, by themselves, specify nothing. All depends upon what you do with them.) Broca depicted himself as an apostle of objectivity, a man who bowed before facts and cast aside superstition and sentimentality. He declared that "there is no faith, however respectable, no interest, however legitimate, which must not accommodate itself to the progress of human knowledge and bend before truth." Women, like it or not, had smaller brains than men and, therefore, could not equal them in intelligence. This fact, Broca argued, may reinforce a common prejudice in male society, but it is also a scientific truth. L. Manouvrier, a black sheep in Broca's fold, rejected the inferiority of women and wrote with feeling about the burden imposed upon them by Broca's numbers:

> Women displayed their talents and their diplomas. They also invoked philosophical authorities. But they were opposed by numbers unknown to Condorcet or to John Stuart Mill. These numbers fell upon poor women like a sledge hammer, and they were accompanied by commentaries and sarcasms more ferocious than the most misogynist imprecations of certain church fathers. The theologians had asked if women had a soul. Several centuries later, some scientists were ready to refuse them a human intelligence.

Broca's argument rested upon two sets of data: the larger brains of men in modern societies, and a supposed increase in male superiority through time. His most extensive data came from autopsies performed personally in four Parisian hospitals. For 292 male brains, he calculated an average weight of 1,325 grams; 140 female brains averaged 1,144 grams for a difference of 181 grams, or 14 percent of the male weight. Broca understood, of course, that part of this difference could be attributed to the greater height of males. Yet he made no attempt to measure the effect of size alone and actually stated that it cannot account for the entire difference because we know, a priori, that women are not as intelligent as men (a premise that the data were supposed to test, not rest upon):

> *We might ask if the small size of the female brain depends exclusively upon the small size of her body. Tiedemann has proposed this explanation. But we must not forget that women are, on the average, a little less intelligent than men, a difference which we should not exaggerate but which is, nonetheless, real. We are therefore permitted to suppose that the relatively small size of the female brain depends in part upon her physical inferiority and in part upon her intellectual inferiority.*

5   In 1873, the year after Eliot published *Middlemarch,* Broca measured the cranial capacities of prehistoric skulls from L'Homme Mort cave. Here he found a difference of only 99.5 cubic centimeters between males and females, while modern populations range from 129.5 to 220.7. Topinard, Broca's chief disciple, explained the increasing discrepancy through time as a result of differing evolutionary pressures upon dominant men and passive women:

> *The man who fights for two or more in the struggle for existence, who has all the responsibility and the cares of tomorrow, who is constantly active in combating the environment and human rivals, needs more brain than the woman whom he must protect and nourish, the sedentary woman, lacking any interior occupations, whose role is to raise children, love, and be passive.*

In 1879, Gustave Le Bon, chief misogynist of Broca's school, used these data to publish what must be the most vicious attack upon women in modern scientific literature (no one can top Aristotle). I do not claim his views were representative of Broca's school, but they were published in France's most respected anthropological journal. Le Bon concluded:

> *In the most intelligent races, as among the Parisians, there are a large number of women whose brains are closer in size to those of gorillas than to the most developed male brains. This inferiority is so obvious that no one can contest it for a moment; only its degree is worth discussion. All psychologists who have studied the intelligence of women, as well as poets and novelists, recognize today that they represent the most inferior forms of human evolution and that they are closer to children and savages than to an adult, civilized man. They excel in fickleness, inconstancy, absence of thought and logic, and incapacity to reason. Without doubt there exist some distinguished women, very superior to the average man, but they are as exceptional as the birth of any monstrosity, as, for example, of a gorilla with two heads; consequently, we may neglect them entirely.*

Nor did Le Bon shrink from the social implications of his views. He was horrified by the proposal of some American reformers to grant women higher education on the same basis as men:

> *A desire to give them the same education, and, as a consequence, to propose the same goals for them, is a dangerous chimera. . . . The day when, misunderstanding the inferior occupations which nature has given her, women leave the home and take part in our battles; on this day a social revolution will begin, and everything that maintains the sacred ties of the family will disappear.*

Sound familiar?[1]

I have reexamined Broca's data, the basis for all this derivative pronouncement, and I find his numbers sound but his interpretation ill-founded, to say the least. The data supporting his claim for increased difference through time can be easily dismissed. Broca based his contention on the samples from L'Homme Mort alone—only seven male and six female skulls in all. Never have so little data yielded such far ranging conclusions.

---

[1]When I wrote this essay, I assumed that Le Bon was a marginal, if colorful, figure. I have since learned that he was a leading scientist, one of the founders of social psychology, and best known for a seminal study on crowd behavior, still cited today (*La psychologie des foules,* 1895), and for his work on unconscious motivation.

10   In 1888, Topinard published Broca's more extensive data on the 10
Parisian hospitals. Since Broca recorded height and age as well as brain
size, we may use modern statistics to remove their effect. Brain weight
decreases with age, and Broca's women were, on average, considerably
older than his men. Brain weight increases with height, and his average man was almost half a foot taller than his average woman. I used
multiple regression, a technique that allowed me to assess simultaneously the influence of height and age upon brain size. In an analysis
of the data for women, I found that, at average male height and age,
a woman's brain would weigh 1,212 grams. Correction for height and
age reduces Broca's measured difference of 181 grams by more than a
third, to 113 grams.

I don't know what to make of this remaining difference because I
cannot assess other factors known to influence brain size in a major
way. Cause of death has an important effect: degenerative disease often
entails a substantial diminution of brain size. (This effect is separate
from the decrease attributed to age alone.) Eugene Schreider, also
working with Broca's data, found that men killed in accidents had
brains weighing, on average, 60 grams more than men dying of in-
fectious diseases. The best modern data I can find (from American
hospitals) records a full 100-gram difference between death by degenerative arteriosclerosis and by violence or accident. Since so many of
Broca's subjects were very elderly women, we may assume that lengthy
degenerative disease was more common among them than among the
men.

More importantly, modern students of brain size still have not
agreed on a proper measure for eliminating the powerful effect of body
size. Height is partly adequate, but men and women of the same
height do not share the same body build. Weight is even worse than
height, because most of its variation reflects nutrition rather than intrinsic size—fat versus skinny exerts little influence upon the brain.
Manouvrier took up this subject in the 1880s and argued that muscular mass and force should be used. He tried to measure this elusive
property in various ways and found a marked difference in favor of
men, even in men and women of the same height. When he corrected
for what he called "sexual mass," women actually came out slightly
ahead in brain size.

Thus, the corrected 113-gram difference is surely too large; the
true figure is probably close to zero and may as well favor women as

men. And 113 grams, by the way, is exactly the average difference between a 5 foot 4 inch and a 6 foot 4 inch male in Broca's data. We would not (especially us short folks) want to ascribe greater intelligence to tall men. In short, who knows what to do with Broca's data? They certainly don't permit any confident claim that men have bigger brains than women.

To appreciate the social role of Broca and his school, we must recognize that his statements about the brains of women do not reflect an isolated prejudice toward a single disadvantaged group. They must be weighed in the context of a general theory that supported contemporary social distinctions as biologically ordained. Women, blacks, and poor people suffered the same disparagement, but women bore the brunt of Broca's argument because he had easier access to data on women's brains. Women were singularly denigrated but they also stood as surrogates for other disenfranchised groups. As one of Broca's disciples wrote in 1881: "Men of the black races have a brain scarcely heavier than that of white women." This juxtaposition extended into many other realms of anthropological argument, particularly to claims that, anatomically and emotionally, both women and blacks were like white children—and that white children, by the theory of recapitulation, represented an ancestral (primitive) adult stage of human evolution. I do not regard as empty rhetoric the claim that women's battles are for all of us.

15   Maria Montessori did not confine her activities to educational re-   15
form for young children. She lectured on anthropology for several years at the University of Rome, and wrote an influential book entitled *Pedagogical Anthropology* (English edition, 1913). Montessori was no egalitarian. She supported most of Broca's work and the theory of innate criminality proposed by her compatriot Cesare Lombroso. She measured the circumference of children's heads in her schools and inferred that the best prospects had bigger brains. But she had no use for Broca's conclusions about women. She discussed Manouvrier's work at length and made much of his tentative claim that women, after proper correction of the data, had slightly larger brains than men. Women, she concluded, were intellectually superior, but men had prevailed heretofore by dint of physical force. Since technology has abolished force as an instrument of power, the era of women may soon be upon us: "In such an epoch there will really be superior human beings, there will really be men strong in morality and in sentiment.

Perhaps in this way the reign of women is approaching, when the enigma of her anthropological superiority will be deciphered. Woman was always the custodian of human sentiment, morality and honor."

This represents one possible antidote to "scientific" claims for the constitutional inferiority of certain groups. One may affirm the validity of biological distinctions but argue that the data have been misinterpreted by prejudiced men with a stake in the outcome, and that disadvantaged groups are truly superior. In recent years, Elaine Morgan has followed this strategy in her *Descent of Woman*, a speculative reconstruction of human prehistory from the woman's point of view—and as farcical as more famous tall tales by and for men.

I prefer another strategy. Montessori and Morgan followed Broca's philosophy to reach a more congenial conclusion. I would rather label the whole enterprise of setting a biological value upon groups for what it is: irrelevant and highly injurious. George Eliot well appreciated the special tragedy that biological labeling imposed upon members of disadvantaged groups. She expressed it for people like herself—women of extraordinary talent. I would apply it more widely—not only to those whose dreams are flouted but also to those who never realize that they may dream—but I cannot match her prose. In conclusion, then, the rest of Eliot's prelude to *Middlemarch:*

> *The limits of variation are really much wider than anyone would imagine from the sameness of women's coiffure and the favorite love stories in prose and verse. Here and there a cygnet is reared uneasily among the ducklings in the brown pond, and never finds the living stream in fellowship with its own oary-footed kind. Here and there is born a Saint Theresa, foundress of nothing, whose loving heart-beats and sobs after an unattained goodness tremble off and are dispersed among hindrances instead of centering in some long-recognizable deed.*

Questions on Meaning

1. How does Gould define "anthropometry"? Why do you think it was popular in the 19th century? What caused it to go out of fashion?
2. What does Gould mean by the assertion that "science is an inferential exercise"? Find an example of scientific inference in the essay.
3. What are Broca's two reasons that women are less intelligent than men? How does Broca argue the first reason? How does his "chief disciple," Topinard, argue the second?

Questions on Rhetorical Strategy and Style

1. Cause and effect is used extensively in this persuasive essay. Find where Broca uses cause and effect—wrongly, Gould would argue—to "prove" the intellectual inferiority of women, and then note how Gould uses a cause and effect strategy to rebut Broca.
2. Find where Gould inserts a rhetorical question into the third paragraph. What theme does he lead into—parenthetically—with this question? As an exercise, replace his question with a declarative sentence and compare the effect of yours with the original.
3. Why did Gould include a discussion of Montessori—a woman—in the essay? How does Montessori's interpretation of Broca's data compare and contrast with Broca's interpretation?

Writing Assignments

1. Reread the quotation by Manouvrier ("Women displayed their talents"). What similar misogynist charges are leveled at women today, perpetuating the myth of the "weaker" sex? How do advertising and the mass media reinforce these stereotypes?
2. Scientific data have been used by scientists to "prove" that blacks are inferior to whites, just as they were applied by Broca to "prove" the inferiority of women. Research theories of black inferiority. How are the data used to show inferiority? Show how scientific inference is or is not being applied.
3. Write an essay about a current scientific dispute—such as irradiating food or the vitamin levels humans require. Research the various arguments in the debate and try to determine if the data are being used properly to develop theories.

Mid-term Break

Seamus Heaney

Seamus Heaney (1939–) was born in Londonderry in Northern Ireland, studied in Belfast at St. Joseph's College, and moved to Dublin in 1976. He has won many honors as a poet, most significantly the Nobel Prize for Literature in 1995 "for works of lyrical beauty and ethical depth, which exalt everyday miracles and the living past." He has taught at Oxford, Berkeley, and Harvard. Noteworthy collections include Haw Lantern *(1987),* Seeing Things *(1991),* Selected Poems: 1966-1987 *(1990),* The Spirit Level *(1996),* Electric Light *(2001), and* District and Circle *(2006). Heaney has also written plays and essays. "Mid-term Break" was first published in 1980.*

1   I sat all morning in the college sick bay
    Counting bells knelling classes to a close.
    At two o'clock our neighbors drove me home.

    In the porch I met my father crying—
5   He had always taken funerals in his stride —
    And Big Jim Evans saying it was a hard blow.

    The baby cooed and laughed and rocked the pram
    When I came in, and I was embarrassed
    By old men standing up to shake my hand

10 And tell me they were "sorry for my trouble,"
    Whispers informed strangers I was the eldest,
    Away at school, as my mother held my hand

In hers and coughed out angry tearless sighs.
At ten o'clock the ambulance arrived
15   With the corpse, stanched and bandaged by the nurses.   15

Next morning 1 went up into the room. Snowdrops
And candles soothed the bedside; I saw him
For the first time in six weeks. Paler now,

Wearing a poppy bruise on his left temple,
20   He lay in the four foot box as in his cot.   20
No gaudy scars, the bumper knocked him clear.

A four foot box, a foot for every year.

Questions on Meaning

1. What event does Heaney recount in this poem? What is the significance of the title?
2. Why does the poet mention that his father "had always taken funerals in his stride"?

Questions on Rhetorical Strategy and Style

1. We can discover much about a poem's meaning by examining its tone. How would you describe Heaney's tone here? What is his attitude toward the event?
2. You might notice that the poet never mentions the child's name. Why?
3. Each stanza in the poem, except for the last, is three lines in length. How does this form serve its overall meaning?

Writing Assignments

1. Write an essay about a sad event in your life. Try to capture your state of mind at the time by describing in detail things you remember seeing and hearing. As you recount these details, consider what dominant impression you want to create.
2. Write an essay in which you recount your memories of returning home for the first time. Was it on the occasion of a significant family event? How did you feel at the time? In what way were things different?

Don't Let Stereotypes Warp Your Judgments

Robert Heilbroner

> *Robert Heilbroner (1919–2005) attended Harvard University and the New School for Social Research, where he taught economics for over thirty years. His books include* the Future as History *(1960),* A Primer of Government Spending: Between Capitalism and Socialism *(1970), and* An Inquiry into the Human Prospect *(1974). This essay, published in* Reader's Digest, *highlights dangers of stereotyping—both to others as well as to ourselves—and suggests how we can correct this tendency.*

1   Is a girl called Gloria apt to be better-looking than one called Bertha? Are criminals more likely to be dark than blond? Can you tell a good deal about someone's personality from hearing his voice briefly over the phone? Can a person's nationality be pretty accurately guessed from his photograph? Does the fact that someone wears glasses imply that he is intelligent?

The answer to all these questions is obviously, "No."

Yet, from all the evidence at hand, most of us believe these things. Ask any college boy if he'd rather take his chances with a Gloria or a Bertha, or ask a college girl if she'd rather blind-date a Richard or a Cuthbert. In fact, you don't have to ask: college students in questionnaires have revealed that names conjure up the same images in their minds as they do in yours—and for as little reason.

Look into the favorite suspects of persons who report "suspicious characters" and you will find a large percentage of them to be "swarthy" or "dark and foreign-looking"—despite the testimony of criminologists that criminals do not tend to be dark, foreign or "wild-eyed." Delve into the main asset of a telephone stock swindler and you will find it to be a marvelously confidence-inspiring telephone

From *Reader's Digest.*

"personality." And whereas we all think we know what an Italian or a Swede looks like, it is the sad fact that when a group of Nebraska students sought to match faces and nationalities of 15 European countries, they were scored wrong in 93 percent of their identifications. Finally, for all the fact that horn-rimmed glasses have now become the standard television sign of an "intellectual," optometrists know that the main thing that distinguishes people with glasses is just bad eyes.

5   Stereotypes are a kind of gossip about the world, a gossip that makes   5
us pre-judge people before we ever lay eyes on them. Hence it is not surprising that stereotypes have something to do with the dark world of prejudice. Explore most prejudices (note that the word means prejudgment) and you will find a cruel stereotype at the core of each one.

For it is the extraordinary fact that once we have typecast the world, we tend to see people in terms of our standardized pictures. In another demonstration of the power of stereotypes to affect our vision, a number of Columbia and Barnard students were shown 30 photographs of pretty but unidentified girls, and asked to rate each in terms of "general liking," "intelligence," "beauty" and so on. Two months later, the same group were shown the same photographs, this time with fictitious Irish, Italian, Jewish and "American" names attached to the pictures. Right away the ratings changed. Faces which were now seen as representing a national group went down in looks and still farther down in likability, while the "American" girls suddenly looked decidedly prettier and nicer.

Why is it that we stereotype the world in such irrational and harmful fashion? In part, we begin to typecast people in our childhood years. Early in life, as every parent whose child has watched a TV Western knows, we learn to spot the Good Guys from the Bad Guys. Some years ago, a social psychologist showed very clearly how powerful these stereotypes of childhood vision are. He secretly asked the most popular youngsters in an elementary school to make errors in their morning gym exercises. Afterwards, he asked the class if anyone had noticed any mistakes during gym period. Oh, yes, said the children. But it was the *unpopular* members of the class—the "bad guys"—they remembered as being out of step.

We not only grow up with standardized pictures forming inside of us, but as grown-ups we are constantly having them thrust upon us. Some of them, like the half-joking, half-serious stereotypes of mothers-in-law, or country yokels, or psychiatrists, are dinned into us by the stock jokes we hear and repeat. In fact, without such stereotypes, there would be a lot fewer jokes. Still other stereotypes are perpetuated by the advertisements we read, the movies we see, the books we read.

And finally, we tend to stereotype because it helps us make sense out of a highly confusing world, a world which William James once described as "one great, blooming, buzzing confusion." It is a curious fact that if we don't *know* what we're looking at, we are often quite literally unable to *see* what we're looking at. People who recover their sight after a lifetime of blindness actually cannot at first tell a triangle from a square. A visitor to a factory sees only noisy chaos where the superintendent sees a perfectly synchronized flow of work. As Walter Lippmann has said, "For the most part we do not first see, and then define; we define first, and then we see."

Stereotypes are one way in which we "define" the world in order to see it. They classify the infinite variety of human beings into a convenient handful of "types" towards whom we learn to act in stereotyped fashion. Life would be a wearing process if we had to start from scratch with each and every human contact. Stereotypes economize on our mental effort by covering up the blooming, buzzing confusion with big recognizable cut-outs. They save us the "trouble" of finding out what the world is like—they give it its accustomed look.

Thus the trouble is that stereotypes make us mentally lazy. As S. I. Hayakawa, the authority on semantics, has written: "The danger of stereotypes lies not in their existence, but in the fact that they become for all people some of the time, and for some people all the time, *substitutes for observation*." Worse yet, stereotypes get in the way of our judgment, even when we do observe the world. Someone who has formed rigid preconceptions of all Latins as "excitable," or all teenagers as "wild," doesn't alter his point of view when he meets a calm and deliberate Genoese, or a serious-minded high school student. He brushes them aside as "exceptions that prove the rule." And, of course, if he meets someone true to type, he stands triumphantly vindicated. "They're all like that," he proclaims, having encountered an excited Latin, an ill-behaved adolescent.

Hence, quite aside from the injustice which stereotypes do to others, they impoverish ourselves. A person who lumps the world into simple categories, who type-casts all labor leaders as "racketeers," all businessmen as "reactionaries," all Harvard men as "snobs," and all Frenchmen as "sexy," is in danger of becoming a stereotype himself. He loses his capacity to be himself—which is to say, to see the world in his own absolutely unique, inimitable and independent fashion.

Instead, he votes for the man who fits his standardized picture of what a candidate "should" look like or sound like, buys the goods that someone in his "situation" in life "should" own, lives the life that others define for him. The mark of the stereotype person is that he never surprises us, that we do indeed have him "typed." And no one fits this straitjacket so perfectly as someone whose opinions about *other people* are fixed and inflexible.

Impoverishing as they are, stereotypes are not easy to get rid of. The world we type-cast may be no better than a Grade B movie, but at least we know what to expect of our stock characters. When we let them act for themselves in the strangely unpredictable way that people do act, who knows but that many of our fondest convictions will be proved wrong?

15   Nor do we suddenly drop our standardized pictures for a blinding vision of the Truth. Sharp swings of ideas about people often just substitute one stereotype for another. The true process of change is a slow one that adds bits and pieces of reality to the pictures in our heads, until gradually they take on some of the blurriness of life itself. Little by little, we learn not that Jews and Negroes and Catholics and Puerto Ricans are "just like everybody else"—for that, too, is a stereotype—but that each and every one of them is unique, special, different and individual. Often we do not even know that we have let a stereotype lapse until we hear someone saying, "all so-and-so's are like such-and-such, and we hear ourselves saying, "Well-maybe."

Can we speed the process along? Of course we can.

First, we can become *aware* of the standardized pictures in our heads, in other peoples' heads, in the world around us.

Second, we can become suspicious of all judgments that we allow exceptions to "prove." There is no more chastening thought than that in the vast intellectual adventure of science, it takes but one tiny exception to topple a whole edifice of ideas.

Third, we can learn to be chary of generalizations about people. As F. Scott Fitzgerald once wrote: "Begin with an individual, and before you know it you have created a type; begin with a type, and you find you have created—nothing."

20   Most of the time, when we type-cast the world, we are not in fact generalizing about people at all. We are only revealing the embarrassing facts about the pictures that hang in the gallery of stereotypes in our own heads.

Questions on Meaning

1. What are some of the common sources of prejudice that Heilbroner identifies?
2. List the negative effects of stereotyping that Heilbroner describes in this essay. What other negatives would you add to this list?
3. Heilbroner says it is not easy to rid ourselves of stereotypes, but that it can be done. What is his three-step process?

Questions on Rhetorical Strategy and Style

1. Find where Heilbroner uses a cause and effect writing strategy to illustrate the impact of ethnicity on such perceived personal characteristics as intelligence and beauty.
2. How does Heilbroner define "stereotypes" and "prejudice"? How are these two terms related?
3. How does Heilbroner use irony to explain that stereotyping not only affects how we see other people but also affects how people see us? Think of ways that you may have inadvertently stereotyped yourself.

Writing Assignments

1. Heilbroner explains that stereotyping is a form of classification that helps us "make sense of a highly confusing world"? List some common "types" of individuals based on visual characteristics (i.e., ethnic group, occupation, attitude, hygiene, etc.), then go to a busy public place—such as the student union, a downtown street corner, or a mass transit stop—and classify people for a few minutes. Next, observe another set of strangers, but his time write descriptions of each person without stereotyping him or her. How do your images of the second group compare with the first group?
2. Research Hayakawa and the study of "general semantics," in particular, theories of observation. Write an essay in which you explain what "general semantics" is and describe how it can affect how we observe people, places, and things.

The Lottery

Shirley Jackson

Shirley Hardie Jackson (1919-1965) was born in San Francisco. She received her B.A. from Syracuse University in 1940, then married literary critic Stanley Edgar Hyman, settling in North Bennington, Vermont, where they raised four children. Both parents continued vigorous literary careers. Jackson published the light and charming works Life among the Savages *(1953) and* Raising Demons *(1957) out of her experiences as a parent. At the same time, she was writing more disturbing works of horror and moral criticism,* The Lottery and Other Stories *(1949) and* The Haunting of Hill House *(1959). She said of "The Lottery" that she was hoping to force readers to see that their own lives contained inhumanity and cruelty.*

1   The morning of June 27th was clear and sunny, with the fresh warmth of a full-summer day; the flowers were blossoming profusely and the grass was richly green. The people of the village began to gather in the square, between the post office and the bank, around ten o'clock; in some towns there were so many people that the lottery took two days and had to be started on June 26th, but in this village, where there were only about three hundred people, the whole lottery took less than two hours, so it could begin at ten o'clock in the morning and still be through in time to allow the villagers to get home for noon dinner.

The children assembled first, of course. School was recently over for the summer, and the feeling of liberty sat uneasily on most of them; they tended to gather together quietly for a while before they broke into boisterous play, and their talk was still of the classroom and the teacher, of books and reprimands. Bobby Martin had already stuffed his pockets full of stones, and the other boys soon followed his example, selecting the smoothest and roundest stones; Bobby and Harry Jones and Dickie Delacroix—the villagers pronounced this name "Dellacroy"—eventually made a great pile of stones in one corner of the square and guarded it against the raids of the other boys. The girls stood aside, talking among themselves, looking over their shoulders at the boys, and the very small children rolled in the dust or clung to the hands of their older brothers or sisters.

Soon the men began to gather, surveying their own children, speaking of planting and rain, tractors and taxes. They stood together, away from the pile of stones in the corner, and their jokes were quiet and they smiled rather than laughed. The women, wearing faded house dresses and sweaters, came shortly after their menfolk. They greeted one another and exchanged bits of gossip as they went to join their husbands. Soon the women, standing by their husbands, began to call to their children, and the children came reluctantly, having to be called four or five times. Bobby Martin ducked under his mother's grasping hand and ran, laughing, back to the pile of stones. His father spoke up sharply, and Bobby came quickly and took his place between his father and his oldest brother.

The lottery was conducted—as were the square dances, the teenage club, the Halloween program—by Mr. Summers, who had time and energy to devote to civic activities. He was a round-faced, jovial man and he ran the coal business, and people were sorry for him, because he had no children and his wife was a scold. When he arrived in the square, carrying the black wooden box, there was a murmur of conversation among the villagers, and he waved and called, "Little late today, folks." The postmaster, Mr. Graves, followed him, carrying a three-legged stool, and the stool was put in the center of the square and Mr. Summers set the black box down on it. The villagers kept their distance, leaving a space between themselves and the stool, and when Mr. Summers said, "Some of you fellows want to give me a hand?" there was a hesitation before two men, Mr. Martin and his oldest son, Baxter, came forward to hold the box steady on the stool while Mr. Summers stirred up the papers inside it.

5   The original paraphernalia for the lottery had been lost long ago, 5
and the black box now resting on the stool had been put into use even
before Old Man Warner, the oldest man in town, was born. Mr. Summers spoke frequently to the villagers about making a new box, but
no one liked to upset even as much tradition as was represented by the
black box. There was a story that the present box had been made with
some pieces of the box that had preceded it, the one that had been
constructed when the first people settled down to make a village here.
Every year, after the lottery, Mr. Summers began talking again about
a new box, but every year the subject was allowed to fade off without
anything's being done. The black box grew shabbier each year; by now
it was no longer completely black but splintered badly along one side
to show the original wood color, and in some places faded or stained.

Mr. Martin and his oldest son, Baxter, held the black box securely
on the stool until Mr. Summers had stirred the papers thoroughly
with his hand. Because so much of the ritual had been forgotten or
discarded, Mr. Summers had been successful in having slips of paper
substituted for the chips of wood that had been used for generations.
Chips of wood, Mr. Summers had argued, had been all very well when
the village was tiny, but now that the population was more than three
hundred and likely to keep on growing, it was necessary to use something that would fit more easily into the black box. The night before
the lottery, Mr. Summers and Mr. Graves made up the slips of paper
and put them in the box, and it was then taken to the safe of Mr. Summers' coal company and locked up until Mr. Summers was ready to
take it to the square next morning. The rest of the year, the box was
put away, sometimes one place, sometimes another; it had spent one
year in Mr. Graves's barn and another year underfoot in the post office, and sometimes it was set on a shelf in the Martin grocery and left
there.

There was a great deal of fussing to be done before Mr. Summers
declared the lottery open. There were the lists to make up—of heads
of families, heads of households in each family, members of each
household in each family. There was the proper swearing-in of Mr.
Summers by the postmaster, as the official of the lottery; at one time,
some people remembered, there had been a recital of some sort, performed by the official of the lottery, a perfunctory, tuneless chant that
had been rattled off duly each year; some people believed that the official of the lottery used to stand just so when he said or sang it, others

believed that he was supposed to walk among the people, but years and years ago this part of the ritual had been allowed to lapse. There had been, also, a ritual salute, which the official of the lottery had had to use in addressing each person who came up to draw from the box, but this also had changed with time, until now it was felt necessary only for the official to speak to each person approaching. Mr. Summers was very good at all this; in his clean white shirt and blue jeans, with one hand resting carelessly on the black box, he seemed very proper and important as he talked interminably to Mr. Graves and the Martins.

Just as Mr. Summers finally left off talking and turned to the assembled villagers, Mrs. Hutchinson came hurriedly along the path to the square, her sweater thrown over her shoulders, and slid into place in the back of the crowd. "Clean forgot what day it was," she said to Mrs. Delacroix, who stood next to her, and they both laughed softly. "Thought my old man was out back stacking wood," Mrs. Hutchinson went on, "and then I looked out the window and the kids were gone, and then I remembered it was the twentyseventh and came a-running." She dried her hands on her apron, and Mrs. Delacroix said, "You're in time, though. They're still talking away up there."

Mrs. Hutchinson craned her neck to see through the crowd and found her husband and children standing near the front. She tapped Mrs. Delacroix on the arm as a farewell and began to make her way through the crowd. The people separated good-humoredly to let her through; two or three people said, in voices just loud enough to be heard across the crowd, "Here comes your Missus, Hutchinson," and "Bill, she made it after all." Mrs. Hutchinson reached her husband, and Mr. Summers, who had been waiting, said cheerfully, "Thought we were going to have to get on without you, Tessie." Mrs. Hutchinson said, grinning, "Wouldn't have me leave m'dishes in the sink, now, would you, Joe?" and soft laughter ran through the crowd as the people stirred back into position after Mrs. Hutchinson's arrival.

10 "Well, now," Mr. Summers said soberly, "guess we better get 10 started, get this over with, so's we can go back to work. Anybody ain't here?"

"Dunbar," several people said. "Dunbar, Dunbar."

Mr. Summers consulted his list. "Clyde Dunbar," he said. "That's right. He's broke his leg, hasn't he? Who's drawing for him?"

"Me, I guess," a woman said, and Mr. Summers turned to look at her. "Wife draws for her husband," Mr. Summers said. "Don't you have a grown boy to do it for you, Janey?" Although Mr. Summers and everyone else in the village knew the answer perfectly well, it was the business of the official of the lottery to ask such questions formally. Mr. Summers waited with an expression of polite interest while Mrs. Dunbar answered.

"Horace's not but sixteen yet," Mrs. Dunbar said regretfully. "Guess I gotta fill in for the old man this year."

15 "Right," Mr. Summers said. He made a note on the list he was 15 holding. Then he asked, "Watson boy drawing this year?"

A tall boy in the crowd raised his hand. "Here," he said. "I'm drawing for m'mother and me." He blinked his eyes nervously and ducked his head as several voices in the crowd said things like "Good fellow, Jack," and "Glad to see your mother's got a man to do it."

"Well," Mr. Summers said, "guess that's everyone. Old Man Warner make it?"

"Here," a voice said, and Mr. Summers nodded.

A sudden hush fell on the crowd as Mr. Summers cleared his throat and looked at the list. "All ready?" he called. "Now, I'll read the names—heads of families first—and the men come up and take a paper out of the box. Keep the paper folded in your hand without looking at it until everyone has had a turn. Everything clear?"

20 The people had done it so many times that they only half listened 20 to the directions; most of them were quiet, wetting their lips, not looking around. Then Mr. Summers raised one hand high and said, "Adams." A man disengaged himself from the crowd and came forward. "Hi, Steve," Mr. Summers said, and Mr. Adams said, "Hi, Joe." They grinned at one another humorlessly and nervously. Then Mr. Adams reached into the black box and took out a folded paper. He held it firmly by one corner as he turned and went hastily back to his place in the crowd, where he stood a little apart from his family, not looking down at his hand.

"Allen," Mr. Summers said. "Anderson . . . Bentham."

"Seems like there's no time at all between lotteries any more," Mrs. Delacroix said to Mrs. Graves in the back row. "Seems like we got through with the last one only last week."

"Time sure goes fast," Mrs. Graves said.

"Clark . . . Delacroix."

25 "There goes my old man," Mrs. Delacroix said. She held her 25
breath while her husband went forward.

"Dunbar," Mr. Summers said, and Mrs. Dunbar went steadily to
the box while one of the women said, "Go on, Janey," and another
said, "There she goes."

"We're next," Mrs. Graves said. She watched while Mr. Graves
came around from the side of the box, greeted Mr. Summers gravely,
and selected a slip of paper from the box. By now, all through the
crowd there were men holding the small folded papers in their large
hands, turning them over and over nervously. Mrs. Dunbar and her
two sons stood together, Mrs. Dunbar holding the slip of paper.

"Harburt . . . Hutchinson."

"Get up there, Bill," Mrs. Hutchinson said, and the people near
her laughed.

30 "Jones." 30

"They do say," Mr. Adams said to Old Man Warner, who stood
next to him, "that over in the north village they're talking of giving up
the lottery."

Old Man Warner snorted. "Pack of crazy fools," he said. "Listening to the young folks, nothing's good enough for *them*. Next thing
you know, they'll be wanting to go back to living in caves, nobody
work any more, live *that* way for a while. Used to be a saying about
'Lottery in June, corn be heavy soon.' First thing you know, we'd all
be eating stewed chickweed and acorns. There's *always* been a lottery,"
he added petulantly. "Bad enough to see young Joe Summers up there
joking with everybody."

"Some places have already quit lotteries," Mrs. Adams said.

"Nothing but trouble in *that*," Old Man Warner said stoutly.
"Pack of young fools."

35 "Martin." And Bobby Martin watched his father go forward. 35
"Overdyke . . . Percy."

"I wish they'd hurry," Mrs. Dunbar said to her older son. "I wish
they'd hurry."

"They're almost through," her son said.

"You get ready to run tell Dad," Mrs. Dunbar said.

Mr. Summers called his own name and then stepped forward precisely and selected a slip from the box. Then he called, "Warner."

40 "Seventy-seventh year I been in the lottery," Old Man Warner 40
said as he went through the crowd. "Seventy-seventh time."

"Watson." The tall boy came awkwardly through the crowd. Someone said, "Don't be nervous, Jack," and Mr. Summers said, "Take your time, son."

"Zanini."

After that, there was a long pause, a breathless pause, until Mr. Summers, holding his slip of paper in the air, said, "All right, fellows." For a minute, no one moved, and then all the slips of paper were opened. Suddenly, all the women began to speak at once, saying, "Who is it?" "Who's got it?" "Is it the Dunbars?" "Is it the Watsons?" Then the voices began to say, "It's Hutchinson. It's Bill," "Bill Hutchinson's got it."

"Go tell your father," Mrs. Dunbar said to her older son.

45   People began to look around to see the Hutchinsons. Bill   45
Hutchinson was standing quiet, staring down at the paper in his hand. Suddenly, Tessie Hutchinson shouted to Mr. Summers, "You didn't give him time enough to take any paper he wanted. I saw you. It wasn't fair."

"Be a good sport, Tessie," Mrs. Delacroix called, and Mrs. Graves said, "All of us took the same chance."

"Shut up, Tessie," Bill Hutchinson said.

"Well, everyone," Mr. Summers said, "that was done pretty fast, and now we've got to be hurrying a little more to get done in time." He consulted his next list. "Bill," he said, "you draw for the Hutchinson family. You got any other households in the Hutchinsons?"

"There's Don and Eva," Mrs. Hutchinson yelled. "Make them take their chance!"

50   "Daughters draw with their husbands' families, Tessie," Mr. Sum-   50
mers said gently. "You know that as well as anyone else."

"It wasn't *fair*," Tessie said.

"I guess not, Joe," Bill Hutchinson said regretfully. "My daughter draws with her husband's family, that's only fair. And I've got no other family except the kids."

"Then, as far as drawing for families is concerned, it's you." Mr. Summers said in explanation, "and as far as drawing for households is concerned, that's you, too. Right?"

"Right," Bill Hutchinson said.

55   "How many kids, Bill?" Mr. Summers asked formally.   55
"Three," Bill Hutchinson said. "There's Bill, Jr., and Nancy, and little Dave. And Tessie and me."

"All right, then," Mr. Summers said. "Harry, you got their tickets back?"

Mr. Graves nodded and held up the slips of paper. "Put them in the box, then," Mr. Summers directed. "Take Bill's and put it in."

"I think we ought to start over," Mrs. Hutchinson said, as quietly as she could. "I tell you it wasn't *fair*. You didn't give him time enough to choose. *Every*body saw that."

60 Mr. Graves had selected the five slips and put them in the box, 60 and he dropped all the papers but those onto the ground, where the breeze caught them and lifted them off.

"Listen, everybody," Mrs. Hutchinson was saying to the people around her.

"Ready, Bill?" Mr. Summers asked, and Bill Hutchinson, with one quick glance around at his wife and children, nodded.

"Remember," Mr. Summers said, "take the slips and keep them folded until each person has taken one. Harry, you help little Dave." Mr. Graves took the hand of the little boy, who came willingly with him up to the box. "Take a paper out of the box, Davy," Mr. Summers said. Davy put his hand into the box and laughed. "Take just *one* paper," Mr. Summers said. "Harry, you hold it for him." Mr. Graves took the child's hand and removed the folded paper from the tight fist and held it while little Dave stood next to him and looked up at him wonderingly.

"Nancy next," Mr. Summers said. Nancy was twelve, and her school friends breathed heavily as she went forward, switching her skirt, and took a slip daintily from the box. "Bill, Jr.," Mr. Summers said, and Billy, his face red and his feet over-large, nearly knocked the box over as he got a paper out. "Tessie," Mr. Summers said. She hesitated for a minute, looking around defiantly, and then set her lips and went up to the box. She snatched a paper out and held it behind her.

65 "Bill," Mr. Summers said, and Bill Hutchinson reached into the 65 box and felt around, bringing his hand out at last with the slip of paper in it.

The crowd was quiet. A girl whispered, "I hope it's not Nancy," and the sound of the whisper reached the edges of the crowd.

"It's not the way it used to be," Old Man Warner said clearly. "People ain't the way they used to be."

"All right," Mr. Summers said. "Open the papers. Harry, you open little Dave's."

Mr. Graves opened the slip of paper and there was a general sigh through the crowd as he held it up and everyone could see that it was blank. Nancy and Bill, Jr., opened theirs at the same time, and both beamed and laughed, turning around to the crowd and holding their slips of paper above their heads.

70 "Tessie," Mr. Summers said. There was a pause, and then Mr. 70 Summers looked at Bill Hutchinson, and Bill unfolded his paper and showed it. It was blank.

"It's Tessie," Mr. Summers said, and his voice was hushed. "Show us her paper, Bill."

Bill Hutchinson went over to his wife and forced the slip of paper out of her hand. It had a black spot on it, the black spot Mr. Summers had made the night before with the heavy pencil in the coal-company office. Bill Hutchinson held it up, and there was a stir in the crowd.

"All right, folks," Mr. Summers said. "Let's finish quickly."

Although the villagers had forgotten the ritual and lost the original black box, they still remembered to use stones. The pile of stones the boys had made earlier was ready; there were stones on the ground with the blowing scraps of paper that had come out of the box. Mrs. Delacroix selected a stone so large she had to pick it up with both hands and turned, to Mrs. Dunbar. "Come on," she said. "Hurry up."

Mrs. Dunbar had small stones in both hands, and she said, gasping for breath, "I can't run at all. You'll have to go ahead and I'll catch up with you."

75 The children had stones already, and someone gave little Davy 75 Hutchinson a few pebbles.

Tessie Hutchinson was in the center of a cleared space by now, and she held her hands out despertely as the villagers moved in on her. "It isn't fair," she said. A stone hit her on the side of the head.

Old Man Warner was saying, "Come on, come on, everyone." Steve Adams was in the front of the crowd of villagers, with Mrs. Graves beside him.

"It isn't fair, it isn't right," Mrs. Hutchinson screamed, and then they were upon her.

Questions on Meaning

1. Why does the story begin with the children, and why does it end with the little boy being given a few stones?
2. Tessie Hutchinson becomes a scapegoat for the community. Look up the word "scapegoat" to see exactly what it means and where it originated.
3. Is this story possible? Could people act so casually about such a horrifying prospect as killing a friend or neighbor? Discuss the possibilities of such behavior.

Questions on Rhetorical Strategy and Style

1. At what point in the story does the reader know that something horrible is about to happen? How does the mood of the whole story lead to that moment? Or does it?
2. The families are divided into prescribed groupings, daughters with husbands' families, children with parents until a certain age. Why do we classify and divide groups of people in these ways? What is to be gained from family groupings? What is lost?
3. A news reporter recently described villagers he had met in Rwanda, where the Tutsi massacres took place. He said that the people told him that they must conform to everyone else's behavior, or they too would be killed. Discuss this kind of argument for military and civil violence. Do you believe it to be a sound argument for any occasion?

Writing Assignments

1. A famous German minister, Diedrich Bonhoeffer, said of the Nazis, "When they came for the Jews, I said nothing; when they came for the Communists, I said nothing; when they came for the Catholics, I said nothing; so when they came for me, there was no one to speak." What does such a statement show about our responsibility for others?
2. Traditions can be good for a society or culture, but they can also cause great damage. Choose a holiday or event and discuss the pros and cons of the traditional approaches to the occasion.
3. The story revolves around an election. Why are elections surrounded with so much ceremony? We have election judges, election officials, and election rules and regulations. Does the right to vote deserve so much time and ceremony? Why or why not?

Interpreter of Maladies

Jhumpa Lahiri

Jhumpa Lahiri (1967–) was born in London and grew up in Rhode Island. Her parents were raised in Bengali, so Lahiri made several extended visits to Calcutta during her youth, visits that dramatically affected her writing. Lahiri received a B.A. in English literature from Barnard College, a master's degree in creative writing from Boston University, and a doctorate in Renaissance studies, also from Boston University. In 1998, The New Yorker *published several of her short stories and, in 1999, named Lahiri one of the twenty best young writers in America. Her first volume of short stories,* Interpreter of Maladies *(1999), won the Pulitzer Prize for Fiction; Lahiri was the first person of South Asian descent to win the prize. Her first novel,* The Namesake *(2003) traces two generations of the Ganguli family as they move from India to Boston. In this short story from* Interpreter of Maladies, *we encounter the Das family on a visit to India in which Mrs. Das reveals her secret.*

1   At the tea stall Mr. and Mrs. Das bickered about who should take Tina to the toilet. Eventually Mrs. Das relented when Mr. Das pointed out that he had given the girl her bath the night before. In the rearview mirror Mr. Kapasi watched as Mrs. Das emerged slowly from his bulky white Ambassador, dragging her shaved, largely bare legs across the back seat. She did not hold the little girl's hand as they walked to the rest room.

They were on their way to see the Sun Temple at Konarak. It was a dry, bright Saturday, the mid-July heat tempered by a steady ocean breeze, ideal weather for sightseeing. Ordinarily Mr. Kapasi would not have stopped so soon along the way, but less than five minutes after he'd picked up the family that morning in front of Hotel Sandy Villa, the little girl had complained. The first thing Mr. Kapasi had noticed when he saw Mr. and Mrs. Das, standing with their children under the portico of the hotel, was that they were very young, perhaps not even thirty. In addition to Tina they had two boys, Ronny and Bobby, who appeared very close in age and had teeth covered in a network of flashing silver wires. The family looked Indian but dressed as foreigners did, the children in stiff, brightly colored clothing and caps with translucent visors. Mr. Kapasi was accustomed to foreign tourists; he was assigned to them regularly because he could speak English. Yesterday he had driven an elderly couple from Scotland, both with spotted faces and fluffy white hair so thin it exposed their sunburnt scalps. In comparison, the tanned, youthful faces of Mr. and Mrs. Das were all the more striking. When he'd introduced himself, Mr. Kapasi had pressed his palms together in greeting, but Mr. Das squeezed hands like an American so that Mr. Kapasi felt it in his elbow. Mrs. Das, for her part, had flexed one side of her mouth, smiling dutifully at Mr. Kapasi, without displaying any interest in him.

As they waited at the tea stall, Ronny, who looked like the older of the two boys, clambered suddenly out of the back seat, intrigued by a goat tied to a stake in the ground.

"Don't touch it," Mr. Das said. He glanced up from his paperback tour book, which said "INDIA" in yellow letters and looked as if it had been published abroad. His voice, somehow tentative and a little shrill, sounded as though it had not yet settled into maturity.

"I want to give it a piece of gum," the boy called back as he trotted ahead.

Mr. Das stepped out of the car and stretched his legs by squatting briefly to the ground. A clean-shaven man, he looked exactly like a magnified version of Ronny. He had a sapphire blue visor, and was dressed in shorts, sneakers, and a T-shirt. The camera slung around his neck, with an impressive telephoto lens and numerous buttons and markings, was the only complicated thing he wore. He frowned, watching as Ronny rushed toward the goat, but appeared to have no intention of intervening. "Bobby, make sure that your brother doesn't do anything stupid."

"I don't feel like it," Bobby said, not moving. He was sitting in the front seat beside Mr. Kapasi, studying a picture of the elephant god taped to the glove compartment.

"No need to worry," Mr. Kapasi said. "They are quite tame." Mr. Kapasi was forty-six years old, with receding hair that had gone completely silver, but his butterscotch complexion and his unlined brow, which he treated in spare moments to dabs of lotus-oil balm, made it easy to imagine what he must have looked like at an earlier age. He wore gray trousers and a matching jacket-style shirt, tapered at the waist, with short sleeves and a large pointed collar, made of a thin but durable synthetic material. He had specified both the cut and the fabric to his tailor—it was his preferred uniform for giving tours because it did not get crushed during his long hours behind the wheel. Through the windshield he watched as Ronny circled around the goat, touched it quickly on its side, then trotted back to the car.

"You left India as a child?" Mr. Kapasi asked when Mr. Das had settled once again into the passenger seat.

10   "Oh, Mina and I were both born in America," Mr. Das announced   10 with an air of sudden confidence. "Born and raised. Our parents live here now, in Assansol. They retired. We visit them every couple years." He turned to watch as the little girl ran toward the car, the wide purple bows of her sundress flopping on her narrow brown shoulders. She was holding to her chest a doll with yellow hair that looked as if it had been chopped, as a punitive measure, with a pair of dull scissors. "This is Tina's first trip to India, isn't it, Tina?"

"I don't have to go to the bathroom anymore," Tina announced.

"Where's Mina?" Mr. Das asked.

Mr. Kapasi found it strange that Mr. Das should refer to his wife by her first name when speaking to the little girl. Tina pointed to where Mrs. Das was purchasing something from one of the shirtless men who worked at the tea stall. Mr. Kapasi heard one of the shirtless men sing a phrase from a popular Hindi love song as Mrs. Das walked back to the car, but she did not appear to understand the words of the song, for she did not express irritation, or embarrassment, or react in any other way to the man's declarations.

He observed her. She wore a red-and-white-checkered skirt that stopped above her knees, slip-on shoes with a square wooden heel, and a close-fitting blouse styled like a man's undershirt. The blouse was decorated at chest-level with a calico appliqué in the shape of a strawberry. She was a short woman, with small hands like paws, her frosty pink fingernails painted to match her lips, and was slightly plump in her figure. Her hair, shorn only a little longer than her husband's, was parted far to one side. She was wearing large dark brown sunglasses with a pinkish tint to them, and carried a big straw bag, almost as big as her torso, shaped like a bowl, with a water bottle poking out of it. She walked slowly, carrying some puffed rice tossed with peanuts and chili peppers in a large packet made from newspapers. Mr. Kapasi turned to Mr. Das.

15 "Where in America do you live?" 15

"New Brunswick, New Jersey."

"Next to New York?"

"Exactly. I teach middle school there."

"What subject?"

20 "Science. In fact, every year I take my students on a trip to the 20 Museum of Natural History in New York City. In a way we have a lot in common, you could say, you and I. How long have you been a tour guide, Mr. Kapasi?"

"Five years."

Mrs. Das reached the car. "How long's the trip?" she asked, shutting the door.

"About two and a half hours," Mr. Kapasi replied.

At this Mrs. Das gave an impatient sigh, as if she had been traveling her whole life without pause. She fanned herself with a folded Bombay film magazine written in English.

25 "I thought that the Sun Temple is only eighteen miles north of 25 Puri," Mr. Das said, tapping on the tour book.

"The roads to Konarak are poor. Actually it is a distance of fifty-two miles," Mr. Kapasi explained.

Mr. Das nodded, readjusting the camera strap where it had begun to chafe the back of his neck.

Before starting the ignition, Mr. Kapasi reached back to make sure the cranklike locks on the inside of each of the back doors were secured. As soon as the car began to move the little girl began to play with the lock on her side, clicking it with some effort forward and backward, but Mrs. Das said nothing to stop her. She sat a bit slouched at one end of the back seat, not offering her puffed rice to anyone. Ronny and Tina sat on either side of her, both snapping bright green gum.

"Look," Bobby said as the car began to gather speed. He pointed with his finger to the tall trees that lined the road. "Look."

"Monkeys!" Ronny shrieked. "Wow!"

They were seated in groups along the branches, with shining black faces, silver bodies, horizontal eyebrows, and crested heads. Their long gray tails dangled like a series of ropes among the leaves. A few scratched themselves with black leathery hands, or swung their feet, staring as the car passed.

"We call them the hanuman," Mr. Kapasi said. "They are quite common in the area."

As soon as he spoke, one of the monkeys leaped into the middle of the road, causing Mr. Kapasi to brake suddenly. Another bounced onto the hood of the car, then sprang away. Mr. Kapasi beeped his horn. The children began to get excited, sucking in their breath and covering their faces partly with their hands. They had never seen monkeys outside of a zoo, Mr. Das explained. He asked Mr. Kapasi to stop the car so that he could take a picture.

While Mr. Das adjusted his telephoto lens, Mrs. Das reached into her straw bag and pulled out a bottle of colorless nail polish, which she proceeded to stroke on the tip of her index finger.

The little girl stuck out a hand. "Mine too. Mommy, do mine too."

"Leave me alone," Mrs. Das said, blowing on her nail and turning her body slightly. "You're making me mess up."

The little girl occupied herself by buttoning and unbuttoning a pinafore on the doll's plastic body.

"All set," Mr. Das said, replacing the lens cap.

The car rattled considerably as it raced along the dusty road, causing them all to pop up from their seats every now and then, but Mrs. Das continued to polish her nails. Mr. Kapasi eased up on the accelerator, hoping to produce a smoother ride. When he reached for the gearshift the boy in front accommodated him by swinging his hairless knees out of the way. Mr. Kapasi noted that this boy was slightly paler than the other children. "Daddy, why is the driver sitting on the wrong side in this car, too?" the boy asked.

"They all do that here, dummy," Ronny said.

"Don't call your brother a dummy," Mr. Das said. He turned to Mr. Kapasi. "In America, you know . . . it confuses them."

"Oh yes, I am well aware," Mr. Kapasi said. As delicately as he could, he shifted gears again, accelerating as they approached a hill in the road. "I see it on *Dallas,* the steering wheels are on the left-hand side."

"What's *Dallas?*" Tina asked, banging her now naked doll on the seat behind Mr. Kapasi.

"It went off the air," Mr. Das explained. "It's a television show."

45 They were all like siblings, Mr. Kapasi thought as they passed a row of date trees. Mr. and Mrs. Das behaved like an older brother and sister, not parents. It seemed that they were in charge of the children only for the day; it was hard to believe they were regularly responsible for anything other than themselves. Mr. Das tapped on his lens cap, and his tour book, dragging his thumbnail occasionally across the pages so that they made a scraping sound. Mrs. Das continued to polish her nails. She had still not removed her sunglasses. Every now and then Tina renewed her plea that she wanted her nails done, too, and so at one point Mrs. Das flicked a drop of polish on the little girl's finger before depositing the bottle back inside her straw bag.

"Isn't this an air-conditioned car?" she asked, still blowing on her hand. The window on Tina's side was broken and could not be rolled down.

"Quit complaining," Mr. Das said. "It isn't so hot."

"I told you to get a car with air-conditioning," Mrs. Das continued. "Why do you do this, Raj, just to save a few stupid rupees. What are you saving us, fifty cents?"

Their accents sounded just like the ones Mr. Kapasi heard on American television programs, though not like the ones on *Dallas.*

50 "Doesn't it get tiresome, Mr. Kapasi, showing people the same thing every day?" Mr. Das asked, rolling down his own window all the way. "Hey, do you mind stopping the car. I just want to get a shot of this guy."

Mr. Kapasi pulled over to the side of the road as Mr. Das took a picture of a barefoot man, his head wrapped in a dirty turban, seated on top of a cart of grain sacks pulled by a pair of bullocks. Both the man and the bullocks were emaciated. In the back seat Mrs. Das gazed out another window, at the sky, where nearly transparent clouds passed quickly in front of one another.

"I look forward to it, actually," Mr. Kapasi said as they continued on their way. "The Sun Temple is one of my favorite places. In that way it is a reward for me. I give tours on Fridays and Saturdays only. I have another job during the week."

"Oh? Where?" Mr. Das asked.

"I work in a doctor's office."

⁵⁵ "You're a doctor?" ⁵⁵

"I am not a doctor. I work with one. As an interpreter."

"What does a doctor need an interpreter for?"

"He has a number of Gujarati patients. My father was Gujarati, but many people do not speak Gujarati in this area, including the doctor. And so the doctor asked me to work in his office, interpreting what the patients say."

"Interesting. I've never heard of anything like that," Mr. Das said.

⁶⁰ Mr. Kapasi shrugged. "It is a job like any other." ⁶⁰

"But so romantic," Mrs. Das said dreamily, breaking her extended silence. She lifted her pinkish brown sunglasses and arranged them on top of her head like a tiara. For the first time, her eyes met Mr. Kapasi's in the rearview mirror: pale, a bit small, their gaze fixed but drowsy.

Mr. Das craned to look at her. "What's so romantic about it?"

"I don't know. Something." She shrugged, knitting her brows together for an instant. "Would you like a piece of gum, Mr. Kapasi?" she asked brightly. She reached into her straw bag and handed him a small square wrapped in green-and-white-striped paper. As soon as Mr. Kapasi put the gum in his mouth a thick sweet liquid burst onto his tongue.

"Tell us more about your job, Mr. Kapasi," Mrs. Das said.

⁶⁵ "What would you like to know, madame?" ⁶⁵

"I don't know," she shrugged, munching on some puffed rice and licking the mustard oil from the corners of her mouth. "Tell us a typical situation." She settled back in her seat, her head tilted in a patch of sun, and closed her eyes. "I want to picture what happens."

"Very well. The other day a man came in with a pain in his throat."

"Did he smoke cigarettes?"

"No. It was very curious. He complained that he felt as if there were long pieces of straw stuck in his throat. When I told the doctor he was able to prescribe the proper medication."

⁷⁰ "That's so neat." ⁷⁰

"Yes," Mr. Kapasi agreed after some hesitation.

"So these patients are totally dependent on you," Mrs. Das said. She spoke slowly, as if she were thinking aloud. "In a way, more dependent on you than the doctor."

"How do you mean? How could it be?"

"Well, for example, you could tell the doctor that the pain felt like a burning, not straw. The patient would never know what you had told the doctor, and the doctor wouldn't know that you had told the wrong thing. It's a big responsibility."

75 "Yes, a big responsibility you have there, Mr. Kapasi," Mr. Das 75 agreed.

Mr. Kapasi had never thought of his job in such complimentary terms. To him it was a thankless occupation. He found nothing noble in interpreting people's maladies, assiduously translating the symptoms of so many swollen bones, countless cramps of bellies and bowels, spots on people's palms that changed color, shape, or size. The doctor, nearly half his age, had an affinity for bell-bottom trousers and made humorless jokes about the Congress party.[1] Together they worked in a stale little infirmary where Mr. Kapasi's smartly tailored clothes clung to him in the heat, in spite of the blackened blades of a ceiling fan churning over their heads.

The job was a sign of his failings. In his youth he'd been a devoted scholar of foreign languages, the owner of an impressive collection of dictionaries. He had dreamed of being an interpreter for diplomats and dignitaries, resolving conflicts between people and nations, settling disputes of which he alone could understand both sides. He was a self-educated man. In a series of notebooks, in the evenings before his parents settled his marriage, he had listed the common etymologies of words, and at one point in his life he was confident that he could converse, if given the opportunity, in English, French, Russian, Portuguese, and Italian, not to mention Hindi, Bengali, Orissi, and Gujarati. Now only a handful of European phrases remained in his memory, scattered words for things like saucers and chairs. English was the only non-Indian language he spoke fluently anymore. Mr. Kapasi knew it was not a remarkable talent. Sometimes he feared that his children knew better English than he did, just from watching television. Still, it came in handy for the tours.

He had taken the job as an interpreter after his first son, at the age of seven, contracted typhoid—that was how he had first made the acquaintance of the doctor. At the time Mr. Kapasi had been teaching English in a grammar school, and he bartered his skills as an interpreter to pay the increasingly exorbitant medical bills. In the end the boy had died one evening in his mother's arms, his limbs burning with fever, but then there was the funeral to pay for, and the other children who were born soon enough, and the newer, bigger house, and the good schools and tutors, and the fine shoes and the television, and the countless other ways he tried to console his wife and to keep her from crying in her sleep, and so when the doctor offered to pay him twice as much as he earned at the grammar school, he accepted. Mr. Kapasi knew that his wife had little regard for his career as an interpreter. He knew it reminded her of the son she'd lost, and that she resented the other lives he helped, in his own small way, to save. If ever she referred to his position, she used the phrase "doctor's assistant," as if the process of interpretation were equal to taking someone's temperature, or changing a bedpan. She never asked him about the patients who came to the doctor's office, or said that his job was a big responsibility.

For this reason it flattered Mr. Kapasi that Mrs. Das was so intrigued by his job. Unlike his wife, she had reminded him of its intellectual challenges. She had also used the word "romantic." She did not behave in a romantic way toward her husband, and yet she had used the word to describe him. He wondered if Mr. and Mrs. Das were a bad match, just as he and his wife were. Perhaps they, too, had little in common apart from three children and a decade of their lives. The signs he recognized from his own marriage were there—the bickering, the indifference, the protracted silences. Her sudden interest in him, an interest she did not express in either her husband or her children, was mildly intoxicating. When Mr. Kapasi thought once again about how she had said "romantic," the feeling of intoxication grew.

He began to check his reflection in the rearview mirror as he drove, feeling grateful that he had chosen the gray suit that morning and not the brown one, which tended to sag a little in the knees. From time to time he glanced through the mirror at Mrs. Das. In addition to glancing at her face he glanced at the strawberry between her breasts, and the golden brown hollow in her throat. He decided to tell Mrs. Das about another patient, and another: the young woman who had complained of a sensation of raindrops in her spine, the gentleman whose birthmark had begun to sprout hairs. Mrs. Das listened attentively, stroking her hair with a small plastic brush that resembled an oval bed of nails, asking more questions, for yet another example. The children were quiet, intent on spotting more monkeys in the trees, and Mr. Das was absorbed by his tour book, so it seemed like a private conversation between Mr. Kapasi and Mrs. Das. In this manner the next half hour passed, and when they stopped for lunch at a roadside restaurant that sold fritters and omelette sandwiches, usually something Mr. Kapasi looked forward to on his tours so that he could sit in peace and enjoy some hot tea, he was disappointed. As the Das family settled together under a magneta umbrella fringed with white and orange tassels, and placed their orders with one of the waiters who marched about in tricornered caps, Mr. Kapasi reluctantly headed toward a neighboring table.

"Mr. Kapasi, wait. There's room here," Mrs. Das called out. She gathered Tina onto her lap, insisting that he accompany them. And so, together they had bottled mango juice and sandwiches and plates of onions and potatoes deep-fried in graham-flour batter. After finishing two omelette sandwiches Mr. Das took more pictures of the group as they ate.

"How much longer?" he asked Mr. Kapasi as he paused to load a new roll of film in the camera.

"About half an hour more."

By now the children had gotten up from the table to look at more monkeys perched in a nearby tree, so there was a considerable space between Mrs. Das and Mr. Kapasi. Mr. Das placed the camera to his face and squeezed one eye shut, his tongue exposed at one corner of his mouth. "This looks funny. Mina, you need to lean in closer to Mr. Kapasi."

85 She did. He could smell a scent on her skin, like a mixture of 85 whiskey and rosewater. He worried suddenly that she could smell his perspiration, which he knew had collected beneath the synthetic material of his shirt. He polished off his mango juice in one gulp and smoothed his silver hair with his hands. A bit of the juice dripped onto his chin. He wondered if Mrs. Das had noticed.

She had not. "What's your address, Mr. Kapasi?" she inquired, fishing for something inside her straw bag.

"You would like my address?"

"So we can send you copies," she said. "Of the pictures." She handed him a scrap of paper which she had hastily ripped from a page of her film magazine. The blank portion was limited, for the narrow strip was crowded by lines of text and a tiny picture of a hero and heroine embracing under a eucalyptus tree.

The paper curled as Mr. Kapasi wrote his address in clear, careful letters. She would write to him, asking about his days interpreting at the doctor's office, and he would respond eloquently, choosing only the most entertaining anecdotes, ones that would make her laugh out loud as she read them in her house in New Jersey. In time she would reveal the disappointment of her marriage, and he his. In this way their friendship would grow, and flourish. He would possess a picture of the two of them, eating fried onions under a magenta umbrella, which he would keep, he decided, safely tucked between the pages of his Russian grammar. As his mind raced, Mr. Kapasi experienced a mild and pleasant shock. It was similar to a feeling he used to experience long ago when, after months of translating with the aid of a dictionary, he would finally read a passage from a French novel, or an Italian sonnet, and understand the words, one after another, unencumbered by his own efforts. In those moments Mr. Kapasi used to believe that all was right with the world, that all struggles were rewarded, that all of life's mistakes made sense in the end. The promise that he would hear from Mrs. Das now filled him with the same belief.

90 When he finished writing his address Mr. Kapasi handed her the paper, but as soon as he did so he worried that he had either misspelled his name, or accidentally reversed the numbers of his postal code. He dreaded the possibility of a lost letter, the photograph never reaching him, hovering somewhere in Orissa, close but ultimately unattainable. He thought of asking for the slip of paper again, just to make sure he had written his address accurately, but Mrs. Das had already dropped it into the jumble of her bag.

They reached Konarak at two-thirty. The temple, made of sandstone, was a massive pyramid-like structure in the shape of a chariot. It was dedicated to the great master of life, the sun, which struck three sides of the edifice as it made its journey each day across the sky. Twenty-four giant wheels were carved on the north and south sides of the plinth. The whole thing was drawn by a team of seven horses, speeding as if through the heavens. As they approached, Mr. Kapasi explained that the temple had been built between A.D. 1243 and 1255, with the efforts of twelve hundred artisans, by the great ruler of the Ganga dynasty, King Narasimhadeva the First, to commemorate his victory against the Muslim army.

"It says the temple occupies about a hundred and seventy acres of land," Mr. Das said, reading from his book.

"It's like a desert," Ronny said, his eyes wandering across the sand that stretched on all sides beyond the temple.

"The Chandrabhaga River once flowed one mile north of here. It is dry now," Mr. Kapasi said, turning off the engine.

95 They got out and walked toward the temple, posing first for pic- 95 tures by the pair of lions that flanked the steps. Mr. Kapasi led them next to one of the wheels of the chariot, higher than any human being, nine feet in diameter.

"'The wheels are supposed to symbolize the wheel of life,'" Mr. Das read. " 'They depict the cycle of creation, preservation, and achievement of realization.' Cool." He turned the page of his book. " 'Each wheel is divided into eight thick and thin spokes, dividing the day into eight equal parts. The rims are carved with designs of birds and animals, whereas the medallions in the spokes are carved with women in luxurious poses, largely erotic in nature.' "

What he referred to were the countless friezes of entwined naked bodies, making love in various positions, women clinging to the necks of men, their knees wrapped eternally around their lovers' thighs. In addition to these were assorted scenes from daily life, of hunting and trading, of deer being killed with bows and arrows and marching warriors holding swords in their hands.

It was no longer possible to enter the temple, for it had filled with rubble years ago, but they admired the exterior, as did all the tourists Mr. Kapasi brought there, slowly strolling along each of its sides. Mr. Das trailed behind, taking pictures. The children ran ahead, pointing to figures of naked people, intrigued in particular by the Nagamithunas, the half-human, half-serpentine couples who were said, Mr. Kapasi told them, to live in the deepest waters of the sea. Mr. Kapasi was pleased that they liked the temple, pleased especially that it appealed to Mrs. Das. She stopped every three or four paces, staring silently at the carved lovers, and the processions of elephants, and the topless female musicians beating on two-sided drums.

Though Mr. Kapasi had been to the temple countless times, it occurred to him, as he, too, gazed at the topless women, that he had never seen his own wife fully naked. Even when they had made love she kept the panels of her blouse hooked together, the string of her petticoat knotted around her waist. He had never admired the backs of his wife's legs the way he now admired those of Mrs. Das, walking as if for his benefit alone. He had, of course, seen plenty of bare limbs before, belonging to the American and European ladies who took his tours. But Mrs. Das was different. Unlike the other women, who had an interest only in the temple, and kept their noses buried in a guide-book, or their eyes behind the lens of a camera, Mrs. Das had taken an interest in him.

100   Mr. Kapasi was anxious to be alone with her, to continue their pri- 100 vate conversation, yet he felt nervous to walk at her side. She was lost behind her sunglasses, ignoring her husband's requests that she pose for another picture, walking past her children as if they were strangers. Worried that he might disturb her, Mr. Kapasi walked ahead, to admire, as he always did, the three life-sized bronze avatars of Surya, the sun god, each emerging from its own niche on the temple facade to greet the sun at dawn, noon, and evening. They wore elaborate head-dresses, their languid, elongated eyes closed, their bare chests draped with carved chains and amulets. Hibiscus petals, offerings from previous visitors, were strewn at their gray-green feet. The last statue, on the northern wall of the temple, was Mr. Kapasi's favorite. This Surya had a tired expression, weary after a hard day of work, sitting astride a horse with folded legs. Even his horse's eyes were drowsy. Around his body were smaller sculptures of women in pairs, their hips thrust to one side.

"Who's that?" Mrs. Das asked. He was startled to see that she was standing beside him.

"He is the Astachala-Surya," Mr. Kapasi said. "The setting sun."

"So in a couple of hours the sun will set right here?" She slipped a foot out of one of her square-heeled shoes, rubbed her toes on the back of her other leg.

"That is correct."

105   She raised her sunglasses for a moment, then put them back on 105 again. "Neat."

Mr. Kapasi was not certain exactly what the word suggested, but he had a feeling it was a favorable response. He hoped that Mrs. Das had understood Surya's beauty, his power. Perhaps they would discuss it further in their letters. He would explain things to her, things about India, and she would explain things to him about America. In its own way this correspondence would fulfill his dream, of serving as an interpreter between nations. He looked at her straw bag, delighted that his address lay nestled among its contents. When he pictured her so many thousands of miles away he plummeted, so much so that he had an overwhelming urge to wrap his arms around her, to freeze with her, even for an instant, in an embrace witnessed by his favorite Surya. But Mrs. Das had already started walking.

"When do you return to America?" he asked, trying to sound placid.
"In ten days."

He calculated: A week to settle in, a week to develop the pictures, a few days to compose her letter, two weeks to get to India by air. According to his schedule, allowing room for delays, he would hear from Mrs. Das in approximately six weeks' time.

110 The family was silent as Mr. Kapasi drove them back, a little past 110 four-thirty, to Hotel Sandy Villa. The children had bought miniature granite versions of the chariot's wheels at a souvenir stand, and they turned them round in their hands. Mr. Das continued to read his book. Mrs. Das untangled Tina's hair with her brush and divided it into two little ponytails.

Mr. Kapasi was beginning to dread the thought of dropping them off. He was not prepared to begin his six-week wait to hear from Mrs. Das. As he stole glances at her in the rear-view mirror, wrapping elastic bands around Tina's hair, he wondered how he might make the tour last a little longer. Ordinarily he sped back to Puri using a shortcut, eager to return home, scrub his feet and hands with sandalwood soap, and enjoy the evening newspaper and a cup of tea that his wife would serve him in silence. The thought of that silence, something to which he'd long been resigned, now oppressed him. It was then that he suggested visiting the hills at Udayagiri and Khandagiri, where a number of monastic dwellings were hewn out of the ground, facing one another across a defile. It was some miles away, but well worth seeing, Mr. Kapasi told them.

"Oh yeah, there's something mentioned about it in this book," Mr. Das said. "Built by a Jain[2] king or something."

"Shall we go then?" Mr. Kapasi asked. He paused at a turn in the road. "It's to the left."

Mr. Das turned to look at Mrs. Das. Both of them shrugged.

115 "Left, left," the children chanted. 115

Mr. Kapasi turned the wheel, almost delirious with relief. He did not know what he would do or say to Mrs. Das once they arrived at the hills. Perhaps he would tell her what a pleasing smile she had. Perhaps he would compliment her strawberry shirt, which he found irresistibly becoming. Perhaps, when Mr. Das was busy taking a picture, he would take her hand.

He did not have to worry. When they got to the hills divided by a steep path thick with trees, Mrs. Das refused to get out of the car. All along the path, dozens of monkeys were seated on stones, as well as on the branches of the trees. Their hind legs were stretched out in front and raised to shoulder level, their arms resting on their arms resting on their knees.

"My legs are tired," she said, sinking low in her seat. "I'll stay here."

"Why did you have to wear those stupid shoes?" Mr. Das said. "You won't be in the pictures."

120 "Pretend I'm there." 120

"But we could use one of these pictures for our Christmas card this year. We didn't get one of all five of us at the Sun Temple. Mr. Kapasi could take it."

"I'm not coming. Anyway, those monkeys give me the creeps."

"But they're harmless," Mr. Das said. He turned to Mr. Kapasi. "Aren't they?"

"They are more hungry than dangerous," Mr. Kapasi said. "Do not provoke them with food, and they will not bother you."

125 Mr. Das headed up the defile with the children, the boys at his 125 side, the little girl on his shoulders. Mr. Kapasi watched as they crossed paths with a Japanese man and woman, the only other tourists there, who paused for a final photograph, then stepped into a nearby car and drove away. As the car disappeared out of view some of the monkeys called out, emitting soft whooping sounds, and then walked on their flat black hands and feet up the path. At one point a group of them formed a little ring around Mr. Das and the children. Tina screamed in delight. Ronny ran in circles around his father. Bobby bent down and picked up a fat stick on the ground. When he extended it, one of the monkeys approached him and snatched it, then briefly beat the ground.

"I'll join them," Mr. Kapasi said, unlocking the door on his side. "There is much to explain about the caves."

"No. Stay a minute," Mrs. Das said. She got out of the back seat and slipped in beside Mr. Kapasi. "Raj has his dumb book anyway." Together, through the windshield, Mrs. Das and Mr. Kapasi watched as Bobby and the monkey passed the stick back and forth between them.

"A brave little boy," Mr. Kapasi commented.

"It's not so surprising," Mrs. Das said.

130 "No?" 130

"He's not his."

"I beg your pardon?"

"Raj's. He's not Raj's son."

Mr. Kapasi felt a prickle on his skin. He reached into his shirt pocket for the small tin of lotus-oil balm he carried with him at all times, and applied it to three spots on his forehead. He knew that Mrs. Das was watching him, but he did not turn to face her. Instead he watched as the figures of Mr. Das and the children grew smaller, climbing up the steep path, pausing every now and then for a picture, surrounded by a growing number of monkeys.

"Are you surprised?" The way she put it made him choose his words with care.

135 "It's not the type of thing one assumes," Mr. Kapasi replied 135 slowly. He put the tin of lotus-oil balm back in his pocket.

"No, of course not. And no one knows, of course. No one at all. I've kept it a secret for eight whole years." She looked at Mr. Kapasi, tilting her chin as if to gain a fresh perspective. "But now I've told you."

Mr. Kapasi nodded. He felt suddenly parched, and his forehead was warm and slightly numb from the balm. He considered asking Mrs. Das for a sip of water, then decided against it.

"We met when we were very young," she said. She reached into her straw bag in search of something, then pulled out a packet of puffed rice. "Want some?"

"No, thank you."

140 She put a fistful in her mouth, sank into the seat a little, and 140 looked away from Mr. Kapasi, out the window on her side of the car. "We married when we were still in college. We were in high school when he proposed. We went to the same college, of course. Back then we couldn't stand the thought of being separated, not for a day, not for a minute. Our parents were best friends who lived in the same town. My entire life I saw him every weekend, either at our house or theirs. We were sent upstairs to play together while our parents joked about our marriage. Imagine! They never caught us at anything, though in a way I think it was all more or less a setup. The things we did those Friday and Saturday nights, while our parents sat downstairs drinking tea . . . I could tell you stories, Mr. Kapasi."

As a result of spending all her time in college with Raj, she continued, she did not make many close friends. There was no one to confide in about him at the end of a difficult day, or to share a passing thought or a worry. Her parents now lived on the other side of the world, but she had never been very close to them, anyway. After marrying so young she was over-whelmed by it all, having a child so quickly, and nursing, and warming up bottles of milk and testing their temperature against her wrist while Raj was at work, dressed in sweaters and corduroy pants, teaching his students about rocks and dinosaurs. Raj never looked cross or harried, or plump as she had become after the first baby.

Always tired, she declined invitations from her one or two college girlfriends, to have lunch or shop in Manhattan. Eventually the friends stopped calling her, so that she was left at home all day with the baby, surrounded by toys that made her trip when she walked or wince when she sat, always cross and tired. Only occasionally did they go out after Ronny was born, and even more rarely did they entertain. Raj didn't mind; he looked forward to coming home from teaching and watching television and bouncing Ronny on his knee. She had been outraged when Raj told her that a Punjabi friend, someone whom she had once met but did not remember, would be staying with them for a week for some job interviews in the New Brunswick area.

Bobby was conceived in the afternoon, on a sofa littered with rubber teething toys, after the friend learned that a London pharmaceutical company had hired him, while Ronny cried to be freed from his playpen. She made no protest when the friend touched the small of her back as she was about to make a pot of coffee, then pulled her against his crisp navy suit. He made love to her swiftly, in silence, with an expertise she had never known, without the meaningful expressions and smiles Raj always insisted on afterward. The next day Raj drove the friend to JFK. He was married now, to a Punjabi girl, and they lived in London still, and every year they exchanged Christmas cards with Raj and Mina, each couple tucking photos of their families into the envelopes. He did not know that he was Bobby's father. He never would.

"I beg your pardon, Mrs. Das, but why have you told me this information?" Mr. Kapasi asked when she had finally finished speaking, and had turned to face him once again.

"For God's sake, stop calling me Mrs. Das. I'm twenty-eight. You probably have children my age."

"Not quite." It disturbed Mr. Kapasi to learn that she thought of him as a parent. The feeling he had had toward her, that had made him check his reflection in the rearview mirror as they drove, evaporated a little.

"I told you because of your talents." She put the packet of puffed rice back into her bag without folding over the top.

"I don't understand," Mr. Kapasi said.

"Don't you see? For eight years I haven't been able to express this to anybody, not to friends, certainly not to Raj. He doesn't even suspect it. He thinks I'm still in love with him. Well, don't you have anything to say?"

150 "About what?" 150

"About what I've just told you. About my secret, and about how terrible it makes me feel. I feel terrible looking at my children, and at Raj, always terrible. I have terrible urges, Mr. Kapasi, to throw things away. One day I had the urge to throw everything I own out the window, the television, the children everything. Don't you think it's unhealthy?"

He was silent.

"Mr. Kapasi, don't you have anything to say? I thought that was your job."

"My job is to give tours, Mrs. Das."

155 "Not that. Your other job. As an interpreter." 155

"But we do not face a language barrier. What need is there for an interpreter?"

"That's not what I mean. I would never have told you otherwise. Don't you realize what it means for me to tell you?"

"What does it mean?"

"It means that I'm tired of feeling so terrible all the time. Eight years, Mr. Kapasi, I've been in pain eight years. I was hoping you could help me feel better, say the right thing. Suggest some kind of remedy."

160 He looked at her, in her red plaid skirt and strawberry T-shirt, 160 a woman not yet thirty, who loved neither her husband nor her children, who had already fallen out of love with life. Her confession depressed him, depressed him all the more when he thought of Mr. Das at the top of the path, Tina clinging to his shoulders, taking pictures of ancient monastic cells cut into the hills to show his students in America, unsuspecting and unaware that one of his sons was not his own. Mr. Kapasi felt insulted that Mrs. Das should ask him to interpret her common, trivial little secret. She did not resemble the patients in the doctor's office, those who came glassy-eyed and desperate, unable to sleep or breathe or urinate with ease, unable,

above all, to give words to their pains. Still, Mr. Kapasi believed it was his duty to assist Mrs. Das. Perhaps he ought to tell her to confess the truth to Mr. Das. He would explain that honesty was the best policy. Honesty, surely, would help her feel better, as she'd put it. Perhaps he would offer to preside over the discussion, as a mediator. He decided to begin with the most obvious question, to get to the heart of the matter, and so he asked, "Is it really pain you feel, Mrs. Das, or is it guilt?"

She turned to him and glared, mustard oil thick on her frosty pink lips. She opened her mouth to say something, but as she glared at Mr. Kapasi some certain knowledge seemed to pass before her eyes, and she stopped. It crushed him; he knew at that moment that he was not even important enough to be properly insulted. She opened the car door and began walking up the path, wobbling a little on her square wooden heels, reaching into her straw bag to eat handfuls of puffed rice. It fell through her fingers, leaving a zigzagging trail, causing a monkey to leap down from a tree and devour the little white grains. In search of more, the monkey began to follow Mrs. Das. Others joined him, so that she was soon being followed by about half a dozen of them, their velvety tails dragging behind.

Mr. Kapasi stepped out of the car. He wanted to holler, to alert her in some way, but he worried that if she knew they were behind her, she would grow nervous. Perhaps she would lose her balance. Perhaps they would pull at her bag or her hair. He began to jog up the path, taking a fallen branch in his hand to scare away the monkeys. Mrs. Das continued walking, oblivious, trailing grains of puffed rice. Near the top of the incline, before a group of cells fronted by a row of squat stone pillars, Mr. Das was kneeling on the ground, focusing the lens of his camera. The children stood under the arcade, now hiding, now emerging from view.

"Wait for me," Mrs. Das called out. "I'm coming."

Tina jumped up and down. "Here comes Mommy!"

"Great," Mr. Das said without looking up. "Just in time. We'll get Mr. Kapasi to take a picture of the five of us."

Mr. Kapasi quickened his pace, waving his branch so that the monkeys scampered away, distracted, in another direction.

"Where's Bobby?" Mrs. Das asked when she stopped.

Mr. Das looked up from the camera. "I don't know. Ronny, where's Bobby?"

Ronny shrugged. "I thought he was right here."

170 "Where is he?" Mrs. Das repeated sharply. "What's wrong with 170 all of you?"

They began calling his name, wandering up and down the path a bit. Because they were calling, they did not initially hear the boy's screams. When they found him, a little farther down the path under a tree, he was surrounded by a group of monkeys, over a dozen of them, pulling at his T-shirt with their long black fingers. The puffed rice Mrs. Das had spilled was scattered at his feet, raked over by the monkeys' hands. The boy was silent, his body frozen, swift tears running down his startled face. His bare legs were dusty and red with welts from where one of the monkeys struck him repeatedly with the stick he had given to it earlier.

"Daddy, the monkey's hurting Bobby," Tina said.

Mr. Das wiped his palms on the front of his shorts. In his nervousness he accidentally pressed the shutter on his camera; the whirring noise of the advancing film excited the monkeys, and the one with the stick began to beat Bobby more intently. "What are we supposed to do? What if they start attacking?"

"Mr. Kapasi," Mrs. Das shrieked, noticing him standing to one side. "Do something, for God's sake, do something!"

175 Mr. Kapasi took his branch and shooed them away, hissing at the 175 ones that remained, stomping his feet to scare them. The animals retreated slowly, with a measured gait, obedient but unintimidated. Mr. Kapasi gathered Bobby in his arms and brought him back to where his parents and siblings were standing. As he carried him he was tempted to whisper a secret into the boy's ear. But Bobby was stunned, and shivering with fright, his legs bleeding slightly where the stick had broken the skin. When Mr. Kapasi delivered him to his parents, Mr. Das brushed some dirt off the boy's T-shirt and put the visor on him the right way. Mrs. Das reached into her straw bag to find a bandage which she taped over the cut on his knee. Ronny offered his brother a fresh piece of gum. "He's fine. Just a little scared, right, Bobby?" Mr. Das said, patting the top of his head.

"God, let's get out of here," Mrs. Das said. She folded her arms across the strawberry on her chest. "This place gives me the creeps."

"Yeah. Back to the hotel, definitely," Mr. Das agreed.

"Poor Bobby," Mrs. Das said. "Come here a second. Let Mommy fix your hair." Again she reached into her straw bag, this time for her hairbrush, and began to run it around the edges of the translucent visor. When she whipped out the hair-brush, the slip of paper with Mr. Kapasi's address on it fluttered away in the wind. No one but Mr. Kapasi noticed. He watched as it rose, carried higher and higher by the breeze, into the trees where the monkeys now sat, solemnly observing the scene below. Mr. Kapasi observed it too, knowing that this was the picture of the Das family he would preserve forever in his mind.

End Notes

1. The oldest surviving political organization in India; the Congress Party, founded in the late nineteenth century, worked toward Indian independence, and then ruled the nation long afterward, under leaders including Jawaharlal Nehru, Indira Gandhi, and Rajiv Gandhi.

2. Jainism is an Indian religion that shares certain ideas with Hinduism and Buddhism, but that understands God not as a creator, but as a universal consciousness.

Questions on Meaning

1. What is your first impression of the Das family? What does Mr. Kapasi notice about them initially and what is his reaction? How does he view Mrs. Das in particular?

2. What does Mr. Kapasi find most strange about the Das family? What does it mean that, "They were all like siblings"? What does this suggest about the loss of traditional values?

3. What is Mr. Kapasi's regular job? How does it relate to his weekend job as a guide for tourists? How does he feel about his regular job?

4. Why does Mrs. Das tell her secret to Mr. Karpasi, a total stranger? How is this secret an example of a malady? What other maladies does the story develop?

Questions on Rhetorical Strategy and Style

1. What is the narrative point of view in the story? Why does the author cast Mr. Kapasi the main character?

2. The author conveys character traits and values through various descriptive elements. Which passages, for example, reveal the most about cultural contrast in the story?

3. What do the monkeys symbolize in the story? Consider the passage where they are first described, and the scene near the conclusion.

4. The story ends as the note is carried off by the wind. What does this image represent? Why does the author leave the reader with this image, and the monkeys, as the image of the Das family Mr. Kapasi will remember?

Writing Assignments

1. Write an analysis of how the story deals with fading traditional values and cultural dislocation. Consider, for example, the trip to the temple and its condition as framework for the story.

2. What perspectives on and definitions of marriage are developed in the story? Write a two-page analysis of the author's treatment of this topic.

I Think, Therefore IM

Jennifer Lee

Jennifer Lee (1976–) was born in New York City. She graduated from Harvard University in 1999 with a degree in mathematics and economics. While at Harvard she spent a year at Beijing University on a fellowship studying international relations. Lee has received a scholarship from the Asian American Journalism Association and has interned at The Boston Globe, The New York Times, Newsday, The Wall Street Journal, *and* The Washington Post. *She joined the staff of* The New York Times *in 2001 as a technology reporter and began writing for the Metro section the next year. The following selection on instant-messaging language originally appeared in the* Times *in September 2002.*

1   Each September Jacqueline Harding prepares a classroom presentation on the common writing mistakes she sees in her students' work.

Ms. Harding, an eighth-grade English teacher at Viking Middle School in Guernee, Ill., scribbles the words that have plagued generations of school children across her whiteboard:

> There. Their. They're.
> Your. You're.
> To. Too. Two.
> Its. It's.

This September, she has added a new list: u, r, ur, b4, wuz, cuz, 2.

When she asked her students how many of them used shortcuts like them in their writing, Ms. Harding said, she was not surprised when most of them raised their hands. This, after all, is their online

---

lingua franca: English adapted for the spitfire conversational style of Internet instant messaging.

Ms. Harding, who has seen such shortcuts creep into student papers over the last two years, said she gave her students a warning: "If I see this in your assignments, I will take points off."

5   "Kids should know the difference," said Ms. Harding, who decided to address this issue head-on this year. "They should know where to draw the line between formal writing and conversational writing."

As more and more teenagers socialize online, middle school and high school teachers like Ms. Harding are increasingly seeing a breezy form of Internet English jump from e-mail into schoolwork. To their dismay, teachers say that papers are being written with shortened words, improper capitalization and punctuation, and characters like &, $ and @.

Teachers have deducted points, drawn red circles and tsk-tsked at their classes. Yet the errant forms continue. "It stops being funny after you repeat yourself a couple of times," Ms. Harding said.

But teenagers, whose social life can rely as much these days on text communication as the spoken word, say that they use instant-messaging shorthand without thinking about it. They write to one another as much as they write in school, or more.

"You are so used to abbreviating things, you just start doing it unconsciously on schoolwork and reports and other things," said Eve Brecker, 15, a student at Montclair High School in New Jersey.

10   Ms. Brecker once handed in a midterm exam riddled with instant-messaging shorthand. "I had an hour to write an essay on *Romeo and Juliet*," she said. "I just wanted to finish before my time was up. I was writing fast and carelessly. I spelled 'you' 'u.'" She got a C.

Even terms that cannot be expressed verbally are making their way into papers. Melanie Weaver was stunned by some of the term papers she received from a 10th-grade class she recently taught as part of an internship. "They would be trying to make a point in a paper, they would put a smiley face in the end," said Ms. Weaver, who teaches at Alvernia College in Reading, PA. "If they were presenting an argument and they needed to present an opposite view, they would put a frown."

As Trisha Fogarty, a sixth-grade teacher at Houlton Southside School in Houlton, Maine, puts it, today's students are "Generation Text."

Almost 60 percent of the online population under age 17 uses instant messaging, according to Nielsen/NetRatings. In addition to cellphone text messaging, Weblogs and e-mail, it has become a popular means of flirting, setting up dates, asking for help with homework and keeping in contact with distant friends. The abbreviations are a natural outgrowth of this rapid-fire style of communication.

"They have a social life that centers around typed communication," said Judith S. Donath, a professor at the Massachusetts Institute of Technology's Media Lab who has studied electronic communication. "They have a writing style that has been nurtured in a teenage social milieu."

15 Some teachers see the creeping abbreviations as part of a continuing assault of technology on formal written English. Others take it more lightly, saying that it is just part of the larger arc of language evolution.

"To them it's not wrong," said Ms. Harding, who is 28. "It's acceptable because it's in their culture. It's hard enough to teach them the art of formal writing. Now we've got to overcome this new instant-messaging language."

Ms. Harding noted that in some cases the shorthand isn't even shorter. "I understand 'cuz,' but what's with the 'wuz'? It's the same amount of letters as 'was,' so what's the point?" she said.

Deborah Bova, who teaches eighth-grade English at Raymond Park Middle School in Indianapolis, thought her eyesight was failing several years ago when she saw the sentence "B4 we perform, ppl have 2 practice" on a student assignment.

"I thought, 'My God, what is this?' " Ms. Bova said. "Have they lost their minds?"

20 The student was summoned to the board to translate the sentence into standard English: "Before we perform, people have to practice." She realized that the students thought she was out of touch. "It was like 'Get with it, Bova,' " she said. Ms. Bova had a student type up a reference list of translations for common instant-messaging expressions. She posted a copy on the bulletin board by her desk and took another one home to use while grading.

Students are sometimes unrepentant.

"They were astonished when I began to point these things out to them," said Henry Assetto, a social studies teacher at Twin Valley High School in Elverson, Pa. "Because I am a history teacher, they did not think a history teacher would be checking up on their grammar or their spelling," said Mr. Assetto, who has been teaching for 34 years.

But Montana Hodgen, 16, another Montclair student, said she was so accustomed to instant-messaging abbreviations that she often read right past them. She proofread a paper last year only to get it returned with the messaging abbreviations circled in red.

"I was so used to reading what my friends wrote to me on Instant Messenger that I didn't even realize that there was something wrong," she said. She said her ability to separate formal and informal English declined the more she used instant messages. "Three years ago, if I had seen that, I would have been 'What is that?' "

25   The spelling checker doesn't always help either, students say. For   25
one, Microsoft Word's squiggly red spell-check lines don't appear beneath single letters and numbers such as u, r, c, 2 and 4. Nor do they catch words which have numbers in them such as "l8r" and "b4" by default.

Teenagers have essentially developed an unconscious "accent" in their typing, Professor Donath said. "They have gotten facile at typing and they are not paying attention."

Teenagers have long pushed the boundaries of spoken language, introducing words that then become passe with adult adoption. Now teenagers are taking charge and pushing the boundaries of written language. For them, expressions like "oic" (oh I see), "nm" (not much), "jk" (just kidding) and "lol" (laughing out loud), "brb" (be right back), "ttyl" (talk to you later) are as standard as conventional English.

"There is no official English language," said Jesse Sheidlower, the North American editor of the *Oxford English Dictionary*. "Language is spread not because anyone dictates any one thing to happen. The decisions are made by the language and the people who use the language."

Some teachers find the new writing style alarming. "First of all, it's very rude, and it's very careless," said Lois Moran, a middle school English teacher at St. Nicholas School in Jersey City.

30   "They should be careful to write properly and not to put these little   30
codes in that they are in such a habit of writing to each other," said Ms. Moran, who has lectured her eighth-grade class on such mistakes.

Others say that the instant-messaging style might simply be a fad, something that students will grow out of. Or they see it as an opportunity to teach students about the evolution of language.

"I turn it into a very positive teachable moment for kids in the class," said Erika V. Karres, an assistant professor at the University of North Carolina at Chapel Hill who trains student teachers. She shows students how English has evolved since Shakespeare's time. "Imagine Langston Hughes's writing in quick texting instead of 'Langston writing,'" she said. "It makes teaching and learning so exciting."

Other teachers encourage students to use messaging shorthand to spark their thinking processes. "When my children are writing first drafts, I don't care how they spell anything, as long as they are writing," said Ms. Fogarty, the sixth-grade teacher from Houlton, Maine. "If this lingo gets their thoughts and ideas onto paper quicker, the more power to them." But during editing and revising, she expects her students to switch to standard English.

Ms. Bova shares the view that instant-messaging language can help free up their creativity. With the help of students, she does not even need the cheat sheet to read the shorthand anymore.

³⁵ "I think it's a plus," she said. "And I would say that with a + sign." ³⁵

145

Questions on Meaning

1. What are the social and technological conditions that have shaped cyberlingo vocabulary and its uses?
2. What does the term "lingua franca" mean? How does it capture the full significance of the text messaging style of young people?
3. Why, in your opinion, are adults frequently appalled when students use an informal or unconventional style in their writing?

Questions on Rhetorical Strategy and Style

1. Why does Lee open her article with the words Ms. Harding puts on the board each September? What is she trying to suggest to her readers?
2. How does the article adhere to the conventions of the newspaper journalism? Does the writer remain balanced and objective? Explain how.
3. Why does the writer quote the editor of the *Oxford English Dictionary?*

Writing Assignments

1. Why do teachers often seem fussy, and even offended, by their students' use of language? Why are they so insistent about the conventions of standard, edited English? Write an essay that explains to your teachers your experience trying to learn these conventions, and why your language is necessary to your sense of identity.
2. Try the exercise used by Erika Karres, the teacher at the University of North Carolina. Take a poem or any piece of writing and translate it into a quick text version. How does the meaning of it change?

From the Poets in the Kitchen

Paule Marshall

Paule Marshall (1929–) grew up in Brooklyn, NY, where she was born Paule Burke to immigrants from Barbados. She graduated from Brooklyn College in 1953 and pursued graduate studies at Hunter College. Marshall first visited Barbados when she was nine years old, and later wrote a series of poems on her impressions of her ancestral home. Primarily a fiction writer, she has published a number of short story collections and novels, including The Chosen Place *(1984),* Reena and Other Stories *(1986),* Soul Clap Hands and Sing *(1988),* Daughters *(1992),* Praisesong for the Widow *(1992), and* Brown Girl, Brownstones *(1996). Marshall's work focuses on a number of themes, particularly gender relations, white supremacy, and post-colonialism. She has received numerous awards, including a Ford Foundation Grant, a Rosenthal Award for the National Institute of Arts and Letters, and a Before Columbus Foundation American Book Award. Marshall has also lectured on Black American literature at Oxford University, Columbia University, Michigan State University, and Cornell University; she has taught creative writing at Yale University, Columbia University, the University of Massachusetts at Boston, and the University of Iowa Writers' Workshop. At present Marshall is professor emeritus of English at Virginia Commonwealth University. In this selection Marshall traces her narrative art to the women who gathered to tell stories in her mother's kitchen.*

Reprinted from *Reena and Other Stories*, by permission of The Feminist Press. Copyright © 1983 by Paule Marshall.

1 Some years ago, when I was teaching a graduate seminar in fiction at Columbia University, a well known male novelist visited my class to speak on his development as a writer. In discussing his formative years, he didn't realize it but he seriously endangered his life by remarking that women writers are luckier than those of his sex because they usually spend so much time as children around their mothers and their mothers' friends in the kitchen.

What did he say that for? The women students immediately forgot about being in awe of him and began readying their attack for the question and answer period later on. Even I bristled. There again was that awful image of women locked away from the world in the kitchen with only each other to talk to, and their daughters locked in with them.

But my guest wasn't really being sexist or trying to be provocative or even spoiling for a fight. What he meant—when he got around to explaining himself more fully—was that, given the way children are (or were) raised in our society, with little girls kept closer to home and their mothers, the woman writer stands a better chance of being exposed, while growing up, to the kind of talk that goes on among women, more often than not in the kitchen; and that this experience gives her an edge over her male counterpart by instilling in her an appreciation for ordinary speech.

It was clear that my guest lecturer attached great importance to this, which is understandable. Common speech and the plain, workaday words that make it up are, after all, the stock in trade of some of the best fiction writers. They are the principal means by which characters in a novel or story reveal themselves and give voice sometimes to profound feelings and complex ideas about themselves and the world. Perhaps the proper measure of a writer's talent is skill in rendering everyday speech—when it is appropriate to the story—as well as the ability to tap, to exploit, the beauty, poetry and wisdom it often contains.

5 "If you say what's on your mind in the language that comes to you from your parents and your street and friends you'll probably say something beautiful." Grace Paley tells this, she says, to her students at the beginning of every writing course.

It's all a matter of exposure and a training of the ear for the would-be writer in those early years of apprenticeship. And according to my guest lecturer, this training, the best of it, often takes place in as unglamorous a setting as the kitchen.

He didn't know it, but he was essentially describing my experience as a little girl. I grew up among poets. Now they didn't look like poets—whatever that breed is supposed to look like. Nothing about them suggested that poetry was their calling. They were just a group of ordinary housewives and mothers, my mother included, who dressed in a way (shapeless housedresses, dowdy felt hats and long, dark, solemn coats) that made it impossible for me to imagine they had ever been young.

Nor did they do what poets were supposed to do—spend their days in an attic room writing verses. They never put pen to paper except to write occasionally to their relatives in Barbados. "I take my pen in hand hoping these few lines will find you in health as they leave me fair for the time being," was the way their letters invariably began. Rather, their day was spent "scrubbing floor," as they described the work they did.

Several mornings a week these unknown bards would put an apron and pair of old house shoes in a shopping bag and take the train or streetcar from our section of Brooklyn out to Flatbush. There, those who didn't have steady jobs would wait on certain designated corners for the white housewives in the neighborhood to come along and bargain with them over pay for a day's work cleaning their houses. This was the ritual even in the winter.

10 Later, armed with the few dollars they had earned, which in their 10 vocabulary became "a few raw-mouth pennies," they made their way back to our neighborhood, where they would sometimes stop off to have a cup of tea or cocoa together before going home to cook dinner for their husbands and children.

The basement kitchen of the brownstone house where my family lived was the usual gathering place. Once inside the warm safety of its walls the women threw off the drab coats and hats, seated themselves at the large center table, drank their cups of tea or cocoa, and talked. While my sister and I sat at a smaller table over in a corner doing our homework, they talked—endlessly, passionately, poetically, and with impressive range. No subject was beyond them. True, they would indulge in the usual gossip; whose husband was running with whom, whose daughter looked slightly "in the way" (pregnant) under her bridal gown as she walked down the aisle. That sort of thing. But they also tackled the great issues of the time. They were always, for example, discussing the state of the economy. It was the mid and late 30's then, and the aftershock of the Depression, with its soup lines and suicides on Wall Street, was still being felt.

Some people, they declared, didn't know how to deal with adversity. They didn't know that you had to "tie up your belly" (hold in the pain, that is) when things got rough and go on with life. They took their image from the bellyband that is tied around the stomach of a newborn baby to keep the navel pressed in.

They talked politics. Roosevelt was their hero. He had come along and rescued the country with relief and jobs, and in gratitude they christened their sons Franklin and Delano and hoped they would live up to the names.

If F.D.R. was their hero, Marcus Garvey was their God. The name of the fiery, Jamaican-born black nationalist of the 20's was constantly invoked around the table. For he had been their leader when they first came to the United States from the West Indies shortly after World War I. They had contributed to his organization, the United Negro Improvement Association (UNIA), out of their meager salaries, bought shares in his ill-fated Black Star Shipping Line, and at the height of the movement they had marched as members of his "nurses' brigade" in their white uniforms up Seventh Avenue in Harlem during the great Garvey Day parades. Garvey: He lived on through the power of their memories.

And their talk was of war and rumors of wars. They raged against World War II when it broke out in Europe, blaming it on the politicians. "It's these politicians. They're the ones always starting up all this lot of war. But what they care? It's the poor people got to suffer and mothers with their sons." If it was *their* sons, they swore they would keep them out of the Army by giving them soap to eat each day to make their hearts sound defective. Hitler? He was for them "the devil incarnate."

Then there was home. They reminisced often and at length about home. The old country. Barbados—or Bimshire, as they affectionately called it. The little Caribbean island in the sun they loved but had to leave. "Poor—poor but sweet" was the way they remembered it.

And naturally they discussed their adopted home. America came in for both good and bad marks. They lashed out at it for the racism they encountered. They took to task some of the people they worked for, especially those who gave them only a hard-boiled egg and a few spoonfuls of cottage cheese for lunch. "As if anybody can scrub floor on an egg and some cheese that don't have no taste to it!"

Yet although they caught H in "this man country," as they called America, it was nonetheless a place where "you could at least see your way to make a dollar." That much they acknowledged. They might even one day accumulate enough dollars, with both them and their husbands working, to buy the brownstone houses which, like my family, they were only leasing at that period. This was their consuming ambition: to "buy house" and to see the children through.

There was no way for me to understand it at the time, but the talk that filled the kitchen those afternoons was highly functional. It served as therapy, the cheapest kind available to my mother and her friends. Not only did it help them recover from the long wait on the corner that morning and the bargaining over their labor, it restored them to a sense of themselves and reaffirmed their self-worth. Through language they were able to overcome the humiliations of the work-day.

20 But more than therapy, that freewheeling, wide-ranging, exuber- 20 ant talk functioned as an outlet for the tremendous creative energy they possessed. They were women in whom the need for self-expression was strong, and since language was the only vehicle readily available to them they made of it an art form that—in keeping with the African tradition in which art and life are one—was an integral part of their lives.

And their talk was a refuge. They never really ceased being baffled and overwhelmed by America—its vastness, complexity and power. Its strange customs and laws. At a level beyond words they remained fearful and in awe. Their uneasiness and fear were even reflected in their attitude toward the children they had given birth to in this country. They referred to those like myself, the little Brooklyn-born Bajans (Barbadians), as "these New York children" and complained that they couldn't discipline us properly because of the laws here. "You can't beat these children as you would like, you know, because the authorities in this place will dash you in jail for them. After all, these is New York children." Not only were we different, American, we had, as they saw it, escaped their ultimate authority.

Confronted therefore by a world they could not encompass, which ever limited their rights as parents, and at the same time finding themselves permanently separated from the world they had known, they took refuge in language. "Language is the only homeland," Czeslaw Milosz, the emigré Polish writer and Nobel Laureate, has said. This is what it became for the women at the kitchen table.

It served another purpose also, I suspect. My mother and her friends were after all the female counterpart of Ralph Ellison's invisible man. Indeed, you might say they suffered a triple invisibility, being black, female and foreigners. They really didn't count in American society except as a source of cheap labor. But given the kind of women they were, they couldn't tolerate the fact of their invisibility, their powerlessness. And they fought back, using the only weapon at their command: the spoken word.

Those late afternoon conversations on a wide range of topics were a way for them to feel they exercised some measure of control over their lives and the events that shaped them. "Soully-gal, talk yuh talk!" they were always exhorting each other. "In this man world you got to take yuh mouth and make a gun!" They were in control, if only verbally and if only for the two hours or so that they remained in our house.

For me, sitting over in the corner, being seen but not heard, which was the rule for children in those days, it wasn't only what the women talked about—the content—but the way they put things—their style. The insight, irony, wit and humor they brought to their stories and discussions and their poet's inventiveness and daring with language— which of course I could only sense but not define back then.

They had taken the standard English taught them in the primary schools of Barbados and transformed it into an idiom, an instrument that more adequately described them—changing around the syntax and imposing their own rhythm and accent so that the sentences were more pleasing to their ears. They added the few African sounds and words that had survived, such as the derisive suck-teeth sound and the word "yam," meaning to eat. And to make it more vivid, more in keeping with their expressive quality, they brought to bear a raft of metaphors, parables, Biblical quotations, sayings and the like:

"The sea ain' got no back door," they would say, meaning that it wasn't like a house where if there was a fire you could run out the back. Meaning that it was not to be trifled with. And meaning perhaps in a larger sense that man should treat all of nature with caution and respect.

"I has read hell by heart and called every generation blessed!" They sometimes went in for hyperbole.

A woman expecting a baby was never said to be pregnant. They never used that word. Rather, she was "in the way" or, better yet, "tumbling big." "Guess who I butt up on in the market the other day tumbling big again!"

And a woman with a reputation of being too free with her sexual favors was known in their book as a "thoroughfare"—the sense of men like a steady stream of cars moving up and down the road of her life. Or she might be dubbed "a free-bee," which was my favorite of the two. I liked the image it conjured up of a woman scandalous perhaps but independent, who flitted from one flower to another in a garden of male beauties, sampling their nectar, taking her pleasure at will, the roles reversed.

And nothing, no matter how beautiful, was ever described as simply beautiful. It was always "beautiful-ugly": the beautiful-ugly dress, the beautiful-ugly house, the beautiful-ugly car. Why the word "ugly," I used to wonder when the thing they were referring to was beautiful, and they knew it. Why the antonym, the contradiction, the linking of opposites? It used to puzzle me greatly as a child.

There is the theory in linguistics which states that the idiom of a people, the way they use language, reflects not only the most fundamental views they hold of themselves and the world but their very conception of reality. Perhaps in using the term "beautiful-ugly" to describe nearly everything, my mother and her friends were expressing what they believed to be a fundamental dualism in life: the idea that a thing is at the same time its opposite, and that these opposites, these contradictions make up the whole. But theirs was not a Manichaean brand of dualism that sees matter, flesh, the body, as inherently evil, because they constantly addressed each other as "soully-gal"—soul; spirit; gal: the body, flesh, the visible self. And it was clear from their tone that they gave one as much weight and importance as the other. They had never heard of the mind/body split.

As for God, they summed up His essential attitude in a phrase. "God," they would say, "don' love ugly and He ain' stuck on pretty."

Using everyday speech, the simple commonplace words—but always with imagination and skill—they gave voice to the most complex ideas. Flannery O'Connor would have approved of how they made ordinary language work, as she put it, "double-time," stretching, shading, deepening its meaning. Like Joseph Conrad they were always trying to infuse new life in the "old old words worn thin . . . by . . . careless usage." And the goals of their oral art were the same as his: "to make you hear, to make you feel . . . to make you *see*." This was their guiding esthetic.

By the time I was 8 or 9, I graduated from the corner of the kitchen to the neighborhood library, and thus from the spoken to the written word. The Macon Street Branch of the Booklyn Public Library was an imposing half block long edifice of heavy gray masonry, with glass-paneled doors at the front and two tall metal torches symbolizing the light that comes of learning flanking the wide steps outside.

The inside was just as impressive. More steps—of pale marble with gleaming brass railings at the center and sides—led up to the circulation desk, and a great pendulum clock gazed down from the balcony stacks that faced the entrance. Usually stationed at the top of the steps like the guards outside Buckingham Palace was the custodian, a stern-faced West Indian type who for years, until I was old enough to obtain an adult card, would immediately shoo me with one hand into the Children's Room and with the other threaten me into silence, a finger to his lips. You would have thought he was the chief librarian and not just someone whose job it was to keep the brass polished and the clock wound. I put him in a story called "Barbados" years later and had terrible things happen to him at the end.

I sheltered from the storm of adolescence in the Macon Street library, reading voraciously, indiscriminately, everything from Jane Austen to Zane Grey, but with a special passion for the long, full-blown, richly detailed 18th- and 19th-century picaresque tales: "Tom Jones," "Great Expectations," "Vanity Fair."

But although I loved nearly everything I read and would enter fully into the lives of the characters—indeed, would cease being myself and become them—I sensed a lack after a time. Something I couldn't quite define was missing. And then one day browsing in the poetry section, I came across a book by someone called Paul Laurence Dunbar, and opening it I found the photograph of a wistful, sad-eyed poet who to my surprise was black. I turned to a poem at random, "Little brown-baby wif spa'klin' / eyes / Come to yo' pappy an' set on his knee." Although I had a little difficulty at first with the words in dialect, the poem spoke to me as nothing I had read before of the closeness, the special relationship I had had with my father, who by then had become an ardent believer in Father Divine and gone to live in Father's "kingdom" in Harlem. Reading it helped to ease somewhat the tight knot of sorrow and longing I carried around in my chest that refused to go away. I read another poem. "'Lias! 'Lias! Bless de Lawd! / Don' you know de day's /erbroad? / Ef you don' get up, you scamp / Dey'll be trouble in dis camp." I laughed. It reminded me of the way my mother sometimes yelled at my sister and me to get out of bed in the mornings.

And another: "Seen my lady home las' night / Jump back, honey, jump back. / Hel' huh han' an' sque'z it tight..." About love between a black man and a black woman. I had never seen that written about before and it roused in me all kinds of delicious feelings and hopes.

And I began to search then for books and stories and poems about "The Race" (as it was put back then), about my people. While not abandoning Thackeray, Fielding, Dickens and the others, I started asking the reference librarian, who was white, for books by Negro writers, although I must admit I did so at first with a feeling of shame—the shame I and many others used to experience in those days whenever the word "Negro" or "colored" came up.

No grade school literature teacher of mine had ever mentioned Dunbar or James Weldon Johnson or Langston Hughes. I didn't know that Zora Neale Hurston existed and was busy writing and being published during those years. Nor was I made aware of people like Frederick Douglass and Harriet Tubman—their spirit and example— or the great 19th-century abolitionist and feminist Sojourner Truth. There wasn't even Negro History Week when I attended P.S. 35 on Decatur Street!

What I needed, what all the kids—West Indian and native black American alike—with whom I grew up needed, was an equivalent of the Jewish shul, someplace where we could go after school—the schools that were shortchanging us—and read works by those like ourselves and learn about our history.

It was around that time also that I began harboring the dangerous thought of someday trying to write myself. Perhaps a poem about an apple tree, although I had never seen one. Or the story of a girl who could magically transplant herself to wherever she wanted to be in the world—such as Father Divine's kingdom in Harlem. Dunbar—his dark, eloquent face, his large volume of poems—permitted me to dream that I might someday write, and with something of the power with words my mother and her friends possessed.

When people at readings and writers' conferences ask me who my major influences were, they are sometimes a little disappointed when I don't immediately name the usual literary giants. True, I am indebted to those writers white and black, whom I read during my formative years and still read for instruction and pleasure. But they were preceded in my life by another set of giants whom I always acknowledge before all others: the group of women around the table long ago. They taught me my first lessons in the narrative art. They trained my ear. They set a standard of excellence. This is why the best of my work must be attributed to them; it stands as testimony to the rich legacy of language and culture they so freely passed on to me in the workshop of the kitchen.

Questions on Meaning

1. Why, according to Marshall, is a mastery of ordinary, everyday speech essential to the writer? How did the language of the women in her mother's kitchen belie those adjectives (ordinary, everyday)? In what ways was their language poetic?

2. In what ways was the talk in the kitchen "functional" for the women? How did both the content and the style of their talk help them to cope with their lives?

3. Why was it so important to the young Marshall to discover African-American writers? How did that discovery encourage her own aspirations? Why does she call her thoughts about becoming a writer "dangerous"?

Questions on Rhetorical Strategy and Style

1. Effective narration relies on vivid characterization. How does Marshall give life to her mother and her mother's friends? How does she portray these women, with their troubles, their triumphs, and their everyday joys? How does their language help to characterize them?

2. Marshall provides several examples of the wit and power of these women's language. Choose two or three of these examples and explain how they support her point about ordinary speech.

3. Consider Marshall's own use of language in this essay. How does her language validate her claim that the primary influence on her writing (the first cause that led to the effect) was the conversation in her mother's kitchen? Use examples to support your response.

Writing Assignments

1. Every writer, whether a famous poet or a writing student, develops in part as a result of early influences. Think of the influences on your writing—perhaps family conversations, teachers, songwriters, or other writers. Write an essay describing the impact that these people have on your writing. Focus not only on your style, but on the subjects about which you enjoy writing and the kinds of writing you lean toward.

2. Read about the major influences on one of your favorite writers; then find evidence of those influences in the writer's work. In a brief essay, discuss how those influences are reflected in the work. Use specific features of and passages from the writer in order to support your interpretation.

3. Marshall spends a good deal of time exploring the nature of the language she heard in her mother's kitchen. Think of people in your life whose language is vivid, witty, or otherwise memorable. Using examples of that speech, write an essay analyzing the impact of that language on its users and on you.

Mysterious Connections that Link Us Together

Azar Nafisi

Azar Nafisi (1950–) was born in Tehran, Iran. As a teenager, her parents sent her to England to be educated. She attended the University of Oklahoma and Oxford University and has taught at three Iranian universities, including the University of Tehran—from which she was fired in 1981 for refusing to wear a veil. She has been the director of the Dialogue Project, a nonprofit group that brings together Palestinians and Jews for monthly dialogue. Currently, Nafisi teaches at the Johns Hopkins School for Advanced International Studies. She has published articles in The New York Times, The Washington Post, The Wall Street Journal, *and* The New Republic. *She is best known for* Reading Lolita in Tehran: A Memoir in Books *(2003) in which she recounts having secretly taught literature in her home to Iranian women. The following was broadcast on National Public Radio in July 2005 as part of the "This I Believe" series.*

1   I believe in empathy. I believe in the kind of empathy that is created through imagination and through intimate, personal relationships. I am a writer and a teacher, so much of my time is spent interpreting stories and connecting to other individuals. It is the urge to know more about ourselves and others that creates empathy. Through imagination and our desire for rapport, we transcend our limitations, freshen our eyes, and are able to look at ourselves and the world through a new and alternative lens.

Whenever I think of the word empathy, I think of a small boy named Huckleberry Finn contemplating his friend and runaway slave, Jim. Huck asks himself whether he should give Jim up or not. Huck was told in Sunday school that people who let slaves go free go to "everlasting fire." But then, Huck says he imagines he and Jim in "the day and night-time, sometimes moonlight, sometimes storms, and we a-floating along, talking and singing and laughing." Huck remembers Jim and their friendship and warmth. He imagines Jim not as a slave but as a human being and he decides that, "alright, then, I'll go to hell."

What Huck rejects is not religion but an attitude of self-righteousness and inflexibility. I remember this particular scene out of *Huck Finn* so vividly today, because I associate it with a difficult time in my own life. In the early 1980s when I taught at the University of Tehran, I, like many others, was expelled. I was very surprised to discover that my staunchest allies were two students who were very active at the University's powerful Muslim Students' Association. These young men and I had engaged in very passionate and heated arguments. I had fiercely opposed their ideological stances. But that didn't stop them from defending me. When I ran into one of them after my expulsion, I thanked him for his support. "We are not as rigid as you imagine us to be Professor Nafisi," he responded. "Remember your own lectures on Huck Finn? Let's just say, he is not the only one who can risk going to hell!"

This experience in my life reinforces my belief in the mysterious connections that link individuals to each other despite their vast differences. No amount of political correctness can make us empathize with a child left orphaned in Darfur or a woman taken to a football stadium in Kabul and shot to death because she is improperly dressed. Only curiosity about the fate of others, the ability to put ourselves in their shoes, and the will to enter their world through the magic of imagination, creates this shock of recognition. Without this empathy there can be no genuine dialogue, and we as individuals and nations will remain isolated and alien, segregated and fragmented.

I believe that it is only through empathy, that the pain experienced by an Algerian woman, a North Korean dissident, a Rwandan child or an Iraqi prisoner, becomes real to me and not just passing news. And it is at times like this when I ask myself, am I—prepared like Huck Finn—to give up Sunday school heaven for the kind of hell that Huck chose?

Questions on Meaning

1. How does Nafisi define empathy? How does it compare with the way you define it?
2. How does the story of Huck Finn illustrate empathy?
3. How did the students from the University of Tehran teach Nafisi a lesson in empathy?

Questions on Rhetorical Strategy and Style

1. Why does Nasifi include the example of the orphaned child from Darfur or the woman shot to death in Kabul? Are we to take these as hypothetical examples?
2. What is the purpose of this essay? How does it illustrate the point she is trying to make about connections among humans with vastly difference backgrounds?

Writing Assignments

1. Write an essay describing an experience illustrative of a complex human emotion, such as empathy. Describe the experience in enough detail so that the reader can identify with it.
2. Nafisi taught literature to Tehran women in secret. What cultural conventions necessitated this? Write an essay dealing with the conditions for women in countries such as Iran.

I Stand Here Ironing

Tillie Olsen

Tillie Olsen (1913–2007) was born in Nebraska in a working class family. She worked at jobs involving manual labor much of her life, educating herself by reading on her own. She published a few short pieces in the 1930s but stopped writing when she married and began raising her four children. More than two decades later she returned to writing and published a collection of stories entitled Tell Me a Riddle *(1956), in which the story "I Stand Here Ironing" was published. In 1984 as editor Olsen published* Mother to Daughter, Daughter to Mother: Mothers on Mothering, *a collection of writings on themes of motherhood. Olsen received several fellowships and held visiting professorships at major universities, where she worked to help younger writers develop.*

1   I stand here ironing, and what you asked me moves tormented back and forth with the iron.

"I wish you would manage the time to come in and talk with me about your daughter. I'm sure you can help me understand her. She's a youngster who needs help and whom I'm deeply interested in helping."

"Who needs help." . . . Even if I came, what good would it do? You think because I am her mother I have a key, or that in some way you could use me as a key? She has lived for nineteen years. There is all that life that has happened outside of me, beyond me.

And when is there time to remember, to sift, to weigh, to estimate, to total? I will start and there will be an interruption and I will have to gather it all together again. Or I will become engulfed with all I did or did not do, with what should have been and what cannot be helped.

5   She was a beautiful baby. The first and only one of our five that   5
was beautiful at birth. You do not guess how new and uneasy her ten-
ancy in her now-loveliness. You did not know her all those years she
was thought homely, or see her poring over her baby pictures, making
me tell her over and over how beautiful she had been—and would be,
I would tell her—and was now, to the seeing eye. But the seeing eyes
were few or nonexistent. Including mine.

I nursed her. They feel that's important nowadays. I nursed all the
children, but with her, with all the fierce rigidity of first motherhood,
I did like the books then said. Though her cries battered me to trem-
bling and my breasts ached with swollenness, I waited till the clock
decreed.

Why do I put that first? I do not even know if it matters, or if it
explains anything.

She was a beautiful baby. She blew shining bubbles of sound. She
loved motion, loved light, loved color and music and textures. She
would lie on the floor in her blue overalls patting the surface so hard
in ecstasy her hands and feet would blur. She was a miracle to me, but
when she was eight months old I had to leave her daytimes with the
woman downstairs to whom she was no miracle at all, for I worked or
looked for work and for Emily's father, who "could no longer endure"
(he wrote in his good-bye note) "sharing want with us."

I was nineteen. It was the pre-relief, pre-WPA world of the depression. I would start running as soon as I got off the streetcar, running up the stairs, the place smelling sour, and awake or asleep to
startle awake, when she saw me she would break into a clogged weeping that could not be comforted, a weeping I can hear yet.

10   After a while I found a job hashing at night so I could be with her   10
days, and it was better. But it came to where I had to bring her to his
family and leave her.

It took a long time to raise the money for her fare back. Then she
got chicken pox and I had to wait longer. When she finally came, I
hardly knew her, walking quick and nervous like her father, looking
like her father, thin, and dressed in a shoddy red that yellowed her skin
and glared at the pockmarks. All the baby loveliness gone.

She was two. Old enough for nursery school they said, and I did
not know then what I know now—the fatigue of the long day, and the
lacerations of group life in the kinds of nurseries that are only parking places for children.

Except that it would have made no difference if I had known. It was the only place there was. It was the only way we could be together, the only way I could hold a job.

And even without knowing, I knew. I knew the teacher that was evil because all these years it has curdled into my memory, the little boy hunched in the corner, her rasp, "why aren't you outside, because Alvin hits you? That's no reason, go out, scaredy." I knew Emily hated it even if she did not clutch and implore "don't go Mommy" like the other children, mornings.

15 She always had a reason why we should stay home. Momma, you look sick. Momma, I feel sick. Momma, the teachers aren't there today, they're sick. Momma, we can't go, there was a fire there last night. Momma, it's a holiday today, no school, they told me.

But never a direct protest, never rebellion. I think of our others in their three-, four-year-oldness—the explosions, the tempers, the denunciations, the demands—and I feel suddenly ill. I put the iron down. What in me demanded that goodness in her? And what was the cost, the cost to her of such goodness?

The old man living in the back once said in his gentle way: "You should smile at Emily more when you look at her." What *was* in my face when I looked at her? I loved her. There were all the acts of love.

It was only with the others I remembered what he said, and it was the face of joy, and not of care or tightness or worry I turned to them—too late for Emily. She does not smile easily, let alone almost always as her brothers and sisters do. Her face is closed and sombre, but when she wants, how fluid. You must have seen it in her pantomimes, you spoke of her rare gift for comedy on the stage that rouses a laughter out of the audience so dear they applaud and applaud and do not want to let her go.

Where does it come from, that comedy? There was none of it in her when she came back to me that second time, after I had had to send her away again. She had a new daddy now to learn to love, and I think perhaps it was a better time.

20 Except when we left her alone nights, telling ourselves she was old enough.

"Can't you go some other time, Mommy, like tomorrow?" she would ask. "Will it be just a little while you'll be gone? Do you promise?"

The time we came back, the front door open, the clock on the floor in the hall. She rigid awake. "It wasn't just a little while. I didn't

164

cry. Three times I called you, just three times, and then I ran downstairs to open the door so you could come faster. The clock talked loud. I threw it away, it scared me what it talked."

She said the clock talked loud again that night I went to the hospital to have Susan. She was delirious with the fever that comes before red measles, but she was fully conscious all the week I was gone and the week after we were home when she could not come near the new baby or me.

She did not get well. She stayed skeleton thin, not wanting to eat, and night after night she had nightmares. She would call for me, and I would rouse from exhaustion to sleepily call back: "You're all right, darling, go to sleep, it's just a dream," and if she still called, in a sterner voice, "now go to sleep, Emily, there's nothing to hurt you." Twice, only twice, when I had to get up for Susan anyhow, I went in to sit with her.

25   Now when it is too late (as if she would let me hold and comfort   25 her like I do the others) I get up and go to her at once at her moan or restless stirring. "Are you awake, Emily? Can I get you something?" And the answer is always the same: "No, I'm all right, go back to sleep, Mother."

They persuaded me at the clinic to send her away to a convalescent home in the country where "she can have the kind of food and care you can't manage for her, and you'll be free to concentrate on the new baby." They still send children to that place. I see pictures on the society page of sleek young women planning affairs to raise money for it, or dancing at the affairs, or decorating Easter eggs or filling Christmas stockings for the children.

They never have a picture of the children so I do not know if the girls still wear those gigantic red bows and the ravaged looks on the every other Sunday when parents can come to visit "unless otherwise notified"—as we were notified the first six weeks.

Oh it is a handsome place, green lawns and tall trees and fluted flower beds. High up on the balconies of each cottage the children stand, the girls in their red bows and white dresses, the boys in white suits and giant red ties. The parents stand below shrieking up to be heard and the children shriek down to be heard, and between them the invisible wall "Not To Be Contaminated by Parental Germs or Physical Affection."

There was a tiny girl who always stood hand in hand with Emily. Her parents never came. One visit she was gone. "They moved her to

Rose Cottage," Emily shouted in explanation. "They don't like you to love anybody here."

30   She wrote once a week, the labored writing of a seven-year-old. "I 30 am fine. How is the baby. If I write my leter nicly I will have a star. Love" There never was a star. We wrote every other day, letters she could never hold or keep but only hear read—once. "We simply do not have room for children to keep any personal possessions," they patiently explained when we pieced one Sunday's shrieking together to plead how much it would mean to Emily, who loved so to keep things, to be allowed to keep her letters and cards.

Each visit she looked frailer. "She isn't eating," they told us.

(They had runny eggs for breakfast or mush with lumps, Emily said later, I'd hold it in my mouth and not swallow. Nothing ever tasted good, just when they had chicken.)

It took us eight months to get her released home, and only the fact that she gained back so little of her seven lost pounds convinced the social worker.

I used to try to hold and love her after she came back, but her body would stay stiff, and after a while she'd push away. She ate little. Food sickened her, and I think much of life too. Oh she had physical lightness and brightness, twinkling by on skates, bouncing like a ball up and down up and down over the jump rope, skimming over the hill; but these were momentary.

35   She fretted about her appearance, thin and dark and foreign- 35 looking at a time when every little girl was supposed to look or thought she should look a chubby blonde replica of Shirley Temple. The doorbell sometimes rang for her, but no one seemed to come and play in the house or be a best friend. Maybe because we moved so much.

There was a boy she loved painfully through two school semesters. Months later she told me how she had taken pennies from my purse to buy him candy. "Licorice was his favorite and I brought him some every day, but he still liked Jennifer better'n me. Why, Mommy?" The kind of question for which there is no answer.

School was a worry to her. She was not glib or quick in a world where glibness and quickness were easily confused with ability to learn. To her overworked and exasperated teachers she was an over-conscientious "slow learner" who kept trying to catch up and was absent entirely too often.

I let her be absent, though sometimes the illness was imaginary. How different from my now-strictness about attendance with the others. I wasn't working. We had a new baby, I was home anyhow. Sometimes, after Susan grew old enough, I would keep her home from school, too, to have them all together.

Mostly Emily had asthma, and her breathing, harsh and labored, would fill the house with a curiously tranquil sound. I would bring the two old dresser mirrors and her boxes of collections to her bed. She would select beads and single earrings, bottle tops and shells, dried flowers and pebbles, old postcards and scraps, all sorts of oddments; then she and Susan would play Kingdom, setting up landscapes and furniture, peopling them with action.

40 Those were the only times of peaceful companionship between 40 her and Susan. I have edged away from it, that poisonous feeling between them, that terrible balancing of hurts and needs I had to do between the two, and did so badly, those earlier years.

Oh there are conflicts between the others too, each one human, needing, demanding, hurting, taking—but only between Emily and Susan, no, Emily toward Susan that corroding resentment. It seems so obvious on the surface, yet it is not obvious. Susan, the second child, Susan, golden- and curly-haired and chubby, quick and articulate and assured, everything in appearance and manner Emily was not; Susan, not able to resist Emily's precious things, losing or sometimes clumsily breaking them; Susan telling jokes and riddles to company for applause while Emily sat silent (to say to me later: that was *my* riddle, Mother, I told it to Susan); Susan, who for all the five years' difference in age was just a year behind Emily in developing physically.

I am glad for that slow physical development that widened the difference between her and her contemporaries, though she suffered over it. She was too vulnerable for that terrible world of youthful competition, of preening and parading, of constant measuring of yourself against every other, of envy, "If I had that copper hair," "If I had that skin. . . ." She tormented herself enough about not looking like the others, there was enough of the unsureness, the having to be conscious of words before you speak, the constant caring—what are they thinking of me? without having it all magnified by the merciless physical drives.

Ronnie is calling. He is wet and I change him. It is rare there is such a cry now. That time of motherhood is almost behind me when the ear is not one's own but must always be racked and listening for the child cry, the child call. We sit for a while and I hold him, looking out over the city spread in charcoal with its soft aisles of light.

"*Shoogily*," he breathes and curls closer. I carry him back to bed, asleep. *Shoogily*. A funny word, a family word, inherited from Emily, invented by her to say: *comfort*.

In this and other ways she leaves her seal, I say aloud. And startle at my saying it. What do I mean? What did I start to gather together, to try and make coherent? I was at the terrible, growing years. War years. I do not remember them well. I was working, there were four smaller ones now, there was not time for her. She had to help be a mother, and housekeeper, and shopper. She had to set her seal. Mornings of crisis and near hysteria trying to get lunches packed, hair combed, coats and shoes found, everyone to school or Child Care on time, the baby ready for transportation. And always the paper scribbled on by a smaller one, the book looked at by Susan then mislaid, the homework not done. Running out to that huge school where she was one, she was lost, she was a drop; suffering over the unpreparedness, stammering and unsure of her classes.

There was so little time left at night after the kids were bedded down. She would struggle over books, always eating (it was in those years she developed her enormous appetite that is legendary in our family) and I would be ironing, or preparing food for the next day, or writing V-mail to Bill, or tending the baby. Sometimes, to make me laugh, or out of her despair, she would imitate happenings or types at school.

I think I said once: "Why don't you do something like this in the school amateur show?" One morning she phoned me at work, hardly understandable through the weeping: "Mother, I did it. I won, I won; they gave me first prize; they clapped and clapped and wouldn't let me go."

Now suddenly she was Somebody, and as imprisoned in her difference as she had been in anonymity.

She began to be asked to perform at other high schools, even in colleges, then at city and statewide affairs. The first one we went to, I only recognized her that first moment when thin, shy, she almost drowned herself into the curtains. Then: Was this Emily? The control, the command, the convulsing and deadly clowning, the spell, then the roaring, stamping audience, unwilling to let this rare and precious laughter out of their lives.

Afterwards: You ought to do something about her with a gift like that—but without money or knowing how, what does one do? We have left it all to her, and the gift has as often eddied inside, clogged and clotted, as been used and growing.

50 She is coming. She runs up the stairs two at a time with her light 50 graceful step, and I know she is happy tonight. Whatever it was that occasioned your call did not happen today.

"Aren't you ever going to finish the ironing, Mother? Whistler painted his mother in a rocker. I'd have to paint mine standing over an ironing board." This is one of her communicative nights and she tells me everything and nothing as she fixes herself a plate of food out of the icebox.

She is so lovely. Why did you want me to come in at all? Why were you concerned? She will find her way.

She starts up the stairs to bed. "Don't get me up with the rest in the morning." "But I thought you were having midterms." "Oh, those," she comes back in, kisses me, and says quite lightly, "in a couple of years when we'll all be atom-dead they won't matter a bit."

She has said it before. She *believes* it. But because I have been dredging the past, and all that compounds a human being is so heavy and meaningful in me, I cannot endure it tonight.

55 I will never total it all. I will never come in to say: She was a child 55 seldom smiled at. Her father left me before she was a year old. I had to work her first six years when there was work, or I sent her home and to his relatives. There were years she had care she hated. She was dark and thin and foreign-looking in a world where the prestige went to blondeness and curly hair and dimples, she was slow where glibness was prized. She was a child of anxious, not proud, love. We were poor and could not afford for her the soil of easy growth. I was a young mother, I was a distracted mother. There were the other children pushing up, demanding. Her younger sister seemed all that she was not. There were years she did not want me to touch her. She kept too much in herself, her life was such she had to keep too much in herself. My wisdom came too late. She has much to her and probably little will come of it. She is a child of her age, of depression, of war, of fear.

Let her be. So all that is in her will not bloom—but in how many does it? There is still enough left to live by. Only help her to know—help make it so there is cause for her to know—that she is more than this dress on the ironing board, helpless before the iron.

Questions on Meaning

1. Who is the "you" the narrator in this story is addressing? How much can you put together from references in the story to fill in the situation that has occasioned the narrator's thoughts on this day?
2. At the end of the story the narrator concludes her daughter Emily is "a child of her age, of depression, of war, of fear." How fully does this explain what Emily is like? What other factors, if any, must be considered?
3. How do you react to the story's ending, the mother's acceptance that there is much in her daughter that will not bloom and this is true of most people? Does the story suggest the mother is being realistic or defeatist in this attitude? Support your answer with details from the story.

Questions on Rhetorical Strategy and Style

1. The story is shaped around a series of memories and thoughts that come to the narrator as she irons and thinks about how someone could understand her daughter. Chart how the story moves repeatedly back and forth between past and present. What effect is gained by this structure?
2. After first showing us the mother's thoughts about Emily throughout the story, the author allows us near the end to see Emily briefly in the present. How do you react when you see and hear her? What effect does the story achieve by contrasting what her mother has been thinking with what we finally actually see?

Writing Assignments

1. The narrator worries near the end of the story that "I will never total it all" to completely understand her daughter. Consider what this means—can we ever total up everything that makes us who we are? If yes, how? If no, why not?
2. Are you a "child of your age"? Write an essay that examines the extent to which the world in which you lived as a child shaped who you are today.

Daddy

Sylvia Plath

Sylvia Plath (1932-1963) grew up in Boston, the daughter of a Boston University entomologist who died when she was eight years old. Plath was a good student, as children of university faculty often are, but she sometimes found herself unable to go on with her writing or her academic work. She attended Smith College, where she was graduated summa cum laude. She then earned a Fulbright Scholarship to Oxford where she met the English poet, Ted Hughes, whom she quickly married. Her poetry and her one novel, The Bell Jar *(1963), indicate the stresses in her life and her marriage. Separated and living with her two small children in a flat in London, she succumbed to those stresses and committed suicide in 1963. Her books of poetry include* A Winter Ship *(1960) and* The Colossus and Other Poems *(1960). "Daddy" (1962) embodies some of the more negative features of feminist attitudes but also expresses a kind of anger that many women suppress.*

1   You do not do, you do not do   1
       Any more, black shoe
       In which I have lived like a foot
       For thirty years, poor and white,
5   Barely daring to breathe or Achoo.   5

       Daddy, I have had to kill you.
       You died before I had time——
       Marble-heavy, a bag full of God,
       Ghastly statue with one grey toe
10   Big as a Frisco seal   10

And a head in the freakish Atlantic
Where it pours bean green over blue
In the waters off beautiful Nauset.
I used to pray to recover you.
Ach, du.

In the German tongue, in the Polish town
Scraped flat by the roller
Of wars, wars, wars.
But the name of the town is common.
My Polack friend

Says there are a dozen or two.
So I never could tell where you
Put your foot, your root,
I never could talk to you.
The tongue stuck in my jaw.

It stuck in a barb wire snare.
Ich, ich, ich, ich,
I could hardly speak.
I thought every German was you.
And the language obscene

An engine, an engine
Chuffing me off like a Jew.
A Jew to Dachau, Auschwitz, Belsen.
I began to talk like a Jew.
I think I may well be a Jew.

The snows of the Tyrol, the clear beer of Vienna
Are not very pure or true.
With my gypsy ancestress and my weird luck
And my Taroc pack and my Taroc pack
I may be a bit of a Jew.

I have always been scared of *you*,
With your Luftwaffe, your gobbledygoo.
And your neat moustache

And your Aryan eye, bright blue.
45 Panzer-man, panzer-man, O You——

Not God but a swastika
So black no sky could squeak through.
Every woman adores a Fascist,
The boot in the face, the brute
50 Brute heart of a brute like you.

You stand at the blackboard, daddy,
In the picture I have of you,
A cleft in your chin instead of your foot
But no less a devil for that, no not
55 Any less the black man who

Bit my pretty red heart in two.
I was ten when they buried you.
At twenty I tried to die
And get back, back, back to you.
60 I thought even the bones would do

But they pulled me out of the sack,
And they stuck me together with glue.
And then I knew what to do.
I made a model of you,
65 A man in black with a Meinkampf look

And a love of the rack and the screw.
And I said I do, I do.
So daddy, I'm finally through.
The black telephone's off at the root,
70 The voices just can't worm through.

If I've killed one man, I've killed two——
The vampire who said he was you
And drank my blood for a year,
Seven years, if you want to know.
75 Daddy, you can lie back now.

There's a stake in your fat black heart
And the villagers never liked you.
They are dancing and stamping on you.
They always *knew* it was you.
Daddy, daddy, you bastard, I'm through.

Questions on Meaning

1. Psychologists suggest that all adults carry images of their parents and early caregivers in their personalities. What kind of man does Plath carry in her psyche? What kind of man does she appear to marry?
2. Most people pass through stages when they have blamed their parents for their problems. Is it fair to blame a parent for dying during a person's childhood? Discuss the idea of anger as Plath expresses it in the poem.
3. At the end of the poem, Plath says, "Daddy, daddy, . . ., I'm through." What is she through with? Has she escaped her obsession with her father, or is she saying that she has been overcome by his image and influence? Use evidence from the poem to argue either way.

Questions on Rhetorical Strategy and Style

1. Plath seems to be showing in this poem that her father has caused her life's distress. What evidence in the poem seems to confirm this causal link?
2. Why does Plath compare her life to the lives of Jews who were captured and carried off to concentration camps during World War II? Discuss this comparison. Does she persuade the reader that her suffering is so severe?

Writing Assignments

1. What is the difference between the words "daddy," "dad," and "father"? Why do we have these separate words? Do a survey of people you know asking them what words they use for their fathers or father figures, then write about the power of such words and their meanings. Discuss what the choice of a particular word can mean. How do these kinds of words change our family values and feelings?
2. Write about the "parent" you carry in your head. It doesn't have to be your biological parent or your caregiver, but think about the part of your personality that makes rules for you. What internalized rules run your life? Where did they come from?
3. "Daddy" works with stereotypes of blue-eyed Germans and images of World War II. What stereotypes of war does your generation carry and how do those images affect the way you see the world? Who is the "enemy" now, and how do we treat certain people unfairly because of those images?

Our Animal Rites

Anna Quindlen

Anna Quindlen (1953–) grew up in Philadelphia and graduated from Barnard College. She first worked as a journalist for The New York Post *and* The New York Times, *where she became a personal opinion columnist. Her writing for the* Times' *"Hers" column covers many topics such as motherhood, family relations, and marriage. The best of her columns have been collected in* Living Out Loud *(1988),* Thinking Out Loud *(1993), and* Loud and Clear *(2004). She won the Pulitzer Prize for Commentary in 1992. Her work in fiction includes the novels* Object Lessons *(1991),* One True Thing *(1994),* Black and Blue *(1998), and* Blessings *(2003). The following essay was written as a column in 1990.*

1   The bear had the adenoidal breathing of an elderly man with a passion for cigars and a tendency toward emphysema. My first thought, when I saw him contemplating me through tiny eyes from a rise just beyond the back porch, was that he looked remarkably bearlike, like a close-up shot from a public television nature program.

I screamed. With heavy tread—pad, pad, pad, harrumph, harrumph—the bear went off into the night, perhaps to search for garbage, cans inexpertly closed and apiaries badly lighted. I sat on the porch, shaking. Everyone asks, "Was he big?" My answer is, "Compared to what?"

What I leave out when I tell the story is my conviction that the bear is still watching. At night I imagine he is staring down from the hillside into the lighted porch, as though he had a mezzanine seat for a performance on which the curtain had already gone up. "A nice female, but not very furry," I imagine him thinking, "I see the cubs have gone to the den for the night."

Sometimes I suspect I think this because the peace and quiet of the country have made me go mad, and if only I could hear a car alarm, an ambulance siren, the sound of a boom box playing "The Power" and its owner arguing with his girlfriend over whether or not he was flirting with Denise at the party, all that would drive the bear clear out of my head.

5 Sometimes I think it is because instead of feeling that the bear is 5 trespassing on my property, in my heart I believe that I am trespassing on his.

That feeling is not apparent to city people, although there is something about the sight of a man cleaning up after a sheepdog with a sheet of newspaper that suggests a kind of horrible atonement. The city is a place built by the people, for the people. There we say people are acting like animals when they do things with guns and bats and knives that your ordinary bear would never dream of doing. There we condescend to our animals, with grooming parlors and cat carriers, using them to salve our loneliness and prepare us for parenthood.

All you who lost interest in the dog after the baby was born, you know who you are.

But out where the darkness has depth, where there are no street lights and the stars leap out of the sky, condescension, a feeling of supremacy, what the animal-rights types call speciesism, is impossible. Oh, hunters try it, and it is pathetic to consider the firepower they require to bring down one fair-sized deer. They get three bear days in the autumn, and afterward there is at least one picture in the paper of a couple of smiling guys in hats surrounding the carcass of an animal that looks, though dead, more dignified than they do.

Each spring, after the denning and the long, cold drowse, we wait to see if the bear that lives on the hill above our house beat the bullets. We discover his triumph through signs: a pile of bear dung on the lawn, impossible to assign to any other animal unless mastodons still roam the earth. A garbage box overturned into the swamp, the cole slaw container licked clean. Symmetrical scratch marks five feet up on a tree.

10   They own this land. Once, long ago, someone put a house on it. 10
That was when we were tentative interlopers, when we put a farmhouse here and a barn there. And then we went nuts, built garden con-
dos with pools and office complexes with parking garages and
developments with names that always included the words Park, Acres,
or Hills. You can't stop progress, especially if it's traveling 65 miles an
hour. You notice that more this time of year, when the possums stiffen
by the side of the road.

Sometimes the animals fight back. I was tickled by the people
who bought a house with a pond and paid a good bit of money for a
little dock from which to swim. It did not take long for them to discover that the snapping turtles were opposed to the addition to their
ecosystem of humans wearing sunscreen. An exterminator was sent
for. The pond was dredged. A guest got bit. The turtles won.

I've read that deer use the same trails all their lives. Someone
comes along and puts a neo-Colonial house in the middle of their deer
paths, and the deer will use the paths anyway, with a few detours. If
you watch, you can see that it is the deer that belong and the house
which does not. The bats, the groundhogs, the weasels, the toads—a
hundred years from now, while our family will likely be scattered, their
descendants might be in this same spot. Somewhere out there the bear
is watching, picking his nits and his teeth, breathing his raggedy bear
breath, and if he could talk, maybe he'd say, "I wonder when they're
going back where they belong."

Questions on Meaning

1. Why does Quindlen seem surprised that the bear "looked remarkably bearlike, like a close-up shot from a public television nature program"?
2. Quindlen comments of animals: "They own this land." Is she arguing that human beings should go somewhere else (and if so, where?). If not, what is her point?
3. What are the animal "rites" the essay's title points to?

Questions on Rhetorical Strategy and Style

1. In at least a couple of places Quindlen personifies the bear by giving it human-like thoughts. What effect does this have in the essay? Does it add to the strength of her argument?
2. Does Quindlen use the techniques of persuasion to attempt to convince the reader? Explain how the essay develops its thesis.

Writing Assignments

1. Quindlen is writing about an area where humans have moved into a natural habitat and seem to be displacing the wildlife there. Some people have argued that humans are not essentially different from some other animal species, which also become dominant over other species and drive them out or prey upon them. Is it "natural" or "unnatural" for humans to become a dominant species in an area? Does the presence of people automatically mean animals must be displaced, or is some sort of ecological harmony possible? Write an essay in which you explore the relationship between people and wildlife.
2. Looking at yourself from the point of view of an animal can be amusing if not instructive. Write a brief description of yourself going about your daily activities—as you might be seen by a pet such as a dog or cat.

The Color of Honey

Janet Raloff

Janet Raloff began her college education as an astronomy major but ultimately earned both a BS.J. and MS.J. from the Medill School of Journalism at Northwestern University. A member of the National Association of Science Writers and a founding board member of the Society of Environmental Journalists, Raloff has been managing editor of Energy Research Reports and a staff writer for Chemistry *magazine, and organ of the American Chemical Society. She has written freelance articles for some four dozen different publications, for which she has won several major writing awards. Raloff writes weekly about science and research-policy issues for* Science News *magazine since July 1996, she has also been writing an electronic column available only on the* Science News *website at www.sciencenews.org. In this essay, Raloff describes honey's healing effects, and the research efforts being made to evaluate its value to consumers.*

1   Many people—including a number of nutritionists—"dismiss honey as nothing more than sugar water," says May R. Berenbaum. "Biologically, however, that makes no sense."
    A concentrated form of nectar, honey is the principal source of nutrition for adult bees, observes Berenbaum, an entomologist at the University of Illinois at Urbana-Champaign. Mixed with pollen, it also serves as the dietary staple of bee larvae. Indeed, honey supplies the insects with a wealth of vitamins, minerals, and other plant-derived nutrients.

"The Color of Honey," by Janet Raloff, reprinted from *Science News*, Vol. 154, September 12, 1998, pp. 170–172.

Chemical analyses by Berenbaum's team now show that some honeys also possess surprising quantities of antioxidants—non-nutritive agents that can retard biologically destructive chemical reactions that cause rancidity in foods and that have been linked to many chronic diseases. When honey is cooked, it appears to acquire additional, functionally important antioxidants, according to related studies now under way at Clemson (S.C.) University.

These new data suggest that substituting honey for refined sugar in foods might provide health and storage benefits. Honey also offers a natural source of antioxidants to manufacturers of skincare products such as sunscreens.

All of this sounds mighty sweet to the United States' beleaguered beekeepers. As their hives have succumbed to blights, the cost of honey production has skyrocketed (SN: 8/8/98, p. 84). At the same time, foreign honey has flooded the U.S. market, keeping the commodity's wholesale price relatively low.

If findings from the antioxidant studies are confirmed, U.S. producers may see substantially greater demand—and prices—for their honey, especially the darker varieties that have often been considered second-rate.

The low status of one honey provided a major impetus for the Urbana studies.

The state of Illinois issues grants for research into ways of increasing the value of existing crops and commodities. "Soy-bean honey, which is what a lot of Illinois beekeepers produce, is not highly prized," Berenbaum notes. It tends to be darker than honeys from bees foraging on clover or orange blossoms, and it lacks their fruity taste. "It has no cachet," she adds, which may explain why this sweetener is usually labeled as deriving from wildflowers, which the bees also visit.

Although honey has been used as a folk remedy for burns, cataracts, ulcers, and wounds—all conditions in which oxidation can play a role—no one had systematically surveyed different honeys to determine whether the antioxidant capacity varies with the nectar source, the Illinois team observes, or even whether antioxidant concentrations in honey are sufficiently high to be of biological significance.

So Berenbaum's group assayed 19 honeys from bees in widely varying geographic locations: Hawaii, Florida, Arizona, Illinois, California, and Washington State. The syrupy sweeteners represented 14

181

different primary floral nectars—from fireweed and mesquite to star thistle and sunflowers.

10   The activity of all water-soluble antioxidants in each honey was 10 compared to that of ascorbic acid, or vitamin C—the gold standard. Because one molecule of ascorbic acid can neutralize two molecules of an oxidant, a micromole of vitamin C is defined as having a potency of 2 microequivalents (μeq). In the summer *Journal of Apicultural Research*, Berenbaum and her Illinois colleagues Steven M. Frankel and Gene E. Robinson report finding a clear trend. Although honeys vary widely in the quantity of water-soluble antioxidants they contain, the scientists found that the darker a honey's color, the higher its antioxidant activity.

A milliliter of Illinois buckwheat honey, by far the darkest tested, contained 4.32×10^{-3} μeq, which is 20 times the antioxidant activity in the same quantity of California sage honey, one of the lightest-colored samples. Sunflower, christmasberry, and water-tupelo honeys, also at the dark end of the color range, were the next richest sources of antioxidants, although their antioxidant content was only 25 to 40 percent as high. Soybean and clover honeys, which fall in the middle of the color range, had only 10 to 12 percent of buckwheat's antioxidant potential.

A few honeys buck the trend, however. Though fairly light, sweet-clover honey is antioxidant-rich, while a darkly golden mesquite version possesses relatively little antioxidant activity. Overall, however, the analysis concludes that color predicts more than 60 percent of the variation in a honey's antioxidant capacity.

While the Illinois scientists did not identify the antioxidants in any given honey, previous studies have shown that nectar tends to contain large quantities of flavonoids—plant pigments and flavoring compounds with antioxidant properties. "My guess is that these flavonoids are not only contributing to the honey's antioxidant activity but are probably the principle contributors," Berenbaum told *Science News*.

Most fruits and vegetables contain antioxidants. Though the average honey's ascorbic-acid equivalency, 0.8×10^{-3} μeq/per milligram comes close to that of tomatoes, Berenbaum's group notes that many fruits and vegetables possess far more. Orange pulp, for instance, has 5.7×10^{-3} μeq/mg, and broccoli and sweet peppers show 13.0×10^{-3} μeq/mg. Dried tea, renowned for its antioxidants, can run to 220×10^{-3} μeq/mg.

15   Moreover, Berenbaum is quick to point out, these figures may ac- 15
tually underestimate those foods' oxidant-quashing activity, since
many of them—unlike honey—also contain large quantities of fatsol-
uble antioxidants such as vitamin E and carotenoids. People also tend
to eat far smaller quantities of honey than they do most fruits and vegetables.

    Still, she notes, per capita sugar consumption in the United States
"is enormous"—roughly 150 pounds per year, according to the latest
Department of Agriculture statistics. "If you were to substitute honey
for all that sugar," she surmises, "the contribution of its antioxidants
might become substantial."

    Although the presence of antioxidants suggests that honey might
be able to limit the ravages of biologically destructive agents, the proof
is in the pudding, or muffins, or sausage, notes Nicki J. Engeseth, a
food scientist at the University of Illinois.

    In one set of experiments, she therefore added honey to fruits and
vegetables that turn brown upon exposure to air. In such foods, an enzyme in the plant tissues triggers a reaction between oxygen and phe-
nolic chemicals. The resulting browning not only makes the food
unappealing but also uses up its vitamin C.

    For this test, she put freshly cut apples, pears, potatoes, or yams
into a blender—grinding them into a soupy homogenate—then
mixed in one of six different types of honey. Though the light colored
acacia honey offered no protection against browning, the darker honeys did.

20   Christmasberry honey retarded the browning enzyme's activity by 20
up to 50 percent, for example. While the honey didn't match the potency of ascorbic acid or sulfites—two commercially popular antioxidants—it did lengthen the time before browning occurred.

    Soy honey also greatly reduced the rate at which the foods turned
brown. Indeed, it proved far more effective than the clover honeys,
even though all possessed similar antioxidant ratings. This suggests,
Engeseth says, that for certain applications, which antioxidants are
present may be as important as their quantity.

    Though buckwheat honey's high antioxidant content suggested it
probably would have had the best chance of retarding enzymatic
browning, "we couldn't use it," Engeseth says, because its "tarry" color
would have darkened foods even in the absence of any oxidation.

In a second experiment, the group investigated honey's ability to slow the oxidation of fats. A form of food spoilage, this process turns fats rancid (SN: 2/9/85, p. 88) and may transform them into a potent risk factor for artery-clogging heart disease (SN: 5/4/85, p. 278).

In this test, the food scientists added honey to ground turkey, making the sweetener 5 percent of the total weight. "We picked poultry," she notes, "because honey is already used in a number of recipes such as honey-smoked turkey." Because lipid oxidation accelerates dramatically once a meat is heated, the Illinois team panfried the concoction.

Three days later, they assayed the meat for oxidation products. Compared to unhoneyed poultry that had been similarly cooked and refrigerated, the honeyed meats exhibited far less rancidity. Again, the darker honeys performed best. Buckwheat honey, permitted in this test, cut oxidation by 70 percent, roughly twice as much as the light-colored acacia honey did. The amount of honey added to the meat was not enough to make it taste sweet, Engeseth notes.

The researchers presented preliminary findings from both studies in June at the Institute of Food Technologists annual meeting in Atlanta.

At the same meeting, Paul Dawson's team from Clemson presented data on an alternative use of honey—not as a source of antioxidants but as a raw ingredient in their production.

While some foods brown upon exposure to air through a series of enzyme-driven reactions, others brown in cooking via a heat-activated transformation of sugars. Known as a Maillard reaction, this browning causes bread crusts to turn golden, the surface of broiled meats to become dark and crispy, and the tops of custards to caramelize. In moderation, the browning enhances both the appearance and flavor of foods.

"Another byproduct of this Maillard reaction is the creation of antioxidant compounds," notes Dawson. Because extra sugar can foster the reaction, his group mixed a large amount of honey into the batter that binds small pieces of turkey into a restructured turkey roll. The honey made up 15 percent by weight of the ingredients but did not impart a sweet flavor to the finished product.

When they assayed the rate of oxidation in slices of the cooked meat after 2 days of refrigeration, the honeyed turkey exhibited only 15 percent as much fat oxidation as the untreated meat.

These data indicate that adding honey "probably would extend the shelf life of such deli-type products by several weeks to a month," Dawson says. Moreover, the honey treatment also appeared to reduce bacterial growth in the product. "We're not sure why," Dawson says, though it may reflect the sweetener's ability to tie up water—as sugars do in jam—rendering it unavailable to microbes.

Though the Clemson studies have focused on techniques likely to aid commercial food processors, Dawson notes that some of the findings might offer ideas to home cooks interested in extending the life of their leftovers. For instance, applying a honey glaze to a roast may retard the oxidation of the uncut meat. Similarly, adding honey to recipes for sausage, meat loaves, and other entrees that include ground meat should retard the rate at which rancid off-flavors develop, he says.

Antioxidant-rich honeys may also find a role in skin-care products, according to David Ropa of Thomas J. Payne Market Development. The Chicago-based consultant prepared a study last year for the National Honey Board in Longmont, Colo.

Honey "can be used to produce alpha hydroxy acids (AHAs), a vital ingredient in the growing market for skin creams and moisturizers," he says. Indeed, manufacturers are currently developing commercial methods to make honey-derived AHAs. The AHAs work, Ropa explains, "by exfoliating the skin and increasing the rate of cell renewal."

Several manufacturers already tap honey in the preparation of moisturizers. Honey "retains moisture and resembles the skin's natural moisturizing factor," notes David Chin, manager of technical marketing in the Somerville, N.J., office of Laboratoires Serobiologiques. Indeed, he says, that's why the French company has used a honey extract in one of its moisturizers for more than 20 years.

Because antioxidants can protect key components of the skin's cells from damage, many firms now add antioxidants to their products, especially sunscreens, Ropa reports. "If honey can act as both an antioxidant and a moisturizer in sunscreens and other skin-care products," he told *Science News*, "the potential for this natural ingredient is enormous."

Though Laboratoires Serobiologiques employs antioxidants in many of its products, it has never considered honey as a possible source, Chin says. If, however, manufacturers can look to this natural product for both moisturizing and antioxidant functions, he told *Science News*, "demand for honey could go flying out of sight—just like a bee."

Questions on Meaning

1. What is an antioxidant, and why are antioxidants so important in human food?
2. How does honey compare as an antioxidant to other fruits and vegetables? Why is honey still important, and what uses can it serve?
3. What advantages are there in using honey in food processing?

Questions on Rhetorical Strategy and Style

1. Raloff is a prominent science writer. When she writes, she is careful to organize her essays around a thesis that is both informative and persuasive. What is the thesis for this essay?
2. The essay mentions many types of honey that come from different plants. List several of these types, noting the qualities of each.
3. Raloff ends with the value of honey to skin care. What advantage is there to putting this point last?

Writing Assignments

1. Go to a health food store to discover the types of honey available. Read the labels and talk with the clerks about honey. What kinds of claims are made for honey and its advantages to health. Write about your findings.
2. The essay claims that honey could replace sugar in many foods. Investigate the cost of sugar versus the cost of honey. What would the difference in cost be if honey were substituted? Write about your findings, perhaps interviewing people to find out how much more they might pay for heathful food.

How to Say Nothing in 500 Words

Paul Roberts

Paul Roberts (1917–1967) wrote clear and helpful writ-
ing textbooks, among them English Syntax *(1954),* Patterns of English *(1956),* Understanding English *(1958)*
and English Sentences *(1962). He approached writing*
with the scientific discipline of a linguist. In the following
excerpt from Understanding English, *note his tendency to*
categorize and classify, to write descriptions and rules. In
this way, the "art" of writing is transformed to the science
(Latin for knowledge) of composition.

Nothing About Something

1   It's Friday afternoon, and you have almost survived another week   1
of classes. You are just looking forward dreamily to the weekend when
the English instructor says: "For Monday you will turn in a five-
hundred-word composition on college football."

Well, that puts a good big hole in the weekend. You don't have
any strong views on college football one way or the other. You get
rather excited during the season and go to all the home games and find
it rather more fun than not. On the other hand, the class has been
reading Robert Hutchins in the anthology and perhaps Shaw's
"Eighty-Yard Run," and from the class discussion you have got the
idea that the instructor thinks college football is for the birds. You are
no fool, you. You can figure out what side to take.

After dinner you get out the portable typewriter that you got for high school graduation. You might as well get it over with and enjoy Saturday and Sunday. Five hundred words is about two double-spaced pages with normal margins. You put in a sheet of paper, think up a title, and you're off:

Why College Football Should Be Abolished

College football should be abolished because it's bad for the school and also bad for the players. The players are so busy practicing that they don't have any time for their studies.

5   This, you feel, is a mighty good start. The only trouble is that it's   5
only thirty-two words. You still have four hundred and sixty-eight to go, and you've pretty well exhausted the subject. It comes to you that you do your best thinking in the morning, so you put away the type-writer and go to the movies. But the next morning you have to do your washing and some math problems, and in the afternoon you go to the game. The English instructor turns up too, and you wonder if you've taken the right side after all. Saturday night you have a date, and Sunday morning you have to go to church. (You shouldn't let English assignments interfere with your religion.) What with one thing and another, it's ten o'clock Sunday night before you get out the typewriter again. You make a pot of coffee and start to fill out your views on college football. Put a little meat on the bones.

Why College Football Should Be Abolished

In my opinion, it seems to me that college football should be abolished. The reason why I think this to be true is because I feel that football is bad for the colleges in nearly every respect. As Robert Hutchins says in his article in our anthology in which he discusses college football, it would be better if the colleges had race horses and had races with one another, because then the horses would not have to attend classes. I firmly agree with Mr. Hutchins on this point, and I am sure that many other students would agree too.

One reason why it seems to me that college football is bad is that it has become too commercial. In the olden times when people played football just for the fun of it, maybe college football was all right, but they do not play football just for the fun of it now as they used to in the old days. Nowadays college football is what you might call a big business. Maybe this is not true at all schools, and I don't think it is especially true here at State, but certainly this is the case at most colleges and universities in America nowadays, as Mr. Hutchins points out in his very interesting article. Actually the coaches and alumni go around to the high schools and offer the high school stars large salaries to come to their colleges and play football for them. There was one case where a high school star was offered a convertible if he would play football for a certain college.

Another reason for abolishing college football is that it is bad for the players. They do not have time to get a college education, because they are so busy playing football. A football player has to practice every afternoon from three to six, and then he is so tired that he can't concentrate on his studies. He just feels like dropping off to sleep after dinner, and then the next day he goes to his classes without having studied and maybe he fails the test.

(Good ripe stuff so far, but you're still a hundred and fifty-one words from home. One more push.)

Also I think college football is bad for the colleges and the universities because not very many students get to participate in it. Out of a college of ten thousand students only seventy-five or a hundred play football, if that many. Football is what you might call a spectator sport. That means that most people go to watch it but do not play it themselves.

(Four hundred and fifteen. Well, you still have the conclusion, and when you retype it, you can make the margins a little wider.)

10   These are the reasons why I agree with Mr. Hutchins   10
that college football should be abolished in American colleges and universities.

On Monday you turn it in, moderately hopeful, and on Friday it
comes back marked "weak in content" and sporting a big "D."

This essay is exaggerated a little, not much. The English instructor will recognize it as reasonably typical of what an assignment on
college football will bring in. He knows that nearly half of the class
will contrive in five hundred words to say that college football is too
commercial and bad for the players. Most of the other half will inform
him that college football builds character and prepares one for life and
brings prestige to the school. As he reads paper after paper all saying
the same thing in almost the same words, all bloodless, five hundred
words dripping out of nothing, he wonders how he allowed himself
to get trapped into teaching English when he might have had a happy
and interesting life as an electrician or a confidence man.

Well, you may ask, what can you do about it? The subject is one
on which you have few convictions and little information. Can you
be expected to make a dull subject interesting? As a matter of fact, this
is precisely what you are expected to do. This is the writer's essential
task. All subjects, except sex, are dull until somebody makes them interesting. The writer's job is to find the argument, the approach, the
angle, the wording that will take the reader with him. This is seldom
easy, and it is particularly hard in subjects that have been much discussed: College Football, Fraternities, Popular Music, Is Chivalry
Dead?, and the like. You will feel that there is nothing you can do with
such subjects except repeat the old bromides. But there are some
things you can do which will make your papers, if not throbbingly
alive, at least less insufferably tedious than they might otherwise be.

Avoid the Obvious Content

Say the assignment is college football. Say that you've decided to
be against it. Begin by putting down the arguments that come to your
mind: it is too commercial, it takes the students' minds off their studies, it is hard on the players, it makes the university a kind of circus
instead of an intellectual center, for most schools it is financially ru-
inous. Can you think of any more arguments just off hand! All right.

191

Now when you write your paper, *make sure that you don't use any of the material on this list*. If these are the points that leap to your mind, they will leap to everyone else's too, and whether you get a "C" or a "D" may depend on whether the instructor reads your paper early when he is fresh and tolerant or late, when the sentence "In my opinion, college football has become too commercial," inexorably repeated, has brought him to the brink of lunacy.

15   Be against college football for some reason or reasons of your own. 15
If they are keen and perceptive ones, that's splendid. But even if they are trivial or foolish or indefensible, you are still ahead so long as they are not everybody else's reasons too. Be against it because the colleges don't spend enough money on it to make it worth while, because it is bad for the characters of the spectators, because the players are forced to attend classes, because the football stars hog all the beautiful women, because it competes with baseball and is therefore un-American and possibly Communist inspired. There are lots of more or less unused reasons for being against college football.

Sometimes it is a good idea to sum up and dispose of the trite and conventional points before going on to your own. This has the advantage of indicating to the reader that you are going to be neither trite nor conventional. Something like this:

> We are often told that college football should be abolished because it has become too commercial or because it is bad for the players. These arguments are no doubt very cogent, but they don't really go to the heart of the matter. Then you go to the heart of the matter.

Take the Less Usual Side

One rather simple way of getting interest into your paper is to take the side of the argument that most of the citizens will want to avoid. If the assignment is an essay on dogs, you can, if you choose, explain that dogs are faithful and lovable companions, intelligent, useful as guardians of the house and protectors of children, indispensable in police work—in short, when all is said and done, man's best friends. Or you can suggest that those big brown eyes conceal, more often than not, a vacuity of mind and an inconstancy of purpose; that the dogs you have known most intimately have been mangy, ill-tempered brutes, incapable of instruction; and that only your nobility of mind and fear of arrest prevent you from kicking the flea-ridden animals when you pass them on the street.

Naturally, personal convictions will sometimes dictate your approach. If the assigned subject is "Is Methodism Rewarding to the individual?" and you are a pious Methodist, you have really no choice. But few assigned subjects, if any, will fall in this category. Most of them will lie in broad areas of discussion with much to be said on both sides. They are intellectual exercises and it is legitimate to argue now one way and now another, as debaters do in similar circumstances. Always take the side that looks to you hardest, least defensible. It will almost always turn out to be easier to write interestingly on that side.

20 This general advice applies where you have a choice of subjects. If 20 you are to choose among "The Value of Fraternities" and "My Favorite High School Teacher" and "What I Think About Beetles," by all means plump for the beetles. By the time the instructor gets to your paper, he will be up to his ears in tedious tales about the French teacher at Bloombury High and assertions about how fraternities build character and prepare one for life. Your views on beetles, whatever they are, are bound to be a refreshing change.

Don't worry too much about figuring out what the instructor thinks about the subject so that you can cuddle up with him. Chances are his views are no stronger than yours. If he does have convictions and you oppose them, his problem is to keep from grading you higher than you deserve in order to show he is not biased. This doesn't mean that you should always cantankerously dissent from what the instructor says; that gets tiresome too. And if the subject assigned is "My Pet Peeve," do not begin, "My pet peeve is the English instructor who assigns papers on 'my pet peeve.'" This was still funny during the War of 1812, but it has sort of lost its edge since then. It is in general good manners to avoid personalities.

Slip out of Abstraction

If you will study the essay on college football . . . you will perceive that one reason for its appalling dullness is that it never gets down to particulars. It is just a series of not very glittering generalities: "football is bad for the colleges," "it has become too commercial," "football is a big business," "it is bad for the players," and so on. Such round phrases thudding against the reader's brain are unlikely to convince him, though they may well render him unconscious.

If you want the reader to believe that college football is bad for the players, you have to do more than say so. You have to display the evil. Take your roommate, Alfred Simkins, the second-string center. Picture poor old Alfy coming home from football practice every evening, bruised and aching, agonizingly tired, scarcely able to shovel the mashed potatoes into his mouth. Let us see him staggering up to the room, getting out his econ textbook, peering desperately at it with his good eye, falling asleep and failing the test in the morning. Let us share his unbearable tension as Saturday draws near. Will he fail, be demoted, lose his monthly allowance, be forced to return to the coal mines? And if he succeeds, what will be his reward? Perhaps a slight ripple of applause when the third-string center replaces him, a moment of elation in the locker room if the team wins, of despair if it loses. What will he look back on when he graduates from college? Toil and torn ligaments. And what will be his future? He is not good enough for pro football, and he is too obscure and weak in econ to succeed in stocks and bonds. College football is tearing the heart from Alfred Simkins and, when it finishes with him, will callously toss aside the shattered hulk.

This is no doubt a weak enough argument for the abolition of college football, but it is a sight better than saying, in three or four variations, that college football (in your opinion) is bad for the players.

Look at the work of any professional writer and notice how consistently he is moving from the generality, the abstract statement, to the concrete example, the facts and figures, the illustration. If he is writing on juvenile delinquency, he does not just tell you that juveniles are (it seems to him) delinquent and that (in his opinion) something should be done about it. He shows you juveniles being delinquent, tearing up movie theatres in Buffalo, stabbing high school principals in Dallas, smoking marijuana in Palo Alto. And more than likely he is moving toward some specific remedy, not just a general wringing of the hands.

It is no doubt possible to be *too* concrete, too illustrative or anecdotal, but few inexperienced writers err this way. For most the soundest advice is to be seeking always for the picture, to be always turning general remarks into seeable examples. Don't say, "Sororities teach girls the social graces." Say "Sorority life teaches a girl how to carry on a conversation while pouring tea, without sloshing the tea into the saucer." Don't say, "I like certain kinds of popular music very much."

Say, "Whenever I hear Gerber Spinklittle play 'Mississippi Man' on the trombone, my socks creep up my ankles."

Get Rid of Obvious Padding

The student toiling away at his weekly English theme is too often tormented by a figure: five hundred words. How, he asks himself, is he to achieve this staggering total? Obviously by never using one word when he can somehow work in ten.

He is therefore seldom content with a plain statement like "Fast driving is dangerous." This has only four words in it. He takes thought, and the sentence becomes:

> In my opinion, fast driving is dangerous.

30 Better, but he can do better still: 30

> In my opinion, fast driving would seem to be rather dangerous.

If he is really adept, it may come out:
> In my humble opinion, though I do not claim to be an expert on this complicated subject, fast driving, in most circumstances, would seem to be rather dangerous in many respects, or at least so it would seem to me.

Thus four words have been turned into forty, and not an iota of content has been added.

35 Now this is a way to go about reaching five hundred words, and 35 if you are content with a "D" grade, it is as good a way as any. But if you aim higher, you must work differently. Instead of stuffing your sentences with straw, you must try steadily to get rid of the padding, to make your sentences lean and tough. If you are really working at it, your first draft will greatly exceed the required total, and then you will work it down, thus:

> It is thought in some quarters that fraternities do not contribute as much as might be expected to campus life.

Some people think that fraternities contribute little to campus life.

The average doctor who practices in small towns or in the country must toil night and day to heal the sick.
Most country doctors work long hours.

When I was a little girl, I suffered from shyness and embarrassment in the presence of others.
I was a shy little girl.

It is absolutely necessary for the person employed as a marine fireman to give the matter of steam pressure his undivided attention at all times.
The fireman has to keep his eye on the steam gauge.

You may ask how you can arrive at five hundred words at this rate. Simply. You dig up more real content. Instead of taking a couple of obvious points off the surface of the topic and then circling warily around them for six paragraphs, you work in and explore, figure out the details. You illustrate. You say that fast driving is dangerous, and then you prove it. How long does it take to stop a car at forty and at eighty? How far can you see at night? What happens when a tire blows?! What happens in a head-on collision at fifty miles an hour! Pretty soon your paper will be full of broken glass and blood and headless torsos, and reaching five hundred words will not really be a problem.

Call a Fool a Fool

Some of the padding in freshman themes is to be blamed not on
anxiety about the word minimum but on excessive timidity. The student writes, "In my opinion, the principal of my high school acted in ways that I believe every unbiased person would have to call foolish." This isn't exactly what he means. What he means is, "My high school principal was a fool." If he was a fool, call him a fool. Hedging the thing about with "in-my-opinion's" and "it-seems-to-me's" and "as-I-see-it's" and "at-least-from-my-point-of-view's" gains you nothing. Delete these phrases whenever they creep into your paper.

The student's tendency to hedge stems from a modesty that in other circumstances would be commendable. He is, he realizes, young and inexperienced, and he half suspects that he is dopey and fuzzy-minded beyond the average. Probably only too true. But it doesn't help to announce your incompetence six times in every paragraph. Decide what you want to say and say it as vigorously as possible, without apology and in plain words.

Linguistic diffidence can take various forms. One is what we call *euphemism*. This is the tendency to call a spade "a certain garden implement" or women's underwear "unmentionables." It is stronger in some eras than others and in some people than others but it always operates more or less in subjects that are touchy or taboo: death, sex, madness, and so on. Thus we shrink from saying "He died last night" but say instead "passed away," "left us," "joined his Maker," "went to his reward." Or we try to take off the tension with a lighter cliché: "kicked the bucket," "cashed in his chips," "handed in his dinner pail." We have found all sorts of ways to avoid saying *mad*: "mentally ill," "touched," "not quite right upstairs," "feeble-minded," "innocent," "simple," "off his trolley," "not in his right mind. "Even such a now plain word as *insane* began as a euphemism with the meaning "not healthy."

Modern science, particularly psychology, contributes many polysyllables in which we can wrap our thoughts and blunt their force. To many writers there is no such thing as a bad schoolboy. Schoolboys are maladjusted or unoriented or misunderstood or in need of guidance or lacking in continued success toward satisfactory integration of the personality as a social unit, but they are never bad. Psychology no doubt makes us better men or women, more sympathetic and tolerant, but it doesn't make writing any easier. Had Shakespeare been confronted with psychology, "To be or not to be" might have come out, "To continue as a social unit or not to do so. That is the personality problem. Whether 'tis a better sign of integration at the conscious level to display a psychic tolerance toward the maladjustments and repressions induced by one's lack of orientation in one's environment or—" But Hamlet would never have finished the soliloquy.

Writing in the modern world, you cannot altogether avoid modern jargon. Nor, in an effort to get away from euphemism, should you salt your paper with four-letter words. But you can do much if you will mount guard against those roundabout phrases, those echoing polysyllables that tend to slip into your writing to rob it of its crispness and force.

Beware of the Pat Expression

50   Other things being equal, avoid phrases like "other things being   50
equal." Those sentences that come to you whole, or in two or three
doughy lumps, are sure to be bad sentences. They are no creation of
yours but pieces of common thought floating in the community soup.

Pat expressions are hard, often impossible, to avoid, because they
come too easily to be noticed and seem too necessary to be dispensed
with. No writer avoids them altogether, but good writers avoid them
more often than poor writers.

By "pat expressions" we mean such tags as "to all practical intents
and purposes," "the pure and simple truth," "from where I sit," "the
time of his life," "to the ends of the earth," "in the twinkling of an
eye," "as sure as you're born," "over my dead body," "under cover of
darkness," "took the easy way out," "when all is said and done," "told
him time and time again," "parted the best of friends," "stand up and
be counted," "gave him the best years of her life," "worked her fingers
to the bone." Like other clichés, these expressions were once forceful.
Now we should use them only when we cant possibly think of anything else.

Some pat expressions stand like a wall between the writer and
thought. Such a one is "the American way of life." Many student writers
feel that when they have said that something accords with the
American way of life or does not they have exhausted the subject. Actually,
they have stopped at the highest level of abstraction. The American
way of life is the complicated set of bonds between a hundred and
eighty million ways. All of us know this when we think about it, but
the tag phrase too often keeps us from thinking about it.

So with many another phrase dear to the politician: "this great
land of ours," "the man in the street," "our national heritage." These
may prove our patriotism or give a clue to our political beliefs, but
otherwise they add nothing to the paper except words.

Colorful Words

55　　The writer builds with words, and no builder uses a raw material 55
more slippery and elusive and treacherous. A writer's work is a constant struggle to get the right word in the right place, to find that particular word that will convey his meaning exactly, that will persuade
the reader or soothe him or startle or amuse him. He never succeeds
altogether—sometimes he feels that he scarcely succeeds at all—but
such successes as he has are what make the thing worth doing.

There is no book of rules for this game. One progresses through
everlasting experiment on the basis of ever-widening experience.
There are few useful generalizations that one can make about words
as words, but there are perhaps a few.

Some words are what we call "colorful." By this we mean that they
are calculated to produce a picture or induce an emotion. They are
dressy instead of plain, specific instead of general, loud instead of soft.
Thus, in place of "Her heart beat," we may write "Her heart *pounded,
throbbed, fluttered, danced.*" Instead of "He sat in his chair," we may
say, "He *lounged, sprawled, coiled.*" Instead of "It was hot," we may say,
"It was *blistering, sultry, muggy, suffocating, steamy, wilting.*"

However, it should not be supposed that the fancy word is always
better. Often it is as well to write "Her heart beat" or "It was hot" if
that is all it did or all it was. Ages differ in how they like their prose.
The nineteenth century liked it rich and smoky. The twentieth has
usually preferred it lean and cool. The twentieth-century writer, like
all writers, is forever seeking the exact word, but he is wary of sounding feverish. He tends to pitch it low, to understate it, to throw it away.
He knows that if he gets too colorful, the audience is likely to giggle.

See how this strikes you: "As the rich, golden glow of the sunset
died away along the eternal western hills, Angela's limpid blue eyes
looked softly and trustingly into Montague's flashing brown ones, and
her heart pounded like a drum in time with the joyous song surging
in her soul." Some people like that sort of thing, but most modern
readers would say, "Good grief," and turn on the television.

Colored Words

60　　Some words we would call not so much colorful as colored—that 60
is, loaded with associations, good or bad. All words—except perhaps

structure words—have associations of some sort. We have said that the meaning of a word is the sum of the contexts in which it occurs. When we hear a word, we hear with it an echo of all the situations in which we have heard it before.

In some words, these echoes are obvious and discussable. The word *mother,* for example, has, for most people, agreeable associations. When you hear *mother* you probably think of home, safety, love, food, and various other pleasant things. If one writes, "She was like a *mother* to me," he gets an effect which he would not get in "She was like an aunt to me." The advertiser makes use of the associations of *mother* by working it in when he talks about his product. The politician works it in when he talks about himself.

So also with such words as *home, liberty, fireside, contentment, patriot, tenderness, sacrifice, childlike, manly, bluff, limpid.* All of these words are loaded with favorable associations that would be rather hard to indicate in a straightforward definition. There is more than a literal difference between "They sat around the fireside" and "They sat around the stove." They might have been equally warm and happy around the stove, but *fireside* suggests leisure, grace, quiet tradition, congenial company, and *stove* does not.

Conversely, some words have bad associations. *Mother* suggests pleasant things, but *mother-in-law* does not. Many mothers-in-law are heroically lovable and some mothers drink gin all day and beat their children insensible, but these facts of life are beside the point. The thing is that *mother* sounds good and *mother-in-law* does not.

Or consider the word *intellectual.* This would seem to be a complimentary term, but in point of fact it is not, for it has picked up associations of impracticality and ineffectuality and general dopiness. So also with such words as *liberal, reactionary, Communist, socialist, capitalist, radical, schoolteacher, truck driver, undertaker, operator, salesman, huckster, speculator.* These convey meanings on the literal level, but beyond that—sometimes, in some places—they convey contempt on the part of the speaker.

65 The question of whether to use loaded words or not depends on what is being written. The scientist, the scholar, try to avoid them; for the poet, the advertising writer, the public speaker, they are standard equipment. But every writer should take care that they do not substitute for thought. If you write, "Anyone who thinks that is nothing but a Socialist (or Communist or capitalist)," you have said nothing ex-

cept that you don't like people who think that, and such remarks are effective only with the most naive readers. It is always a bad mistake to think your readers more naive than they really are.

Colorless Words

But probably most student writers come to grief not with words that are colorful or those that are colored but with those that have no color at all. A pet example is *nice*, a word we would find it hard to dispense with in casual conversation but which is no longer capable of adding much to a description. Colorless words are those of such general meaning that in a particular sentence they mean nothing. Slang adjectives, like *cool* ("That's real cool") tend to explode all over the language. They are applied to everything, lose their original force, and quickly die.

Beware also of nouns of very general meaning, like *circumstances, cases, instances, aspects, factors, relationships, attitudes, eventualities,* etc. In most circumstances you will find that those cases of writing which contain too many instances of words like these will in this and other aspects have factors leading to unsatisfactory relationships with the reader resulting in unfavorable attitudes on his part and perhaps other eventualities, like a grade of "D." Notice also what "etc." means. It means "I'd like to make this list longer, but I can't think of any more examples."

Questions on Meaning

1. Did the description of the student struggling with an English assignment remind you of yourself? In what ways? If it did not, describe the ways your writing process works with assignments like "College Football."
2. List the "rules" Roberts offers for successful college writing. Which of them do you already follow? Which have you been taught but so far not used much? Which are new to you? Which do you feel you may want to adopt?

Questions on Rhetorical Strategy and Style

1. Roberts's essay is a process analysis, like a set of directions for assembling something, complete with a troubleshooting section. The best test of a process analysis is to try to follow the directions. So try writing and revising a paragraph using the process that Roberts describes. Once you have finished, report any problems you encountered.
2. Sets of directions usually require the writer to use the second person pronoun "you." Try revising one of Roberts's paragraphs to put it in first person, "I," or third person, "one," or "he or she." Note that when Roberts uses third person, he allows the masculine pronoun, "he," to stand for both genders. That is now considered sexist usage.

Writing Assignments

1. List and explain any additional steps in writing that you find necessary to your comfort or personal creativity or focus.
2. Most writing processes are not as linear—that is not so tidy and orderly—as process analysis leads us to infer. Recall the process by which you wrote the essay you completed most recently, or the one you remember most clearly. In an essay intended to clarify your writing processes for yourself, your peers, and your teacher, describe the process of writing that essay.
3. Roberts uses a form of wry humor often associated with English teachers (e.g., "Many mothers-in-law are heroically loveable and some mothers drink gin all day and beat their children insensible, but these facts of life are beside the point. The thing is that mother sounds good and mother-in-law does not.") Find other examples of his humor to get the idea, and write a process analysis essay that uses this tone.

Letter to the President

Jackie Robinson

Jackie Robinson was born in Georgia in 1919 but grew up in California. There he became the first four-letter athlete—an athlete who receives varsity letters in four distinct sports—at the University of California, Los Angeles. He joined the Brooklyn Dodgers, breaking the color barrier in professional baseball. In 1962, after playing for 10 years, he became the first black to be inducted into the Baseball Hall of Fame. In the following letter to President Eisenhower, Robinson explains that African Americans can no longer wait for the civil rights they deserve.

May 13, 1958

The President
The White House
Washington, D. C.

My dear Mr. President:

1   I was sitting in the audience at the Summit Meeting of Negro Leaders yesterday when you said we must have patience. On hearing you say this, I felt like standing up and saying, "Oh no! Not again."

I respectfully remind you sir, that we have been the most patient of all people. When you said we must have self-respect, I wondered how we could have self-respect and remain patient considering the treatment accorded us through the years.

"Letter to The President" by Jackie Robinson, Online at: <www.nara.gov/exhall/ featured-document/robinson/robinson.html>

17 million Negroes cannot do as you suggest and wait for the hearts of men to change. We want to enjoy now the rights that we feel we are entitled to as Americans. This we cannot do unless we pursue aggressively goals which all other Americans achieved over 150 years ago.

As the chief executive of our nation, I respectfully suggest that you unwittingly crush the spirit of freedom in Negroes by constantly urging forbearance and give hope to those pro-segregation leaders like Governor Faubus who would take from us even those freedoms we now enjoy. Your own experience with Governor Faubus is proof enough that forbearance and not eventual integration is the goal the pro-segration leaders seek.

In my view, an unequivocal statement backed up by action such as you demonstrated you could take last fall in dealing with Governor Faubus if it became necessary, would let it be known that American is determined to provide—in the near future—for Negroes—the freedoms we are entitled to under the constitution.

Respectfully yours,

Jackie Robinson

JR:cc

Questions on Meaning

1. Robinson was a great sports hero, one of the first black men to break the color barrier in baseball. Why would that fact make this letter to President Dwight D. Eisenhower more effective?
2. Governor Faubus of Arkansas fought integration of southern schools. Robinson said that such men wanted blacks to agree to "forbearance," or patience. Why did Robinson find this objectionable?
3. Robinson wrote that "17 million" black Americans could not wait for the "hearts of men to change." What did this statement imply about how people's minds are changed? Do you think Robinson was right?

Questions on Rhetorical Strategy and Style

1. The letter begins with a simple statement: "Oh, no! Not again." Why was this opening line so effective?
2. Black rhetoricians since Robinson have used powerful repetition and colorful language to make their points. What methods did Robinson use? For example, what effect does "I respectfully remind you sir" have on the reader? What rhetorical stance was Robinson taking?
3. The letter ends with an appeal to the U.S. Constitution. Why would that approach be particularly effective in a letter to the president?

Writing Assignments

1. Write a letter to an official protesting something you object to or asking for some social goal that you consider important.
2. Interview older African-American citizens who lived through the Civil Rights movement. Write a paper about their experiences.
3. Do some research on Robinson the man, to find out about his life and times. Then write about how this letter does or does not express Robinson's actual beliefs and values.

From: The School Days of an Indian Girl

Zitkala-Sa

Zitkala-Sa (1876–1938) was born as Gertrude Simmons on the Pine Ridge Reservation in South Dakota to a full-blooded Sioux mother and a white father who abandoned the family. At the age of eight she enrolled in a Quaker boarding school for American Indians, later attending normal (teacher-training) school and finally accepting scholarships to Earlham College in Indiana, where she excelled in oratory. An accomplished musician, Zitkala-Sa also attended the Boston Conservatory of Music before beginning a brief teaching career at the Carlisle Indian School. The exploitation of student labor at the school, as well as the suppression of native custom and language, led her to write several articles critical of the school for Atlantic Monthly *and* Harper's Monthly *under the pen name Zitkala-Sa (Red Bird). After marrying another mixed-blood Sioux, Raymond Bonnin, Zitkala-Sa became an activist with the Society of American Indians and edited* American Indian Magazine. *Her collection of personal narratives and tribal legends, titled* American Indian Stories, *was published in 1921; she also wrote the libretto for an opera,* Sun Dance. *In the following selection Zitkala-Sa recounts the terrors and humiliations undergone by young American Indian children at the hands of white missionaries determined to lead them "from savagery to civilization."*

Excerpt from "The School Days of an Indian Girl," reprinted from *Atlantic*, 85, February, 1900, pp. 185–194.

I. The Land of Red Apples

1   There were eight in our party of bronzed children who were
going East with the missionaries. Among us were three young
braves, two tall girls, and we three little ones, Judéwin,
Thowin, and I.

We had been very impatient to start on our journey to the Red
Apple Country, which, we were told, lay a little beyond the great cir-
cular horizon of the Western prairie. Under a sky of rosy apples we
dreamt of roaming as freely and happily as we had chased the cloud
shadows on the Dakota plains. We had anticipated much pleasure
from a ride on the iron horse, but the throngs of staring palefaces disturbed and troubled us.

On the train, fair women, with tottering babies on each arm,
stopped their haste and scrutinized the children of absent mothers.
Large men, with heavy bundles in their hands, halted near by, and riv-
eted their glassy blue eyes upon us.

I sank deep into the corner of my seat, for I resented being
watched. Directly in front of me, children who were no larger than I
hung themselves upon the backs of their seats, with their bold white
faces toward me. Sometimes they took their forefingers out of their
mouths and pointed at my moccasined feet. Their mothers, instead of
reproving such rude curiosity, looked closely at me, and attracted their
children's further notice to my blanket. This embarrassed me, and
kept me constantly on the verge of tears.

5   I sat perfectly still, with my eyes downcast, daring only now and
then to shoot long glances around me. Chancing to turn to the window at my side, I was quite breathless upon seeing one familiar object. It was a telegraph pole which strode by at short paces. Very near
my mother's dwelling, along the edge of a road thickly bordered with
wild sunflowers, some poles like these had been planted by white men.
Often I had stopped, on my way down the road, to hold my ear
against the pole, and, hearing its low moaning, I used to wonder what
the paleface had done to hurt it. Now I sat watching for each pole that
glided by to be the last one.

In this way I had forgotten my uncomfortable surroundings,
when I heard one of my comrades call out my name. I saw the mis-

sionary standing very near, tossing candies and gums into our midst. This amused us all, and we tried to see who could catch the most of the sweet-meats. The missionary's generous distribution of candies was impressed upon my memory by a disastrous result which followed. I had caught more than my share of candies and gums, and soon after our arrival at the school I had a chance to disgrace myself, which, I am ashamed to say, I did.

Though we rode several days inside of the iron horse, I do not recall a single thing about our luncheons.

It was night when we reached the school grounds. The lights from the windows of the large buildings fell upon some of the icicled trees that stood beneath them. We were led toward an open door, where the brightness of the lights within flooded out over the heads of the excited palefaces who blocked the way. My body trembled more from fear than from the snow I trod upon.

Entering the house, I stood close against the wall. The strong glaring light in the large whitewashed room dazzled my eyes. The noisy hurrying of hard shoes upon a bare wooden floor increased the whirring in my ears. My only safety seemed to be in keeping next to the wall. As I was wondering in which direction to escape from all this confusion, two warm hands grasped me firmly, and in the same moment I was tossed high in midair. A rosy-cheeked paleface woman caught me in her arms. I was both frightened and insulted by such trifling. I stared into her eyes, wishing her to let me stand on my own feet, but she jumped me up and down with increasing enthusiasm. My mother had never made a plaything of her wee daughter. Remembering this I began to cry aloud.

10   They misunderstood the cause of my tears, and placed me at a   10
white table loaded with food. There our party were united again. As I did not hush my crying, one of the older ones whispered to me, "Wait until you are alone in the night."

It was very little I could swallow besides my sobs, that evening.

"Oh, I want my mother and my brother Dawée! I want to go to my aunt!" I pleaded; but the ears of the palefaces could not hear me.

From the table we were taken along an upward incline of wooden boxes, which I learned afterward to call a stairway. At the top was a quiet hall, dimly lighted. Many narrow beds were in one straight line down the entire length of the wall. In them lay sleeping brown faces, which peeped just out of the coverings. I was tucked into bed with one of the tall girls, because she talked to me in my mother tongue and seemed to soothe me.

I had arrived in the wonderful land of rosy skies, but I was not happy, as I had thought I should be. My long travel and the bewildering sights had exhausted me. I fell asleep, heaving deep, tired sobs. My tears were left to dry themselves in streaks, because neither my aunt nor my mother was near to wipe them away.

II The Cutting of My Long Hair

15   The first day in the land of apples was a bitter-cold one; for the snow   15
still covered the ground, and the trees were bare. A large bell rang for breakfast, its loud metallic voice crashing through the belfry overhead and into our sensitive ears. The annoying clatter of shoes on bare floors gave us no peace. The constant clash of harsh noises, with an undercurrent of many voices murmuring an unknown tongue, made a bedlam within which I was securely tied. And though my spirit tore itself in struggling for its lost freedom, all was useless.

A paleface woman, with white hair, came up after us. We were placed in a line of girls who were marching into the dining room. These were Indian girls, in stiff shoes and closely clinging dresses. The small girls wore sleeved aprons and shingled hair. As I walked noiselessly in my soft moccasins, I felt like sinking to the floor, for my blanket had been stripped from my shoulders. I looked hard at the Indian girls, who seemed not to care that they were even more immodestly dressed than I, in their tightly fitting clothes. While we marched in, the boys entered at an opposite door. I watched for the three young braves who came in our party. I spied them in their ranks, looking as uncomfortable as I felt.

A small bell was tapped, and each of the pupils drew a chair from under the table. Supposing this act meant they were to be seated, I pulled out mine and at once slipped into it from one side. But when I turned my head, I saw that I was the only one seated, and all the rest at our table remained standing. Just as I began to rise, looking shyly around to see how chairs were to be used, a second bell was sounded. All were seated at last, and I had to crawl back into my chair again. I heard a man's voice at one end of the hall, and I looked around to see him. But all the others hung their heads over their plates. As I glanced at the long chain of tables, I caught the eyes of a paleface woman upon me. Immediately I dropped my eyes, wondering why I was so keenly watched by the strange woman. The man ceased his mutterings, and then a third bell was tapped. Every one picked up his knife and fork and began eating. I began crying instead, for by this time I was afraid to venture anything more.

But this eating by formula was not the hardest trial in that first day. Late in the morning, my friend Judéwin gave me a terrible warning. Judéwin knew a few words of English; and she had overheard the paleface woman talk about cutting our long, heavy hair. Our mothers had taught us that only unskilled warriors who were captured had their hair shingled by the enemy. Among our people, short hair was worn by mourners, and shingled hair by cowards!

We discussed our fate some moments, and when Judéwin said, "We have to submit, because they are strong," I rebelled.

20 "No, I will not submit! I will struggle first!" I answered. 20

I watched my chance, and when no one noticed I disappeared. I crept up the stairs as quietly as I could in my squeaking shoes,—my moccasins had been exchanged for shoes. Along the hall I passed, without knowing whither I was going. Turning aside to an open door, I found a large room with three white beds in it. The windows were covered with dark green curtains, which made the room very dim. Thankful that no one was there, I directed my steps toward the corner farthest from the door. On my hands and knees I crawled under the bed, and cuddled myself in the dark corner.

From my hiding place I peered out, shuddering with fear whenever I heard footsteps near by. Though in the hall loud voices were calling my name, and I knew that even Judéwin was searching for me, I did not open my mouth to answer. Then the steps were quickened and the voices became excited. The sounds came nearer and nearer. Women and girls entered the room. I held my breath, and watched them open closed doors and peep behind large trunks. Some one threw up the curtains, and the room was filled with sudden light. What caused them to stoop and look under the bed I do not know. I remember being dragged out, though I resisted by kicking and scratching wildly. In spite of myself, I was carried downstairs and tied fast in a chair.

I cried aloud, shaking my head all the while until I felt the cold blades of the scissors against my neck, and heard them gnaw off one of my thick braids. Then I lost my spirit. Since the day I was taken from my mother I had suffered extreme indignities. People had stared at me. I had been tossed about in the air like a wooden puppet. And now my long hair was shingled like a coward's! In my anguish I moaned for my mother, but no one came to comfort me. Not a soul reasoned quietly with me like my own mother used to do: for now I was only one of many little animals driven by a herder.

Questions on Meaning

1. Zitkala-Sa recalls two particular indignities to which she was subjected during her journey: being stared at by the white people on the train and being tossed in the air by the missionary teacher. Why is she offended by these things? Why are the white people unable to understand her offense?
2. How does the author emphasize the significance of clothing to her people? How does she react to the clothing worn by the children at the school?
3. When her hair is cut off, the author states that she lost her spirit. In what ways is she speaking metaphorically? In what ways might she be speaking literally, given her traditions?

Questions on Rhetorical Strategy and Style

1. This narrative is told from the point of view of a child. Find several passages in which this point of view is evident and explain their significance to the story.
2. Zitkala-Sa describes certain features of the boarding school in great detail: the bright lights of the main room at night, the rows of beds in the dormitory, and the room in which she hides. Why does she focus on these details? Of what significance are they to the little girl?

Writing Assignments

1. Recall an incident from your childhood in which you found yourself in unfamiliar surroundings. Write a narrative describing your response to the place, using the kind of detail found in this story.
2. Read about the Christian boarding schools established in the late nineteenth century to educate American Indian children. Write an essay describing the schools, focusing on the motivation of the missionaries, the treatment of the children, and the nature of the education provided to the children.

The Inheritance of Tools

Scott Russell Sanders

Scott Russell Sanders (1945–) was born in Memphis, Tennessee, attended Brown University and took a Ph.D. at Cambridge University. He writes on a variety of subjects for "little" magazines such as The Georgia Review *and* The North American Review *and for more commercial publications such as* Omni *and* Isaac Asimov's Science FictionMagazine. *His published books include* Wonders Hidden: Audubon's Early Years *(1984),* Hear the Wind Blow: American Folksongs Retold *(1985), and* The Paradise of Bombs *(1987). His writing is characteristically rich in detail and focused on the ironies and complexities of human experience. The essay that follows first appeared in* The North American Review *in 1986 and uses a story within a story to pay tribute to his father's teaching.*

1   At just about the hour when my father died, soon after dawn one February morning when ice coated the windows like cataracts, I banged my thumb with a hammer. Naturally I swore at the hammer, the reckless thing, and in the moment of swearing I thought of what my father would say: "If you'd try hitting the nail it would go in a whole lot faster. Don't you know your thumb's not as hard as that hammer?" We both were doing carpentry that day, but far apart. He was building cupboards at my brother's place in Oklahoma; I was at home in Indiana, putting up a wall in the basement to make a bedroom for my daughter. By the time my mother called with news of his death—the long distance wires whittling her voice

until it seemed too thin to bear the weight of what she had to say—my thumb was swollen. A week or so later a white scar in the shape of a crescent moon began to show above the cuticle, and month by month it rose across the pink sky of my thumbnail. It took the better part of a year for the scar to disappear, and every time I noticed it I thought of my father.

The hammer had belonged to him, and to his father before him. The three of us have used it to build houses and barns and chicken coops, to upholster chairs and crack walnuts, to make doll furniture and bookshelves and jewelry boxes. The head is scratched and pockmarked, like an old plowshare that has been working rocky fields, and it gives off the sort of dull sheen you see on fast creek water in the shade. It is a finishing hammer, about the weight of a bread loaf, too light, really, for framing walls, too heavy for cabinet work, with a curved claw for pulling nails, a rounded head for pounding, a fluted neck for looks, and a hickory handle for strength.

The present handle is my third one, bought from a lumberyard in Tennessee, down the road from where my brother and I were helping my father build his retirement house. I broke the previous one by trying to pull sixteen-penny nails out of floor joists—a foolish thing to do with a finishing hammer, as my father pointed out. "You ever hear of a crowbar?" he said. No telling how many handles he and my grandfather had gone through before me. My grandfather used to cut down hickory trees on his farm, saw them into slabs, cure the planks in his hayloft, and carve handles with a drawknife. The grain in hickory is crooked and knotty, and therefore tough, hard to split, like the grain in the two men who owned this hammer before me.

After proposing marriage to a neighbor girl, my grandfather used this hammer to build a house for his bride on a stretch of river bottom in northern Mississippi. The lumber for the place, like the hickory for the handle, was cut on his own land. By the day of the wedding he had not quite finished the house, and so right after the ceremony he took his wife home and put her to work. My grandmother had worn her Sunday dress for the wedding, with a fringe of lace tacked on around the hem in honor of the occasion. She removed this lace and folded it away before going out to help my grandfather nail siding on the house. "There she was in her good dress," he told me some fifty-odd years after that wedding day, "holding up them long pieces of clapboard while I hammered, and together we got the place covered up before dark." As the family grew to four, six, eight, and eventually thirteen, my grandfather used this hammer to enlarge his house room by room, like a chambered nautilus expanding its shell.

5   By and by the hammer was passed along to my father. One day   5 he was up on the roof of our pony barn nailing shingles with it, when I stepped out the kitchen door to call him for supper. Before I could yell, something about the sight of him straddling the spine of that roof and swinging the hammer caught my eye and made me hold my tongue. I was five or six years old, and the world's commonplaces were still news to me. He would pull a nail from the pouch at his waist, bring the hammer down, and a moment later the *thunk* of the blow would reach my ears. And that is what had stopped me in my tracks and stilled my tongue, that momentary gap between seeing and hearing the blow. Instead of yelling from the kitchen door, I ran to the barn and climbed two rungs up the ladder—as far as I was allowed to go—and spoke quietly to my father. On our walk to the house he explained that sound takes time to make its way through air. Suddenly the world seemed larger, the air more dense, if sound could be held back like any ordinary traveler.

By the time I started using this hammer, at about the age when I discovered the speed of sound, it already contained houses and mysteries for me. The smooth handle was one my grandfather had made. In those days I needed both hands to swing it. My father would start a nail in a scrap of wood, and I would pound away until I bent it over.

"Looks like you got ahold of some of those rubber nails," he would tell me. "Here, let me see if I can find you some stiff ones." And he would rummage in a drawer until he came up with a fistful of more cooperative nails. "Look at the head," he would tell me. "Don't look at your hands, don't look at the hammer. Just look at the head of that nail and pretty soon you'll learn to hit it square."

Pretty soon I did learn. While he worked in the garage cutting dovetail joints for a drawer or skinning a deer or tuning an engine, I would hammer nails. I made innocent blocks of wood look like porcupines. He did not talk much in the midst of his tools, but he kept up a nearly ceaseless humming, slipping in and out of a dozen tunes in an afternoon, often running back over the same stretch of melody again and again, as if searching for a way out. When the humming did cease, I knew he was faced with a task requiring great delicacy or concentration, and I took care not to distract him.

He kept scraps of wood in a cardboard box—the ends of two-by-fours, slabs of shelving and plywood, odd pieces of molding—and everything in it was fair game. I nailed scraps together to fashion what I called boats or houses, but the results usually bore only faint resemblance to the visions I carried in my head. I would hold up these constructions to show my father, and he would turn them over in his hands admiringly, speculating about what they might be. My cobbled-together guitars might have been alien spaceships, my barns might have been models of Aztec temples, each wooden contraption might have been anything but what I had set out to make.

10   Now and again I would feel the need to have a chunk of wood   10
shaped or shortened before I riddled it with nails, and I would clamp it in a vise and scrape at it with a handsaw. My father would let me lacerate the board until my arm gave out, and then he would wrap his hand around mine and help me finish the cut, showing me how to use my thumb to guide the blade, how to pull back on the saw to keep it from binding, how to let my shoulder do the work.

"Don't force it," he would say, "just drag it easy and give the teeth a chance to bite."

As the saw teeth bit down, the wood released its smell, each kind with its own fragrance, oak or walnut or cherry or pine—usually pine because it was the softest, easiest for a child to work. No matter how weathered and gray the board, no matter how warped and cracked, inside there was this smell waiting, as of something freshly baked. I gathered every smidgen of sawdust and stored it away in coffee cans, which I kept in a drawer of the workbench. When I did not feel like hammering nails, I would dump my sawdust on the concrete floor of the garage and landscape it into highways and farms and towns, running miniature cars and trucks along miniature roads. Looming as huge as a colossus, my father worked over and around me, now and again bending down to inspect my work, careful not to trample my creations. It was a landscape that smelled dizzyingly of wood. Even after a bath my skin would carry the smell, and so would my father's hair, when he lifted me for a bedtime hug.

I tell these things not only from memory but also from recent observation, because my own son now turns blocks of wood into nailed porcupines, dumps cans full of sawdust at my feet and sculpts highways on the floor. He learns how to swing a hammer from the elbow instead of the wrist, how to lay his thumb beside the blade to guide a saw, how to tap a chisel with a wooden mallet, how to mark a hole with an awl before starting a drill bit. My daughter did the same before him, and even now, on the brink of teenage aloofness, she will occasionally drag out my box of wood scraps and carpenter something. So I have seen my apprenticeship to wood and tools re-enacted in each of my children, as my father saw his own apprenticeship renewed in me.

The saw I use belonged to him, as did my level and both of my squares, and all four tools had belonged to his father. The blade of the saw is the bluish color of gun barrels, and the maple handle, dark from the sweat of hands, is inscribed with curving leaf designs. The level is a shaft of walnut two feet long, edged with brass and pierced by three round windows in which air bubbles float in oil-filled tubes of glass. The middle window serves for testing if a surface is horizontal, the others for testing if a surface is plumb or vertical. My grandfather used to carry this level on the gun rack behind the seat in his pickup, and when I rode with him I would turn around to watch the bubbles dance. The larger of the two squares is called a framing square, a flat steel elbow, so beat up and tarnished you can barely make out the rows of numbers that show how to figure the cuts on rafters. The smaller one is called a try square, for marking angles, with a blued steel blade for the shank and a brass-faced block of cherry for the head.

15   I was taught early on that a saw is not to be used apart from a 15 square: "If you're going to cut a piece of wood," my father insisted, "you owe it to the tree to cut it straight."

Long before studying geometry, I learned there is a mystical virtue in right angles. There is an unspoken morality in seeking the level and the plumb. A house will stand, a table will bear weight, the sides of a box will hold together, only if the joints are square and the members upright. When the bubble is lined up between two marks etched in the glass tube of a level, you have aligned yourself with the forces that hold the universe together. When you miter the corners of a picture frame, each angle must be exactly forty-five degrees, as they are in the perfect triangles of Pythagoras, not a degree more or less. Otherwise the frame will hang crookedly, as if ashamed of itself and of its maker. No matter if the joints you are cutting do not show. Even if you are butting two pieces of wood together inside a cabinet, where no one except a wrecking crew will ever see them, you must take pains to ensure that the ends are square and the studs are plumb.

I took pains over the wall I was building on the day my father died. Not long after that wall was finished—paneled with tongue-and-groove boards of yellow pine, the nail holes filled with putty and the wood all stained and sealed—I came close to wrecking it one afternoon when my daughter ran howling up the stairs to announce that her gerbils had escaped from their cage and were hiding in my brand new wall. She could hear them scratching and squeaking behind her bed. Impossible! I said. How on earth could they get inside my drum-tight wall? Through the heating vent, she answered. I went downstairs, pressed my ear to the honey-colored wood, and heard the *scritch scritch* of tiny feet.

"What can we do?" my daughter wailed. "They'll starve to death, they'll die of thirst, they'll suffocate."

"Hold on," I soothed. "I'll think of something."

While I thought and she fretted, the radio on her bedside table delivered us the headlines: Several thousand people had died in a city in India from a poisonous cloud that had leaked overnight from a chemical plant. A nuclear-powered submarine had been launched. Rioting continued in South Africa. An airplane had been hijacked in the Mediterranean. Authorities calculated that several thousand homeless people slept on the streets within sight of the Washington Monument. I felt my usual helplessness in the face of all these calamities. But here was my daughter, weeping because her gerbils were holed up in a wall. This calamity I could handle.

"Don't worry," I told her. "We'll set food and water by the heating vent and lure them out. And if that doesn't do the trick, I'll tear the wall apart until we find them."

She stopped crying and gazed at me. "You'd really tear it apart? Just for my gerbils? The *wall?*" Astonishment slowed her down only for a second, however, before she ran to the workbench and began tugging at drawers, saying, "let's see, what'll we need? Crowbar. Hammer. Chisels. I hope we don't have to use them—but just in case."

We didn't need the wrecking tools. I never had to assault my handsome wall, because the gerbils eventually came out to nibble at a dish of popcorn. But for several hours I studied the tongue-and-groove skin I had nailed up on the day of my father's death, considering where to begin prying. There were no gaps in that wall, no crooked joints.

I had botched a great many pieces of wood before I mastered the right angle with a saw, botched even more before I learned to miter a joint. The knowledge of these things resides in my hands and eyes and the webwork of muscles, not in the tools. There are machines for sale—powered miter boxes and radial-arm saws, for instance—that will enable any casual soul to cut proper angles in boards. The skill is invested in the gadget instead of the person who uses it, and this is what distinguishes a machine from a tool. If I had to earn my keep by making furniture or building houses, I suppose I would buy powered saws and pneumatic nailers; the need for speed would drive me to it. But since I carpenter only for my own pleasure or to help neighbors or to remake the house around the ears of my family, I stick with hand tools. Most of the ones I own were given to me by my father, who also taught me how to wield them. The tools in my work-bench are a double inheritance, for each hammer and level and saw is wrapped in a cloud of knowing.

25   All of these tools are a pleasure to look at and to hold. Merchants would never paste NEW! NEW! NEW! signs on them in stores. Their designs are old because they work, because they serve their purpose well. Like folk songs and aphorisms and the grainy bits of language, these tools have been pared down to essentials. I look at my claw hammer, the distillation of a hundred generations of carpenters, and consider that it holds up well beside those other classics—Greek vases, Gregorian chants, *Don Quixote,* barbed fish hooks, candles, spoons. Knowledge of hammering stretches back to the earliest humans who squatted beside fires, chipping flints. Anthropologists have a lovely name for those unworked rocks that served as the earliest hammers. *Dawn stones,* they are called. Their only qualification for the work, aside from hardness, is that they fit the hand. Our ancestors used them for grinding corn, tapping awls, smashing bones. From dawn stones to the claw hammer is a great leap in time, but no great distance in design or imagination.

On that iced-over February morning when I smashed my thumb with the hammer, I was down in the basement framing the wall that my daughter's gerbils would later hide in. I was thinking of my father, as I always did whenever I built anything, thinking how he would have gone about the work, hearing in memory what he would have said about the wisdom of hitting the nail instead of my thumb. I had the studs and plates nailed together all square and trim, and was lifting the wall into place when the phone rang upstairs. My wife answered, and in a moment she came to the basement door and called down softly to me. The stillness in her voice made me drop the framed wall and hurry upstairs. She told me my father was dead. Then I heard the details over the phone from my mother. Building a set of cupboards for my brother in Oklahoma, he had knocked off work early the previous afternoon because of cramps in his stomach. Early this morning, on his way into the kitchen of my brother's trailer, maybe going for a glass of water, so early that no one else was awake, he slumped down on the linoleum and his heart quit.

For several hours I paced around inside my house, upstairs and down, in and out of every room, looking for the right door to open and knowing there was no such door. My wife and children followed me and wrapped me in arms and backed away again, circling and staring as if I were on fire. Where was the door, the door, the door? I kept wondering. My smashed thumb turned purple and throbbed, making me furious. I wanted to cut it off and rush outside and scrape away the snow and hack a hole in the frozen earth and bury the shameful thing.

I went down into the basement, opened a drawer in my workbench, and stared at the ranks of chisels and knives. Oiled and sharp, as my father would have kept them, they gleamed at me like teeth. I took up a clasp knife, pried out the longest blade, and tested the edge on the hair of my forearm. A tuft came away cleanly, and I saw my father testing the sharpness of tools on his own skin, the blades of axes and knives and gouges and hoes, saw the red hair shaved off in patches from his arms and the backs of hands. "That will cut bear," he would say. He never cut a bear with his blades, now my blades, but he cut deer, dirt, wood. I closed the knife and put it away. Then I took up the hammer and went back to work on my daughter's wall, snugging the bottom plate against a chalk line on the floor, shimming the top plate against the joists overhead, plumbing the studs with my level, making sure before I drove the first nail that every line was square and true.

Questions on Meaning

1. Would you say that Sanders's essay is more about inheritance or more about loss? Explain your answer.
2. What larger lesson was Sanders's father teaching as he taught Sanders carpentry?
3. Does Sanders's reaction to the news of his father's death seem odd to you? Comment on his actions.

Questions on Rhetorical Strategy and Style

1. Sanders uses the news of his father's death as a frame to contain a second narrative about tools and their uses. What effects are achieved by setting the two stories together? How does it affect each story individually and both as a coherent essay?
2. Narration involves description, and Sanders uses both literal and figurative description. Re-read the beginning and the end of the essay, noting figurative descriptions such as ". . . ice coated the windows like cataracts. . . ." Explain how each figurative description contributes to the impact of the story of his father's death.
3. What do Sanders's quotations of his father's advice tell you about the father's character?

Writing Assignments

1. Tell the story of an important passage in your life, one that caused you to recall earlier moments or lessons. Use a frame structure to combine the story of the passage with the flashback sequences to earlier times.
2. Describe the way you taught someone a physical skill like carpentry. As you describe the process, comment on the kinds of problems your student encountered and how you helped handle those problems.

Food Product Design

Eric Schlosser

Eric Schlosser (1960–) was born in Manhattan. He studied American history at Princeton and British imperial history at Oxford University. He began his journalism career at The Atlantic Monthly *and is today a correspondent for that magazine. His work has also appeared in many magazines, including* The New Yorker, The Nation, Vanity Fair, *and* Rolling Stone. *Schlosser has lectured at colleges and universities around the country and has addressed the U.S. Senate on the risk to the U.S. food supply from bioterrorism. He has won awards for his journalism, including a National Magazine Award, the Loeb Award for business journalism, and a Sidney Hillman Foundation Award for Reporting. Other works include* Reefer Madness: Sex, Drugs, and Cheap Labor in the American Black Market *(2003); and* Chew on This: Everything You Don't Want to Know about Fast Food *(2006). The following selection is taken from Schlosser's best-known book,* Fast Food Nation: The Dark Side of the All-American Meal *(2001). It began as a two-part investigative piece published in* Rolling Stone. *As a best-selling book it has changed the image many have of the fast-food and meat-packing industries, and also exposed shoddy working conditions for employees. A Hollywood movie based on* Fast Food Nation *was released in 2006. The fast-food industry has, in response, prepared a public relations attack on Schlosser and his work in the hope of reversing the effects of his journalism on public perception. In this excerpt from* Fast Food Nation, *the author explains the "chemical wizardry" of the companies that keeps people coming back for more.*

---

1   The taste of McDonald's french fries has long been praised by   1
customers, competitors, and even food critics.[1] James Beard
loved McDonald's fries.[2] Their distinctive taste does not stem
from the type of potatoes that McDonald's buys, the technology that
processes them, or the restaurant equipment that fries them. Other
chains buy their french fries from the same large processing companies, use Russet Burbanks, and have similar fryers in their restaurant
kitchens. The taste of a fast food fry is largely determined by the
cooking oil.[3] For decades, McDonald's cooked its french fries in a
mixture of about 7 percent cottonseed oil and 93 percent beef tallow.
The mix gave the fries their unique flavor—and more saturated beef
fat per ounce than a McDonald's hamburger.[4]

    Amid a barrage of criticism over the amount of cholesterol in
their fries, McDonald's switched to pure vegetable oil in 1990. The
switch presented the company with an enormous challenge: how to
make fries that subtly taste like beef without cooking them in tallow.
A look at the ingredients now used in the preparation of McDonald's
french fries suggests how the problem was solved.[5] Toward the end of
the list is a seemingly innocuous, yet oddly mysterious phrase: "natural flavor." That ingredient helps to explain not only why the fries
taste so good, but also why most fast food—indeed, most of the food
Americans eat today—tastes the way it does.

    Open your refrigerator, your freezer, your kitchen cupboards, and
look at the labels on your food. You'll find "natural flavor" or "artificial
flavor" in just about every list of ingredients. The similarities between
these two broad categories of flavor are far more significant than their
differences. Both are man-made additives that give most processed
food most of its taste. The initial purchase of a food item may be driven by its packaging or appearance, but subsequent purchases are
determined mainly by its taste. About 90 percent of the money that
Americans spend on food is used to buy processed food.[6] But the canning, freezing, and dehydrating techniques used to process food
destroy most of its flavor. Since the end of World War II, a vast industry has arisen in the United States to make processed food palatable.
Without this flavor industry, today's fast food industry could not exist.
The names of the leading American fast food chains and their best-
selling menu items have become famous worldwide, embedded in our
popular culture. Few people, however, can name the companies that
manufacture fast food's taste.

The flavor industry is highly secretive. Its leading companies will not divulge the precise formulas of flavor compounds or the identities of clients. The secrecy is deemed essential for protecting the reputation of beloved brands. The fast food chains, understandably, would like the public to believe that the flavors of their food somehow originate in their restaurant kitchens, not in distant factories run by other firms.

5   The New Jersey Turnpike runs through the heart of the flavor   5
industry, an industrial corridor dotted with refineries and chemical plants. International Flavors & Fragrances (IFF), the world's largest flavor company, has a manufacturing facility off Exit 8A in Dayton, New Jersey; Givaudan, the world's second-largest flavor company, has a plant in East Hanover. Haarmann & Reimer, the largest German flavor company, has a plant in Teterboro, as does Takasago, the largest Japanese flavor company. Flavor Dynamics has a plant in South Plainfield; Frutarom is in North Bergen; Elan Chemical is in Newark. Dozens of companies manufacture flavors in the corridor between Teaneck and South Brunswick. Indeed, the area produces about two-thirds of the flavor additives sold in the United States.[7]

The IFF plant in Dayton is a huge pale blue building with a modern office complex attached to the front. It sits in an industrial park, not far from a BASF plastics factory, a Jolly French Toast factory, and a plant that manufactures Liz Claiborne cosmetics. Dozens of tractor-trailers were parked at the IFF loading dock the afternoon I visited, and a thin cloud of steam floated from the chimney. Before entering the plant, I signed a nondisclosure form, promising not to reveal the brand names of products that contain IFF flavors. The place reminded me of Willy Wonka's chocolate factory. Wonderful smells drifted through the hallways, men and women in neat white lab coats cheerfully went about their work, and hundreds of little glass bottles sat on laboratory tables and shelves. The bottles contained powerful but fragile flavor chemicals, shielded from light by the brown glass and the round plastic caps shut tight. The long chemical names on the little white labels were as mystifying to me as medieval Latin. They were the odd-sounding names of things that would be mixed and poured and turned into new substances, like magic potions.

I was not invited to see the manufacturing areas of the IFF plant, where it was thought I might discover trade secrets. Instead, I toured various laboratories and pilot kitchens, where the flavors of well-established brands are tested or adjusted, and where whole new flavors are created.

IFF's snack and savory lab is responsible for the flavor of potato chips, corn chips, breads, crackers, breakfast cereals, and pet food. The confectionery lab devises the flavor for ice cream, cookies, candies, toothpastes, mouthwashes, and antacids. Everywhere I looked, I saw famous, widely advertised products sitting on laboratory desks and tables. The beverage lab is full of brightly colored liquids in clear bottles. It comes up with the flavor for popular soft drinks, sport drinks, bottled teas, and wine coolers, for all-natural juice drinks, organic soy drinks, beers, and malt liquors. In one pilot kitchen I saw a dapper food technologist, a middle-aged man with an elegant tie beneath his lab coat, carefully preparing a batch of cookies with white frosting and pink-and-white sprinkles. In another pilot kitchen I saw a pizza oven, a grill, a milk-shake machine, and a french fryer identical to those I'd seen behind the counter at countless fast food restaurants.

In addition to being the world's largest flavor company, IFF manufactures the smell of six of the ten best-selling fine perfumes in the United States, including Estée Lauder's Beautiful, Clinique's Happy, Lancôme's Trésor, and Calvin Klein's Eternity.[8] It also makes the smell of household products such as deodorant, dishwashing detergent, bath soap, shampoo, furniture polish, and floor wax. All of these aromas are made through the same basic process: the manipulation of volatile chemicals to create a particular smell. The basic science behind the scent of your shaving cream is the same as that governing the flavor of your TV dinner.

The aroma of a food can be responsible for as much as 90 percent of its flavor.[9] Scientists now believe that human beings acquired the sense of taste as a way to avoid being poisoned. Edible plants generally taste sweet; deadly ones, bitter. Taste is supposed to help us differentiate food that's good for us from food that's not. The taste buds on our tongues can detect the presence of half a dozen or so basic tastes, including: sweet, sour, bitter, salty, astringent, and umami (a taste discovered by Japanese researchers, a rich and full sense of deliciousness triggered by amino acids in foods such as shellfish, mushrooms, potatoes, and seaweed).[10] Taste buds offer a relatively limited means of detection, however, compared to the human olfactory system, which can perceive thousands of different chemical aromas. Indeed "flavor" is primarily the smell of gases being released by the chemicals you've just put in your mouth.

10   The act of drinking, sucking, or chewing a substance releases its   10 volatile gases. They flow out of the mouth and up the nostrils, or up the passageway in the back of the mouth, to a thin layer of nerve cells called

the olfactory epithelium, located at the base of the nose, right between the eyes. The brain combines the complex smell signals from the epithelium with the simple taste signals from the tongue, assigns a flavor to what's in your mouth, and decides if it's something you want to eat.

Babies like sweet tastes and reject bitter ones; we know this because scientists have rubbed various flavors inside the mouths of infants and then recorded their facial reactions. A person's food preferences, like his or her personality, are formed during the first few years of life, through a process of socialization. Toddlers can learn to enjoy hot and spicy food, bland health food, or fast food, depending upon what the people around them eat. The human sense of smell is still not fully understood and can be greatly affected by psychological factors and expectations. The color of a food can determine the perception of its taste. The mind filters out the overwhelming majority of chemical aromas that surround us, focusing intently on some, ignoring others. People can grow accustomed to bad smells or good smells; they stop noticing what once seemed overpowering. Aroma and memory are somehow inextricably linked. A smell can suddenly evoke a long-forgotten moment. The flavors of childhood foods seem to leave an indelible mark, and adults often return to them, without always knowing why. These "comfort foods" become a source of pleasure and reassurance, a fact that fast food chains work hard to promote. Childhood memories of Happy Meals can translate into frequent adult visits to McDonald's, like those of the chain's "heavy users," the customers who eat there four or five times a week.[11]

The human craving for flavor has been a largely unacknowledged and unexamined force in history. Royal empires have been built, unexplored lands have been traversed, great religions and philosophies have been forever changed by the spice trade. In 1492 Christopher Columbus set sail to find seasoning. Today the influence of flavor in the world marketplace is no less decisive. The rise and fall of corporate empires—of soft drink companies, snack food companies, and fast food chains—is frequently determined by how their products taste.

The flavor industry emerged in the mid-nineteenth century, as processed foods began to be manufactured on a large scale. Recognizing the need for flavor additives, the early food processors turned to perfume companies that had years of experience working with essential oils and volatile aromas. The great perfume houses of England, France, and the Netherlands produced many of the first flavor compounds. In the early part of the twentieth century, Germany's powerful chemical industry assumed the technological lead in flavor production. Legend has it that a German scientist discovered methyl anthranilate, one of the first artificial flavors, by accident while mixing chemicals in his laboratory. Suddenly the lab was filled with the sweet smell of grapes. Methyl anthranilate later became the chief flavoring compound of grape Kool-Aid. After World War II, much of the perfume industry shifted from Europe to the United States, settling in New York City near the garment district and the fashion houses. The flavor industry came with it, subsequently moving to New Jersey to gain more plant capacity. Man-made flavor additives were used mainly in baked goods, candies, and sodas until the 1950s, when sales of processed food began to soar. The invention of gas chromatographs and mass spectrometers—machines capable of detecting volatile gases at low levels—vastly increased the number of flavors that could be synthesized. By the mid-1960s the American flavor industry was churning out compounds to supply the taste of Pop Tarts, Bac-Os, Tab, Tang, Filet-O-Fish sandwiches, and literally thousands of other new foods.

The American flavor industry now has annual revenues of about $1.4 billion.[12] Approximately ten thousand new processed food products are introduced every year in the United States. Almost all of them require flavor additives. And about nine out of every ten of these new food products fail.[13] The latest flavor innovations and corporate realignments are heralded in publications such as *Food Chemical News, Food Engineering, Chemical Market Reporter,* and *Food Product Design.* The growth of IFF has mirrored that of the flavor industry as a whole. IFF was formed in 1958, through the merger of two small companies. Its annual revenues have grown almost fifteenfold since the early 1970s, and it now has manufacturing facilities in twenty countries.[14]

15   The quality that people seek most of all in a food, its flavor, is usu-   15
ally present in a quantity too infinitesimal to be measured by any traditional culinary terms such as ounces or teaspoons. Today's sophisticated spectrometers, gas chromatographs, and headspace vapor analyzers provide a detailed map of a food's flavor components, detecting chemical aromas in amounts as low as one part per billion. The human nose, however, is still more sensitive than any machine yet invented. A nose can detect aromas present in quantities of a few parts per trillion—an amount equivalent to 0.000000000003 percent. Complex aromas, like those of coffee or roasted meat, may be composed of volatile gases from

nearly a thousand different chemicals. The smell of a strawberry arises from the interaction of at least 350 different chemicals that are present in minute amounts. The chemical that provides the dominant flavor of bell pepper can be tasted in amounts as low as .02 parts per billion; one drop is sufficient to add flavor to five average size swimming pools.[15] The flavor additive usually comes last, or second to last, in a processed food's list of ingredients. As a result, the flavor of a processed food often costs less than its packaging. Soft drinks contain a larger proportion of flavor additives than most products. The flavor in a twelve-ounce can of Coke costs about half a cent.[16]

The color additives in processed foods are usually present in even smaller amounts than the flavor compounds. Many of New Jersey's flavor companies also manufacture these color additives, which are used to make processed foods look appealing. Food coloring serves many of the same purposes as lipstick, eye shadow, mascara—and is often made from the same pigments. Titanium dioxide, for example, has proved to be an especially versatile mineral. It gives many processed candies, frosting, and icing their bright white color; it is a common ingredient in women's cosmetics; and it is the pigment used in many white oil paints and house paints. At Burger King, Wendy's, and McDonald's, coloring agents have been added to many of the soft drinks, salad dressings, cookies, condiments, chicken dishes, and sandwich buns.

Studies have found that the color of a food can greatly affect how its taste is perceived. Brightly colored foods frequently seem to taste better than bland-looking foods, even when the flavor compounds are identical. Foods that somehow look off-color often seem to have off tastes. For thousands of years, human beings have relied on visual cues to help determine what is edible. The color of fruit suggests whether it is ripe, the color of meat whether it is rancid. Flavor researchers sometimes use colored lights to modify the influence of visual cues during taste tests. During one experiment in the early 1970s, people were served an oddly tinted meal of steak and French fries that appeared normal beneath colored lights. Everyone thought the meal tasted fine until the lighting was changed. Once it became apparent that the steak was actually blue and the fries were green, some people became ill.

The Food and Drug Administration does not require flavor companies to disclose the ingredients of their additives, so long as all the chemicals are considered by the agency to be GRAS (Generally Regarded As Safe). This lack of public disclosure enables the companies to maintain the secrecy of their formulas. It also hides the fact that flavor compounds sometimes contain more ingredients than the foods being given their taste. The ubiquitous phrase "artificial strawberry flavor" gives little hint of the chemical wizardry and manufacturing skill that can make a highly processed food taste like a strawberry.

A typical artificial strawberry flavor, like the kind found in a Burger King strawberry milk shake, contains the following ingredients: amyl acetate, amyl butyrate, amyl valerate, anethol, anisyl formate, benzyl acetate, benzyl isobutyrate, butyric acid, cinnamyl isobutyrate, cinnamyl valerate, cognac essential oil, diacetyl, dipropyl ketone, ethyl acetate, ethyl amylketone, ethyl butyrate, ethyl cinnamate, ethyl heptanoate, ethyl heptylate, ethyl lactate, ethyl methylphenylglycidate, ethyl nitrate, ethyl propionate, ethyl valerate, heliotropin, hydroxyphenyl-2-butanone (10 percent solution in alcohol), α-ionone, isobutyl anthranilate, isobutyl butyrate, lemon essential oil, maltol, 4-methylacetophenone, methyl anthranilate, methyl benzoate, methyl cinnamate, methyl heptine carbonate, methyl naphthyl ketone, methyl salicylate, mint essential oil, neroli essential oil, nerolin, neryl isobutyrate, orris butter, phenethyl alcohol, rose, rum ether, γ-undecalactone, vanillin, and solvent.[17]

20 Although flavors usually arise from a mixture of many different 20 volatile chemicals, a single compound often supplies the dominant aroma. Smelled alone, that chemical provides an unmistakable sense of the food. Ethyl-2-methyl butyrate, for example, smells just like an apple. Today's highly processed foods offer a blank palette: whatever chemicals you add to them will give them specific tastes. Adding methyl-2-peridylketone makes something taste like popcorn. Adding ethyl-3-hydroxybutanoate makes it taste like marshmallow. The possibilities are now almost limitless. Without affecting the appearance or nutritional value, processed foods could even be made with aroma chemicals such as hexanal (the smell of freshly cut grass) or 3-methyl butanoic acid (the smell of body odor).

The 1960s were the heyday of artificial flavors. The synthetic versions of flavor compounds were not subtle, but they did not need to be, given the nature of most processed food. For the past twenty years food processors have tried hard to use only "natural flavors" in their products. According to the FDA, these must be derived entirely from natural sources—from herbs, spices, fruits, vegetables, beef, chicken, yeast, bark, roots, etc. Consumers prefer to see natural flavors on a label, out of a belief that they are healthier. The distinction between artificial and natural flavors can be somewhat arbitrary and absurd, based more on how the flavor has been made than on what it actually contains. "A natural flavor," says Terry Acree, a professor of food science at Cornell University, "is a flavor that's been derived with an out-of-date technology."[18] Natural flavors and artificial flavors sometimes contain exactly the same chemicals, produced through different methods. Amyl acetate, for example, provides the dominant note of banana flavor. When you distill it from bananas with a solvent, amyl acetate is a natural flavor. When you produce it by mixing vinegar with amyl alcohol, adding sulfuric acid as a catalyst, amyl acetate is an artificial flavor. Either way it smells and tastes the same. The phrase "natural flavor" is now listed among the ingredients of everything from Stonyfield Farm Organic Strawberry Yogurt to Taco Bell Hot Taco Sauce.

A natural flavor is not necessarily healthier or purer than an artificial one. When almond flavor (benzaldehyde) is derived from natural sources, such as peach and apricot pits, it contains traces of hydrogen cyanide, a deadly poison. Benzaldehyde derived through a different process—by mixing oil of clove and the banana flavor, amyl acetate—does not contain any cyanide. Nevertheless, it is legally considered an artificial flavor and sells at a much lower price. Natural and artificial flavors are now manufactured at the same chemical plants, places that few people would associate with Mother Nature. Calling any of these flavors "natural" requires a flexible attitude toward the English language and a fair amount of irony.

The small and elite group of scientists who create most of the flavor in most of the food now consumed in the United States are called "flavorists." They draw upon a number of disciplines in their work: biology, psychology, physiology, and organic chemistry. A flavorist is a chemist with a trained nose and a poetic sensibility. Flavors are created by blending scores of different chemicals in tiny amounts, a process governed by scientific principles but demanding a fair amount of art. In an age when delicate aromas, subtle flavors, and microwave ovens do not easily coexist, the job of the flavorist is to conjure illusions about processed food and, in the words of one flavor company's literature, to ensure "consumer likeability."[19] The flavorists with whom I spoke were charming, cosmopolitan, and ironic. They were also discreet, in keeping with the dictates of their trade. They were the sort of scientist who not only enjoyed fine wine, but could also tell you the chemicals that gave each vintage its unique aroma. One flavorist compared his work to composing music. A well-made flavor compound will have a "top note," followed by a "dry-down," and a "leveling-off," with different chemicals responsible for each stage. The taste of a food can be radically altered by minute changes in the flavoring mix. "A little odor goes a long way," one flavorist said.

In order to give a processed food the proper taste, a flavorist must always consider the food's "mouthfeel"—the unique combination of textures and chemical interactions that affects how the flavor is perceived. The mouthfeel can be adjusted through the use of various fats, gums, starches, emulsifiers, and stabilizers. The aroma chemicals of a food can be precisely analyzed, but mouthfeel is much harder to measure. How does one quantify a french fry's crispness? Food technologists are now conducting basic research in rheology, a branch of physics that examines the flow and deformation of materials. A number of companies sell sophisticated devices that attempt to measure mouthfeel. The TA.XT2i Texture Analyzer, produced by the Texture Technologies Corporation, performs calculations based on data derived from as many as 250 separate probes.[20] It is essentially a mechanical mouth. It gauges the most important rheological properties of a food—the bounce, creep, breaking point, density, crunchiness, chewiness, gumminess, lumpiness, rubberiness, springiness, slipperiness, smoothness, softness, wetness, juiciness, spreadability, springback, and tackiness.

Some of the most important advances in flavor manufacturing are now occurring in the field of biotechnology. Complex flavors are being made through fermentation, enzyme reactions, fungal cultures, and tissue cultures. All of the flavors being created through these methods— including the ones being synthesized by funguses—are considered natural flavors by the FDA.[21] The new enzyme-based processes are responsible for extremely lifelike dairy flavors. One company now offers not just butter flavor, but also fresh creamy butter, cheesy butter, milky butter, savory melted butter, and super-concentrated butter flavor, in liquid or powder form. The development of new fermentation techniques, as well as new techniques for heating mixtures of sugar and amino acids, have led to the creation of much more realistic meat flavors. The McDonald's Corporation will not reveal the exact origin of the natural flavor added to its french fries. In response to inquiries from *Vegetarian Journal,* however, McDonald's did acknowledge that its fries derive some of their characteristic flavor from "animal products."[22]

Other popular fast foods derive their flavor from unexpected sources. Wendy's Grilled Chicken Sandwich, for example, contains beef extracts.[23] Burger King's BK Broiler Chicken Breast Patty contains "natural smoke flavor."[24] A firm called Red Arrow Products Company specializes in smoke flavor, which is added to barbecue sauces and processed meats. Red Arrow manufactures natural smoke flavor by charring sawdust and capturing the aroma chemicals released into the air. The smoke is captured in water and then bottled, so that other companies can sell food which seems to have been cooked over a fire.

The Vegetarian Legal Action Network recently petitioned the FDA to issue new food labeling requirements for foods that contain natural flavors. The group wants food processors to list the basic origins of their flavors on their labels. At the moment, vegetarians often have no way of knowing whether a flavor additive contains beef, pork, poultry, or shellfish. One of the most widely used color additives—whose presence is often hidden by the phrase "color added"—violates a number of religious dietary restrictions, may cause allergic reactions in susceptible people, and comes from an unusual source. Cochineal extract (also known as carmine or carminic acid) is made from the desiccated bodies of female Dactlyopius coccus Costa, a small insect harvested mainly in Peru and the Canary Islands. The bug feeds on red cactus berries and color from the berries accumulated in the females and their unhatched larvae. The insects are collected, dried, and ground into pigment. It takes about 70,000 of them to produce one pound of carmine, which is used to make processed foods look pink, red, or purple. Dannon strawberry yogurt gets its color from carmine, as do many frozen fruit bars, candies, fruit fillings, and Ocean Spray pink-grapefruit juice drink.

In a meeting room at IFF, Brian Grainger let me sample some of the company's flavors. It was an unusual taste test; there wasn't any food to taste. Grainger is a senior flavorist at IFF, a soft-spoken chemist with graying hair, an English accent, and a fondness for understatement. He could easily be mistaken for a British diplomat or the owner of a West End brasserie with two Michelin stars. Like many in the flavor industry, he has an Old World, old-fashioned sensibility which seems out of step with our brand-conscious, egocentric age. When I suggested that IFF should put its own logo on the products that contain its flavors—instead of allowing other brands to enjoy the consumer loyalty and affection inspired by those flavors—Grainger politely disagreed, assuring me such a thing would never be done. In the absence of public credit or acclaim, the small and secretive fraternity of flavor chemists praises one another's work. Grainger can often tell, by analyzing the flavor formula of a product, which of his counterparts at a rival firm devised it. And he enjoys walking down supermarket aisles, looking at the many products that contain his flavors, even if no one else knows it.

Grainger had brought a dozen small glass bottles from the lab. After he opened each bottle, I dipped a fragrance testing filter into it. The filters were long white strips of paper designed to absorb aroma chemicals without producing off-notes. Before placing the strips of paper before my nose, I closed my eyes. Then I inhaled deeply, and one food after another was conjured from the glass bottles. I smelled fresh cherries, black olives, sautéed onions, and shrimp. Grainger's most remarkable creation took me by surprise. After closing my eyes, I suddenly smelled a grilled hamburger. The aroma was uncanny, almost miraculous. It smelled like someone in the room was flipping burgers on a hot grill. But when I opened my eyes, there was just a narrow strip of white paper and a smiling flavorist.

Why the Fries Taste Good

30   *Food: A Culinary History* (New York: Columbia University Press,   30
1999), edited by Jean-Louis Flandrin and Massimo Montanari, traces the cultural and technological changes in food preparation from prehistoric campfires to the kitchens at McDonald's. A good account of the history of American food processing can be found in John M. Connor and William A. Schiek, *Food Processing: An Industrial Powerhouse in Transition* (New York: John Wiley & Sons, 1997). Harvey Levenstein's *Paradox of Plenty: A Social History of Eating in Modern America* (New York: Oxford University Press, 1993) has a fine chapter on the implications of postwar advances in food processing. For consolidation in the food processing industry and its effects on American farmers, I learned a great deal from the following sources: Charles R. Handy and Alden C. Manchester, "Structure and Performance of the Food System Beyond the Farm Gate," Commodities Economics Division White Paper, USDA Economic Research Service, April 1990; Alden C. Manchester, "The Transformation of U.S. Food Marketing," in *Food and Agricultural Markets: The Quiet Revolution,* edited by Lyle

P. Schertz and Lynn M. Daff (Washington, D.C.: National Planning Association, 1994); *Concentration in Agriculture, A Report of the USDA Advisory Committee on Agricultural Concentration* (Washington, D.C.: USDA Agricultural Marketing Service, June 1996); *A Time to Act: Report of the USDA National Commission on Small Farms* (Washington, D.C.: United States Department of Agriculture, 1998); and William Heffernan, "Consolidation in the Food and Agriculture System," Report to the National Farmers Union, February 5, 1999. A telephone interview, extending for hours, with J. R. Simplot provided much information on the details of his life and the origins of the potato industry in Idaho. Simplot was blunt, charismatic, entertaining, and seemingly tireless. Fred Zerza, the vice president for public and government relations at the J. R. Simplot Company, helped confirm the accuracy of Simplot's remarks. I also relied on "Origins of the J. R. Simplot Company," J. R. Simplot Company, 1997; and James W. Davis, *Aristocrat in Burlap: A History of the Potato in Idaho* (Boise: Idaho Potato Commission, 1992). Paul Patterson, an extension professor of agricultural economics at the University of Idaho, graciously explained to me how potatoes are grown, processed, and sold today. Bert Moulton, at the Potato Growers of Idaho, gave me a sense of the challenges that farmers in his state must now confront. I am grateful to Ben Strand, at the Simplot Food Group, and Bud Mandeville, at Lamb Weston, for giving me tours of their french fry facilities.

The reference books on flavor technology were a pleasure to read; they reminded me of medieval texts on the black arts. Among the works I consulted were *Fenaroli's Handbook of Flavor Ingredients,* vol. 2 (Ann Arbor, Mich.: CRC Press, 1995); Henry B. Heath, *Source Book of Flavors* (Westport, Conn.: Avi Publishing, 1981); Martin S. Peterson and Arnold H. Johnson, *Encyclopedia of Food Science* (Westport, Conn.: Avi Publishing, 1978); Y. H. Hui, *Encyclopedia of Food Science and Technology,* vol. 2 (New York: John Wiley & Sons, 1992); Carl W. Hall, A. W. Farrall, and A. L. Rippen, *Encyclopedia of Food Engineering* (Westport, Conn.: Avi Publishing, 1986); *Flavor Science: Sensible Principles and Techniques,* edited by Terry E. Acree and Roy Teranishi (Washington, D.C.: American Chemical Society, 1993); *Biotechnology for Improved Foods and Flavors,* edited by Gary R. Takeoka, Roy Teranishi, Patrick J. Williams, and Akio Kobayashi (Washington, D.C.: American Chemical Society, 1995); *Flavor Analyses Developments in Isolation and Characterization,* edited by Cynthia J. Mussinan and

Michael J. Novello (Washington, D.C.: American Chemical Society, 1998). I found many useful articles on the flavor industry in journals such as *Food Product Design, Food Engineering, Food Processing, Food Manufacture, Chemistry and Industry, Chemical Market Reporter,* and *Soap-Cosmetics-Chemical Specialties* (now published as *Soap & Cosmetics*). A good overview of the flavor business can be found in *Industry and Trade Summary: Flavor and Fragrance Materials* (Washington, D.C.: U.S. International Trade Commission, USITC Publication 3162, March 1999). Ellen Ruppel Shell wrote a fine article on the work of flavorists more than a decade ago: "Chemists Whip Up a Tasty Mess of Artificial Flavors," *Smithsonian,* May 1986. Terry Acree, a professor of food science technology at Cornell University, was a wonderful resource on the subjects of smell, taste, flavor, and the flavor industry. Bob Bauer, executive director of the National Association of Fruits, Flavors, and Syrups, outlined when and where the flavor industry settled in New Jersey. At International Flavors & Fragrances, I am grateful to Nancy Ciancaglini, Diane Mora, and Brian Grainger, who patiently answered many questions. The flavorists at other firms whom I interviewed shall remain anonymous.

End Notes

1. Since the publication of *Fast Food Nation,* the McDonald's Corporation has been more forthcoming about the ingredients in their fries. For the origins of the new policy, see pages 278–80 of the Afterword.
2. See Elizabeth Mehren, "From Whisks to Molds, James Beard's Personal Possessions to Be Auctioned," *Los Angeles Times,* September 12, 1985.
3. See Olivia Wu, "Fats and Oils in a New Light," *Restaurants and Institutions,* January 15, 1997; and Candy Sagon, "Fry, Fry Again: The Secret of Great French Fries? Frying and more Frying," *Washington Post,* July 9, 1997.
4. A small McDonald's hamburger weighed 102 grams and had 3.6 grams of saturated fat; a small order of fries weighed 68 grams and had 5.05 grams of saturated fat. See "Where's the Fat," *USA Today,* April 5, 1990; Marian Burros, "The Slimming of Fat Fast Food," *New York Times,* July 25, 1990; and Michael F. Jacobson and Sarah Fritscher, *The Completely Revised and Updated Fast-Food Guide* (New York: Workman Publishing, 1991).
5. See "McDonald's Nutrition Facts," McDonald's Corporation, July 1997.
6. See "Personal Consumption Expenditures Table, 1999," Bureau of Economic Analysis, U.S. Department of Commerce.
7. Cited in Joyce Jones, "Labs Conjure Up Fragrances and Flavors to Add Allure," *New York Times,* December 26, 1993.
8. Interview with Nancy Ciancaglini, International Flavors & Fragrances.

9. Cited in Ruth Sambrook, "Do You Smell What I Smell? The Science of Smell and Taste," Institute of Food Research March 1999.

10. See Marilynn Larkin, "Truncated Glutamate Receptor Holds Key to the Fifth Primary Taste," *Lancet,* January 29, 2000; and Andy Coghlan, "In Good Taste," *New Scientist,* January 29, 2000.
    Babies like sweet tastes: See Julie A. Mennella and Gary K. Beauchamp, "Early Flavor Experiences: When Do They Start?" *Nutrition Today,* September 1994.

11. See Jennifer Ordonez, "Hamburger Joints Call Them 'Heavy Users,'" *Wall Street Journal,* January 12, 2000.

12. Interview with Nancy Ciancaglini. *Approximately ten thousand new processed food products:* Cited in Susan Carroll, "Flavors Market Is Poised for Recovery This Year," *Chemical Market Report,* July 19, 1999.

13. Cited in Andrew Bary, "Take a Whiff: Why International Flavors & Fragrances Looks Tempting Right Now," *Barron's,* July 20, 1998.

14. *Its annual revenues have grown almost fifteenfold:* IFF's sales were about $103 million in 1970 and about $1.4 billion in 1999. The first figure comes from "Company History," IFF Advertising and Public Relations. The second is cited in Catherine Curan, "Perfume Company Banks on CEO's Nose for Business," *Crain's NY Business,* June 26, 2000.

15. The chemical is isobutylmethoxy pyrazine. Its minute taste recognition threshold is noted in "Flavor Chemistry Seminar," International Flavors & Fragrances.

16. An industry source provided me with the cost of the flavor in a six-pack of Coke, and I did the rest of the math.

17. This recipe comes from *Fenaroli's Handbook of Flavor Ingredients,* vol. 2, p. 831.

18. Interview with Terry Acree.

19. Quoted in "What Is Flavor? An IFF Consumer Insights Perspective."

20. For a description of such contraptions, see Ray Marsili, "Texture and Mouthfeel: Making Rheology Real," *Food Product Design,* August 1993.

21. See Leticia Mancini, "Expanding Flavor Horizons," *Food Engineering,* November 1991; and Kitty Kevin, "A Brave New World: Capturing the Flavor Bug: Flavors from Microorganisms," *Food Processing,* March 1995.

22. See Jeanne-Marie Bartas, "Vegan Menu Items at Fast Food and Family-Style Restaurants—Part 2," *Vegetarian Journal,* January/February 1998.

23. See "Wendy's Nutrition/Ingredient Guide," Wendy's International, Inc., 1997.

24. See "Nutritional Information," Burger King, 1999.

Questions on Meaning

1. Where does the title of this selection come from? Why do you think the author chose it?
2. According to the author, what percentage of our nation's food is considered processed? Why is this fact a cause for concern?
3. What is the difference between natural and artificial flavors? How did you react to the author's description of how these flavors are created?
4. What is the Universal TA-XT2 Texture Analyzer? What is the field called "rheology"?

Questions on Rhetorical Strategy and Style

1. Why does the author include heavy doses and long lists of technical and scientific diction and data in this selection? What effect might this have on the reader? How is this strategy both objective and emotional?
2. How does the author characterize the companies that form the "flavor industry"? Why does the IFF company remind him of Willy Wonka's chocolate factory? What impression is that analogy intended to create?
3. What is the purpose of the author's brief profile of the senior flavorist Brian Grainger? Why does this selection end with it?

Writing Assignments

1. Write a two-page response to this selection. Where are you inclined to agree with the author's concerns about the fast food industry? On the other hand, where did you question his use of evidence?
2. Write a paper describing the role of the FDA in our society. In your opinion, is the FDA doing enough to protect consumers? Does it have enough leverage or authority? In what ways is it, in your opinion, bogged down by bureaucracy and politics?

Me Talk Pretty One Day

David Sedaris

David Sedaris is considered a master of satire and his readings sell out concert halls across the country. He has a CD entitled David Sedaris at Carnegie Hall. *He read his stories on stage and on the radio, and has had plays produced in New York at La Mama and at Lincoln Center. He has written essays for* Esquire *and* The New Yorker. *His works include* Book of Liz *(2002),* Me Talk Pretty One Day *(2001),* Holidays on Ice *(1998) and* Naked *(1998). He won an Obie Award for a theater production created with his sister, Amy Sedaris, called* One Women Shoe. *Sedaris is a regular contributor to National Public Radio's "This American Life."*

1   At the age of forty-one, I am returning to school and have to think of myself as what my French textbook calls "a true debutant." After paying my tuition, I was issued a student ID, which allows me a discounted entry fee at movie theaters, puppet shows, and Festyland, a far-flung amusement park that advertises with billboards picturing a cartoon stegosaurus sitting in a canoe and eating what appears to be a ham sandwich.

I've moved to Paris with hope of learning the language. My school is an easy ten-minute walk from my apartment, and on the first day of class I arrived early, watching as the returning students greeted one another in the school lobby. Vacations were recounted, and questions were raised concerning mutual friends with names like Kang and Vlatnya. Regardless of their nationalities, everyone spoke in

Reprinted from *Me Talk Pretty One Day*, by permission of Little, Brown & Company. Copyright © 2000 by David Sedaris.

what sounded to me like excellent French. Some accents were better than others, but the students exhibited an ease and confidence I found intimidating. As an added discomfort, they were all young, attractive, and well dressed, causing me to feel not unlike Pa Kettle trapped backstage after a fashion show.

The first day of class was nerve-racking because I knew I'd be expected to perform. That's the way they do it here—it's everybody in the language pool, sink or swim. The teacher marched in, deeply tanned from a recent vacation, and proceeded to rattle off a series of administrative announcements. I've spent quite a few summers in Normandy, and I took a monthlong French class before leaving New York. I'm not completely in the dark, yet I understood only half of what this woman was saying.

"If you have not *meimslsxp* or *lgpdmurct* by this time, then you should not be in this room. Has everyone *apzkiubjxow?* Everyone? Good, we shall begin." She spread out her lesson plan and sighed, saying, "All right, then, who knows the alphabet?"

It was startling because (a) I hadn't been asked that question in a while and (b) I realized, while laughing, that I myself did *not* know the alphabet. They're the same letters, but in France they're pronounced differently. I know the shape of the alphabet but had no idea what it actually sounded like.

"Ahh." The teacher went to the board and sketched the letter *a.* "Do we have anyone in the room whose first name commences with an *ahh?*"

Two Polish Annas raised their hands, and the teacher instructed them to present themselves by stating their names, nationalities, occupations, and a brief list of things they liked and disliked in this world. The first Anna hailed from an industrial town outside of Warsaw and had front teeth the size of tombstones. She worked as a seamstress, enjoyed quiet times with friends, and hated the mosquito.

"Oh, really," the teacher said. "How very interesting. I thought that everyone loved the mosquito, but here, in front of all the world, you claim to detest him. How is it that we've been blessed with someone as unique and original as you? Tell us, please."

The seamstress did not understand what was being said but knew that this was an occasion for shame. Her rabbity mouth huffed for breath, and she stared down at her lap as though the appropriate comeback were stitched somewhere alongside the zipper of her slacks.

10   The second Anna learned from the first and claimed to love sun- 10
shine and detest lies. It sounded like a translation of one of those
Playmate of the Month data sheets, the answers always written in the
same loopy handwriting: "Turn-ons: Mom's famous five-alarm chili!
Turnoffs: insecurity and guys who come on too strong!!!!"

The two Polish Annas surely had clear notions of what they loved
and hated, but like the rest of us, they were limited in terms of vocabulary, and this made them appear less than sophisticated. The teacher
forged on, and we learned that Carlos, the Argentine bandonion
player, loved wine, music, and in his words, "making sex with the wom-
ens of the world." Next came a beautiful young Yugoslav who identified herself as an optimist, saying that she loved everything that life
had to offer.

The teacher licked her lips, revealing a hint of the saucebox we
would later come to know. She crouched low for her attack, placed
her hands on the young woman's desk, and leaned close, saying, "Oh
yeah? And do you love your little war?"

While the optimist struggled to defend herself, I scrambled to
think of an answer to what had obviously become a trick question.
How often is one asked what he loves in this world? More to the point,
how often is one asked and then publicly ridiculed for his answer? I
recalled my mother, flushed with wine, pounding the tabletop late
one night, saying, "Love? I love a good steak cooked rare. I love my
cat, and I love . . ." My sisters and I leaned forward, waiting to hear
our names. "Tums," our mother said. "I love Tums."

The teacher killed some time accusing the Yugoslavian girl of
masterminding a program of genocide, and I jotted frantic notes in
the margins of my pad. While I can honestly say that I love leafing
through medical textbooks devoted to severe dermatological conditions, the hobby is beyond the reach of my French vocabulary, and
acting it out would only have invited controversy.

15   When called upon, I delivered an effortless list of things that I 15
detest: blood sausage, intestinal pâtés, brain pudding. I'd learned these
words the hard way. Having given it some thought, I then declared my
love for IBM typewriters, the French word for *bruise,* and my electric
floor waxer. It was a short list, but still I managed to mispronounce
IBM and assign the wrong gender to both the floor waxer and the
typewriter. The teacher's reaction led me to believe that these mistakes
were capital crimes in the country of France.

"Were you always this *palicmkrexis?*" she asked. "Even a *fiuscrzsa ticiwelmun* knows that a typewriter is feminine."

I absorbed as much of her abuse as I could understand, think-ing—but not saying—that I find it ridiculous to assign a gender to an inanimate object incapable of disrobing and making an occasional fool of itself. Why refer to crack pipe or Good Sir Dishrag when these things could never live up to all that their sex implied?

The teacher proceeded to belittle everyone from German Eva, who hated laziness, to Japanese Yukari, who loved paintbrushes and soap. Italian, Thai, Dutch, Korean, and Chinese—we all left class fool-ishly believing that the worst was over. She'd shaken us up a little, but surely that was just an act designed to weed out the deadweight. We didn't know it then, but the coming months would teach us what it was like to spend time in the presence of a wild animal, something completely unpredictable. Her temperament was not based on a series of good and bad days but, rather, good and bad moments. We soon learned to dodge chalk and protect our heads and stomachs whenever she approached us with a question. She hadn't yet punched anyone, but it seemed wise to protect ourselves against the inevitable.

Though we were forbidden to speak anything but French, the teacher would occasionally use us to practice any of her five fluent languages.

"I hate you," she said to me one afternoon. Her English was flaw-less. "I really, really hate you." Call me sensitive, but I couldn't help but take it personally.

After being singled out as a lazy *kfdtinvfm,* I took to spending four hours a night on my homework, putting in even more time whenever we were assigned an essay. I suppose I could have gotten by with less, but I was determined to create some sort of identity for myself: David the hard worker, David the cut-up. We'd have one of those "complete this sentence" exercises, and I'd fool with the thing for yours, invariably settling on something like "A quick run around the lake? I'd love to! Just give me a moment while I strap on my wooden leg." The teacher, through word and action, conveyed the message that if this was my idea of an identity, she wanted nothing to do with it.

My fear and discomfort crept beyond the borders of the class-room and accompanied me out onto the wide boulevards. Stopping for a coffee, asking directions, depositing money in my bank account:

these things were out of the question, as they involved having to speak. Before beginning school, there'd been no shutting me up, but now I was convinced that everything I said was wrong. When the phone rang, I ignored it. If someone asked me a question, I pretended to be deaf. I knew my fear was getting the best of me when I started wondering why they don't sell cuts of meat in vending machines.

My only comfort was the knowledge that I was not alone. Huddled in the hallways and making the most of our pathetic French, my fellow students and I engaged in the sort of conversation commonly overheard in refugee camps.

"Sometime me cry alone at night."

"That be common for I, also, but be more strong, you. Much work and someday you talk pretty. People start love you soon. Maybe tomorrow, okay."

Unlike the French class I had taken in New York, here there was no sense of competition. When the teacher poked a shy Korean in the eyelid with a freshly sharpened pencil, we took no comfort in the fact that, unlike Hyeyoon Cho, we all knew the irregular past tense of the verb *to defeat*. In all fairness, the teacher hadn't meant to stab the girl, but neither did she spend much time apologizing, saying only, "Well, you should have been *vkkdyo* more *kdeynfulh*."

Over time it became impossible to believe that any of us would ever improve. Fall arrived and it rained every day, meaning we would now be scolded for the water dripping from our coats and umbrellas. It was mid-October when the teaching singled me out, saying, "Every day spent with you is like having a cesarean section." And it struck me that, for the first time since arriving in France, I could understand every word that someone was saying.

Understanding doesn't mean that you can suddenly speak the language. Far from it. It's a small step, nothing more, yet its rewards are intoxicating and deceptive. The teacher continued her diatribe and I settled back, bathing in the subtle beauty of each new curse and insult.

"You exhaust me with your foolishness and reward my efforts with nothing but pain, do you understand me?"

The world opened up, and it was with great joy that I responded, "I know the thing that you speak exact now. Talk me more, you, plus, please, plus."

Questions on Meaning

1. Have you ever been in a situation where you could not fluently speak a language and thus felt awkward and powerless? What was this experience like for you? Explain in detail. How did you manage to maintain your sense of identity?
2. Explain the attitude of the teacher. It appears plainly rude, but it is also a reflection of more complicated and problematic traditions. As students, what do you make of the teacher's behavior?
3. What understanding does the author come to at the end? What "world opened up" and why was it joyful?

Questions on Rhetorical Strategy and Style

1. An important characteristic of this essay is its humor. What manner of humor is it? How does it serve to advance the author's perspective?
2. When the teacher asks the students if they know the alphabet, the author realizes that he does not. What is the symbolic significance of this reference to the basic units of language?
3. A good portion of the essay is devoted to the two Annas, the Argentine bandonion player, and the Yugoslav optimist. What purpose do they serve the essay? Discuss each one separately.

Writing Assignments

1. The author's experience might be unusual in some respects, but in one sense, it is a typical story of the return of a so-called nontraditional student. If you have a similar experience, write an essay describing it. If you know such a student, interview him or her and write a profile of that person's experiences.
2. The essay is an example of a literacy narrative. These are essays that describe someone's experience with acquiring a literacy that results in empowerment. A famous example of such a narrative is the essay "Learning to Read and Write" by Frederick Douglass. Write your own narrative of how you came to be a reader and a writer. In your essay, detail specific experiences that illustrate your story.

The End of the Affair

David Sedaris

David Sedaris (1956–), famed commentator on National Public Radio's "This American Life," grew up in a family that was both bizarre and perfectly ordinary. This family life and his own coming to terms with himself, his sexuality, and his own worldview have led to gloriously funny memoirs: Dress Your Family in Corduroy and Denim *(2004);* Me Talk Pretty One Day *(2000); and* Naked *(1997). Sedaris creates a wonderful world of the postmodern American family in all its zany permutations and combinations.*

Two people attend a film together and experience romantic tragedy in wildly different ways. The difference in response leads to misunderstandings and to insights for the author. No one sees the world through the same eyes, no matter what the situation.

1   On a summer evening in Paris, Hugh and I went to see *The End of the Affair,* a Neil Jordan adaptation of the Graham Greene novel. I had trouble keeping my eyes open because I was tired and not completely engaged. Hugh had trouble keeping his eyes open because they were essentially swollen shut: He sobbed from beginning to end, and by the time we left the theater, he was completely dehydrated. I asked if he always cried during comedies, and he accused me of being grossly insensitive, a charge I'm trying to plea-bargain down to simply obnoxious.

Looking back, I should have known better than to accompany Hugh to a love story. Such movies are always a danger, as unlike battling aliens or going undercover to track a serial killer, falling in love is something most adults have actually experienced at some point in their lives. The theme is universal and encourages the viewer to make a number of unhealthy comparisons, ultimately raising the question "Why can't *our* lives be like that?" It's a box best left unopened, and its avoidance explains the continued popularity of vampire epics and martial-arts extravaganzas.

The End of the Affair made me look like an absolute toad. The movie's voracious couple was played by Ralph Fiennes and Julianne Moore, who did everything but eat each other. Their love was doomed and clandestine, and even when the bombs were falling, they looked radiant. The picture was fairly highbrow, so I was surprised when the director employed a device most often seen in TV movies of the week: Everything's going along just fine and then one of the characters either coughs or sneezes, meaning that within 20 minutes he or she will be dead. It might have been different had Julianne Moore suddenly started bleeding from the eyes, but coughing, in and of itself, is fairly pedestrian. When she did it, Hugh cried. When I did it, he punched me in the shoulder and told me to move. "I can't wait until she dies," I whispered. I don't know if it was their good looks or their passion, but something about Julianne Moore and Ralph Fiennes put me on the defensive.

I'm not as unfeeling as Hugh accuses me of being, but things change once you've been together for more than 10 years. They rarely make movies about long-term couples, and for good reason: Our lives are boring. The courtship had its moments, but now we've become the predictable Part II no one in his right mind would ever pay to see ("Look, they're opening their electric bill!") Hugh and I have been together for so long that in order to arouse extraordinary passion, we need to engage in physical combat. Once, he hit me on the back of the head with a broken wineglass, and I fell to the floor pretending to be unconscious. That was romantic, or would have been had he rushed to my side rather than stepping over my body to fetch the dustpan.

Call me unimaginative, but I still can't think of anyone else I'd rather be with. On our worst days, I figure things will work themselves out. Otherwise, I really don't give our problems much thought. Neither of us would ever publicly display affection; we're just not that type. We can't profess love without talking through hand puppets, and we'd never consciously sit down to discuss our relationship. These, to me, are good things. They were fine with Hugh as well, until he saw that damned movie and was reminded that he has other options.

The picture ended at about 10, and afterward we went for coffee at a little place across the street from the Luxembourg Gardens. I was ready to wipe the movie out of my mind, but Hugh was still under its spell. He looked as though his life had not only passed him by but paused along the way to spit in his face. Our coffee arrived, and as he blew his nose into a napkin, I encouraged him to look on the bright side. "Listen," I said, "we maybe don't live in wartime London, but in terms of the occasional bomb scare, Paris is a pretty close second. We both love bacon and country music, what more could you possibly want?"

What more could he want? It was an incredibly stupid question and when he failed to answer, I was reminded of just how lucky I truly am. Movie characters might chase each other through the fog or race down the stairs of burning buildings, but that's for beginners. Real love amounts to withholding the truth, even when you're offered the perfect opportunity to hurt someone's feelings. I wanted to say something to this effect, but my hand puppets were back home in their drawer. Instead, I pulled my chair a few inches closer, and we sat silently at our little table on the square, looking for all the world like two people in love.

Questions on Meaning

1. Why do you think that a movie with a heterosexual couple in wartime London evokes such a romantic response from gay Hugh?
2. The key feelings in the relationship are, according to Sedaris, expressed through hand puppets. Why is this important to the humor of the piece?
3. Why is it so important that Hugh does not pick a fight at the end of the piece? How does this response show that the two are in love?

Questions on Rhetorical Strategy and Style

1. The essay demonstrates many aspects of humor writing. How does Sedaris use the examples of his sleeping eyes and Hugh's tearful eyes to set up the humorous style of the essay?
2. The essay begins and ends with images, especially the hand puppets. How do these images construct the meaning and the mood of the essay?
3. In the middle of the essay, Sedaris explains why he is so amused with the sentimental movie: The plot is predictable and a little silly. How does he show the predictability of the movie's plot?

Writing Assignments

1. Write about a movie that you have found either unintentionally amusing or completely boring. Why did you react the way that you did? What was wrong with the movie for you?
2. Recount an example of a situation in which you have disagreed with a lover or a good friend. How was the conflict resolved? What effect did the disagreement have on the relationship?
3. Read other essays by Sedaris, and write about his perspective on the world. If possible, listen to an episode of National Public Radio's *This American Life* in which Sedaris reads one of his essays. Write about Sedaris's humor and his view of the world. What techniques does he use to produce humor? Why does he tend to win the reader's and listener's sympathy?

The Case for Curling Up with a Book

Carol Shields

Carol Shields (1935–2003) was born in Chicago and grew up in Oak Park, Illinois. She studied at Hanover College, the University of Exeter (England), and the University of Ottawa, and now lives in Winnipeg. Shields has won many prizes and awards for her fiction, including a Pulitzer Prize for The Stone Diaries *(1993) and both the National Book Critics Circle Award and the Prix de Lire in 1998 for* Larry's Party *(1997). In July of 2003, she died from complications of breast cancer. Her final novel,* Unless, *was published in 2002 and was nominated for, among others, the* Booker Prize. *In the following essay Shields writes eloquently on the experience of absorbing reading.*

1   **S**ome years ago a Canadian politician, one of our more admirable figures, announced that he was cutting back on his public life because it interfered with his reading. *His reading*[—]notice the possessive pronoun, like saying his arm or his leg[—]and notice too, the assumption that human beings carry, like a kind of cerebral brief case, this built-in commitment to time and energy[:] *their reading.*

I'm told that people no longer know how to curl up with a book. The body has forgotten how to curl. Either we snack on paperbacks while waiting for the bus or we hunch over our books with a yellow underliner in hand. Or, more and more, we sit before a screen and "interact."

Curling up with a book can be accomplished in a variety of ways: in bed for instance, with a towel on a sunlit beach, or from an armchair parked next to a good reading lamp. What it absolutely requires

---

"The Case for Curling Up with a Book," by Carol Shields from *The Journal*, Spring 1997. Reprinted by permission of the Bella Pomer Agency, Canada.

is a block of uninterrupted time, solitary time and our society some-times looks with pity on the solitary, that woman alone at the movies, that poor man sitting by himself at his restaurant table. Our hearts go out to them, but reading, by definition, can only be done alone. I would like to make the case today for solitary time, for a life with space enough to curl up with a book.

Reading, at least since human beings learned to read silently (and what a cognitive shift that was!) requires an extraordinary effort at pay-ing attention, at remaining alert. The object of our attention matters less, in a sense, than the purity of our awareness. As the American writer Sven Birkerts says, it is better, better in terms of touching the self within us, that we move from a state of half-distraction to one of full atten-tion. When we read with attention, an inner circuit of the brain is satisfyingly completed. We feel our perceptions sharpen and acquire edge. Reading, as many of you have discovered, is one of the very few things you can do only by shining your full awareness on the task. We can make love, cook, listen to music, shop for groceries, add up columns of figures all with our brain, our self that is, divided and dis-tracted. But print on the page demands *all* of us. It is so complex, its cognitive circuitry so demanding; the black strokes on the white page must be apprehended and translated into ideas, and ideas fitted into patterns, the patterns then shifted and analyzed. The eye travels back-ward for a moment; this in itself is a technical marvel, rereading a sentence or a paragraph, extracting the sense, the intention, the essence of what is offered.

5   And ironically, this singleness of focus delivers a doubleness of per-ception. You are invited into a moment sheathed in nothing but itself. Reading a novel, *curled up* with a novel, you are simultaneously in your arm chair and in, for instance, the garden of Virginia Woolf in the year 1927, or a shabby Manitoba farmhouse conjured by Margaret Laurence, . . . participating fully in another world while remaining conscious of the core of your self, that self that may be hardwired into our bodies or else developed slowly, created over the long distance of our lives.

We are connected through our work, through our familial chain and, by way of the Internet, to virtually everyone in the world. So what of the private self which comes tantalizingly alive under the circle of the reading lamp, that self that we only occasionally touch and then with trepidation. We use the expression "being lost in a book," but we are really closer to a state of being found. Curled up with a novel about an

East Indian family for instance, we are not so much escaping our own splintered and decentred world as we are enlarging our sense of self, our multiplying possibilities and expanded experience. People are, after all, tragically limited: we can live in only so many places, work at a small number of jobs or professions; we can love only a finite number of people. Reading, and particularly the reading of fiction (perhaps I really do have a sales pitch here) lets us be other, to touch and taste the other, to sense the shock and satisfaction of otherness. A novel lets us be ourselves and yet enter another person's boundaried world, to share in a private gaze between reader and writer. *Your* reading, and here comes the possessive pronoun again, can be part of your life and there will be times when it may be the best part. . . .

[A] written text, as opposed to electronic information, has formal order, tone, voice, irony, persuasion. We can inhabit a book; we can possess it and be possessed by it. The critic and scholar Martha Nussbaum believes that attentive readers of serious fiction cannot help but be compassionate and ethical citizens. The rhythms of prose train the empathetic imagination and the rational emotions. . . .

Almost all of [us are] plugged into the electronic world in one way or another, reliant on it for its millions of bytes of information. But a factoid, a nugget of pure information, or even the ever-widening web of information, while enabling us to perform, does relatively little to nourish us. A computer connects facts but cannot reflect upon them. There is no depth, no embeddedness. It is, literally, software, plaintext, language prefabricated and sorted into byte sizes. It does not, in short, aspire; it rarely sings. Enemies of the book want to see information freed from the prison of the printed page, putting faith instead in free floating information and this would be fine if we weren't human beings, historical beings, thinking beings with a hunger for diversion, for narrative, for consolation, for exhortation.

We need literature on the page because it allows us to experience more fully, to imagine more deeply, enabling us to live more freely. Reading, [we] are in touch with [our best selves], and I think, too, that reading shortens the distance we must travel to discover that our most private perceptions are, in fact, universally felt. *Your* reading will intersect with the axis of *my* reading and of his reading and of her reading. Reading, then, offers us the ultimate website, where attention, awareness, reflection, understanding, clarity, and civility come together in a transformative experience.

Questions on Meaning

1. Explain Shields' assertion that a reader is closer to the state of being found rather than lost in a book.
2. Describe the mental state that reading evokes, according to Shields.
3. Why does Shields feel that solitude is so important to reading?

Questions on Strategy and Style

1. What, according to Shields, differentiates Internet reading from curling up with a book?
2. Why is it particularly effective to tell the story of a Canadian politician who cut back on public life to attend to his reading? What does that tell you about his view of reading?
3. What point is Shields making in describing reading as "the ultimate website"?

Writing Assignments

1. Spend some time surfing the Internet and some time reading a good book that interests you. Then do some journaling about the two experiences. Write an essay that contrasts the two forms of reading, using the material in your journal to help fill out the details of the essay.
2. Ask elder siblings, parents, and grandparents about their reading habits. Write a report that describes the changes in reading across the generations.
3. Recall your favorite childhood books and the places where you read them (or where they were read to you). Then write a memoir about curling up with a book.

Responsibility

Russell Smith

Russell Smith (1963–) was born in South Africa and became a Canadian citizen in 1972. He was educated at Queen's University in Ontario and at the universities of Poitiers and Paris in France. Smith has spent much of his career as a journalist writing about the urban scene in Toronto. He has published two novels, How Insensitive *(1994), and* Noise *(1998). "Responsibility" appeared in 1999 in a collection of short stories entitled* Young Men. *In it we encounter a son and his mother trying to come to terms with each other's values.*

1 "Perhaps you don't value it now, but as you get older money becomes more important," said his mother. She was sitting in the breakfast nook with her tea, looking out at the bird feeder. James too was looking out at the garden, standing at the sliding doors. Anyone who talked in the kitchen did so while looking at the garden.

"I'm sure that's true, but you see, believe it or not, I'm hoping to make money from my writing, eventually. I know that seems ridiculous to you and Dad." He waited for her to contradict him. "Some people actually make a great deal of money from what I . . . the kind of writing I'm trying to do. I'm talking to some people about a documentary, about my music column, it could be a book, it could . . ." He clenched his jaw shut. He felt helpless. "It could be the kind of book that would sell outside this little . . . anyway. Yes, it's a bigger risk, yes, but actually it could pay off very well, if you do something successful. So actually I'm being *more* ambitious than you and Dad were."

"I guess it's just the risk I worry about."

It was no longer surprising that this conversation came up, even that it came up on the Sunday afternoons of his visits, that it came up just as simultaneous relief and tension about the trip back to the city were growing with a mental hum, ripening in him, in his nervous and circulatory systems like some slowly developing and ultimately convulsive disease, just as they were all about to begin the bargaining about which parent in which car would drive him to the bus station and dump him in its stained limbo air and promise of metamorphosis, this was so familiar it was no longer surprising; what was surprising was how unfailingly and deeply it seared him with a fine painful clear sense of abandonment, as would some long penetrating parental angioscopic device, every time, and made him think, every time, that perhaps now, this time, was the time it would all come out, it would come clear exactly what it was about what he did that so disappointed her, and why her disappointment so irritated—no, worse, let's be honest—so hurt him. He said quickly, "And you worry about my lifestyle, that I'm not married and—"

5 "I don't care that you're not married, if you're happy." 5

"Yes you do. Don't pretend you don't. Of course you do. You'd like me to be married and have kids and a minivan and come over on Sundays and talk about eavestroughing with Dad."

"*I* don't think you could *handle* kids," said his mother with the restrained tone of someone producing an ace.

"No, I couldn't," said James.

She was silent for a moment. Then she said, "But when you do have children, you'll want to be able to provide for them, and I think you should think of that now."

10 He turned to her and said gently, "Mom, what would you say if I 10 told you I might never have children? Do you think there's something wrong with that?"

She was silent again. She twirled a strand of hair around a finger, which meant that she was agitated. She would never sit down for so long in mid-morning unless she was upset. The tea in her cup was getting cold.

"You think that's somehow morally wrong, not to have children, don't you?" said James. He felt merciless; he felt this was the time to get it all out.

"No," she said quickly, "not at all. It's you I'm thinking of. I just think that you would be happier with children. Having children . . .

253

it takes you out of yourself. You would stop chasing after every girl you met and—"

"What if I don't want to stop chasing after every girl I meet? You seem to feel that I have to at a certain point, because everybody does. Why? What if it makes me happy?"

"It won't make you happy forever."

"Will children?"

She was silent again. "Look, all I know is that all this tension in your life, all that awful time you had with Alison and that girl in the city when they wouldn't speak to each other and—"

"Yes," said James, "I know, go on."

"All that wouldn't happen if you had a family. You wouldn't have time for it. And all I know is that when you have a child, that's the most important thing. If your child is happy, then you're happy, it's as simple as that. And you're—what is it that Joanne Winterson always said? You're only as happy as your most unhappy child. It's true." She took quick sips at her tea, which by now was surely cold.

"Sounds terrific." He puffed out his cheeks. "Just remind me again why this is a better system?"

"Oh, don't be so snooty. You're so *arrogant*."

"What? Sorry. I'm not following you."

"Yes you are. You know exactly what I mean. You're so condescending."

James turned back to the garden. "I have no idea what you're talking about." But he did. He made an effort to make an effort to think about trying to be nicer. He said, "I don't mean to be nasty about anyone's choices. As long as you *make* choices."

"What about Jennifer? Doesn't she want children?"

James took a deep breath. "Well, not right now she doesn't. She's trying to get her own career going, she's in the same boat as me. We have more . . ." He stopped himself. He said, "She's just too busy, and she doesn't have the money or the stability in her life for it. She doesn't want kids right now."

"Well, she's over thirty now. She doesn't have much time left."

"So maybe she won't. Maybe she won't have time. I'm not sure, because we haven't talked about it a lot, but I think that right now at least she isn't too worried about it. She's thinking about herself, about her career. Like me."

"Oh! But . . ." His mother leaned over the table to pour more tea. She spilled the tea and said, *"Bother."* She was frowning and biting her lip; she really was agitated and maybe about to cry. He wasn't sure what it was all about and he got agitated too. He handed her a cloth. At least they were getting somewhere.

30 "But what?" He sat down at the table.   30

She wiped the table with furious speed. "What she wants, what you want," she said, shaking her head. "You people—it's always what *you* want. You just think you can play around and have fun forever."

"Yes. Perhaps we do. What should we do instead?" His heart was beating fast.

She didn't answer.

"What is it, exactly, Mom, that upsets you? That I don't have enough responsibilities in life? Is that it?"

35 There was a long silence and then she said in a faint voice, "Yes." 35

"I have too much fun. I don't have enough to tie me down."

"James, if your father and I had felt like you," she said urgently, looking at him, "then you wouldn't even *be* here!"

"Right." James rubbed his face with his hands. "The logic of this is growing too much for me." He sighed. "Mom. You don't under-stand what I'm . . . Look at it this way. Imagine you had never had me. Or Kurt. Then you wouldn't, you wouldn't feel a responsibility to us, right? Because we wouldn't—"

"I can't imagine that," she said in a higher voice, her indignant voice. "Lucky for you, I couldn't imagine that."

40 "That's my point, Mom. That you're not imagining what I'm—" 40

"You think," she said rapidly, "that you can just live this student life forever, have no—"

"Why not? Why can't I—"

"But it's not all fun. At a certain point you have to pay the piper. At a certain point you just have to stop fooling around and accept your responsibilities."

James looked at her. She was fidgeting with a doily. "What responsibilities? My family responsibilities?"

45 *"Yes."*   45

"Mom, this is what I'm trying to get at. Think about it. If I don't have a wife or kids then who do I have a responsibility to?"

There was a long silence. She was fingering the doily on the tray that held the salt and pepper shakers and the bowl of sugar and the tiny antique silver spoons from the ancestral Germany that was unknown to them all, moving her eyes from the doily out to the bird feeder where there were no birds and back again.

"What is it?" he said more gently. "Is it that you think I have a responsibility to Jennifer, or maybe to you?"

"No, no, not to me, certainly."

50 "Is it just that you feel I have a responsibility to *have* kids? So that I can feel a responsibility to them? This is what I mean about logical—"

"No, no, I'm not saying that. I'm not saying you *have* to."

He waited. She did not go on. "I don't have to."

"No."

"Okay, so what—why—"

55 "I don't know." Her voice sounded weak now. "I'm not sure. I'm not sure—I don't know what I mean." She played with the doily.

James thought about this. He looked at the doily, which she had inherited from her mother who had crocheted in it Portage la Prairie, a place he had never been, and wondered for some reason how old she had been when it had been crocheted. He had a black-and-white picture of his mother in a rather Chanel-like tweed suit, leaning against the hood of a large American car, against an unblemished sky and a flat wheaty horizon of laughably pure rural nowhere. He wondered how old she had been in that photograph; probably younger, yes, much younger than him. "Are you saying, Mom, maybe that . . . maybe it's just that you, when you were young, I mean younger, you felt you didn't . . ." He stopped himself. He wanted to say, You *didn't have a choice.*

"Oh, we didn't even think about it. Everyone had children. It was all—it was what we wanted."

"Right." He paused. He had to go very carefully here. "But have you ever thought about how, about how things might have . . . about what you might have done if you hadn't"—he took a deep breath—"had me and Kurt."

She stood up abruptly and stood in the window, while James thought, She never does that, never takes a moment to stare at the garden without a vacuum cleaner or a duster in her hand. Her arms were folded and her shoulders hunched. She said, "You sound as if you *want* me to think about that."

60 "No." He didn't know what she was getting at, but the safe answer was no. "No, no. I just, I'm thinking of me, in my case—"

"If I hadn't got married? Is that what you mean?"

"I don't know. Was it impossible to get married and not have children? Not that I'm saying that's what you should—"

"Well, I suppose it wasn't impossible. But I wanted children. Your dad wanted children. And, you know, Jamie"—she gave a small laugh—"I was very flattered, you know, that Hans wanted to marry me. He was, I knew he was going to be very successful. You didn't turn down opportunity, in those days."

James laughed, too. As the refrigerator began to hum unevenly, he became aware of a cloud of worry too vague to describe, forming over his head. "It meant your problems were solved."

65 "Sure. And he wanted children too, you know, it wasn't just 65 my idea."

"Yes. Okay. But what, I guess I mean to ask, what if you hadn't got married?"

"I suppose I would have had to get some kind of job."

James asked slowly, "Did you want . . . to do that?"

"No. I suppose not." She paused. "I don't know."

70 He held himself very still. Her voice had gone small as she had 70 said it. His worry buzzed and shifted overhead. He didn't know what was approaching them here, but it was something grey and tight. He thought of the bus station, its cigarette air.

"I guess you don't respect at all what I did," she said in a wavering voice. "Bringing you two boys up."

"Of course I do, Mom. Of course I do. I know how much work it is, how hard—"

"No you don't."

It was James's turn to be silent.

75 She said, in a voice that fluttered and broke, "There was a time 75 when people thought it was valuable, to run a house and sew and clean and cook for two boys and a man, and educate the boys, the way I read to you—"

"Mom," said James, agitated, "of course I value that. Of course I respect—"

"No you don't. You don't think it meant—it's not important to you. You think if it's not some big career it's not difficult and it's, it's some kind of cop-out."

"No," said James.

"I've heard you say it. When you found out Alison had a child you said it was a cop-out."

80   James opened his mouth and closed it. It was true, not only that 80 he had said it, but that he believed it. It was a cop-out.

"The work of about twenty-two years. A cop-out."

He looked at the doily, her moving hands.

"And you're not the only one," she said quietly. "I can tell people laugh at me. The younger wives at Dad's firm."

James went cold. "No they don't. They wouldn't."

85   "They think we're ridiculous, me and Joanne and . . . all of my 85 friends. I can tell. And maybe they're right."

"Oh, Mom, don't be—"

"You know, Jamie, I was thinking about this last week. I was trying to remember all the jobs I've had in my life. All the paying jobs." She counted on her fingers. "I used to babysit, as a teenager. I must have earned less than a dollar an hour. And I was in a nursing course when I met Dad, but I worked in an office in the summers. So that was two summers, about four months' total. And then I worked at the kindergarten, where you and Kurt went, for about two years, part-time, for a little extra cash, when we were just starting out."

James listened to the anxious fridge.

"So," she said, "I counted it all up. All the money I've ever earned. Myself. And I figured it came to a total of about three thousand five hundred dollars. In my whole life. That's all I've ever earned myself. I never thought about it, until now. I guess, I guess that's all the young women see. The other things we did, what we did, it's not important to anyone any more. I guess."

90   The refrigerator grunted, shuddered and stopped humming. The 90 kitchen was silent.

He said as gently as he could, "Yes it is, Mom. I don't think the money's important. I do think it was a disappointing choice for Alison, because she had her music, and her . . ." He trailed off. He did not want to imply that his mother had had nothing else to do. But it was true. "She gave up her music. But you, there were fewer opportunities at that—"

"And I didn't have anything I could have done? Is that what you mean? And Alison shouldn't have done the most important thing in the world?" She balled her little hand into a fist and made to punch his shoulder, but of course she didn't. "You're all so selfish." Her voice wavered again.

"What?" said James, alarmed. "Who is? Alison?"

"It's just that . . . you're all so arrogant about everything. It's just not very . . . it's not very *nice*." Her voice cracked and he realized she was in tears.

95   He stood behind her and put a hand on her shoulder. His worry 95 was gone, and in its place he had a pure, liquid anguish, a sense that the air itself was sad, over the silent garden, that forces were moving all around him like invisible rain. He said, "What isn't nice, Mom? Tell me."

"I can't explain it. It's just that . . ." She sniffled. "Nice people . . ." She paused and coughed. Then she said, loud and cracking, as if in physical distress, *"Nice people don't do things for themselves."*

She was really sobbing.

He felt as if the floor of his stomach had opened, and there was darkness below it.

He patted her shoulder. She sobbed and shook. There was nothing else to do but pat her shoulder. He looked around the immaculate kitchen, the slate-tiled floor, the island and the overhead wrought-iron pot hooks she had campaigned so hard to have his father put in. The sandy wall, the pristine counters. The pot lids were stacked in the pot-lid rack; the utensils hung from hooks over the island. "I'm sorry, Mom," he said. "*You're* nice."

100   He tried a laugh and she giggled, too, a sniffling giggle as if she 100 was embarrassed, and wiped her eyes and blew her nose. He exhaled in relief, for if she was blowing her nose already, the whole thing was okay. He glanced at his watch: there was a bus back to the city at 3:15.

He put his arm around her shoulder and they looked at the empty garden, the wrought-iron chairs. He wondered what she was going to do that afternoon, after he got back on his bus. His dad had had to go into the office. And Kurt was gone, probably gone for good now, even when he got back from Whistler he would be looking for a job in the city. James wondered for a second if he should stay, maybe take her out to the craft shops. He thought of the drive through the industrial park, the deserted highways, the hot little shops. He thought of the handmade towel racks and calico quilts and apple dolls they would look at. The photo frames in amusing shapes. If they drove out of town, they would have to stop and buy corn and squash, for it was that time, which would go into soups and preserves and pie fillings which only his dad would eat.

He stared at the garden. There were no birds at the bird feeder. The house was dead quiet; the whole neighbourhood was silent as a tomb. And he knew then that he wasn't nice, he wasn't a nice person, because all he wanted to do was get out, get the hell out of there.

Questions on Meaning

1. We quickly learn that the mother and son have discussed the topic of responsibility before. However, it seems that lately the topic has come up more frequently. What does this suggest about how relations are developing?

2. At one point in the story, the son looks at a photo of his mother when she was young, "leaning against the unblemished sky and a flat wheaty horizon." What does this image represent? The mother and the son have two different value systems. Why is it often difficult for people, even loved ones, to reconcile such conflicts?

3. What perspectives on the concept of responsibility are represented in this story? In what ways do the mother's and son's values on this subject conflict? Where, perhaps, do they converge?

Questions on Rhetorical Strategy and Style

1. The reference to the garden frames this story, that is, it opens and closes it. What is its significance in the story? Typically, we think of a garden as appealing to the senses. Yet here, the image of the garden expresses something quite different. What does it suggest about this family?

2. Early in the story, the author lets readers know that this conversation has taken place before. Why is this important for us to know? What language informs readers of the son's attitude and frame of mind?

3. The story uses the third person. This strategy creates distance between the writer and his subject. Would you say the narrative perspective is subject, objective, or omniscient? Explain your response.

Writing Assignments

1. Write down a dialogue you remember well enough to recreate. Attempt to convey what is happening in the scene through the speech itself and by descriptions of actions, gestures, and states of mind. Is there a conflict of some kind? Does the dialogue reveal what transaction is taking place?

2. Write a third-person narrative of a situation involving several people. In your narrative, take time to introduce each character and establish, through descriptive detail, the setting.

Beauty

Susan Sontag

*Susan Sontag (1933–2004) was born in New York City and
reared in Arizona and California. She attended the University of California at Berkeley, the University of Chicago
(from which she graduated at age 18), received a graduate
degree from Harvard University, and served as an instructor
and writer-in-residence at several colleges. Accomplished as
both a fiction and nonfiction writer, Sontag was best known
for her social commentary, which often focused on trends in
literature, art, and film. Her books include* Against Interpretation and Other Essays *(1966),* Death Kit *(1967),*
Trip to Hanoi *(1968),* The Style of Radical Will *(1969),*
On Photography *(1976),* Illness as a Metaphor *(1978),*
AIDS and Its Metaphors *(1989),* The Volcano Lover
(1992), and Alice in Bed *(1993). She won the National
Book Award for* In America *in 2004. She also wrote and
directed four movies:* Duet for Cannibals *(1969),* Brother
Carl *(1971),* Promised Lands *(1974), and* Unguided
Tour *(1975). In this 1975 essay, Sontag argued that our so-
ciety traps women into an endless preoccupation with out-
ward appearance by associating beauty with femininity.*

1   For the Greeks, beauty was a virtue: a kind of excellence. Persons
then were assumed to be what we now have to call—lamely, en-
viously—whole persons. If it did occur to the Greeks to distinguish between a person's "inside" and "outside," they still expected that
inner beauty would be matched by beauty of the other kind. The well-
born young Athenians who gathered around Socrates found it quite
paradoxical that their hero was so intelligent, so brave, so honorable,

so seductive—and so ugly. One of Socrates' main pedagogical acts was to be ugly—and teach those innocent, no doubt splendid-looking disciples of his how full of paradoxes life really was.

They may have resisted Socrates' lesson. We do not. Several thousand years later, we are more wary of the enchantments of beauty. We not only split off—with the greatest facility—the "inside" (character, intellect) from the "outside" (looks); but we are actually surprised when someone who is beautiful is also intelligent, talented, good.

It was principally the influence of Christianity that deprived beauty of the central place it had in classical ideals of human excellence. By limiting excellence (*virtus* in Latin) to *moral* virtue only, Christianity set beauty adrift—as an alienated, arbitrary, superficial enchantment. And beauty has continued to lose prestige. For close to two centuries it has become a convention to attribute beauty to only one of the two sexes: the sex which, however Fair, is always Second. Associating beauty with women has put beauty even further on the defensive, morally.

A beautiful woman, we say in English. But a handsome man. "Handsome" is the masculine equivalent of—and refusal of—a compliment which has accumulated certain demeaning overtones, by being reserved for women only. That one can call a man "beautiful" in French and in Italian suggests that Catholic countries—unlike those countries shaped by the Protestant version of Christianity—still retain some vestiges of the pagan admiration for beauty. But the difference, if one exists, is of degree only. In every modern country that is Christian or post-Christian, women *are* the beautiful sex—to the detriment of the notion of beauty as well as of women.

5 To be called beautiful is thought to name something essential to women's character and concerns. (In contrast to men—whose essence is to be strong, or effective, or competent.) It does not take someone in the throes of advanced feminist awareness to perceive that the way women are taught to be involved with beauty encourages narcissism, reinforces dependence and immaturity. Everybody (women and men) knows that. For it is "everybody," a whole society, that has identified being feminine with caring about how one *looks*. (In contrast to being masculine—which is identified with caring about what one *is* and *does* and only secondarily, if at all, about how one looks.) Given these stereotypes, it is no wonder that beauty enjoys, at best, a rather mixed reputation.

It is not, of course, the desire to be beautiful that is wrong but the obligation to be—or to try. What is accepted by most women as a flattering idealization of their sex is a way of making women feel inferior to what they actually are—or normally grow to be. For the ideal of beauty is administered as a form of self-oppression. Women are taught to see their bodies in *parts,* and to evaluate each part separately. Breasts, feet, hips, waistline, neck, eyes, nose, complexion, hair, and so on—each in turn is submitted to an anxious, fretful, often despairing scrutiny. Even if some pass muster, some will always be found wanting. Nothing less than perfection will do.

In men, good looks is a whole, something taken in at a glance. It does not need to be confirmed by giving measurements of different regions of the body, nobody encourages a man to dissect his appearance, feature by feature. As for perfection, that is considered trivial—almost unmanly. Indeed, in the ideally good-looking man a small imperfection or blemish is considered positively desirable. According to one movie critic (a woman) who is a declared Robert Redford fan, it is having that cluster of skin-colored moles on one cheek that saves Redford from being merely a "pretty face." Think of the depreciation of women—as well as of beauty—that is implied in that judgment.

"The privileges of beauty are immense," said Cocteau. To be sure, beauty is a form of power. And deservedly so. What is lamentable is that it is the only form of power that most women are encouraged to seek. This power is always conceived in relation to men; it is not the power to do but the power to attract. It is a power that negates itself. For this power is not one that can be chosen freely—at least, not by women—or renounced without social censure.

To preen, for a woman, can never be just a pleasure. It is also a duty. It is her work. If a woman does real work—and even if she has clambered up to a leading position in politics, law, medicine, business, or whatever—she is always under pressure to confess that she still works at being attractive. But in so far as she is keeping up as one of the Fair Sex, she brings under suspicion her very capacity to be objective, professional, authoritative, thoughtful. Damned if they do—women are. And damned if they don't.

10   One could hardly ask for more important evidence of the dangers   10
of considering persons as split between what is "inside" and what is "outside" than that interminable half-comic half-tragic tale, the oppression of women. How easy it is to start off by defining women as caretakers of their surfaces, and then to disparage them (or find them adorable) for being "superficial." It is a crude trap, and it has worked

for too long. But to get out of the trap requires that women get some critical distance from that excellence and privilege which is beauty, enough distance to see how much beauty itself has been abridged in order to prop up the mythology of the "feminine." There should be a way of saving beauty *from* women—and *for* them.

Questions on Meaning

1. Why does Sontag say that beauty carries "demeaning overtones"? Was this always so throughout history?
2. Sontag points out that beauty is a form of power. Why does she feel that this power can work against women? How can beauty be detrimental to a woman in the workplace?
3. What does Sontag say that Socrates tried to teach his students about beauty, ugliness, and life's paradoxes? If Socrates' beauty was not physical, where did it lie?

Questions on Rhetorical Strategy and Style

1. In explaining why beauty is a form of self-oppression for women, Sontag compares and contrasts how women and men are seen and see themselves. What major differences does she expose in terms of the quest for perfection?
2. Find where Sontag uses cause and effect to describe the impact of Christianity on perceptions of beauty. How does she compare the *virtue* of beauty of the ancient Greeks with the Christian view?

Writing Assignments

1. How does Sontag relate the perceptions of beauty to women's character? How does this compare with perceptions associated with the term *masculine*?
2. What role does physical beauty play in your life? How much time and money do you spend on your appearance—clothes, makeup, hair styling, etc.? How does your interest in your appearance compare with your friends' interest in their appearance? What is your motivation (or lack thereof) for your attention (inattention) to your appearance?
3. When Sontag wrote this essay in 1975, feminists such as Sontag were alerting Americans to the stigmas and stereotypes in society that harmed women. How is the concept of "femininity" attached to perceptions of "beauty" today? Have things changed? How do advertising and the media affect women's ability to be seen as a "whole" person in the classical Greek sense of the word?
4. Choose a person you admire greatly—a parent, teacher, neighbor, friend, politician, or friend—and write an essay describing the elements that make him or her a "whole" person. Why are you

attracted to this person? Do you aspire to be like him or her? What characteristics of this person reflect his or her "inner beauty"?

The Blue-Winged Teal

Wallace Stegner

Wallace Stegner (1909-1993) was born in Iowa and died in Santa Fe, New Mexico. He was educated at the University of Utah, the University of California, and Iowa State University, where he received a Ph.D. in 1935. His list of literary awards is lengthy, most significantly two O. Henry prizes, the National Books award, and the Pulitzer prize for the novel Angle of Repose *(1971). A fellowship exists in his name at Stanford University. His last published novel was* Crossing to Safety *(1987). His stories were gathered in the* Collected Stories of Wallace Stegner *(1990) and in 1992 he published* Where the Bluebird Sings to the Lemonade Springs: Living and Writing in the West. *Stegner made an important contribution to the literature and the thinking on the American West. In the short story that follows, Stegner gives us a view of a difficult father and son relationship in small-town America.*

1   Still in waders, with the string of ducks across his shoulder, he   1
stood hesitating on the sidewalk in the cold November wind. His
knees were stiff from being cramped up all day in the blind, and
his feet were cold. Today, all day, he had been alive; now he was back
ready to be dead again.

Lights were on all up and down the street, and there was a rush
of traffic and a hurrying of people past and around him, yet the town
was not his town, the people passing were strangers, the sounds of
evening in this place were no sounds that carried warmth or familiarity. Though he had spent most of his twenty years in the town, knew

---

"The Blue-Winged Tail" from *Collected Stories of Wallace Stegner* by Wallace Stegner. Published and with permission by Random House, 1990.

hundreds of its people, could draw maps of its streets from memory, he wanted to admit familiarity with none of it.

Then what was he doing here, in front of this poolhall loaded down with nine dead ducks? What had possessed him in the first place to borrow gun and waders and car from his father and go hunting? If he had wanted to breathe freely for a change, why hadn't he kept right on going? What was there in this place to draw him back? A hunter had to have a lodge to bring his meat to and people who would be glad of his skill. He had this poolhall and his father, John Lederer, Prop.

He stepped out of a woman's path and leaned against the door. Downstairs, in addition to his father, he would find old Max Schmeckebier, who ran a cheap blackjack game in the room under the sidewalk. He would find Giuseppe Sciutti, the Sicilian barber, closing his shop or tidying up the rack of *Artists and Models* and *The Nudist*. He would probably find Billy Hammond, the night clerk from the Windsor Hotel, having his sandwich and beer and pie, or moving alone around a pool table, whistling abstractedly, practicing shots. If the afternoon blackjack game had broken up, there would be Navy Edwards, dealer and bouncer for Schmeckebier. At this time of evening there might be a few counter customers and a cop collecting his tribute of a beer or that other tribute that Schmeckebier paid to keep the cardroom open.

5 And he would find, sour contrast with the bright sky and the wind of the tule marshes, the cavelike room with its back corners in darkness, would smell that smell compounded of steam heat and cuechalk dust, of sodden butts in cuspidors, of coffee and meat and beer smells from the counter, of cigarette smoke so unaired that it darkened the walls. From anywhere back of the middle tables there would be the pervasive reek of toilet disinfectant. Back of the counter his father would be presiding, throwing the poolhall light switch to save a few cents when the place was empty, flipping it on to give an air of brilliant and successful use when feet came down the stairs past Sciutti's shop.

The hunter moved his shoulder under the weight of the ducks, his mind full for a moment with the image of his father's face, darkly pale, fallen in on its bones, and the pouched, restless, suspicious eyes that seemed always looking for someone. Over the image came the face of his mother, dead now and six weeks buried. His teeth clicked at the thought of how she had held the old man up for thirty years, kept him at a respectable job, kept him from slipping back into the poolroom-Johnny he had been when she married him. Within ten days of her death he had hunted up this old failure of a poolhall.

In anger the hunter turned, thinking of the hotel room he shared with his father. But he had to eat. Broke as he was, a student yanked from his studies, he had no choice but to eat on the old man. Besides, there were the ducks. He felt somehow that the thing would be incomplete unless he brought his game back for his father to see.

His knees unwilling in the stiff waders, he went down the steps, descending into the light shining through Joe Sciutti's door, and into the momentary layer of clean bay rum smell, talcum smell, hair tonic smell, that rose past the still-revolving barber pole in the angle of the stairs.

Joe Sciutti was sweeping wads of hair from his tile floor, and hunched over the counter beyond, their backs to the door, were Schmeckebier, Navy Edwards, Billy Hammond, and an unknown customer. John Lederer was behind the counter, mopping alertly with a rag. The poolroom lights were up bright, but when Lederer saw who was coming he flipped the switch and dropped the big room back into dusk.

10 As the hunter came to the end of the counter their heads turned 10 towards him. "Well, I'm a son of a bee," Navy Edwards said, and scrambled off his stool. Next to him Billy Hammond half stood up so that his pale yellow hair took a halo from the backbar lights. "Say!" Max Schmeckebier said. "Say, dot's goot, dot's pooty goot, Henry!"

But Henry was watching his father so intently he did not turn to them. He slid the string of ducks off his shoulder and swung them up on to the wide walnut bar. They landed solidly—offering or tribute or ransom or whatever they were. For a moment it was as if this little act were private between the two of them. He felt queerly moved, his stomach tightened in suspense or triumph. Then the old man's pouchy eyes slipped from his and the old man came quickly forward along the counter and laid hands on the ducks.

He handled them as if he were petting kittens, his big white hands stringing the heads one by one from the wire.

"Two spoonbill," he said, more to himself than to others crowding around. "Shovelducks. Don't see many of those any more. And two, no three, hen mallards and one drake. Those make good eating."

Schmeckebier jutted his enormous lower lip. Knowing him for a stingy, crooked, suspicious little man, Henry almost laughed at the air he could put on, the air of a man of probity about to make an honest judgment in a dispute between neighbors. "I take a budderball," he said thickly. "A liddle budderball, dot is vot eats goot."

15   An arm fell across Henry's shoulders, and he turned his head to   15
see the hand with red hairs rising from its pores, the wristband of a gray silk shirt with four pearl buttons. Navy Edwards' red face was close to his. "Come clean now," Navy said. "You shot 'em all sitting, didn't you, Henry?"

"I just waited till they stuck their heads out of their holes and let them have it," Henry said.

Navy walloped him on the back and convulsed himself laughing. Then his face got serious again, and he bore down on Henry's shoulder. "By God, you could've fooled me," he said. "If I'd been makin' book on what you'd bring in I'd've lost my shirt."

"Such a pretty shirt, too," Billy Hammond said.

Across the counter John Lederer cradled a little drab duck in his hand. Its neck, stretched from the carrier, hung far down, but its body was neat and plump and its feet were waxy. Watching the sallow face of his father, Henry thought it looked oddly soft.

20   "Ain't that a beauty, though?" the old man said. "There ain't a   20
prettier duck made than a blue-wing teal. You can have all your wood ducks and redheads, all the flashy ones." He spread a wing until the hidden band of bright blue showed. "Pretty?" he said, and shook his head and laughed suddenly, as if he had not expected to. When he laid the duck down beside the others his eyes were bright with sentimental moisture.

So now, Henry thought, you're right in your element. You always did want to be one of the boys from the poolroom pouring out to see the elk on somebody's running board, or leaning on a bar with a schooner of beer talking baseball or telling the boys about the big German Brown somebody brought in in a cake of ice. We haven't any elk or German Browns right now, but we've got some nice ducks, a fine display along five feet of counter. And who brought them in? The student, the alien son. It must gravel you.

He drew himself a beer. Several other men had come in, and he saw three more stooping to look in the door beyond Sciutti's. Then they too came in. Three tables were going; his father had started to hustle, filling orders. After a few minutes Schmeckebier and Navy went into the cardroom with four men. The poolroom lights were up bright again, there was an ivory click of balls, a rumble of talk. The smoke-filled air was full of movement.

Still more people dropped in, kids in high school athletic sweaters and bums from the fringes of skid road. They all stopped to look at the ducks, and Henry saw glances at his waders, heard questions and answers. John Lederer's boy. Some of them spoke to him, deriving importance from contact with him. A fellowship was promoted by the ducks strung out along the counter. Henry felt it himself. He was so mellowed by the way they spoke to him that when the players at the first table thumped with their cues, he got off his stool to rack them up and collect their nickels. It occurred to him that he ought to go to the room and get into a bath, but he didn't want to leave yet. Instead he came back to the counter and slid the nickels towards his father and drew himself another beer.

"Pretty good night tonight," he said. The old man nodded and slapped his rag on the counter, his eyes already past Henry and fixed on two youths coming in, his mouth fixing itself for the greeting and the "Well, boys, what'll it be?"

Billy Hammond wandered by, stopped beside Henry a moment. "Well, time for my nightly wrestle with temptation," he said.

"I was just going to challenge you to a game of call-shot."

"Maybe tomorrow," Billy said, and let himself out carefully as if afraid a noise would disturb someone—a mild, gentle, golden-haired boy who looked as if he ought to be in some prep school learning to say "Sir" to grown-ups instead of clerking in a girlie hotel. He was the only one of the poolroom crowd that Henry half liked. He thought he understood Billy Hammond a little.

He turned back to the counter to hear his father talking with Max Schmeckebier. "I don't see how we could on this rig. That's the hell of it, we need a regular oven."

"In my room in back," Schmeckebier said. "Dot old electric range."

"Does it work?"

"Sure. Vy not? I t'ink so."

"By God," John Lederer said. "Nine ducks, that ought to give us a real old-fashioned feed." He mopped the counter, refilled a coffee cup, came back to the end and pinched the breast of a duck, pulled out a wing and looked at the band of blue hidden among the drab feathers. "Just like old times, for a change," he said, and his eyes touched Henry's in a look that might have meant anything from a challenge to an apology.

Henry had no desire to ease the strain that had been between them for months. He did not forgive his father the poolhall, or forget the way the old man had sprung back into the old pattern, as if his wife had been a jailer and he was now released. He neither forgot nor forgave the red-haired woman who sometimes came to the poolhall late at night and waited on a bar stool while the old man closed up. Yet now when his father remarked that the ducks ought to be drawn and plucked right away, Henry got to his feet.

"I could do ten while you were doing one," his father said.

The blood spread hotter in Henry's face, but he bit off what he might have said. "All right," he said. "You do them and I'll take over the counter for you."

So here he was, in the poolhall he had passionately sworn he would never do a lick of work in, dispensing Mrs. Morrison's meat pies and tamales smothered in chile, clumping behind the counter in the waders which had been the sign of his temporary freedom. Leaning back between orders, watching the Saturday night activity of the place, he half understood why he had gone hunting, and why it had seemed to him essential that he bring his trophies back here.

That somewhat disconcerted understanding was still troubling him when his father came back. The old man had put on a clean apron and brushed his hair. His pouched eyes, brighter and less houndlike than usual, darted along the bar, counting, and darted across the bright tables, counting again. His eyes met Henry's, and both smiled. Both of them, Henry thought, were a little astonished.

Later, propped in bed in the hotel room, he put down the magazine he had been reading and stared at the drawn blinds, the sleazy drapes, and asked himself why he was here. The story he had told others, and himself, that his mother's death had interrupted his school term and he was waiting for the new term before going back, he knew to be an evasion. He was staying because he couldn't get away, or wouldn't. He hated his father, hated the poolhall, hated the people he was thrown with. He made no move to hobnob with them, or hadn't until tonight, and yet he deliberately avoided seeing any of the people who had been his friends for years. Why?

He could force his mind to the barrier, but not across it. Within a half minute he found himself reading again, diving deep, and when he made himself look up from the page he stared for a long time at his father's bed, his father's shoes under the bed, his father's soiled shirts hanging in the open closet. All the home he had any more was this little room. He could not pretend that as long as he stayed here the fragments of his home and family were held together. He couldn't fool himself that he had any function in his father's life any more, or his father in his, unless his own hatred and his father's uneasy suspicion were functions. He ought to get out and get a job until he could go back to school. But he didn't.

40 Thinking made him sleepy, and he knew what that was, too. Sleep 40 was another evasion, like the torpor and monotony of his life. But he let drowsiness drift over him, and drowsily he thought of his father behind the counter tonight, vigorous and jovial, Mine Host, and he saw that the usual fretful petulance had gone from his face.

He snapped off the bed light and dropped the magazine on the floor. Then he heard the rain, the swish and hiss of traffic in the wet street. He felt sad and alone, and he disliked the coldness of his own isolation. Again he thought of his father, of the failing body that had once been tireless and bull-strong, of the face before it had sagged and grown dewlaps of flesh on the square jaws. He thought of the many failures, the jobs that never quite worked out, the schemes that never quite paid off, and of the eyes that could not quite meet, not quite hold, the eyes of his cold son.

Thinking of this, and remembering when they had been a family and when his mother had been alive to hold them together, he felt pity, and he cried.

His father's entrance awakened him. He heard the fumbling at the door, the creak, the quiet click, the footsteps that groped in darkness, the body that bumped into something and halted, getting its bearings. He heard the sighing weight of his father's body on the bed, his father's sighing breath as he bent to untie his shoes. Feigning sleep, he lay unmoving, breathing deeply and steadily, but an anguish of fury had leaped in him as sharp and sudden as a sudden fear, for he smelled the smells his father brought with him: wet wool, stale tobacco, liquor;

and above all, more penetrating than any, spreading through the room and polluting everything there, the echo of cheap musky perfume.

The control Henry imposed upon his body was like an ecstasy. He raged at himself for the weak sympathy that had troubled him all evening. One good night, he said to himself now, staring furiously upward. One lively Saturday night in the joint and he can't contain himself, he has to go top off the evening with his girl friend. And how? A drink in her room? A walk over to some illegal after-hours bar on Rum Alley? Maybe just a trip to bed, blunt and immediate?

His jaws ached from the tight clamping of his teeth, but his orderly breathing went in and out, in and out, while the old man sighed into bed and creaked a little, rolling over, and lay still. The taint of perfume seemed even stronger now. The sow must slop it on by the cupful. And so cuddly. Such a sugar baby. How's my old sweetie tonight? It's been too long since you came to see your baby. I should be real mad at you. The check against the lapel, the unreal hair against the collar, the perfume like some gaseous poison tainting the clothes it touched.

The picture of his mother's bureau drawers came to him, the careless simple collection of handkerchiefs and gloves and lace collars and cuffs, and he saw the dusty blue sachet packets and smelled the faint fragrance. That was all the scent she had ever used.

My God, he said, how can he stand himself?

After a time his father began to breathe heavily, then to snore. In the little prison of the room his breathing was obscene—loose and bubbling, undisciplined, animal. Henry with an effort relaxed his tense arms and legs, let himself sink. He tried to concentrate on his own breathing, but the other dominated him, burst out and died and whiffled and sighed again. By now he had resolution in him like an iron bar. Tomorrow, for sure, for good, he would break out of his self-imposed isolation and see Frank, see Welby. They would lend him enough to get to the coast. Not another day in this hateful relationship. Not another night in this room.

He yawned. It must be late, two or three o'clock. He ought to get to sleep. But he lay uneasily, his mind tainted with hatred as the room was tainted with perfume. He tried cunningly to elude his mind, to get to sleep before it could notice, but no matter how he composed himself for blankness and shut his eyes and breathed deeply, his mind was out again in a half minute, bright-eyed, lively as a weasel, and he was helplessly hunted again from hiding place to hiding place.

50   Eventually he fell back upon his old device.   50

He went into a big dark room in his mind, a room shadowy with great half-seen tables. He groped and found a string above him and pulled, and light fell suddenly in a bright cone from the darker cone of the shade. Below the light lay an expanse of dark green cloth, and this was the only lighted thing in all that darkness. Carefully he gathered bright balls into a wooden triangle, pushing them forward until the apex lay over a round spot on the cloth. Quietly and thoroughly he chalked a cue: the inlaid handle and the smooth taper of the shaft were very real to his eyes and hands. He lined up the cue ball, aimed, drew the cue back and forth in smooth motions over the bridge of his left hand. He saw the balls run from the spinning shock of the break, and carom, and come to rest, and he hunted up the yellow I-ball and got a shot at it between two others. He had to cut it very fine, but he saw the shot go true, the I angle off cleanly into the side pocket. He saw the cue ball rebound and kiss and stop, and he shot the 2 in a straight shot for the left corner pocket, putting drawers on the cue ball to get shape for the 3.

Yellow and blue and red, spotted and striped, he shot pool balls into pockets as deep and black and silent as the cellars of his consciousness. He was not now quarry that his mind chased, but an actor, a willer, a doer, a man in command. By an act of will or of flight he focused his whole awareness on the game he played. His mind undertook it with intent concentration. He took pride in little two-cushion banks, little triumphs of accuracy, small successes of foresight. When he had finished one game and the green cloth was bare he dug the balls from the bin under the end of the table and racked them and began another.

Eventually, he knew, nothing would remain in his mind but the clean green cloth traced with running color and bounded by simple problems, and sometime in the middle of an intricately planned combination shot he would pale off into sleep.

At noon, after the rain, the sun seemed very bright. It poured down from a clearing sky, glittered on wet roofs, gleamed in reflection from pavements and sidewalks. On the peaks beyond the city there was a purity of snow.

55   Coming down the hill, Henry noticed the excessive brightness 55
and could not tell whether it was really as it seemed, or whether his
plunge out of the dark and isolated hole of his life had restored a lost
capacity to see. A slavery, or a paralysis, was ended; he had been for
three hours in the company of a friend; he had been eyed with concern; he had been warmed by solicitude and generosity. In his pocket
he had fifty dollars, enough to get him to the coast and let him renew
his life. It seemed to him incredible that he had alternated between
dismal hotel and dismal poolroom so long. He could not understand
why he had not before this moved his legs in the direction of the hill.
He perceived that he had been sullen and morbid, and he concluded
with some surprise that even Schmeckebier and Edwards and the rest
might have found him a difficult companion.

      His father too. The fury of the night before had passed, but he
knew he would not bend again towards companionship. That antipa-
thy was too deep. He would never think of his father again without
getting the whiff of that perfume. Let him have it; it was what he
wanted, let him have it. They could part without an open quarrel,
maybe, but they would part without love. They could part right now,
within an hour.

      Two grimy stairways led down into the cellar from the alley he
turned into. One went to the furnace room, the other to the poolhall.
The iron rail was blockaded with filled ash cans. Descent into Aver-
nus, he said to himself, and went down the left-hand stair.

      The door was locked. He knocked, and after some time knocked
again. Finally someone pulled on the door from inside. It stuck, and
was yanked irritably inward. His father stood there in his shirt sleeves,
a cigar in his mouth.

      "Oh," he said. "I was wondering what had become of you."

60   The basement air was foul and heavy, dense with the reek from 60
the toilets. Henry saw as he stepped inside that at the far end only the
night light behind the bar was on, but that light was coming from
Schmeckebier's door at this end too, the two weak illuminations dif-
fusing in the shadowy poolroom, leaving the middle in almost absolute dark. It was the appropriate time, the appropriate place, the
stink of his prison appropriately concentrated. He drew his lungs full
of it with a kind of passion, and he said, "I just came down to—"

      "Who is dot?" Schmeckebier called out. He came to his door,
wrapped to the armpits in a bar apron, with a spoon in his hand, and

he bent, peering out into the dusk like a disturbed dwarf in an un-
derhill cave. "John? Who? Oh, Henry. Shust in time, shust in time. It
is not long now." His lower lip waggled, and he pulled it up, apparently with an effort.

Henry said, "What's not long?"

"Vot?" Schmeckebier said, and thrust his big head far out. "You
forgot about it?"

"I must have," Henry said.

65 "The duck feed," his father said impatiently. 65

They stood staring at one another in the dusk. The right moment
was gone. With a little twitch of the shoulder Henry let it go. He
would wait a while, pick his time. When Schmeckebier went back to
his cooking, Henry saw through the doorway the lumpy bed, the big
chair with a blanket folded over it, the roll-top desk littered with pots
and pans, the green and white enamel of the range. A rich smell of
roasting came out and mingled oddly with the chemical stink of toilet disinfectant.

"Are we going to eat in there?" he asked.

His father snorted. "How could we eat in there? Old Maxie lived
in the ghetto too damn long. By God, I never saw such a boar's nest."

"Vot's duh matter? Vot's duh matter?" Schmeckebier said. His big
lip thrust out, he stooped to look into the oven, and John Lederer
went shaking his head up between the tables to the counter. Henry
followed him, intending to make the break when he got the old man
alone. But he saw the three plates set up on the bar, the three glasses
of tomato juice, the platter of olives and celery, and he hesitated. His
father reached with a salt shaker and shook a little salt into each glass
of tomato juice.

70 "All the fixings," he said. "Soon as Max gets those birds out of the 70
oven we can take her on."

Now it was easy to say, "As soon as the feed's over I'll be shoving
off." Henry opened his mouth to say it, but was interrupted this time
by a light tapping at the glass door beyond Sciutti's shop. He swung
around angrily and saw duskily beyond the glass the smooth blond
hair, the even smile.

"It's Billy," he said. "Shall I let him in?"

"Sure," the old man said. "Tell him to come and have a duck with
us."

But Billy Hammond shook his head when Henry asked him. He was shaking his head almost as he came through the door. "No, thanks, I just ate. I'm full of chow mein. This is a family dinner anyway. You go on ahead."

75 "Got plenty," John Lederer said, and made a motion as if to set a 75 fourth place at the counter.

"Who is dot?" Schmeckebier bawled from the back. "Who come in? Is dot Billy Hammond? Set him up a blate."

"By God, his nose sticks as far into things as his lip," Lederer said. Still holding the plate, he roared back, "Catch up with the parade, for Christ sake, or else tend to your cooking." He looked at Henry and Billy and chuckled.

Schmeckebier had disappeared, but now his squat figure blotted the lighted doorway again. "Vot? Vot you say?"

"Vot?" John Lederer said. "Vot, vot, vot? Vot does it matter vot I said? Get the hell back to your kitchen."

80 He was, Henry saw, in a high humor. The effect of last night was 80 still with him. He was still playing Mine Host. He looked at the two of them and laughed so naturally that Henry almost joined him. "I think old Maxie's head is full of duck dressing," he said, and leaned on the counter. "I ever tell you about the time we came back from Reno together? We stopped off in the desert to look at a mine, and got lost on a little dirt road so we had to camp. I was trying to figure out where we were, and started looking for stars, but it was clouded over, hard to locate anything. So I ask old Maxie if he can see the Big Dipper anywhere. He thinks about that maybe ten minutes with his lip stuck out and then he says, 'I t'ink it's in duh water bucket.'"

He did the grating gutturals of Schmeckebier's speech so accurately that Henry smiled in spite of himself. His old man made another motion with the plate at Billy Hammond. "Better let me set you up a place."

"Thanks," Billy said. His voice was as polite and soft as his face, and his eyes had the ingenuous liquid softness of a girl's. "Thanks, I really just ate. You go on, I'll shoot a little pool if it's all right."

Now came Schmeckebier with a big platter held in both hands. He bore it smoking through the gloom of the poolhall and up the steps to the counter, and John Lederer took it from him there and with a flourish speared one after another three tight-skinned brown ducks and slid them on to the plates set side by side for the feast. The one frugal light from the backbar shone on them as they sat down. Henry looked over his shoulder to see Billy Hammond pull the cord and flood a table with a sharp-edged cone of brilliance. Deliberately, already absorbed, he chalked a cue. His lips pursed, and he whistled, and, whistling, bent to take aim.

Lined up in a row, they were not placed for conversation, but John Lederer kept attempting it, leaning forward over his plate to see Schmeckebier or Henry. He filled his mouth with duck and dressing and chewed, shaking his head with pleasure, and snapped off a bite of celery with a crack like a breaking stick. When his mouth was clear he leaned and said to Schmeckebier, "Ah, *das schmeckt gut*, hey, Maxie?"

85 "*Ja*," Schmeckebier said, and sucked grease off his lip and only then turned in surprise. "Say, you speak German?"

"Sure, I speak German," Lederer said. "I worked three weeks once with an old squarehead brickmason that taught me the whole language. He taught me about *sehr gut* and *nicht wahr* and *besser I bleiben* right *hier*, and he always had his *Frau* make me up a lunch full of *kalter Aufschnitt* and *gemixte pickeln*. I know all about German."

Schmeckebier stared a moment, grunted, and went back to his eating. He had already stripped the meat from the bones and was gnawing the carcass.

"Anyway," John Lederer said, "*es schmeckt* God damn good." He got up and went around the counter and drew a mug of coffee from the urn. "Coffee?" he said to Henry.

"Please."

90 His father drew another mug and set it before him. "Maxie?"

Schmeckebier shook his head, his mouth too full for talk. For a minute, after he had set out two little jugs of cream, Lederer stood as if thinking. He was watching Billy Hammond move quietly around the one lighted table, whistling. "Look at that sucker," Lederer said. "I bet he doesn't even know where he is."

By the time he got around to his stool he was back at the German. "*Schmeckebier*," he said. "What's that mean?"

"Uh?"

"What's your name mean? Tastes beer? Likes beer?"

95 Schmeckebier rolled his shoulders. The sounds he made eating were like sounds from a sty. Henry was half sickened, sitting next to him, and he wished the old man would let the conversation drop. But apparently it had to be a feast, and a feast called for chatter.

"That's a hell of a name, you know it?" Lederer said, and already he was up again and around the end of the counter. "You couldn't get into any church with a name like that." His eyes fastened on the big drooping greasy lip, and he grinned.

"Schmeckeduck, that ought to be your name," he said. "What's German for duck? *Vogel?* Old Man Schmeckevogel. How about number two?"

Schmeckebier pushed his plate forward and Lederer forked a duck out of the steam table. Henry did not take a second.

"You ought to have one," his father told him. "You don't get grub like this every day."

100 "One's my limit," Henry said. 100

For a while they worked at their plates. Back of him Henry heard the clack of balls hitting, and a moment later the rumble as a ball rolled down the chute from a pocket. The thin, abstracted whistling of Billy Hammond broke off, became words:

> *Annie doesn't live here any more.*
> *You must be the one she waited for.*
> *She said I would know you by the blue in your eye—*

"Talk about one being your limit," his father said. "When we lived in Nebraska we used to put on some feeds. You remember anything about Nebraska at all?"

105 "A little," Henry said. He was irritated at being dragged into rem- 105
iniscences, and he did not want to hear how many ducks the town hog could eat at a sitting.

"We'd go out, a whole bunch of us," John Lederer said. "The sloughs were black with ducks in those days. We'd come back with a buggyful, and the womenfolks'd really put us on a feed. Fifteen, twenty, thirty people. Take a hundred ducks to fill 'em up." He was silent a moment, staring across the counter, chewing. Henry noticed that he had tacked two wings of a teal up on the frame of the backbar mirror, small, strong bows with a band of bright blue half hidden in them. The old man's eyes slanted over, caught Henry's looking at the wings.

"Doesn't seem as if we'd had a duck feed since we left there," he said. His forehead wrinkled; he rubbed his neck, leaning forward over his plate, and his eyes met Henry's in the backbar mirror. He spoke to

282

the mirror, ignoring the gobbling image of Schmeckebier between his own reflection and Henry's.

"You remember that set of china your mother used to have? The one she painted herself? Just the plain white china with the one design on each plate?"

Henry sat stiffly, angry that his mother's name should even be mentioned between them in this murky hole, and after what had passed. Gabble, gabble, gabble, he said to himself. If you can't think of anything else to gabble about, gabble about your dead wife. Drag her through the poolroom too. Aloud he said, "No, I guess I don't."

110   "Blue-wing teal," his father said, and nodded at the wings tacked 110 to the mirror frame. "Just the wings, like that. Awful pretty. She thought a teal was about the prettiest little duck there was."

His vaguely rubbing hand came around from the back of his neck and rubbed along the cheek, pulling the slack flesh and distorting the mouth. Henry said nothing, watching the pouched hound eyes in the mirror.

It was a cold, skin-tightening shock to realize that the hound eyes were cloudy with tears. The rubbing hand went over them, shaded them like a hatbrim, but the mouth below remained distorted. With a plunging movement his father was off the stool.

"Oh, God damn!" he said in a strangling voice, and went past Henry on hard, heavy feet, down the steps and past Billy Hammond, who neither looked up nor broke the sad thin whistling.

Schmeckebier had swung around. "Vot's duh matter? Now vot's duh matter?"

115   With a short shake of the head, Henry turned away from him, 115 staring after his father down the dark poolhall. He felt as if orderly things were breaking and flying apart in his mind; he had a moment of white blind terror that this whole scene upon whose reality he counted was really a dream, something conjured up out of the bottom of his consciousness where he was accustomed to comfort himself into total sleep. His mind was still full of the anguished look his father had hurled at the mirror before he ran.

The hell with you, the look had said. The hell with you, Schmeckebier, and you, my son Henry. The hell with your ignorance, whether you're stupid or whether you just don't know all you think you know. You don't know enough to kick dirt down a hole. You know nothing at all, you know less than nothing because you know things wrong.

He heard Billy's soft whistling, saw him move around his one lighted table—a well-brought-up boy from some suburban town, a polite soft gentle boy lost and wandering among pimps and prostitutes, burying himself for some reason among people who never even touched his surface. Did he shoot pool in his bed at night, tempting sleep, as Henry did? Did his mind run carefully to angles and banks and englishes, making a reflecting mirror of them to keep from looking through them at other things?

Almost in terror he looked out across the sullen cave, past where the light came down in an intense isolated cone above Billy's table, and herd the lugubrious whistling that went on without intention of audience, a recurrent and deadening and only half-conscious sound. He looked toward the back, where his father had disappeared in the gloom, and wondered if in his bed before sleeping the old man worked through a routine of little jobs: cleaning the steam table, ordering a hundred pounds of coffee, jacking up the janitor about the mess in the hall. He wondered if it was possible to wash yourself to sleep with restaurant crockery, work yourself to sleep with chores, add yourself to sleep with columns of figures, as you could play yourself to sleep with a pool cue and a green table and fifteen colored balls. For a moment, in the sad old light with the wreckage of the duck feast at his elbow, he wondered if there was anything more to his life, or his father's life, or Billy Hammond's life, or anyone's life, than playing the careful games that deadened you into sleep.

Schmeckebier, beside him, was still groping in the fog of his mind for an explanation of what had happened. "Vere'd he go?" he said, and nudged Henry fiercely. "Vot's duh matter?"

Henry shook him off irritably, watching Billy Hammond's oblivious bent head under the light. He heard Schmeckebier's big lip flop and heard him sucking his teeth.

"I tell you," the guttural voice said. "I got somet'ing dot fixes him if he feels bum."

He too went down the stairs past the lighted table and into the gloom at the back. The light went on in his room, and after a minute or two his voice was shouting, "John! Say, come here, uh? Say, John!"

Eventually John Lederer came out of the toilet and they walked together between the tables. In his fist Schmeckebier was clutching a square bottle. He waved it in front of Henry's face as they passed, but Henry was watching his father. He saw the crumpled face, oddly rigid, like the face of a man in the grip of a barely controlled rage, but his father avoided his eyes.

"Kümmel," Schmeckebier said. He set four ice-cream dishes on the counter and poured three about a third full of clear liquor. His squinted eyes lifted and peered towards Billy Hammond, but Henry said, on an impulse, "Let him alone. He's walking in his sleep."

So there were only the three. They stood together a moment and raised their glasses. "Happy days," John Lederer said automatically. They drank.

Schmeckebier smacked his lips, looked at them one after another, shook his head in admiration of the quality of his kümmel, and waddled back towards his room with the bottle. John Lederer was already drawing hot water to wash the dishes.

In the core of quiet which was not broken even by the clatter of crockery and the whistling of Billy Hammond, Henry said what he had to say. "I'll be leaving," he said. "Probably tonight."

But he did not say it in anger, or with the cold command of himself that he had imagined in advance. He said it like a cry, and with the feeling he might have had on letting go the hand of a friend too weak and too exhausted to cling any longer to their inadequate shared driftwood in a wide cold sea.

Questions on Meaning

1. What is Henry's mood as he approaches the poolhall at the opening of this story? Why does Stegner spend time describing the
   people and the ambiance of the place?
2. Stegner also refers to Henry as the "hunter." Why?
3. What kind of relationship does Henry have with his father? Why
   is he reluctant to return to the poolhall? How long would you estimate he has been away?

Questions on Rhetorical Strategy and Style

1. This story includes several characters less developed than Henry.
   How are they essential to the story's success?
2. A crucial scene takes place in the hotel room. What happens there
   and how does it contribute to the plot development?
3. What is significant about the blue-winged teal? In what way does
   it help Henry to understand his father? How do you interpret the
   ending?

Writing Assignments

1. This story deals with familiar ideas about returning home and
   tension between fathers and sons. In a brief, informal essay, explain why these themes may be so common.
2. Write a story about conflict between a parent and child. Have the
   two characters meet together in some specific locale and have
   them talk about their relationship. Describe the setting in detail
   to reflect the mood of the conversation.

Mother Tongue

Amy Tan

Amy Tan was born in Oakland, California in 1952, several years after her mother and father immigrated from China. She was raised in various cities in the San Francisco Bay Area. When she was eight, her essay, "What the Library Means to Me," won first prize among elementary school participants, for which Tan received a transistor radio and publication in the local newspaper. Upon the deaths of her brother and father in 1967 and 1968 from brain tumors, the family began a haphazard journey through Europe, before settling in Montreux, Switzerland, where Tan graduated in her junior year in 1969.

For the next seven years, Tan attended five schools. She first went to Linfield College in McMinnville, Oregon, and there, on a blind date, met her future husband, Lou DeMattei. She followed him to San Jose, where she enrolled in San Jose City College. She next attended San Jose State University, and, while working two part-time jobs, she became an English honor's students and a President's Scholar, while carrying a semester course load of 21 units. In 1972 she graduated with honors, receiving a B.A. with a double major in English and Linguistics. She was awarded a scholarship to attend the Summer Linguistics Institute at the University of California, Santa Cruz. In 1973, she earned her M.A. in Linguistics, also from San Jose State University, and was then awarded a Graduate Minority Fellowship under the affirmative action program at the University of California, Berkeley, where she enrolled as a doctoral student in linguistics.

First published in *Threepenny Review*, 1990. Copyright © 1990 by Amy Tan.

1   I am not a scholar of English or literature. I cannot give you much   1
      more than personal opinions on the English language and its vari-
      ations in this country or others.

 I am a writer. And by that definition, I am someone who has always loved language. I am fascinated by language in daily life. I spend
a great deal of my time thinking about the power of language—the
way it can evoke an emotion, a visual image, a complex idea, or a simple truth. Language is the tool of my trade. And I use them all—all
the Englishes I grew up with.

 Recently, I was made keenly aware of the different Englishes I do
use. I was giving a talk to a large group of people, the same talk I had
already given to half a dozen other groups. The nature of the talk was
about my writing, my life, and my book, *The Joy Luck Club*. The talk
was going along well enough, until I remembered one major difference that made the whole talk sound wrong. My mother was in the
room. And it was perhaps the first time she had heard me give a
lengthy speech, using the kind of English I have never used with her.
I was saying things like, "The intersection of memory upon imagination" and "There is an aspect of my fiction that relates to thus-and-
thus"—a speech filled with carefully wrought grammatical phrases,
burdened, it suddenly seemed to me, with nominalized forms, past
perfect tenses, conditional phrases, all the forms of standard English
that I had learned in school and through books, the forms of English
I did not use at home with my mother.

 Just last week, I was walking down the street with my mother, and
I again found myself conscious of the English I was using, and the
English I do use with her. We were talking about the price of new and
used furniture and I heard myself saying this: "Not waste money that
way." My husband was with us as well, and he didn't notice any switch
in my English. And then I realized why. It's because over the twenty
years we've been together I've often used that same kind of English
with him, and sometimes he even uses it with me. It has become our
language of intimacy, a different sort of English that relates to family
talk, the language I grew up with.

5   So you'll have some idea of what this family talk I heard sounds   5
like, I'll quote what my mother said during a recent conversation
which I videotaped and then transcribed. During this conversation,
my mother was talking about a political gangster in Shanghai who had
the same last name as her family's, Du, and how the gangster in his

early years wanted to be adopted by her family, which was rich by comparison. Later, the gangster became more powerful, far richer than my mother's family, and one day showed up at my mother's wedding to pay his respects. Here's what she said in part:

"Du Yusong having business like fruit stand. Like off the street kind. He is Du like Du Zong—but not Tsung-ming Island people. The local people call putong, the river east side, he belong to that side local people. That man want to ask Du Zong father take him in like become own family. Du Zong father wasn't look down on him, but didn't take seriously, until that man big like become a mafia. Now important person, very hard to inviting him. Chinese way, came only to show respect, don't stay for dinner. Respect for making big celebration, he shows up. Mean gives lots of respect. Chinese custom. Chinese social life that way. If too important won't have to stay too long. He come to my wedding. I didn't see, I heard it. I gone to boy's side, they have YMCA dinner. Chinese age I was nineteen."

You should know that my mother's expressive command of English belies how much she actually understands. She reads the *Forbes* report, listens to *Wall Street Week*, converses daily with her stockbroker, reads all of Shirley MacLaine's books with ease—all kinds of things I can't begin to understand. Yet some of my friends tell me they understand 50 percent of what my mother says. Some say they understand 80 to 90 percent. Some say they understand none of it, as if she were speaking pure Chinese. But to me, my mother's English is perfectly clear, perfectly natural. It's my mother tongue. Her language, as I hear it, is vivid, direct, full of observation and imagery. That was the language that helped shape the way I saw things, expressed things, made sense of the world.

Lately, I've been giving more thought to the kind of English my mother speaks. Like others, I have described it to people as "broken" or "fractured" English. But I wince when I say that. It has always bothered me that I can think of no way to describe it other than "broken," as if it were damaged and needed to be fixed, as if it lacked a certain wholeness and soundness. I've heard other terms used, "limited English," for example. But they seem just as bad, as if everything is limited, including people's perceptions of the limited English speaker.

I know this for a fact, because when I was growing up, my mother's "limited" English limited *my* perception of her. I was ashamed of her English. I believed that her English reflected the quality of what she had to say. That is, because she expressed them imperfectly her thoughts were imperfect. And I had plenty of empirical evidence to support me: the fact that people in department stores, at banks, and at restaurants did not take her seriously, did not give her good service, pretended not to understand her, or even acted as if they did not hear her.

10   My mother has long realized the limitations of her English as well.   10
When I was fifteen, she used to have me call people on the phone to pretend I was she. In this guise, I was forced to ask for information or even to complain and yell at people who had been rude to her. One time it was a call to her stockbroker in New York. She had cashed out her small portfolio and it just so happened we were going to go to New York the next week, our very first trip outside California. I had to get on the phone and say in an adolescent voice that was not very convincing, "This is Mrs. Tan."

And my mother was standing in the back whispering loudly, "Why he don't send me check, already two weeks late. So mad he lie to me, losing me money."

And then I said in perfect English, "Yes, I'm getting rather concerned. You had agreed to send the check two weeks ago, but it hasn't arrived."

Then she began to talk more loudly. "What he want, I come to New York tell him front of his boss, you cheating me?" And I was trying to calm her down, make her be quiet, while telling the stockbroker, "I can't tolerate any more excuses. If I don't receive the check immediately, I am going to have to speak to your manager when I'm in New York next week." And sure enough, the following week there we were in front of this astonished stockbroker, and I was sitting there red-faced and quiet, and my mother, the real Mrs. Tan, was shouting at his boss in her impeccable broken English.

We used a similar routine just five days ago, for a situation that was far less humorous. My mother had gone to the hospital for an appointment, to find out about a benign brain tumor a CAT scan had revealed a month ago. She said she had spoken very good English, her best English, no mistakes. Still, she said, the hospital did not apologize when they said they had lost the CAT scan and she had come for nothing. She said they did not seem to have any sympathy when she told them she was anxious to know the exact diagnosis, since her husband and son had both died of brain tumors. She said they would not give her any more information until the next time and she would have to make another appointment for that. So she said she would not leave until the doctor called her daughter. She wouldn't budge. And when the doctor finally called her daughter, me, who spoke in perfect English—lo and behold—we had assurances the CAT scan would be found, promises that a conference call on Monday would be held, and apologies for any suffering my mother had gone through for a most regrettable mistake.

15   I think my mother's English almost had an effect on limiting my   15
possibilities in life as well. Sociologists and linguists probably will tell you that a person's developing language skills are more influenced by peers. But I do think that the language spoken in the family, especially in immigrant families which are more insular, plays a large role in shaping the language of the child. And I believe that it affected my results on achievement tests, IQ tests, and the SAT. While my English skills were never judged as poor, compared to math, English could not be considered my strong suit. In grade school I did moderately well, getting perhaps B's, sometimes B-pluses, in English and scoring perhaps in the sixtieth or seventieth percentile on achievement tests. But those scores were not good enough to override the opinion that my true abilities lay in math and science, because in those areas I achieved A's and scored in the ninetieth percentile or higher.

This was understandable. Math is precise, there is only one correct answer. Whereas, for me at least, the answers on English tests were always a judgment call, a matter of opinion and personal experience. Those tests were constructed around items like fill-in-the-blank sentence completion, Such as, "Even though Tom was _____, Mary thought he was _____." And the correct answer always seemed to be the most bland combinations of thoughts, for example, "Even though Tom was shy, Mary thought he was charming," with the grammatical structure "even though" limiting the correct answer to some sort of semantic opposites, so you wouldn't get answers like, Even though Tom was foolish, Mary thought he was ridiculous." Well, according to my mother, there were very few limitations as to what Tom could have been and what Mary might have thought of him. So I never did well on tests like that.

The same was true with word analogies, pairs of words in which you were supposed to find some sort of logical, semantic relationship—

for example, "*Sunset* is to *nightfall* as _____ is to _____."
And here you would be presented with a list of four possible pairs, one
of which showed the same kind of relationship: *red* is to *stoplight*, *bus*
is to *arrival*, *chills* is to *fever*, *yawn* is to *boring*. Well, I could never think
that way. I knew what the tests were asking, but I could not block out
of my mind the images already created by the first pair, "*sunset* is to
nightfall"—and I would see a burst of colors against a darkening sky,
the moon rising, the lowering of a curtain of stars. And all the other
pairs of words—red, bus, stoplight, boring—just threw up a mass of
confusing images, making it impossible for me to sort out something
as logical as saying: "A sunset precedes nightfall" is the same as "a chill
precedes a fever." The only way I would have gotten that answer right
would have been to imagine an associative situation, for example, my
being disobedient and staying out past sunset, catching a chill at night,
which turns into feverish pneumonia as punishment, which indeed did
happen to me.

I have been thinking about all this lately, about my mother's English,
about achievement tests. Because lately I've been asked, as a writer,
why there are not more Asian Americans represented in American literature. Why are there few Asian Americans enrolled in creative writing programs? Why do so many Chinese students go into engineering?
Well, these are broad sociological questions I can't begin to answer.
But I have noticed in surveys—in fact, just last week—that Asian students, as a whole, always do significantly better on math achievement
tests than in English. And this makes me think that there are other
Asian American students whose English spoken in the home might
also be described as "broken" or "limited." And perhaps they also have
teachers who are steering them away from writing and into math and
science, which is what happened to me.

Fortunately, I happen to be rebellious in nature and enjoy the
challenge of disproving assumptions made about me. I became an
English major my first year in college, after being enrolled as pre-med.
I started writing nonfiction as a freelancer the week after I was told by
my former boss that writing was my worst skill and I should hone my
talents toward account management.

20 But it wasn't until 1985 that I finally began to write fiction. And 20
at first I wrote using what I thought to be wittily crafted sentences,
sentences that would finally prove I had mastery over the English

language. Here's an example from the first draft of a story that later made its way into *The Joy Luck Club,* but without this line: "That was my mental quandary in its nascent state." A terrible line, which I can barely pronounce.

Fortunately, for reasons I won't get into today, I later decided I should envision a reader for the stories I would write. And the reader I decided upon was my mother, because these were stories about mothers. So with this reader in mind—and in fact she did read my early drafts—I began to write stories using all the Englishes I grew up with: the English I spoke to my mother, which for lack of a better term might be described as "simple"; the English she used with me, which for lack of a better term might be described as "broken"; my translation of her Chinese, which could certainly be described as "watered down"; and what I imagined to be her translation of her Chinese if she could speak in perfect English, her internal language, and for that I sought to preserve the essence, but neither an English nor a Chinese structure. I wanted to capture what language ability tests can never reveal: her intent, her passion, her imagery, the rhythms of her speech and the nature of her thoughts.

Apart from what any critic had to say about my writing, I knew I had succeeded where it counted when my mother finished reading my book and gave me her verdict: "So easy to read."

Questions on Meaning

1. Until near the end of the essay, Tan describes essentially only two "Englishes": the English with which she speaks to others, as in the speech she delivers, and the English of her mother. At the end we learn of a multitude of other Englishes. What are these? What are the differences among them?
2. Why was Tan ashamed of her mother's English when she was growing up?
3. What does Tan have to say about her math scores being higher than her language scores?

Questions on Rhetorical Strategy and Style

4. Tan uses the writing strategy of narration to reveal how others reacted to her mother's language skills, such as the treatment she received at the hospital. Reread that scene and explain how it effectively develops Tan's point.
5. Tan says that she wanted in her writing to capture her mother's "intent, her passion, her imagery, the rhythms of her speech and the nature of her thoughts." Evaluate this essay by this standard: do we get a glimpse of her mother's character here? How does Tan use language in this essay to capture a small part of her mother?

Writing Assignments

1. Tan makes the point that teachers may be steering Asian American students into math and science because their language scores may mistakenly be suggesting they have lower aptitude in studies involving language. Could such "steering" by teachers and guidance counselors be faulty with other students as well? Think of some other examples of situations in which test scores could give false impressions about a person's natural abilities and aptitudes.
2. Tan describes how people judged her mother as a result of her "broken English." What other ways do people judge strangers by appearances? Do clothing and physical appearance give true insight into what a person is like? Write an essay in which you explore the issue of how we come to know what people are like and the extent to which it is meaningful to make assumptions based on how people look and sound.

3. Tan explains at length how she never understood word analogy tests because her mind just did not work that way. Is this more than just a matter of using English? Are there differences in how people think that can throw off such responses to standardized tests, such as those used to measure intelligence? Write an essay in which you explain your ideas, based on your own experience, about whether standardized tests accurately measure people's abilities and aptitudes.

Men and Women Talking on the Job

Deborah Tannen

Deborah Tannen (1945–), born in Brooklyn, New York, received her Ph.D. in linguistics from the University of California at Berkeley and teaches at Georgetown University. Her research into how people communicate has brought her critical and popular acclaim, and she has appeared on several television programs and has written for The New York Times, *the* Washington Post, *and* Vogue. *Her book* That's Not What I Meant *(1987) analyzes the effects of conversational styles on relationships.* You Just Don't Understand *(1990) examines differences in how men and women converse.* Talking From 9 to 5 *(1994), from which the following essay is excerpted, resulted from her research into conversational styles in work settings and their impact on how work is performed and who gets ahead. Because of differences in communication styles between men and women in general, how they express themselves on the job can become a crucial work issue.*

1   A my was a manager with a problem: She had just read a final   1
report written by Donald, and she felt it was woefully inadequate. She faced the unsavory task of telling him to do it over. When she met with Donald, she made sure to soften the blow by beginning with praise, telling him everything about his report that was

good. Then she went on to explain what was lacking and what needed to be done to make it acceptable. She was pleased with the diplomatic way she had managed to deliver the bad news. Thanks to her thoughtfulness in starting with praise, Donald was able to listen to the criticism and seemed to understand what was needed. But when the revised report appeared on her desk, Amy was shocked. Donald had made only minor, superficial changes, and none of the necessary ones. The next meeting with him did not go well. He was incensed that she was now telling him his report was not acceptable and accused her of having misled him. "You told me before it was fine," he protested.

Amy thought she had been diplomatic; Donald thought she had been dishonest. The praise she intended to soften the message "This is unacceptable" sounded to him like the message itself: "This is fine." So what she regarded as the main point—the needed changes—came across to him as optional suggestions, because he had already registered her praise as the main point. She felt he hadn't listened to her. He thought she had changed her mind and was making him pay the price.

Work days are filled with conversations about getting the job done. Most of these conversations succeed, but too many end in impasses like this. It could be that Amy is a capricious boss whose wishes are whims, and it could be that Donald is a temperamental employee who can't hear criticism no matter how it is phrased. But I don't think either was the case in this instance. I believe this was one of innumerable misunderstandings caused by differences in conversational style. Amy delivered the criticism in a way that seemed to her self-evidently considerate, a way she would have preferred to receive criticism herself: taking into account the other person's feelings, making sure he knew that her ultimate negative assessment of his report didn't mean she had no appreciation of his abilities. She offered the praise as a sweetener to help the nasty-tasting news go down. But Donald didn't expect criticism to be delivered in that way, so he mistook the praise as her overall assessment rather than a preamble to it.

This conversation could have taken place between two women or two men. But I do not think it is a coincidence that it occurred between a man and a woman. This book will explain why. First, it gives a view of the role played by talk in our work lives. To do this, I show the workings of conversational style, explaining the ritual nature of conversation[1] and the confusion that arises when rituals are not shared and therefore not recognized as such, I take into account the many influences on conversational style, but I focus in particular on the differing rituals that typify women and men (although, of course, not all individual men and women behave in ways that are typical). Conversational rituals common among men often involve using opposition such as banter, joking, teasing, and playful put-downs, and expending effort to avoid the one-down position in the interaction. Conversational rituals common among women are often ways of maintaining an appearance of equality, taking into account the effect of the exchange on the other person, and expending effort to downplay the speaker's authority so they can get the job done without flexing their muscles in an obvious way.

5   When everyone present is familiar with these conventions, they work well. But when ways of speaking are not recognized as conventions, they are taken literally, with negative results on both sides. Men whose oppositional strategies are interpreted literally may be seen as hostile when they are not, and their efforts to ensure that they avoid appearing one-down may be taken as arrogance. When women use conversational strategies designed to avoid appearing boastful and to take the other person's feelings into account, they may be seen as less confident and competent than they really are. As a result, both women and men often feel they are not getting sufficient credit for what they have done, are not being listened to, are not getting ahead as fast as they should.

When I talk about women's and men's characteristic ways of speaking, I always emphasize that both styles make sense and are equally valid in themselves, though the difference in styles may cause trouble in interaction. In a sense, when two people form a private

---

[1]"... *the ritual nature of conversation* ... " As my colleague Rom Harré pointed out to me, it would be useful to note, for readers interested in finer distinctions, that I am using the term "ritual" rather loosely to capture the automatic, nonliteral, conventionalized nature of conversational language. There are, of course, a number of different levels on which this operates. Technically, a "ritual" per se is a symbolic means of accomplishing a social act. Other ways in which talk is not meant literally include what scholars refer to as "phatic speech," which refers to relatively "empty" verbiage whose main purpose is the maintenance of social relations, or recognizing the other as a person.

relationship of love or friendship, the bubble of their interaction is a world unto itself, even though they both come with the prior experience of their families, their community, and a lifetime of conversations. But someone who takes a job is entering a world that is already functioning, with its own characteristic style already in place. Although there are many influences such as regional background, the type of industry involved, whether it is a family business or a large corporation, in general, workplaces that have previously had men in positions of power have already established male-style interaction as the norm. In that sense, women, and others whose styles are different, are not starting out equal, but are at a disadvantage. Though talking at work is quite similar to talking in private, it is a very different enterprise in many ways.

Negotiating from the Inside Out or the Outside In

Two co-workers who were on very friendly terms with each other were assigned to do a marketing survey together. When they got the assignment, the man began by saying, "I'll do the airline and automobile industry, and you can do the housewares and direct-mail market." The woman was taken aback. "Hey," she said. "It sounds like you've got it all figured out. As a matter of fact, *I'd* like to do airlines and autos. I've already got a lot of contacts in those areas." "Oh," he said, a little chagrined and a lot surprised. She continued, "I wish you wouldn't come on so strong." "Well, how would you have started?" he asked. She said, "I wouldn't have just said what I wanted to do. I would have asked, 'What parts do you want to do?'" This made no sense to him. "Then what are you complaining about? If you had asked me what parts I wanted to do, I would have said, 'I'll do the airlines and autos.' We would have ended up in the same place anyway."

The woman saw his point. But if the conversation had gone that way, she still would have been frustrated. To her, the question "What parts of the survey would you like to do?" is not an invitation to grab the parts he wants and run away with them. It's an invitation to talk about the various parts—which ones interest him, which he has experience in, which he would like to learn more about. Then he would ask, "What do you want to do?" and she would say what interests her, where her experience lies, and where she'd like to get more experience. Finally, they would divvy up the parts in a way that gave them both some of what they wanted, while taking advantage of both their expertise.

Making decisions is a crucial part of any workday. Daily, weekly, monthly, decisions must be made with never enough information and never enough time. People have very different ways of reaching decisions, and none is clearly better than others. But when two people with different styles have to make decisions together, both styles may have worse results than either would have if their styles were shared, unless the differences are understood and accommodated.

10 Beginning by stating what you will do is a style of negotiating that 10 starts inside and works its way out. If others have different ideas, you expect them to say so, and you'll negotiate. Opening with a question like "What would you like to do?" or "What do you think?" is a style that begins by being vague and works its way in. It specifically invites others to express their perspective. Either style can work well. What makes the machine go TILT! is the difference in styles. Someone who expects negotiation to proceed from the inside and work its way out hears a vague question as an invitation to decide; someone who tends to negotiate from the outside in hears a specific claim as a nonnegotiable demand. In this sense, both styles are indirect—they depend on an unspoken understanding of how the subsequent conversation is expected to go. This is a sense in which conversation is ritualized: It follows a preset sequencing scheme that seems self-evidently appropriate.

More on Negotiating Styles

The managers of a medium-size company got the go-ahead to hire a human-resources coordinator, and two managers who worked well together were assigned to make the choice. As it turned out, Maureen and Harold favored different applicants, and both felt strongly about their preferences. Maureen argued with assurance and vigor that the person she wanted to hire was the most creative and innovative, and that he had the most appropriate experience. Harold argued with equal conviction that the applicant he favored had a vision of management that fit with the company's, whereas her candidate might be a thorn in their side. They traded arguments for some time, neither convincing the other. Then Harold said that hiring the applicant Maureen wanted would make him so uncomfortable that he would have to consider resigning. Maureen respected Harold. What's more, she liked him and considered him a friend. So she felt that his admission of such strong feelings had to be taken into account. She said what seemed to her the only thing she could say under the circumstances: "Well, I certainly don't want you to feel uncomfortable here; you're one of the pillars of the place. If you feel that strongly about it, I can't argue with that." Harold's choice was hired.

In this case, the decision-making power went not to the manager who had the highest rank in the firm (their positions were parallel) and not necessarily to the one whose judgment was best, but to the one whose arguing strategies were most effective in the negotiation. Maureen was an ardent and persuasive advocate for her view, but she assumed that she and Harold would have to come to an agreement in order to make a decision, and that she had to take his feelings into account. Since Harold would not back down, she did. Most important, when he argued that he would have to quit if she got her way, she felt she had no option but to yield.

What was crucial was not Maureen's and Harold's individual styles in isolation but how their styles interacted—how they played in concert with the other's style. Harold's threat to quit ensured his triumph—when used with someone who would not call his bluff. If he had been arguing with someone who regarded this threat as simply another move in the negotiation rather than as a nonnegotiable expression of deep feelings that had to be respected, the result might have been different. For example, had she said, "That's ridiculous; of course you're not going to quit!" or "If that's how shallow your commitment to this firm is, then we'd be better off without you," the decision might well have gone the other way.

When you talk to someone whose style is similar to yours, you can fairly well predict the response you are going to get. But when you talk to someone whose style is different, you can't predict, and often can't make sense of, the response. Hearing the reaction you get, if it's not the one you expected, often makes you regret what you said. Harold later told Maureen that he was sorry he had used the argument he did. In retrospect he was embarrassed, even a bit ashamed of himself. His retrospective chagrin was like what you feel if you slam down something in anger and are surprised and regretful to see that it breaks. You wanted to make a gesture, but you didn't expect it to come out with such force. Harold regretted what he said precisely because it caused Maureen to back down so completely. He'd known he was upping the ante—he felt he had to do something to get them out of the loop of recycling arguments they were in—but he had not expected it to end the negotiation summarily; he expected Maureen to meet his move with a balancing move of her own. He did not predict the impact that personalizing his argument would have on her. For her part, Maureen did not think of Harold's threat as just another move in a negotiable argument; she heard it as a personal plea that she could not reject. Their different approaches to negotiation put her at a disadvantage in negotiating with him.

"How Certain Are You of That?"

15 Negotiating is only one kind of activity that is accomplished through 15 talk at work. Other kinds of decision-making are also based as much on ways of talking as on the content of the arguments. The CEO of a corporation explained to me that he regularly has to make decisions based on insufficient information—and making decisions is a large part of his work life. Much of his day is spent hearing brief presentations following which he must either approve or reject a course of action. He has to make a judgment in five minutes about issues the presenters have worked on for months. "I decide," he explained, "based on how confident they seem. If they seem very confident, I call it a go. If they seem unsure, I figure it's too risky and nix it."

Here is where the rule of competence and the role of communication go hand in hand. Confidence, after all, is an internal feeling. How can you judge others' confidence? The only evidence you have to go on is circumstantial—how they talk about what they know. You judge by a range of signs, including facial expression and body posture, but most of all, speech. Do they hesitate? Do they speak up or swallow half their words? Is their tone of voice declamatory or halting? Do they make bald statements ("This is a winner! We've got to go for it!") or hedge ("Um . . . from what I can tell, I think it'll work, but we'll never know for sure until we try")? This seems simple enough. Surely, you can tell how confident people are by paying attention to how they speak, just as you can tell when someone is lying.

Well, maybe not. Psychologist Paul Ekman has spent years studying lying, and he has found that most people are very sure they can tell when others are lying. The only trouble is, most can't. With a few thus-far inexplicable exceptions, people who tell him they are absolutely sure they can tell if someone is lying are as likely to be wrong as to be right—and he has found this to be as true for judges as for the rest of us.

In the same way, our ability to determine how confident others are is probably quite limited. The CEO who does not take into account the individual styles of the people who make presentations to him will find it difficult, if not impossible, to make the best judgment. Different people will talk very differently, not because of the absolute level of their confidence or lack of it, but because of their habitual ways of speaking. There are those who sound sure of themselves even when inside they're not sure at all, and others who sound tentative even when they're very sure indeed. So being aware of differences in ways of speaking is a prerequisite for making good decisions as well as good presentations.

Feasting on Humble Pie

Although these factors affecting decision-making are the same for men and women, and every individual has his or her own style, it seems that women are more likely to downplay their certainty, men more likely to downplay their doubts. From childhood, girls learn to temper what they say so as not to sound too aggressive—which means too certain. From the time they are little, most girls learn that sounding too sure of themselves will make them unpopular with their peers. Groups of girls, as researchers who have studied girls at play have found, will penalize and even ostracize a girl who seems too sure she's right. Anthropologist Marjorie Harness Goodwin found that girls criticize other girls who stand out by saying, "She thinks she's cute," or "She thinks she's something." Talking in ways that display self-confidence is not approved for girls.[2]

It is not only peers who disapprove of girls talking in ways that call attention to their accomplishments. Adults too can be critical of such behavior in girls, as was a woman who wrote a letter that was published

---

[2]"... *girls criticize other girls who stand out* ..." Marjorie Harness Goodwin spent a year and a half observing the girls and boys in her inner-city black Philadelphia neighborhood and found the girls sanctioning other girls who seemed to stand out by saying, in the dialect of their community, "She thinks she cute," Goodwin found, for example, that girls criticized a girl who dressed too well and did too well in school.

in a magazine. The letter-writer was responding to an article about a ten-year-old girl named Heather DeLoach who became a child celebrity by tap-dancing in a bee costume on a rock video.[3] Heather was portrayed in the magazine as still being awed by others' fame ("I got to meet Pauly Shore and Janet Jackson, and I got Madonna's autograph, but I wasn't allowed to take pictures") and unawed by her own ("I see myself so much on TV that when the Bee Girl comes on, I just click right through the channel"). Sounding very much like other girls, she hedged when mentioning her good grades ("sort of like straight-A"). But she was also quoted as saying, "I'm extremely talented. I guess when the director first set eyes on me, he liked me. I try my best to be an actress, and I'm just great. I'm the one and only Bee Girl."

Although the article did not explain what question the interviewer asked to elicit Heather's truthful description of herself, the disapproving reader zeroed in on those words and admonished, "Heather De-Loach, the Bee Girl, describes herself as 'extremely talented' and 'just great.' Perhaps 10-year-old Heather should stop being a *bumble*bee and start being a *humble* bee." Not only did this reader tell the child star to start being more humble, but she also told her to stop being a bumblebee—that is, doing what she's so good at that it's bringing her attention, reward, and too much—or too obvious—self-confidence.

Reactions like these teach girls how they are expected to talk in order to be liked. It is not surprising that when she spoke in this guileless way, Heather DeLoach was ten. By the time she gets through junior high school and puberty, chances are she will have learned to talk differently, a transformation—and loss of confidence—that white middle-class American girls experience at that stage of their lives, according to a great deal of current research.[4] But it is crucial to bear in mind that ways of talking are not literal representations of mental

---

[3]The article about ten-year-old Heather DeLoach appeared in *People* magazine, November 29, 1993, p. 102. The letter criticizing her for not being humble was published in the same magazine, December 20,1993, p. 8.

[4]The crisis of confidence that girls undergo during adolescence was first brought to public attention by psychologist Carol Gilligan and her colleagues (see the essays in *Making Connections,* edited by Gilligan, Lyons, and Haruner). Journalist Judy Mann discusses the evidence for and causes of this troubling phenomenon in *The Difference,* and provides an eloquent personal expansion on it with reference to her own daughter. Psychotherapist Mary Pipher tells the stories of adolescent girls she has seen in psychotherapy in *Reviving Ophelia.*

states, and refraining from boasting may not reveal a true lack of confidence. A pair of studies by a team of psychologists makes this clear.

Laurie Heatherington and her colleagues had student experimenters ask hundreds of incoming college students to predict how they thought their first year at college would go by forecasting the grades they expected to get. In some cases, the predictions were made anonymously: They were put in writing and placed in an envelope. In others, they were made publicly, either orally to the experimenter or by writing on a paper that the experimenter promptly read. The researchers found that women predicted lower grades for themselves than men did—but only when they made their predictions publicly. The predictions the women students made in private did not differ from the men's, just as the grades they actually earned as the year progressed did not differ from the men's. In other words, their lower predictions evidenced not lack of confidence but reluctance to reveal the level of confidence they felt.

The same researchers conducted a second study that captured women's characteristic balancing act between their own interests and those of the person they are talking to. In half the cases, the experimenters told their own grade-point averages to the students they interviewed, and the grades they claimed to have gotten were comparatively low. Lo and behold, when women students thought they were talking to someone who had gotten low grades, they lowered their predictions of what they expected their own grades to be. Whether or not the experimenter claimed to have gotten low grades did not affect the predictions made by men students.

25 The first of these ingenious experiments dramatizes that the social inhibition against seeming to boast can make women appear less confident than they really are. And the second study shows that part of the reason many women censor themselves from proclaiming their confidence is that they are balancing their own interests with those of the person they are talking to. In other words, they modify their speech to take into account the impact of what they say on the other person's feelings.

There may be something peculiarly white middle class and American about the cultural constraint against women boasting. Those who have studied the remarkable change in how girls talk about their own talents and prospects during the crucial junior high school years have noted that the pattern is not necessarily found, or is not as strong, among black American teenage girls.[5] And anthropologist Thomas Kochman notes that talking about one's own accomplishments can be a highly valued source of humor for members of the cultural group he calls "community blacks," as illustrated by the widely publicized self-congratulatory verbal performances of the African-American prize-fighter Muhammad Ali. But every culture makes distinctions that outsiders may miss. Kochman contrasts acceptable African-American "boasting" to the kind of self-aggrandizement that is negatively sanctioned by the same community as "bragging."

To emphasize the cultural relativity of attitudes toward boasting, I should mention, too, the reaction of a British man who was certain that in his country, a boy who spoke like Heather DeLoach would be as likely as a girl to be chastised. Indeed, this Briton remarked, the British often find Americans annoyingly boastful.

For middle-class American women, though, the constraint is clear: Talking about your own accomplishments in a way that calls attention to yourself is not acceptable. This social constraint became both a source of criticism and a dodge for figure-skater Nancy Kerrigan when an inordinate amount of media attention was focused on her during the 1994 winter Olympics. *Newsweek* magazine called her "ungracious" for saying of her own performance, "I was flawless," and of her competitor's, "Oksana wasn't clean." But when a microphone picked up what Kerrigan thought was private grumbling about how "corny" and "dumb" it was to parade through Disney World with life-size cartoon characters, her "handlers" issued a statement that "she was referring merely to her mom's insistence that she wear her silver medal. She feared it would 'look like bragging.' "[6]

The expectation that women should not display their own accomplishments brings us back to the matter of negotiating that is so important in the workplace. A man who owned a medium-sized company remarked that women who came to ask him for raises often supported their requests by pointing to a fellow worker on the same level who earned more. He considered this a weak bargaining strategy because he could always identify a different coworker at that level who

---

[5]" . . . *have noted that the pattern is not necessarily found, or is not as strong, among black American teenage girls.*" See, for example, The AAUW Report, *How Schools Short-change Girls,* p. 13.

[6]"*She feared it would 'look like bragging.'* " *Newsweek,* March 14, 1994, p. 79.

earned less. They would do better, he felt, to argue for a raise on the basis of how valuable their own work is to the company. Yet it is likely that many women would be less comfortable "blowing their own horn" than making a claim based on fairness.

Follow the Leader

30 Similar expectations constrain how girls express leadership. Being a leader often involves giving directions to others, but girls who tell other girls what to do are called "bossy." It is not that girls do not exert influence on their group—of course they do—but, as anthropologists like Marjorie Harness Goodwin have found, many girls discover they get better results if they phrase their ideas as suggestions rather than orders, and if they give reasons for their suggestions in terms of the good of the group. But while these ways of talking make girls—and, later, women—more likable, they make women seem less competent and self-assured in the world of work. And women who do seem competent and self-assured are as much in danger of being negatively labeled as are girls. After her retirement, Margaret Thatcher was described in the press as "bossy." Whereas girls are ready to stick this label on each other because they don't think any girl should boss the others around, it seems odd to apply it to Thatcher, who, after all, was the boss. And this is the rub: Standards of behavior applied to women are based on roles that do not include being boss.

Boys are expected to play by different rules, since the social organization of boys is different. Boys' groups tend to be more obviously hierarchical: Someone is one-up, and someone is one-down. Boys don't typically accuse each other of being "bossy" because the high-status boys are expected to give orders and push the low-status boys around. Daniel Maltz and Ruth Borker summarize research by many scholars showing that boys tend to jockey for center stage, challenge those who get it, and deflect challenges. Giving orders and telling the others what to do are ways of getting and keeping the high-status role. Another way of getting high status is taking center stage by telling stories, jokes, and information. Along with this, many boys learn to state their opinions in the strongest possible terms and find out if they're wrong by seeing if others challenge them. These ways of talking translate into an impression of confidence.

The styles typical of women and men both make sense given the context in which they were learned, but they have very different consequences in the workplace. In order to avoid being put in the one-down position, many men have developed strategies for making sure they get the one-up position instead, and this results in ways of talking that serve them well when it comes to hiring and promotion. In relation to the examples I have given, women are more likely to speak in the styles that are less effective in getting recognized and promoted. But if they speak in the styles that are effective when used by men—being assertive, sounding sure of themselves, talking up what they have done to make sure they get credit for it—they run the risk that everyone runs if they do not fit their culture's expectations for appropriate behavior: They will not be liked and may even be seen as having psychological problems.

Both women and men pay a price if they do not behave in ways expected of their gender: Men who are not very aggressive are called "wimps," whereas women who are not very aggressive are called "feminine." Men who are aggressive are called "go-getters," though if they go too far, from the point of view of the viewer, they may be called "arrogant." This can hurt them, but not nearly as much as the innumerable labels for women who are thought to be too aggressive—starting with the most hurtful one: bitch.

Even the compliments that we receive are revealing. One woman who had designed and implemented a number of innovative programs was praised by someone who said, "You have such a gentle way of bringing about radical change that people don't realize what's happening—or don't get threatened by it." This was a compliment, but it also hinted at the downside of the woman's gentle touch: Although it made it possible for her to be effective in instituting the changes she envisioned, her unobtrusive style ensured a lack of recognition. If people don't realize what's happening, they won't give her credit for what she has accomplished.

35   Not only advancement and recognition, but hiring is affected by   35
ways of speaking. A woman who supervised three computer programmers mentioned that her best employee was another woman whom she had hired over the objections of her own boss. Her boss had preferred a male candidate, because he felt the man would be better able to step into her supervisory role if needed. But she had taken a

dislike to the male candidate. For one thing, she had felt he was inappropriately flirtatious with her. But most important, she had found him arrogant, because he spoke as if he already had the job, using the pronoun "we" to refer to the group that had not yet hired him.

I have no way of knowing whether the woman hired was indeed the better of these two candidates, or whether either she or the man was well suited to assume the supervisory role, but I am intrigued that the male boss was impressed with the male candidate's take-charge self-presentation, while the woman supervisor was put off by it. And it seems quite likely that whatever it was about his way of talking that struck her as arrogant was exactly what led her boss to conclude that this man would be better able to take over her job if needed.

This example brings to mind a small item in an unusual memoir: the autobiography of an Australian woman with autism. In her remarkable memoir *Somebody Somewhere,* Donna Williams explains that although her autism made it difficult for her to process language, she managed to function in the world by mimicking the speech she heard around her. However, she regarded her successful performances not as her own doing but as the work of two imaginary personas, Carol and Willie. Although there is no evidence that Williams herself thought of these two "characters" (as she called them) as female and male, when reading her account of the kinds of things they could say and do, I repeatedly noticed that Carol performed stereotypically female behavior (she cocked her head, filled the air with social chatter, and, above all, smiled), while Willie played the stereotypically male part (he was strong, detached, and accumulated facts to impress people). So it struck me as amusing, but also troubling, when I read in Williams's memoir that it was Willie who went for interviews but Carol who held down jobs. This is not to imply that men do not deserve the jobs they get, but that ways of talking typically associated with men are more likely to impress many job interviewers as well as those making decisions about promotions to managerial levels.

I believe these patterns explain why it is common to hear that a particular woman lacks confidence or that a particular man is arrogant. Though we think of these as individual weaknesses, underconfidence and arrogance are disproportionately observed in women and men respectively, because they result from an overabundance of ways of speaking that are expected of females and males. Boys are expected to put themselves forward, emphasize the qualities that make them look good, and deemphasize those that would show them in a less favorable light. Too much of this is called arrogance. Girls are expected to be "humble"—not try to take the spotlight, emphasize the ways they are just like everyone else, and deemphasize ways they are special. A woman who does this really well comes off as lacking in confidence. Ironically, those who learn the lessons best are most in danger of falling into traps laid by conversational conventions.

Questions on Meaning

1. What are the different "conversational rituals" of men and women when talking to members of the same sex? What problems can arise when a man talks with a women and neither understands the rituals of the other? What is the difference between negotiating "from the inside out" and "from the outside in"?
2. Why is self-confidence so important in business communication? What account for women seemingly showing less self-confidence in how they communicate their ideas?
3. What is the difference in men's and women's leadership styles?

Questions on Rhetorical Strategy and Style

1. Tannen frequently cites studies by psychologists and other social scientists. How do these help develop her essay? What writing strategy generally uses this approach?
2. Tannen typically follows a writing strategy in which she explains an idea or observation and then goes on to clarify it by tracing backward to its causes and then forward to its effects. Reread the section of the essay with the heading "Feasting on Humble Pie" and analyze how Tannen uses these and other rhetorical styles to explain how women are more humble than men.

Writing Assignments

1. Tannen makes some interesting observations about how men do not hesitate to speak highly of their own accomplishments, whereas women tend to demur and avoid boasting. Test out this observation with your own peers. Ask a few other students what their favorite class is, and then ask them how well they are doing in that class. Try to ask an equal number of men and women. Do you observe differences in how positively they speak of their per-formance in the class? If your own observations do not match Tannen's, how do you account for the difference?
2. Assume for this exercise that you are the office manager of a mid-size company and that you have been observing the types of com-munication problems about which Tannen writes. In the interests of improving communication and making decision making more effective in the office, you decide to meet with key men and women in the office and offer advice on how they can better work

with members of the opposite sex. Write two short scripts to prepare for these meetings: what you plan to say to the men, and
what you plan to say to the women. Do the first draft on your
own; do not reread Tannen's essay or paraphrase her arguments.
Then use her essay to guide your revision.

3. All writers who generalize about differences between men and
women, or blacks and whites, or Americans and the French, or
any other human groups are in reality making comments only
about *most* or *many* men and women and so on. Therefore all such
generalizations run the risk of not being true when applied to a
given person, who may or may not be like the *most* expressed in
the generalization. How can such generalizations, then, be useful—if you simply may be wrong when you try to apply them to
real individuals? For example, should a woman assume the man
she is about to speak to is like most men and is assertive in his negotiating style, even though this runs a risk if it happens he has a
cooperative style instead? How can one escape this dilemma?
Think about this issue, and write an essay explaining how such
generalizations can be applied in the real world—how abstract
knowledge can be translated into practical tactics.

The Ethic of Compassion
The Dalai Lama

His Holiness the Dalai Lama (1935–) was born a peasant in Taktser, Tibet under the birth name of Lhamo Dhondrub. He is the fourteenth Dalai Lama (spiritual leader of Tibet, reincarnation of the thirteenth Dalai Lama, and an incarnation of the Buddha of Compassion). He lives in Dharamsala, India. He was recognized at age two as the Dalai Lama and was enthroned on February 22, 1940. He completed the Geshe Lharampa Degree (equivalent to a Doctorate of Buddhist Philosophy) in 1959 and became head of Tibet—but was driven out by a Chinese invasion. He has worked on behalf of Tibet from India, asking the United Nations for help and working to bring Buddhist beliefs back to the country. He received the Albert Schweitzer Humanitarian Award (1987); Raoul Wallenberg Congressional Human Rights Award (1989); the Nobel Peace Prize (1989); Franklin D. Roosevelt Freedom Medal (1994); and the Hessian Peace Prize (2005). His books include Kindness, Clarity and Insight *(Snow Lion, 1984);* Compassion and the Individual *(Wisdom Publications, 1991); and* The Power of Compassion *(Harper Collins, 1995).*

Compassion is good when first considered, for it is easy to feel compassion for one who suffers. Compassion is harder to muster for wealthy and powerful people and even harder to feel when true compassion leads to a career change or an even greater life upheaval.

1   We noted earlier that all the world's major religions stress the 1
importance of cultivating love and compassion. In the Buddhist philosophical tradition, different levels of attainment

Reprinted from *Ethics for the New Millennium,* by permission of Riverhead Books, an imprint of Penguin Group (USA) Inc. and The Wylie Agency. Copyright © 1999, 2001 by Kyabje Tenzin Gyatso, 14th Dalai Lama of Tibet.

are described. At a basic level, compassion (*nying je*) is understood mainly in terms of empathy—our ability to enter into and, to some extent, share others' suffering. But Buddhist—and perhaps others—believe that this can be developed to such a degree that not only does our compassion arise without any effort, but it is unconditional, undifferentiated, and universal in scope. A feeling of intimacy toward all other sentient beings, including of course those who would harm us, is generated, which is likened in the literature to the love a mother has for her only child.

But this sense of equanimity toward all others is not seen as an end in itself. Rather, it is seen as the springboard to a love still greater. Because our capacity for empathy is innate, and because the ability to reason is also an innate faculty, compassion shares the characteristics of consciousness itself. The potential we have to develop it is therefore stable and continuous. It is not a resource which can be used up—as water is used up when we boil it. And though it can be described in terms of activity, it is not like a physical activity which we train for, like jumping, where once we reach a certain height we can go no further. On the contrary, when we enhance our sensitivity toward others' suffering through deliberately opening ourselves up to it, it is believed that we can gradually extend out compassion to the point where the individual feels so moved by even the subtlest suffering of others that they come to have an over-whelming sense of responsibility toward those others. This causes the one who is compassionate to dedicate themselves entirely to helping others overcome both their suffering and the causes of their suffering. In Tibetan, this ultimate level of attainment is called *nying je chenmo*, literally "great compassion."

Now I am not suggesting that each individual must attain these advanced states of spiritual development in order to lead an ethically wholesome life. I have described *nying je chenmo* not because it is a precondition of ethical conduct but rather because I believe that pushing the logic of compassion to the highest level can act as a powerful inspiration. If we can just keep the aspiration to develop *nying je chenmo*, or great compassion, as an ideal, it will naturally have a significant impact on our outlook. Based on the simple recognition that, just as I do, so do all others desire to be happy and not to suffer, it will serve as a constant reminder against selfishness and partiality. It will remind us that there is little to be gained from being kind and generous because we hope to win something in return. It will remind us that actions motivated by the desire to create a good name for ourselves are still selfish, however much they may appear to be acts of kindness. It will also remind us that there is nothing exceptional about acts of charity toward those we already feel close to. And it will help us to recognize that the bias we naturally feel toward our families and friends is actually a highly unreliable thing on which to base ethical conduct. If we reserve ethical conduct for those whom we feel close to, the danger is that we will neglect our responsibilities toward those outside this circle.

Why is this? So long as the individuals in question continue to meet our expectations, all is well. But should they fail to do so, someone we consider a dear friend one day can become our sworn enemy the next. As we saw earlier, we have a tendency to react badly to all who threaten fulfillment of our cherished desires, though they may be our closest relations. For this reason, compassion and mutual respect offer a much more solid basis for our relations with others. This is also true of partnerships. If our love for someone is based largely on attraction, whether it be their looks or some other superficial characteristic, our feelings for that person are liable, over time, to evaporate. When they lose the quality we found alluring, or when we find ourselves no longer satisfied by it, the situation can change completely, this despite their being the same person. This is why relationships based purely on attraction are almost always unstable. On the other hand, when we begin to perfect our compassion, neither the other's appearance nor their behavior affects our underlying attitude.

Consider, too, that habitually our feelings toward others depend very much on their circumstances. Most people, when they see someone who is handicapped, feel sympathetic toward that person. But then when they see others who are wealthier, or better educated, or better placed socially, they immediately feel envious and competitive toward them. Our negative feelings prevent us from seeing the sameness of ourselves and all others. We forget that just like us, whether fortunate or unfortunate, distant or near, they desire to be happy and not to suffer.

The struggle is thus to overcome these feelings of partiality. Certainly, developing genuine compassion for our loved ones is the obvious and appropriate place to start. The impact our actions have on our close ones will generally be much greater than on others, and therefore our responsibilities toward them are greater. Yet we need to recognize that, ultimately, there are no grounds for discriminating in their favor. In this sense, we are all in the same position as a doctor confronted by ten patients suffering the same serious illness. They are each equally deserving of treatment. The reader should not suppose that what is being advocated here is a state of detached indifference, however. The further essential challenge, as we begin to extend our compassion toward all others, is to maintain the same level of intimacy as we feel toward those closest to us. In other words, what is being suggested is that we need to strive for even-handedness in our approach toward all others, a level ground into which we can plant the seed of *nying je chenmo,* of great love and compassion.

If we can begin to relate to others on the basis of such equanimity, our compassion will not depend on the fact that so and so is my husband, my wife, my relative, my friend. Rather, a feeling of closeness toward all others can be developed based on the simple recognition that, just like myself, all wish to be happy and to avoid suffering. In other words, we will start to relate to others on the basis of their sentient nature. Again, we can think of this in terms of an ideal, one which it is immensely difficult to attain. But, for myself, I find it one which is profoundly inspiring and helpful.

Let us now consider the role of compassionate love and kind-heartedness in our daily lives. Does the ideal of developing it to the point where it is unconditional mean that we must abandon our own interests entirely? Not at all. In fact, it is the best way of serving them—indeed, it could even be said to constitute the wisest course for fulfilling self-interest. For if it is correct that those qualities such as love, patience, tolerance, and forgiveness are what happiness consists in, and if it is also correct that *nying je,* or compassion, as I have defined it, is both the source and the fruit of these qualities, then the more we are compassionate, the more we provide for our own happiness. Thus, any idea that concern for others, though a noble quality, is a matter for our private lives only, is simply short-sighted. Compassion belongs to every sphere of activity, including, of course, the workplace.

Here, though, I must acknowledge the existence of a perception—shared by many, it seems—that compassion is, if not actually an impediment, at least irrelevant to professional life. Personally, I would argue that not only is it relevant, but that when compassion is lacking, our activities are in danger of becoming destructive. This is because when we ignore the question of the impact our actions have on others' well-being, inevitably we end up hurting them. The ethic of compassion helps provide the necessary foundation and motivation for both restraint and the cultivation of virtue. When we begin to develop a genuine appreciation of the value of compassion, our outlook on others begins automatically to change. This alone can serve as a powerful influence on the conduct of our lives. When, for example, the temptation to deceive others arises, our compassion for them will prevent us from entertaining the idea. And when we realize that our work itself is in danger of being exploited to the detriment of others, compassion will cause us to disengage from it. So to take an imaginary case of a scientist whose research seems likely to be a source of suffering, they will recognize this and act accordingly, even if this means abandoning the project.

10 I do not deny that genuine problems can arise when we dedicate 10 ourselves to the ideal of compassion. In the case of a scientist who felt unable to continue in the direction their work was taking them, this could have profound consequences both for themselves and for their families. Likewise, those engaged in the caring professions—in medicine, counseling, social work, and so on—or even those looking after someone at home may sometimes become so exhausted by their duties that they feel overwhelmed. Constant exposure to suffering, coupled occasionally with a feeling of being taken for granted, can induce feelings of helplessness and even despair. Or it can happen that individuals may find themselves performing outwardly generous actions merely for the sake of it—simply going through the motions, as it were. Of course this is better than nothing. But when left unchecked, this can lead to insensitivity toward others' suffering. If this starts to happen, it is best to disengage for a short while and make a deliberate effort to reawaken that sensitivity. In this it can be helpful to remember that despair is never a solution. It is, rather, the ultimate failure. Therefore, as the Tibetan expression has it, even if the rope breaks nine times, we must splice it back together a tenth time. In this way, even if ultimately we do fail, at least there will be no feelings of regret. And when we combine this insight with a clear appreciation of our potential to benefit others, we find that we can begin to restore our hope and confidence.

Some people may object to this ideal on the grounds that by entering into others' suffering, we bring suffering on ourselves. To an extent, this is true. But I suggest that there is an important qualitative distinction to be made between experiencing one's own suffering and experiencing suffering in the course of sharing in others'. In the case of one's own suffering, given that it is involuntary, there is a sense of oppression: it seems to come from outside us. By contrast, sharing in someone else's suffering must at some level involve a degree of voluntariness, which itself is indicative of a certain inner strength. For this reason, the disturbance it may cause is considerably less likely to paralyze us than our own suffering.

Of course, even as an ideal, the notion of developing unconditional compassion is daunting. Most people, including myself, must struggle even to reach the point where putting others' interests on a par with our own becomes easy. We should not allow this to put us off, however. And while undoubtedly there will be obstacles on the way to developing a genuinely warm heart, there is the deep consolation of knowing that in doing so we are creating the conditions for our own happiness. As I mentioned earlier, the more we truly desire to benefit others, the greater the strength and confidence we develop and the greater the peace and happiness we experience. If this still seems unlikely, it is worth asking ourselves how else we are to do so. With violence and aggression? Of course not. With money? Perhaps up to a point, but no further. But with love, by sharing in others' suffering, by recognizing ourselves clearly in all others—especially those who are disadvantaged and those whose rights are not respected—by helping them to, be happy: yes. Through love, through kindness, through compassion we establish understanding between ourselves and others. This is how we forge unity and harmony.

Compassion and love are not mere luxuries. As the source both of inner and external peace, they are fundamental to the continued survival of our species. On the one hand, they constitute non-violence in action. On the other, they are the source of all spiritual qualities: of forgiveness, tolerance, and all the virtues. Moreover, they are the very thing that gives meaning to our activities and makes them constructive. There is nothing amazing about being highly educated; there is nothing amazing about being rich. Only when the individual has a warm heart do these attributes become worthwhile.

So to those who say that the Dalai Lama is being unrealistic in advocating this ideal of unconditional love, I urge them to experiment with it nonetheless. They will discover that when we reach beyond the confines of narrow self-interest, our hearts become filled with strength. Peace and joy become our constant companion. It breaks down barriers of every kind and in the end destroys the notion of my interest as independent from others' interest. But most important, so far as ethics is concerned, where love of one's neighbor, affection, kindness, and compassion live, we find that ethical conduct is automatic. Ethically wholesome actions arise naturally in the context of compassion.

Questions on Meaning

1. Compassion means to empathize with another, to feel that person's joy, pain, and hope. Why does the author say that feeling compassion for the disabled or the poor is easy? Why is it hard to feel sympathy for those we envy?

2. What would happen to our ordinary, selfish lives if we were to start feeling real compassion? Would we be able to use the environment and the rest of the world as we do now? What would we have to change?

3. What does the individual gain by feeling compassion? Is the kind of peace and love that are described in this essay really what people want? Why do most of us live lives that are aimed at making money and winning, rather than loving?

Questions on Rhetorical Strategy and Style

1. The tone of this essay is very gentle and kind, but the message is quite tough. How does the author warn the reader in the introduction that the essay is going to be demanding and maybe a bit disturbing?

2. The essay moves to a cause and effect structure: If one feels true compassion, the feeling may cause one to have to change one's life. The feeling, though a good one, may lead to uncomfortable results. How does this causality affect the reader of the essay? Is a reader likely to change behavior in light of this cause and effect explanation?

3. The end of the essay promises that great good can come from feeling compassion. How does the writer hope to persuade the reader that these benefits are worthwhile? Does this ending promise better things for the world if many readers are persuaded? Is it even possible?

Writing Assignments

1. A wise person once said that we should feel compassion rather than guilt, for we will act from compassion, but we will merely suffer from guilt. Think of someone you know whom you consider compassionate. Write about what that person does with life. What kind of work does the person do? What kind of entertainment and leisure activities does that person pursue?

2. Write about a world leader whom you consider compassionate. Show how this feeling is displayed in the person's actions. What would happen to world politics if everyone acted with compassion?
3. Consider a world conflict, either one occurring now or one in history. Write about how the events could be or would have been different had the parties shown more compassion and less aggression.

Being a Man

Paul Theroux

Paul Theroux (1941–) divides his time between England and his native Massachusetts. He has written novels, including the well-regarded The Mosquito Coast; *short stories which were recently collected in his* The Collected Stories *(1997); and many magazine articles. In this essay he explores with vengeful enthusiasm the stereotypical social role reserved for American males.*

1   There is a pathetic sentence in the chapter "Fetishism" in Dr. Norman Cameron's book *Personality Development and Psychopathology.* It goes, "Fetishists are nearly always men; and the commonest fetish is a woman's shoe," I cannot read that sentence without thinking that it is just one more awful thing about being a man—and perhaps it is an important thing to know about us.

I have always disliked being a man. The whole idea of manhood in America is pitiful, in my opinion. This version of masculinity is a little like having to wear an ill-fitting coat for one's entire life (by contrast, I imagine femininity to be an oppressive sense of nakedness). Even the expression "Be a man!" strikes me as insulting and abusive. It means: Be stupid, be unfeeling, obedient, soldierly and stop thinking. Man means "manly"—how can one think about men without considering the terrible ambition of manliness? And yet it is part of every man's life. It is a hideous and crippling lie; it not only insists on difference and connives at superiority, it is also by its very nature destructive—emotionally damaging and socially harmful.

The youth who is subverted, as most are, into believing in the masculine ideal is effectively separated from women and he spends the rest of his life finding women a riddle and a nuisance. Of course, there is a female version of this male affliction. It begins with mothers

From *Sunrise and Seamonsters* by Paul Theroux. Published by Houghton Mifflin Company. Copyright © 1985 by Cape Cod Scriveners Company.

encouraging little girls to say (to other adults) "Do you like my new dress?" In a sense, little girls are traditionally urged to please adults with a kind of coquettishness, while boys are enjoined to behave like monkeys towards each other. The nine-year-old coquette proceeds to become womanish in a subtle power game in which she learns to be sexually indispensable, socially decorative and always alert to a man's sense of inadequacy.

Femininity—being lady-like—implies needing a man as witness and seducer; but masculinity celebrates the exclusive company of men. That is why it is so grotesque; and that is also why there is no manliness without inadequacy—because it denies men the natural friendship of women.

It is very hard to imagine any concept of manliness that does not belittle women, and it begins very early. At an age when I wanted to meet girls—let's say the treacherous years of thirteen to sixteen—I was told to take up a sport, get more fresh air, join the Boy Scouts, and I was urged not to read so much. It was the 1950s and if you asked too many questions about sex you were sent to camp—boy's camp, of course: the nightmare. Nothing is more unnatural or prison-like than a boy's camp, but if it were not for them we would have no Elks' Lodges, no pool rooms, no boxing matches, no Marines.

And perhaps no sports as we know them. Everyone is aware of how few in number are the athletes who behave like gentlemen. Just as high school basketball teaches you how to be a poor loser, the manly attitude towards sports seems to be little more than a recipe for creating bad marriages, social misfits, moral degenerates, sadists, latent rapists and just plain louts. I regard high school sports as a drug far worse than marijuana, and it is the reason that the average tennis champion, say, is a pathetic oaf.

Any objective study would find the quest for manliness essentially right-wing, puritanical, cowardly, neurotic and fueled largely by a fear of women. It is also certainly philistine. There is no book-hater like a Little League coach. But indeed all the creative arts are obnoxious to the manly ideal, because at their best the arts are pursued by uncompetitive and essentially solitary people. It makes it very hard for a creative youngster, for any boy who expresses the desire to be alone seems to be saying that there is something wrong with him.

It ought to be clear by now that I have something of an objection to the way we turn boys into men. It does not surprise me that when the President of the United States has his customary weekend off he dresses like a cowboy—it is both a measure of his insecurity and his willingness to please. In many ways, American culture does little more for a man than prepare him for modeling clothes in the L. L. Bean catalogue. I take this as a personal insult because for many years I found it impossible to admit to myself that I wanted to be a writer. It was my guilty secret, because being a writer was incompatible with being a man.

There are people who might deny this, but that is because the American writer, typically, has been so at pains to prove his manliness that we have come to see literariness and manliness as mingled qualities. But first there was a fear that writing was not a manly profession—indeed, not a profession at all. (The paradox in American letters is that it has always been easier for a woman to write and for a man to be published.) Growing up, I had thought of sports as wasteful and humiliating, and the idea of manliness was a bore. My wanting to become a writer was not a flight from that oppressive role-playing, but I quickly saw that it was at odds with it. Everything in stereotyped manliness goes against the life of the mind. The Hemingway personality is too tedious to go into here, and in any case his exertions are well-known, but certainly it was not until this aberrant behavior was examined by feminists in the 1960s that any male writer dared question the pugnacity in Hemingway's fiction. All the bullfighting and arm wrestling and elephant shooting diminished Hemingway as a writer, but it is consistent with a prevailing attitude in American writing: one cannot be a male writer without first proving that one is a man.

10   It is normal in America for a man to be dismissive or even somewhat apologetic about being a writer. Various factors make it easier. There is a heartiness about journalism that makes it acceptable—journalism is the manliest form of American writing and, therefore, the profession the most independent-minded women seek (yes, it is an illusion, but that is my point). Fiction-writing is equated with a kind of dispirited failure and is only manly when it produces wealth—money is masculinity. So is drinking. Being a drunkard is another assertion, if misplaced, of manliness. The American male writer is traditionally proud of his heavy drinking. But we are also a very literal-minded people. A man proves his manhood in America in old-fashioned ways. He kills lions, like Hemingway; or he hunts ducks,

like Nathanael West; or he makes pronouncements like, "A man should carry enough knife to defend himself with," as James Jones once said to a *Life* interviewer. Or he says he can drink you under the table. But even tiny drunken William Faulkner loved to mount a horse and go fox hunting, and Jack Kerouac roistered up and down Manhattan in a lumberjack shirt (and spent every night of *The Subterraneans* with his mother in Queens). And we are familiar with the lengths to which Norman Mailer is prepared, in his endearing way, to prove that he is just as much a monster as the next man.

When the novelist John Irving was revealed as a wrestler, people took him to be a very serious writer; and even a bubble reputation like Eric (*Love Story*) Segal's was enhanced by the news that he ran the marathon in a respectable time. How surprised we would be if Joyce Carol Oates were revealed as a sumo wrestler or Joan Didion active in pumping iron. "Lives in New York City with her three children" is the typical woman writer's biographical note, for just as the male writer must prove he has achieved a sort of muscular manhood, the woman writer—or rather her publicists—must prove her motherhood.

There would be no point in saying any of this if it were not generally accepted that to be a man is somehow—even now in feminist-influenced America—a privilege. It is on the contrary an unmerciful and punishing burden. Being a man is bad enough; being manly is appalling (in this sense, women's lib has done much more for men than for women). It is the sinister silliness of men's fashions, and a clubby attitude in the arts. It is the subversion of good students. It is the so-called "Dress Code" of the Ritz-Carlton Hotel in Boston, and it is the institutionalized cheating in college sports. It is the most primitive insecurity.

And this is also why men often object to feminism but are afraid to explain why: of course women have a justified grievance, but most men believe—and with reason—that their lives are just as bad.

Questions on Meaning

1. List the negative qualities of the American male that Theroux mentions. Does the list correspond to reality as you know it?
2. What are the losses to men who try to live up to the stereotype Theroux describes?

Questions on Rhetorical Strategy and Style

1. This piece of writing could be called a diatribe—a bitter and abusive denunciation. Locate and list particular word choices that suggest bitterness. What experiences do you think are behind Theroux's feelings?
2. Theroux's intention here is primarily to express his opinion rather than to persuade an audience. If he were going to rewrite this essay with a more persuasive intent, which points would be the most important to retain? Which would he have to cut out?
3. What are the more positive meanings of the expression, "Be a man"?

Writing Assignments

1. Write an essay in which you define the concept of "man" based on the men you know. List some of the more important and representative men in your life and note the qualities they share. Illustrate your discussion with descriptions of the men's belief and behavior.
2. Write an essay that defines the concept of "man" by dividing it into types of men. Your typology may be based on age or generation (e.g., the middle-aged man, the man of the nineties), geography (the Western man, the urban man), tastes (the conservative man, the GQ man), or some other set of factors that seems important to you.

Everyday Use

Alice Walker

Alice Walker (1944–) was born in Georgia to sharecropper parents. She attended Spelman College and Sarah Lawrence College and was active in the civil rights movement of the 1960s. Publishing her first novel, The Third Life of Grange Copeland, *at the age of 26, she has been a prolific writer since. In all, she has published five novels, two short story collections, two collections of essays, and several books of poems. Her novel* The Color Purple *(1982) is perhaps her best known, having won the American Book Award, the Pulitzer Prize, and the Candace Award of the National Coalition of 100 Black Women. The novel was also made into a prize-winning film by director Steven Spielberg. Walker's topics run the gamut of human experience and include some harsh realities such as incest and racial violence as well as relationships within families and society. "Everyday Use" is a short story published in* In Love and Trouble *(1973). In it Walker deals with a number of themes common in her work: changes between generations, family tensions, African-American heritage. You should notice right away that in this story Walker is writing from the point of view of a woman other than herself.*

for your grandmama

1   I will wait for her in the yard that Maggie and I made so clean and   1
wavy yesterday afternoon. A yard like this is more comfortable
than most people know. It is not just a yard. It is like an extended
living room. When the hard clay is swept clean as a floor and the fine
sand around the edges lined with tiny, irregular grooves, anyone can

From *In Love & Trouble: Stories of Black Women.* Published by Harcourt Brace Jovanovich, Inc. Copyright © Harcourt Brace & Company and Wendy Weil Agency.

come and sit and look up into the elm tree and wait for the breezes that never come inside the house.

Maggie will be nervous until after her sister goes: she will stand hopelessly in corners, homely and ashamed of the burn scars down her arms and legs, eying her sister with a mixture of envy and awe. She thinks her sister has held life always in the palm of one hand, that "no" is a word the world never learned to say to her.

You've no doubt seen those TV shows where the child who has "made it" is confronted, as a surprise, by her own mother and father, tottering in weakly from backstage. (A pleasant surprise, of course: What would they do if parent and child came on the show only to curse out and insult each other?) On TV mother and child embrace and smile into each other's faces. Sometimes the mother and father weep, the child wraps them in her arms and leans across the table to tell how she would not have made it without their help, I have seen these programs.

Sometimes I dream a dream in which Dee and I are suddenly brought together on a TV program of this sort. Out of a dark and soft-seated limousine I am ushered into to a bright room filled with many people. There I meet a smiling, gray, sporty man like Johnny Carson who shakes my hand and tells me what a fine girl I have. Then we are on the stage and Dee is embracing me with tears in her eyes. She pins on my dress a large orchid, even though she has told me once that she thinks orchids are tacky flowers.

5   In real life I am a large, big-boned woman with rough, man-   5 working hands. In the winter I wear flannel nightgowns to bed and overalls during the day. I can kill and clean a hog as mercilessly as a man. My fat keeps me hot in zero weather. I can work outside all day, breaking ice to get water for washing; I can eat pork liver cooked over the open fire minutes after it comes steaming from the hog. One winter I knocked a bull calf straight in the brain between the eyes with a sledge hammer and had the meat hung up to chill before nightfall. But of course all this does not show on television. I am the way my daughter would want me to be: a hundred pounds lighter, my skin like an uncooked barley pancake. My hair glistens in the hot bright lights. Johnny Carson has much to do to keep up with my quick and witty tongue.

But that is a mistake. I know even before I wake up. Who ever knew a Johnson with a quick tongue? Who can even imagine me looking a strange white man in the eye? It seems to me I have talked to them always with one foot raised in flight, with my head turned in whichever way is farthest from them. Dee, though. She would always look anyone in the eye. Hesitation was no part of her nature.

"How do I look, Mama?" Maggie says, showing just enough of her thin body enveloped in pink skirt and red blouse for me to know she's there, almost hidden by the door.
"Come out into the yard," I say.
Have you ever seen a lame animal, perhaps a dog run over by some careless person rich enough to own a car, sidle up to someone who is ignorant enough to be kind to him? That is the way my Maggie walks. She has been like this, chin on chest, eyes on ground, feet in shuffle, ever since the fire that burned the other house to the ground.

10   Dee is lighter than Maggie, with nicer hair and a fuller figure.   10
She's a woman now, though sometimes I forget. How long ago was it that the other house burned? Ten, twelve years? Sometimes I can still hear the flames and feel Maggie's arms sticking to me, her hair smoking and her dress falling off her in little black papery flakes. Her eyes seemed stretched open, blazed open by the flames reflected in them. And Dee. I see her standing off under the sweet gum tree she used to dig gum out of, a look of concentration on her face as she watched the last dingy gray board of the house fall in toward the red-hot brick chimney. Why don't you do a dance around the ashes? I'd wanted to ask her. She had hated the house that much.

I used to think she hated Maggie, too. But that was before we raised the money, the church and me, to send her to Augusta to school. She used to read to us without pity; forcing words, lies, other folks' habits, whole lives upon us two, sitting trapped and ignorant underneath her voice. She washed us in a river of make-believe, burned us with a lot of knowledge we didn't necessarily need to know. Pressed us to her with the serious way she read, to shove us away at just the moment, like dimwits, we seemed about to understand.

Dee wanted nice things. A yellow organdy dress to wear to her graduation from high school; black pumps to match a green suit she'd made from an old suit somebody gave me. She was determined to stare down any disaster in her efforts. Her eyelids would not flicker for minutes at a time. Often I fought off the temptation to shake her. At sixteen she had a style of her own: and knew what style was.

I never had an education myself. After second grade the school was closed down. Don't ask me why: in 1927 colored asked fewer questions than they do now. Sometimes Maggie reads to me. She stumbles along good-naturedly but can't see well. She knows she is not bright. Like good looks and money, quickness passed her by. She will marry John Thomas (who has mossy teeth in an earnest face) and then I'll be free to sit here and I guess just sing church songs to myself. Although I never was a good singer. Never could carry a tune. I was always better at a man's job. I used to love to milk till I was hooked in the side in '49. Cows are soothing and slow and don't bother you, unless you try to milk them the wrong way.

I have deliberately turned my back on the house. It is three rooms, just like the one that burned, except the roof is tin; they don't make shingle roofs any more. There are no real windows, just some holes cut in the sides, like the portholes in a ship, but not round and not square, with rawhide holding the shutters up on the outside. This house is in a pasture, too, like the other one. No doubt when Dee sees it she will want to tear it down. She wrote me once that no matter where we "choose" to live, she will manage to come see us. But she will never bring her friends. Maggie and I thought about this and Maggie asked me, "Mama, when did Dee ever *have* any friends?"

15 She had a few. Furtive boys in pink shirts banging about on wash-day after school. Nervous girls who never laughed. Impressed with her they worshiped the well-turned phrase, the cute shape, the scalding humor that erupted like bubbles in lye. She read to them.

When she was courting Jimmy T she didn't have much time to pay to us, but turned all her faultfinding power on him. He *flew* to marry a cheap city girl from a family of ignorant flashy people. She hardly had time to recompose herself.

When she comes I will meet—but there they are!

Maggie attempts to make a dash for the house, in her shuffling way, but I stay her with my hand. "Come back here," I say. And she stops and tries to dig a well in the sand with her toe.

It is hard to see them clearly through the strong sun. But even the first glimpse of leg out of the car tells me it is Dee. Her feet were always neat-looking, as if God himself had shaped them with a certain style. From the other side of the car comes a short, stocky man. Hair is all over his head a foot long and hanging from his chin like a kinky mule tail. I hear Maggie suck in her breath. "Uhnnnh," is what it sounds like. Like when you see the wriggling end of a snake just in front of your foot on the road. "Uhnnnh."

20   Dee next. A dress down to the ground, in this hot weather. A 20 dress so loud it hurts my eyes. There are yellows and oranges enough to throw back the light of the sun. I feel my whole face warming from the heat waves it throws out. Earrings gold, too, and hanging down to her shoulders. Bracelets dangling and making noises when she moves her arm up to shake the folds of the dress out of her armpits. The dress is loose and flows, and as she walks closer, I like it. I hear Maggie go "Uhnnnh" again. It is her sister's hair. It stands straight up like the wool on a sheep. It is black as night and around the edges are two long pigtails that rope about like small lizards disappearing behind her ears.

    "Wa-su-zo-Tean-o!" she says, coming on in that gliding way the dress makes her move. The short stocky fellow with the hair to his navel is all grinning and he follows up with "Asalamalakim, my mother and sister!" He moves to hug Maggie but she falls back, right up against the back of my chair. I feel her trembling there and when I look up I see the perspiration falling off her chin.

    "Don't get up," says Dee. Since I am stout it takes something of a push. You can see me trying to move a second or two before I make it. She turns, showing white heels through her sandals, and goes back to the car. Out she peeks next with a Polaroid. She stoops down quickly and lines up picture after picture of me sitting there in front of the house with Maggie cowering behind me. She never takes a shot without making sure the house is included. When a cow comes nibbling around the edge of the yard she snaps it and me and Maggie *and* the house. Then she puts the Polaroid in the back seat of the car, and comes up and kisses me on the forehead.

    Meanwhile Asalamalakim is going through motions with Maggie's hand. Maggie's hand is as limp as a fish, and probably as cold, despite the sweat, and she keeps trying to pull it back. It looks like Asalamalakim wants to shake hands but wants to do it fancy. Or maybe be don't know how people shake hands. Anyhow, he soon gives up on Maggie.

    "Well," I say. "Dee."

25   "No, Mama," she says. "Not 'Dee,' Wangero Leewanika Kemanjo!" 25 "What happened to 'Dee'?" I wanted to know.

"She's dead," Wangero said. "I couldn't bear it any longer, being named after the people who oppress me."

"You know as well as me you was named after your aunt Dicie," I said. Dicie is my sister. She named Dee. We called her "Big Dee" after Dee was born.

"But who was she named after?" asked Wangero.

30 "I guess after Grandma Dee," I said.

"And who was she named after?" asked Wangero.

"Her mother," I said, and saw Wangero was getting tired. "That's about as far back as I can trace it," I said. Though, in fact, I probably could have carried it back beyond the Civil War through the branches.

"Well," said Asalamalakim, "there you are."

"Uhnnnh," I heard Maggie say.

35 "There I was not," I said, "before 'Dicie' cropped up in our family, so why should I try to trace it that far back?"

He just stood there grinning, looking down on me like somebody inspecting a Model A car. Every once in a while he and Wangero sent eye signals over my head.

"How do you pronounce this name?" I asked.

"You don't have to call me by it if you don't want to," said Wangero.

"Why shouldn't I?" I asked. "If that's what you want us to call you, we'll call you."

40 "I know it might sound awkward at first," said Wangero.

"I'll get used to it," I said. "Ream it out again."

Well, soon we got the name out of the way. Asalamalakim had a name twice as long and three times as hard. After I tripped over it two or three times he told me to just call him Hakim-a-barber. I wanted to ask him was he a barber, but I didn't really think he was, so I didn't ask.

"You must belong to those beef-cattle peoples down the road," I said. They said "Asalamalakim" when they met you, too, but they didn't shake hands. Always too busy: feeding the cattle, fixing the fences, putting up salt-lick shelters, throwing down hay. When the white folks poisoned some of the herd the men stayed up all night with rifles in their hands. I walked a mile and a half just to see the sight.

Hakim-a-barber said, "I accept some of their doctrines, but farming and raising cattle is not my style." (They didn't tell me, and I didn't ask, whether Wangero [Dee] had really gone and married him.)

45   We sat down to eat and right away he said he didn't eat collards 45
and pork was unclean. Wangero, though, went on through the chitlins
and corn bread, the greens and everything else. She talked a blue streak
over the sweet potatoes. Everything delighted her. Even the fact that
we still used the benches her daddy made for the table when we
couldn't afford to buy chairs.

     "Oh, Mama!" she cried. Then turned to Hakim-a-barber. "I never
knew how lovely these benches are. You can feel the rump prints," she
said, running her hands underneath her and along the bench. Then
she gave a sigh and her hand closed over Grandma Dee's butter dish.
"That's it!" she said. "I knew there was something I wanted to ask you
if I could have." She jumped up from the table and went over in the
corner where the churn stood, the milk in it clabber by now. She
looked at the churn and looked at it.

     "This churn top is what I need," she said. "Didn't Uncle Buddy
whittle it out of a tree you all used to have?"

     "Yes," I said.

     "Uh huh," she said happily. "And I want the dasher, too."

50   "Uncle Buddy whittle that, too?" asked the barber.   50

Dee (Wangero) looked up at me.

     "Aunt Dee's first husband whittled the dash," said Maggie so low
you almost couldn't hear her. "His name was Henry, but they called
him Stash."

     "Maggie's brain is like an elephant's," Wangero said, laughing. "I
can use the churn top as a centerpiece for the alcove table," she said,
sliding a plate over the churn, "and I'll think of something artistic to
do with the dasher."

     When she finished wrapping the dasher the handle stuck out. I
took it for a moment in my hands. You didn't even have to look close
to see where hands pushing the dasher up and down to make butter
had left a kind of sink in the wood. In fact, there were a lot of small
sinks; you could see where thumbs and fingers had sunk into the
wood. It was beautiful light yellow wood, from a tree that grew in the
yard where Big Dee and Stash had lived.

55   After dinner Dee (Wangero) went to the trunk at the foot of my 55
bed and started rifling through it. Maggie hung back in the kitchen
over the dishpan. Out came Wangero with two quilts. They had been
pieced by Grandma Dee and then Big Dee and me had hung them on
the quilt frames on the front porch and quilted them. One was in the

Lone Star pattern. The other was Walk Around the Mountain. In both of them were scraps of dresses Grandma Dee had worn fifty and more years ago. Bits and pieces of Granpa Jarrell's Paisley shirts. And one teeny faded blue piece, about the size of a penny matchbox, that was from Great Grandpa' Ezra's uniform that he wore in the Civil War.

"Mama," Wangero said sweet as a bird. "Can I have these old quilts?"

I heard something fall in the kitchen, and a minute later the kitchen door slammed.

"Why don't you take one or two of the others?" I asked. "These old things was just done by me and Big Dee from some tops your grandma pieced before she died."

"No," said Wangero. "I don't want those. They are stitched around the borders by machine."

60   "That'll make them last better," I said   60

"That's not the point," said Wangero. "These are all pieces of dresses Grandma used to wear. She did all this stitching by hand. Imagine!" She held the quilts securely in her arms, stroking them.

"Some of the pieces, like those lavender ones, come from old clothes her mother handed down to her," I said, moving up to touch the quilts. Dee (Wangero) moved back just enough so that I couldn't reach the quilts. They already belonged to her.

"Imagine!" she breathed again, clutching them closely to her bosom.

"The truth is," I said. "I promised to give them quilts to Maggie, for when she marries John Thomas."

65   She gasped like a bee had stung her.   65

"Maggie can't appreciate these quilts!" she said. "She'd probably be backward enough to put them to everyday use."

"I reckon she would," I said. "God knows I been saving 'em for long enough with nobody using 'em. I hope she will!" I didn't want to bring up how I had offered Dee (Wangero) a quilt when she went away to college. Then she had told me they were old-fashioned, out of style.

"But they're *priceless!*" she was saying now, furiously; for she has a temper. "Maggie would put them on the bed and in five years they'd be in rags. Less than that!"

"She can always make some more," I said. "Maggie knows how to quilt."

70   Dee (Wangero) looked at me with hatred. "You just will not un- 70
derstand. The point is these quilts, *these* quilts!"

"Well," I said, stumped. "What would *you* do with them?"

"Hang them," she said. As if that was the only thing you *could* do
with quilts.

Maggie by now was standing in the door. I could almost hear the
sound her feet made as they scraped over each other.

"She can have them, Mama," she said, like somebody used to
never winning anything, or having anything reserved for her. "I can
'member Grandma Dee without the quilts."

75   I looked at her hard. She had filled her bottom lip with checker- 75
berry snuff and it gave her face a kind of dopey, hangdog look. It was
Grandma Dee and big Dee who taught her how to quilt herself. She
stood there with her scarred hands hidden in the folds of her skirt. She
looked at her sister with something like fear but she wasn't mad at her.
This was Maggie's portion. This was the way she knew God to work.

When I looked at her like that something hit me in the top of my
head and ran down to the soles of my feet. Just like when I'm in
church and the spirit of God touches me and I get happy and shout.
I did something I never had done before: hugged Maggie to me, then
dragged her on into the room, snatched the quilts out of Miss
Wangero's hands and dumped them into Maggie's lap. Maggie just sat
there on my bed with her mouth open.

"Take one or two of the others," I said to Dee.

But she turned without a word and went out to Hakim-a-barber.

"You just don't understand," she said, as Maggie and I came out
to the car.

80   "What don't I understand?" I wanted to know. 80

"Your heritage," she said. And then she turned to Maggie, kissed
her, and said, "You ought to try to make something of yourself, too,
Maggie. It's really a new day for us. But from the way you and Mama
still live you'd never know it."

She put on some sunglasses that hid everything above the tip of
her nose and her chin.

Maggie smiled; maybe at the sunglasses. But a real smile, not
scared. After we watched the car dust settle I asked Maggie to bring
me a dip of snuff. And then the two of us sat there just enjoying, until
it was time to go in the house and go to bed.

Questions on Meaning

1. Describe the differences in Wangero's and her mother's attitudes toward the quilt. Is either more "right" than the other?
2. What do you make of the character "Hakim-a-barber"? He is not as fully described as the three women, but he still plays an important role in the story. What is it?
3. Is Mrs. Johnson, the mother, a happy person? Content with her life? What does the story seem to say about the way that she lives?

Questions on Rhetorical Strategy and Style

1. The story compares and contrasts Maggie and Dee in many ways. Describe how they seem to represent two different types of women. What is important about their differences?
2. The quilt in this story becomes a symbol—to Wangero, at least—of African-American heritage. What other physical things in the setting seem also to have this larger, symbolic value? Explain how Walker uses the symbolism of these physical objects to develop her thesis about their heritage.
3. The story moves through four small sections at the beginning into one extended scene when Dee arrives home. What is the function of the opening parts?

Writing Assignments

1. The story contrasts a poor rural life and a less poor urban life. The traditional rural, farming life is said to be disappearing, as modern "corporate farms" take over agriculture and individual family farms cease to exist. What do you think about a whole lifestyle and heritage disappearing? What about efforts to preserve knowledge and understanding of this tradition? Are such efforts important? Why or why not?
2. Relationships between siblings form a great theme in literature and film, perhaps in part because this relationship typically starts out in the innocence and happiness of childhood but can go so awry as siblings develop in different directions, the world intercedes, and tensions creep in. If you have a brother or sister near you in age, think about how your relationship has changed over time. If not, choose a sibling relationship from a written or cinematic work. What do you feel about growing apart? Is this

inevitable? Does it really matter? Write an essay in which you try to define your ideas about sibling relationships and their importance (or lack of importance).

The Place Where I Was Born

Alice Walker

Alice Walker (1944–) was born in Georgia to sharecrop-
per parents. She attended Spelman College and Sarah
Lawrence College and was active in the civil rights move-
ment of the 1960s. Publishing her first novel, The Third
Life of Grange Copeland, *at the age of 26, she has been*
a prolific writer since. In all, she has published five novels,
two short story collections, two collections of essays, and sev-
eral books of poems. Her novel The Color Purple
(1982) is perhaps her best known, having won the Amer-
ican Book Award, the Pulitzer Prize, and the Candace
Award of the National Coalition of 100 Black Women.
The novel was also made into a prize-winning film by di-
rector Steven Spielberg. Walker's topics run the gamut of
human experience and include some harsh realities such as
incest and racial violence as well as relationships within
families and society. In the following essay, first published
in the June, 1991 Essence, *Walker compares her present*
home to her childhood home and reveals something larger
about the meaning of place.

1   I am a displaced person. I sit here on a swing on the deck of my
house in northern California admiring how the fog has turned the
valley below into a lake. For hours nothing will be visible below
me except this large expanse of vapor; then slowly, as the sun rises and
gains in intensity, the fog will start to curl up and begin its slow rolling
drift toward the ocean. People here call it the dragon; and, indeed, a
dragon is what it looks like, puffing and coiling, winged, flaring and
in places thin and discreet, as it races before the sun, back to its ocean

coast den. Mornings I sit here in awe and great peace. The mountains across the valley come and go in the mist; the redwoods and firs, oaks and giant bays appear as clumpish spires, enigmatic shapes of green, like the stone forests one sees in Chinese paintings of Guilin.

It is incredibly beautiful where I live. Not fancy at all, or exclusive. But from where I sit on my deck I can look down on the backs of hawks, and the wide, satiny wings of turkey vultures glistening in the sun become my present connection to ancient Egyptian Africa. The pond is so still below me that the trees reflected in it seem, from this distance, to be painted in its depths.

All this—the beauty, the quiet, the cleanliness, the peace—is what I love. I realize how lucky I am to have found it here. And yet, there are days when my view of the mountains and redwoods makes me nostalgic for small rounded hills easily walked over, and for the look of big-leaf poplar and the scent of pine.

I am nostalgic for the land of my birth, the land I left forever when I was 13—moving first to the town of Eatonton, Georgia, and then, at 17, to the city of Atlanta.

5   I cried one day as I talked to a friend about a tree I loved as a child.   5
A tree that had sheltered my father on his long cold walk to school each morning: It was midway between his house and the school and because there was a large cavity in its trunk, a fire could be made inside it. During my childhood, in a tiny, overcrowded house in a tiny dell below it, I looked up at it frequently and felt reassured by its age, its generosity despite its years of brutalization (the fires, I knew, had to hurt), and its tall, old-growth pine nobility. When it was struck by lightning and killed, and then was cut down and made into firewood, I grieved as if it had been a person. Secretly. Because who among the members of my family would not have laughed at my grief?

I have felt entirely fortunate to have had this companion, and even today remember it with gratitude. But why the tears? my friend wanted to know. And it suddenly dawned on me that perhaps it *was* sad that it was a tree and not a member of my family to whom I was so emotionally close.

As a child I assumed I would always have the middle Georgia landscape to live in, as Br'er Rabbit, a native also, and relative, had his brier patch. It was not to be. The pain of racist oppression, and its consequence, economic impoverishment, drove me to the four corners of the earth in search of justice and peace, and work that affirmed my whole being. I have come to rest here, weary from travel, on a deck—not a southern front porch—overlooking another world.

I am content; and yet, I wonder what my life would have been like if I had been able to stay home.

I remember early morning fogs in Georgia, not so dramatic as California ones, but magical too because out of the southern fog of memory tramps my dark father, smiling and large, glowing with root-edness, and talking of hound dogs, biscuits and coons. And my equally rooted mother bustles around the corner of our house preparing to start a wash, the fire under the black wash pot extending a circle of warmth in which I, a grave-eyed child, stand. There is my sister Ruth, beautiful to me and dressed elegantly for high school, in gray felt skirt and rhinestone brooch, hurrying up the road to catch the yellow school bus which glows like a large glowworm in the early morning fog.

Questions on Meaning

1. Why does Walker say she left Georgia? Why does she use one brief paragraph to explain her reasons for leaving?
2. Walker describes both her parents as "rooted" in Georgia. Is Walker herself rooted in some respect? Speculate about differences between her and her parents that led to her leaving and their apparent staying.
3. What do you make of the story of the large tree in the middle of the essay? How does this description fit in with the rest of the essay? Walker comments that she was emotionally closer to the tree than to members of her family—why do you think that was so?

Questions on Rhetorical Strategy and Style

1. Walker begins the essay with a description of the fog near her northern California home and closes it with a description of the fog near her childhood home in Georgia. What is the effect of this image on your reading experience? Reread these fog passages and analyze the mood and meaning that emerge from them.
2. Walker uses the rhetorical device of comparison and contrast in describing her present home and her childhood home. In addition to the fog, what aspects of each home are compared? What meaning emerges from this comparison? What is the effect of an incomplete comparison, such as when Walker comments that Georgia held the "pain of racist oppression" but does not explicitly state what she has experienced in California; what are you meant to conclude?

Writing Assignments

1. Remember a place that was special to you in your childhood. How clearly and specifically can you describe it now? Write a paragraph or two of physical description, avoiding the temptation to explain what it means to you but allowing the images to reveal this meaning through the description itself. How well do you feel you can capture the spirit of the place? Why is it that even apparently simple physical descriptions require such careful attention to writing?
2. An implied theme in Walker's essay is that place affects people's behavior. Consider your own experience. Choose two different

places you have lived, perhaps your current college setting and the place where you grew up, and think about differences in people in those two places. Write an essay in which you analyze these differences while comparing and contrasting those different groups of people.

Cloning for Medicine

Ian Wilmut

Ian Wilmut (1944–) grew up in Coventry, England, the son of a mathematics teacher and housewife. He earned an honors degree in agricultural science at the University of Nottingham and a Ph.D. from Cambridge University, specializing in methods of deep-freeze preservation of boar semen. Wilmut completed other scientific work, on deep-freeze techniques with animal embryos and on the causes of prenatal death in sheep and pigs, before turning to his highly publicized work in cloning. He and his team of scientists at the Roslin Institute near Edinburgh, Scotland announced the birth of Dolly—the first cloned mammal—in 1997 and generated a controversy that continues to spark heated ethical debate. In this article, he presents a "popularized" discussion of work that is discussed in highly technical fashion elsewhere. Note that as he presents the technical information in a readable way, he includes musings on the ethical questions that scientists are sometimes assumed to ignore.

1   In the summer of 1995 the birth of two lambs at my institution, the Roslin Institute near Edinburgh in Midlothian, Scotland, heralded what many scientists believe will be a period of revolutionary opportunities in biology and medicine. Megan and Morag, both carried to term by a surrogate mother, were not produced from the union of a sperm and an egg. Rather their genetic material came from cultured cells originally derived from a nine-day-old embryo. That made Megan and Morag genetic copies, or clones, of the embryo.

"Cloning for Medicine" by Ian Wilmut, published in *Scientific American*, December 1998.

Before the arrival of the lambs, researchers had already learned how to produce sheep, cattle and other animals by genetically copying cells painstakingly isolated from early-stage embryos. Our work promised to make cloning vastly more practical, because cultured cells are relatively easy to work with. Megan and Morag proved that even though such cells are partially specialized, or differentiated, they can be genetically reprogrammed to function like those in an early embryo. Most biologists had believed that this would be impossible.

We went on to clone animals from cultured cells taken from a 26-day-old fetus and from a mature ewe. The ewe's cells gave rise to Dolly, the first mammal to be cloned from an adult. Our announcement of Dolly's birth in February 1997 attracted enormous press interest, perhaps because Dolly drew attention to the theoretical possibility of cloning humans. This is an outcome I hope never comes to pass. But the ability to make clones from cultured cells derived from easily obtained tissue should bring numerous practical benefits in animal husbandry and medical science, as well as answer critical biological questions.

How to Clone

Cloning is based on nuclear transfer, the same technique scientists have used for some years to copy animals from embryonic cells. Nuclear transfer involves the use of two cells. The recipient cell is normally an unfertilized egg taken from an animal soon after ovulation. Such eggs are poised to begin developing once they are appropriately stimulated. The donor cell is the one to be copied. A researcher working under a high-power microscope holds the recipient egg cell by suction on the end of a fine pipette and uses an extremely fine micropipette to suck out the chromosomes, sausage-shaped bodies that incorporate the cell's DNA. (At this stage, chromosomes are not enclosed in a distinct nucleus.) Then, typically, the donor cell, complete with its nucleus, is fused with the recipient egg. Some fused cells start to develop like a normal embryo and produce offspring if implanted into the uterus of a surrogate mother.

5 In our experiments with cultured cells, we took special measures   5
to make the donor and recipient cells compatible. In particular, we tried to coordinate the cycles of duplication of DNA and those of the production of messenger RNA, a molecule that is copied from DNA

and guides the manufacture of proteins. We chose to use donor cells whose DNA was not being duplicated at the time of the transfer. To arrange this, we worked with cells that we forced to become quiescent by reducing the concentration of nutrients in their culture medium. In addition, we delivered pulses of electric current to the egg after the transfer, to encourage the cells to fuse and to mimic the stimulation normally provided by a sperm.

After the birth of Megan and Morag demonstrated that we could produce viable offspring from embryo-derived cultures, we filed for patents and started experiments to see whether offspring could be produced from more completely differentiated cultured cells. Working in collaboration with PPL Therapeutics, also near Edinburgh, we tested fetal fibroblasts (common cells found in connective tissue) and cells taken from the udder of a ewe that was three and a half months pregnant. We selected a pregnant adult because mammary cells grow vigorously at this stage of pregnancy, indicating that they might do well in culture. Moreover, they have stable chromosomes, suggesting that they retain all their genetic information. The successful cloning of Dolly from the mammary-derived culture and of other lambs from the cultured fibroblasts showed that the Roslin protocol was robust and repeatable.

All the cloned offspring in our experiments looked, as expected, like the breed of sheep that donated the originating nucleus, rather than like their surrogate mothers or the egg donors. Genetic tests prove beyond doubt that Dolly is indeed a clone of an adult. It is most likely that she was derived from a fully differentiated mammary cell, although it is impossible to be certain because the culture also contained some less differentiated cells found in small numbers in the mammary gland. Other laboratories have since used an essentially similar technique to create healthy clones of cattle and mice from cultured cells, including ones from nonpregnant animals.

Although cloning by nuclear transfer is repeatable, it has limitations. Some cloned cattle and sheep are unusually large, but this effect has also been seen when embryos are simply cultured before gestation. Perhaps more important, nuclear transfer is not yet efficient. John B. Gurdon, now at the University of Cambridge, found in nuclear-transfer experiments with frogs almost 30 years ago that the number of embryos surviving to become tadpoles was smaller when donor cells were taken from animals at a more advanced developmental stage. Our first results with mammals showed a similar pattern. All the cloning studies described so far show a consistent pattern of deaths during embryonic and fetal development, with laboratories reporting only 1 to 2 percent of embryos surviving to become live offspring. Sadly, even some clones that survive through birth die shortly afterward.

Clones with a Difference

The cause of these losses remains unknown, but it may reflect the complexity of the genetic reprogramming needed if a healthy offspring is to be born. If even one gene inappropriately expresses or fails to express a crucial protein at a sensitive point, the result might be fatal. Yet reprogramming might involve regulating thousands of genes in a process that could involve some randomness. Technical improvements, such as the use of different donor cells, might reduce the toll.

10 The ability to produce offspring from cultured cells opens up relatively easy ways to make genetically modified, or transgenic, animals. Such animals are important for research and can produce medically valuable human proteins.

The standard technique for making transgenic animals is painfully slow and inefficient. It entails microinjecting a genetic construct—a DNA sequence incorporating a desired gene—into a large number of fertilized eggs. A few of them take up the introduced DNA so that the resulting offspring express it. These animals are then bred to pass on the construct [see "Transgenic Livestock as Drug Factories," by William H. Velander, Henryk Lubon and William N. Drohan; SCIENTIFIC AMERICAN, January 1997].

In contrast, a simple chemical treatment can persuade cultured cells to take up a DNA construct. If these cells are then used as donors for nuclear transfer, the resulting cloned offspring will all carry the construct. The Roslin Institute and PPL Therapeutics have already used this approach to produce transgenic animals more efficiently than is possible with microinjection.

We have incorporated into sheep the gene for human factor IX, a blood-clotting protein used to treat hemophilia B. In this experiment we transferred an antibiotic-resistance gene to the donor cells along with the factor IX gene, so that by adding a toxic dose of the antibiotic neomycin to the culture, we could kill cells that had failed to take up the added DNA. Yet despite this genetic disruption, the proportion of embryos that developed to term after nuclear transfer was in line with our previous results.

The first transgenic sheep produced this way, Polly, was born in the summer of 1997. Polly and other transgenic clones secrete the human protein in their milk. These observations suggest that once techniques for the retrieval of egg cells in different species have been perfected, cloning will make it possible to introduce precise genetic changes into any mammal and to create multiple individuals bearing the alteration.

15 Cultures of mammary gland cells might have a particular advantage as donor material. Until recently, the only practical way to assess whether a DNA construct would cause a protein to be secreted in milk was to transfer it into female mice, then test their milk. It should be possible, however, to test mammary cells in culture directly. That will speed up the process of finding good constructs and cells that have incorporated them so as to give efficient secretion of the protein.

Cloning offers many other possibilities. One is the generation of genetically modified animal organs that are suitable for transplantation into humans. At present, thousand of patients die every year before a replacement heart, liver or kidney becomes available. A normal pig organ would be rapidly destroyed by a "hyperacute" immune reaction if transplanted into a human. This reaction is triggered by proteins on the pig cells that have been modified by an enzyme called alpha-galactosyl transferase. It stands to reason, then, that an organ from a pig that has been genetically altered so that it lacks this enzyme might be well tolerated if doctors gave the recipient drugs to suppress other, less extreme immune reactions.

Another promising area is the rapid production of large animals carrying genetic defects that mimic human illnesses, such as cystic fibrosis. Although mice have provided some information, mice and humans have different genes for cystic fibrosis. Sheep are expected to be more valuable for research into this condition, because their lungs resemble those of humans. Moreover, because sheep live for years, scientists can evaluate their long-term responses to treatments.

Creating animals with genetic defects raises challenging ethical questions. But it seems clear that society does in the main support research on animals, provided that the illnesses being studied are serious ones and that efforts are made to avoid unnecessary suffering.

The power to make animals with a precisely engineered genetic constitution could also be employed more directly in cell-based therapies for important illnesses, including Parkinson's disease, diabetes and muscular dystrophy. None of these conditions currently has any fully effective treatment. In each, some pathological process damages specific cell populations, which are unable to repair or replace themselves. Several novel approaches are now being explored that would provide new cells—ones taken from the patient and cultured, donated by other humans or taken from animals.

20   To be useful, transferred cells must be incapable of transmitting   20
new disease and must match the patient's physiological need closely. Any immune response they produce must be manageable. Cloned animals with precise genetic modifications that minimize the human immune response might constitute a plentiful supply of suitable cells. Animals might even produce cells with special properties, although any modifications would risk a stronger immune reaction.

Cloning could also be a way to produce herds of cattle that lack the prion protein gene. This gene makes cattle susceptible to infection with prions, agents that cause bovine spongiform encephalitis (BSE), or mad cow disease. Because many medicines contain gelatin or other products derived from cattle, health officials are concerned that prions from infected animals could infect patients. Cloning could create herds that, lacking the prion protein gene, would be a source of ingredients for certifiable prion-free medicines.

The technique might in addition curtail the transmission of genetic disease. Many scientists are now working on therapies that would supplement or replace defective genes in cells, but even successfully treated patients will still pass on defective genes to their offspring. If a couple was willing to produce an embryo that could be treated by advanced forms of gene therapy, nuclei from modified embryonic cells could be transferred to eggs to create children who would be entirely free of a given disease.

Some of the most ambitious medical projects now being considered envision the production of universal human donor cells. Scientists know how to isolate from very early mouse embryos undifferentiated stem cells, which can contribute to all the different tissues of the adult. Equivalent cells can be obtained for some other species, and humans are probably no exception. Scientists are learning how to differentiate stem cells in culture, so it may be possible to manufacture cells to repair or replace tissue damaged by illness.

Making Human Stem Cells

Stem cells matched to an individual patient could be made by creating an embryo by nuclear transfer just for that purpose, using one of the patient's cells as the donor and a human egg as the recipient. The embryo would be allowed to develop only to the stage needed to separate and culture stem cells from it. At that point, an embryo has only a few hundred cells, and they have not started to differentiate. In particular, the nervous system has not begun to develop, so the embryo has no means of feeling pain or sensing the environment. Embryo-derived cells might be used to treat a variety of serious diseases caused by damage to cells, perhaps including AIDS as well as Parkinson's, muscular dystrophy and diabetes.

25   Scenarios that involve growing human embryos for their cells are 25 deeply disturbing to some people, because embryos have the potential to become people. The views of those who consider life sacred from conception should be respected, but I suggest a contrasting view. The embryo is a cluster of cells that does not become a sentient being until much later in development, so it is not yet a person. In the U.K., the Human Genetics Advisory Commission has initiated a major public consultation to assess attitudes toward this use of cloning.

Creating an embryo to treat a specific patient is likely to be an expensive proposition, so it might be more practical to establish permanent, stable human embryonic stem-cell lines from cloned embryos. Cells could then be differentiated as needed. Implanted cells derived this way would not be genetically perfect matches, but the immune reaction would probably be controllable. In the longer term, scientists might be able to develop methods for manufacturing genetically matched stem cells for a patient by "dedifferentiating" them directly, without having to utilize an embryo to do it.

Several commentators and scientists have suggested that it might in some cases be ethically acceptable to clone existing people. One scenario envisages generating a replacement for a dying relative. All such possibilities, however, raise the concern that the clone would be treated as less than a complete individual, because he or she would likely be subjected to limitations and expectations based on the family's knowledge of the genetic "twin." Those expectations might be false, because human personality is only partly determined by genes. The clone of an extrovert could have a quite different demeanor. Clones of athletes, movie stars, entrepreneurs or scientists might well choose different careers because of chance events in early life.

Some pontificators have also put forward the notion that couples in which one member is infertile might choose to make a copy of one or the other partner. But society ought to be concerned that a couple might not treat naturally a child who is a copy of just one of them. Because other methods are available for the treatment of all known types of infertility, conventional therapeutic avenues seem more appropriate. None of the suggested uses of cloning for making copies of existing people is ethically acceptable to my way of thinking, because they are not in the interests of the resulting child. It should go without saying that I strongly oppose allowing cloned human embryos to develop so that they can be tissue donors.

It nonetheless seems clear that cloning from cultured cells will offer important medical opportunities. Predictions about new technologies are often wrong: societal attitudes change; unexpected developments occur. Time will tell. But biomedical researchers probing the potential of cloning now have a full agenda.

Questions on Meaning

1. In reading scientific writing, scientific terminology is one of the obstacles to overcome. Collaborate with a classmate to develop a glossary of the unfamiliar terms in this article.
2. How does a clone differ biologically from offspring that are conceived and born naturally? According to Wilmut, what medical uses may clones serve in the future?

Questions on Rhetorical Strategy and Style

1. Describe the process of transgenic cloning.
2. Describe the cause–effect relationship between using quiescent donor cells and achieving greater success with cloning.

Writing Assignments

1. Wilmut acknowledges that animal experimentation raises ethical issues, but he suggests that the social benefits of experimentation justify the process. Define the ethical issues that arise from animal experimentation. Go beyond simple imperatives such as "it's not right to hurt animals," to state the reasons behind the ethical stance.
2. Write an editorial that clearly explains cloning and takes an ethical position on the use of cloned animals to serve human health needs.

When We Were Very Young: Archaeologists Uncover Traces of Childhood

Samuel M. Wilson

*Samuel Wilson (1956–) teaches in the Anthropology De-
partment at the University of Texas at Austin. An archaeologist and historical anthropologist, he studies the
prehistory of the Caribbean where he has carried out research on the small island of Nevis for several years. His
books include* The Emperor's Giraffe and Other Stories
of Culture Contact *(1999) and* The Aboriginal People
of the Caribbean *(1997). He publishes widely in academic journals and also writes frequent columns for* Natural
History *magazine, of which the following is a recent representative. This essay illustrates his interest in what artifacts from former inhabitants can tell us about the world
we live in today.*

1   Among the artifacts left behind by the Iroquois people who lived   1
in southern Ontario in late prehistoric times was a miniature
pot made from a lump of clay. A tiny thumb or finger, too
small to be a grown-up's, had shaped the inside of the pot, leaving the
impression of a tiny fingernail. Archaeologists have also recovered
small clay versions of smoking pipes, impractical because they lack
holes. These were children's toys—small and ephemeral, easily over-
looked in the refuse of the past. Just as male scholars were typically

"When We Were Very Young: Archaeologists Uncover Traces of Childhood," by
Samuel M. Wilson, reprinted from *Natural History*, November 1999, pp. 58–61.

once blind to the presence of women in the archaeological record, grown-up archaeologists often don't look for children in the past.

The inhabitants of Cerén, a Mayan site in western El Salvador, fled in A.D. 595, leaving everything in place—crops in the field, pots of food, their most cherished goods. A nearby volcanic eruption covered the whole settlement with ash. Carefully excavated by archaeologist Payson Sheets and his colleagues, this site gives us a remarkable glimpse of life in the Mayan Classic period. One of the houses at Cerén contained a complete inventory of the artifacts of everyday life. Next to an interior doorway, just (in my view) where a kid would sit, was a diminutive pot and a scattering of twenty small shards of pottery. Reporting on these finds, Christian J. Zier remarks (with due scholarly caution) that they "may be the playthings of a child and could indicate that this is a child's room. This statement is tentative at best and will remain so."

In my own excavations in North America and the Caribbean, I have found odds and ends that did not fall into any obvious category: a collection of colored rocks, a few fossilized casts of the inside of shellfish, a half-burned lump of clay with a hole in it, poorly made little arrowheads. Not until I had children and saw their piles of treasure did the finds start to make sense. At times I have come close to throwing away something my children prized, thinking it was a piece of junk, and as an archaeologist I may have done just that with the artifacts of children who lived long ago.

Various unusual things are relegated to the category of "enigmatic finds" and get stuck at the end of archaeological reports. Going over the artifacts from the Israeli site of Tell Jemmeh, Smithsonian archaeologist Gus Van Beek noticed some rounded disks an inch or two across. They were made from pieces of broken pottery and had two holes drilled through them. Earlier archaeologists had taken them for buttons or had simply described them as "perforated disks." But Van Beek saw in them a "buzz," a simple toy he recalled from childhood. To play, you loop string through the two holes and hold one end of the loop in each hand. When the string is wound up and you pull the two ends of the loop apart, the disk in the middle will spin and make a buzzing sound. Van Beek identified archaeological examples of this toy at other sites in the Near East, as well as in Pakistan, India, China, Japan, and Korea. Buzzes have been found in the sites of Native American peoples in North and South America, and even in the remains of British army camps from the Revolutionary War.

5   Children's toys today include many low-tech items that are com-   5
mon around the world. Rattles, whistles, bull-roarers (a slat of wood
tied to the end of a thong and whirled around the head), balls, tops,
and buzzes are fun to play with by themselves. There are also the
pieces and markers that go along with games. The most common
kinds of toys, however, allow children to do things that grownups do,
but on a miniature scale: small versions of hunting and fishing gear,
model boats, baskets, dolls, pots, and plates.

In his *Laws*, Plato argued that "the man who is to make a good
builder must play at building toy houses, and to make a good farmer
he must play at tilling land; and those who are rearing them must provide each child with toy tools modeled on real ones" (translation by
R. G. Bury). I wonder whether Plato ever gave a boy or girl an "educational" toy and then watched as the child made a temple to Diony-
sus out of the box it came in.

In the dry shelters of the Lower Pecos region on the Texas-Mex-
ico border, normally perishable artifacts made of wood, fiber, and
leather have been well preserved. Archaeologist Ken Brown studied
more than a hundred such artifacts, identifying child-size versions of
digging sticks, wood and fiber snares, and netted backpack frames. He
sees these as tools for teaching children how to behave and survive in
the world and, perhaps, even make a small contribution to the group's
quest for food.

In 1879 a famine wiped out the village of Kukulik on Saint
Lawrence Island, south of the Bering Strait between Alaska and
Siberia. Excavation of the site in the 1930s brought to light an extraordinary range of artifacts made of wood, bone, and other materials.
Among the objects were dolls, miniature kayaks, and small carved
bears and seals. Similarly, the prehistoric Thule of Canada and Greenland left behind numerous dolls and miniatures of adult artifacts. In
a recent study, archaeologist Robert W. Park, of the University of Wa-
terloo, Ontario, compared these to the traditional toys of the Inuit,
the Thule's descendants.

A great many archaeologists are justifiably wary of viewing any
given miniature artifact as a plaything. Miniature versions of everyday objects can have potent ritual significance. An exhibit at the
Idaho State Historical Museum in Boise ("Backtracking: Ancient Art
of Southern Idaho") included a number of human figurines identified
as possible dolls. Some Shoshone people who visited the exhibit, de-

scendants of makers of the artifacts, saw them as the powerful representations of the supernatural character Nu'-numbi and perhaps taken from a shaman's paraphernalia.

10   Probably the most famous of prehistoric artifacts that are thought   10
to be toys are the wheeled dogs and other animals from pre-Conquest tombs in Mexico. They have attracted a lot of attention because they show that ancient Mesoamericans understood the principle of the wheel—even though they put it to no practical application, perhaps because they lacked draft animals and lived in mountainous terrain. Archaeologist Francisco Javier Hernandez argued in an extensive study that these were ritual objects (of now unknown meaning) made to be used in burials. This is probably also the case with the elaborate dioramas buried with Egyptian royalty in the third and fourth millennia B.C., in which miniature figures carried the things people would need in the next world.

The idea that artifacts we identify as toys might once have had deeper meanings connects with the influential argument put forward by French historian Philippe Ariès in his 1960 classic, *Centuries of Childhood*. He contended that the Western conception of childhood as a distinct stage of human development and as a protected time of make-believe and play has emerged only in the past few centuries.

A child's early years would indeed have been different in the past, if only because mortality rates and demographics were generally different. In Roman society, for instance, infant mortality may have been as high as one-third of live births, and half the population was under the age of twenty. Some have argued that in prehistory, and even in recent centuries, parents showed relative indifference toward younger children precisely because so few survived. But burials of children with grave goods show that children were cherished as early as Upper Paleolithic times. At the Russian site of Sungir, for example, a man, a girl, and a boy were buried together with ivory spears, stone tools, small animal carvings, and thousands of beads carved from the tusks of mammoths. The grave dates to about 23,000 years ago. Such deliberate burials became more common during the Upper Paleolithic, and through them, children become more visible in the archaeological record.

Although Upper Paleolithic people may not have considered childhood to be a carefree and innocent stage of life, they apparently did distinguish it from adulthood and marked the transition through ritual. Some of the painted caves of northern Spain and southwestern France, including the recently discovered caves of the Ardèche in France, preserve footprints of young people. And the cavern called Gargas, in the Pyrenees, has hundreds of handprints stenciled onto the walls—some, judging by their size, the hands of adolescents or children. These traces may have been left by young people at the time of their initiation into adulthood.

An awareness of childhood can contribute to the more general effort, current in archaeology, to look for individuals in prehistory, to trace families and lineages through time and discover what motivated people to behave the way they did. Formerly, archaeologists tended to view past societies as a composite of integrated subsystems—economy, demography, politics, social organization, and so on. By focusing more on individuals and the choices they confronted, we come face to face with the concrete agents of change in human prehistory. In doing so, perhaps we shall even discover that children were among their societies' most important innovators.

Questions on Meaning

1. The essay notes the many playthings that have been discovered in archeological digs. Early peoples buried toys with dead children. What kinds of toys have been discovered, and what do these toys say about their users and about the parents of the children?
2. Traditionally historians have assumed that children were not so much appreciated in times when infant mortality was high. What evidence does this essay give to the contrary?
3. How do anthropologists know when the concept of the wheel began to appear? What does it mean that the concept preceded the actual use of the wheel in agriculture?

Questions on Rhetorical Strategy and Style

1. The thesis of this essay does not appear until the end of the essay. Why does the author wait until the end of the essay to make his point?
2. The author presents several examples. List these examples, noting the reason for each example.
3. The author gives precise locations and uses detailed names and references. What kind of reader is likely to want this kind of information?

Writing Assignments

1. Try to remember some of your favorite toys. Make a list of the toys you remember, and write about them while reflecting on what they meant to your childhood.
2. Reread a children's book that you enjoyed in your youngest years. Write about your reactions to the book now and about what it means to you.
3. Go to a preschool or day care center and observe children playing with their toys. Then write an essay about their choices of toys and types of play.

The Right Stuff
Tom Wolfe

*Tom Wolfe (1931–), born in Virginia, received his Ph.D.
in American Studies from Yale University. He has worked
as a newspaper reporter in New York and Washington and
has published essays in magazines such as* Esquire *and*
Rolling Stone. *His publications include* The Bonfire of
the Vanities *(1987),* The Electric Kool-Aid Acid Test
(1968), Radical Chic and Mau Mauing the Flak Catch-
ers *(1970),* A Man in Full *(1998),* Hooking Up *(2000),
and* I Am Charlotte Simmons *(2005), The essay excerpted
here is from one of his most acclaimed books,* The Right
Stuff *(1979), which describes the American space program
and the development of astronauts from military test pilots.
In these nonfiction books Wolfe writes in what is often
called the "new journalism," a style of writing in which a
true story is written with techniques of fiction, including
characterization, scene building, dialogue, and narration.
Wolfe is also known for his polished, clever, often exuber-
ant style as well as a satiric tone. Readers are sometimes not
quite sure what to take seriously, or how seriously to take
it. You may find yourself wondering the same at times
about this quality of "the right stuff" in this passage describing the beginning of flight training.*

1   A young man might go into military flight training believing   1
that he was entering some sort of technical school in which he
was simply going to acquire a certain set of skills. Instead, he
found himself all at once enclosed in a fraternity. And in this fraternity, even though it was military, men were not rated by their outward

rank as ensigns, lieutenants, commanders, or whatever. No, herein the world was divided into those who had it and those who did not. This quality, this *it,* was never named, however, nor was it talked about in any way.

As to just what this ineffable quality was . . . well, it obviously involved bravery. But it was not bravery in the simple sense of being willing to risk your life. The idea seemed to be that any fool could do that, if that was all that was required, just as any fool could throw away his life in the process. No, the idea here (in the all-enclosing fraternity) seemed to be that a man should have the ability to go up in a hurtling piece of machinery and put his hide on the line and then have the moxie, the reflexes, the experience, the coolness, to pull it back in the last yawning moment—and then go up again *the next day,* and the next day, and every next day, even if the series should prove infinite and, ultimately, in its best expression, do so in a cause that means something to thousands, to a people, a nation, to humanity, to God. Nor was there a test to show whether or not a pilot had this righteous quality. There was, instead, a seemingly infinite series of tests. A career in flying was like climbing one of those ancient Babylonian pyramids made up of a dizzy progression of steps and ledges, a ziggurat, a pyramid extraordinarily high and steep; and the idea was to prove at every foot of the way up that pyramid that you were one of the elected and anointed ones who had *the right stuff* and could move higher and higher and even—ultimately, God willing, one day—that you might be able to join that special few at the very top, that elite who had the capacity to bring tears to men's eyes, the very Brotherhood of the Right Stuff itself.

None of this was to be mentioned, and yet it was acted out in a way that a young man could not fail to understand. When a new flight (i.e., a class) of trainees arrived at Pensacola, they were brought into an auditorium for a little lecture. An officer would tell them: "Take a look at the man on either side of you." Quite a few actually swiveled their heads this way and that in the interest of appearing diligent. Then the officer would say: "One of the three of you is not going to make it!"—meaning, not get his wings. That was the opening theme, the *motif* of primary training. We already know that one-third of you do not have the right stuff—it only remains to find out who.

Furthermore, that was the way it turned out. At every level in one's progress up that staggeringly high pyramid, the world was once more divided into those men who had the right stuff to continue the climb and those who had to be *left behind* in the most obvious way. Some were eliminated in the course of the opening classroom work, as either not smart enough or not hardworking enough, and were left behind. Then came the basic flight instruction, in single-engine, propeller-driven trainers, and a few more—even though the military tried to make this stage easy—were washed out and left behind. Then came more demanding levels, one after the other, formation flying, instrument flying, jet training, all-weather flying, gunnery, and at each level more were washed out and left behind. By this point easily a third of the original candidates had been, indeed, eliminated . . . from the ranks of those who might prove to have the right stuff.

5   In the Navy, in addition to the stages that Air Force trainees went   5 through, the neophyte always had waiting for him, out in the ocean, a certain grim gray slab; namely, the deck of an aircraft carrier; and with it perhaps the most difficult routine in military flying, carrier landings. He was shown films about it, he heard lectures about it, and he knew that carrier landings were hazardous. He first practiced touching down on the shape of a flight deck painted on an airfield. He was instructed to touch down and gun right off. This was safe enough—the shape didn't move, at least—but it could do terrible things to, let us say, the gyroscope of the soul. *That shape!—It's so damned small!* And more candidates were washed out and left behind. Then came the day, without warning, when those who remained were sent out over the ocean for the first of many days of reckoning with the slab. The first day was always a clear day with little wind and a calm sea. The carrier was so steady that it seemed, from up there in the air, to be resting on pilings, and the candidate usually made his first carrier landing successfully, with relief and even *élan.* Many young candidates looked like terrific aviators up to that very point— and it was not until they were actually standing on the carrier deck that they first began to wonder if they had the proper stuff, after all. In the training film the flight deck was a grand piece of gray geometry, perilous, to be sure, but an amazing abstract shape as one looks down upon it on the screen. And yet once the newcomer's two feet were on it . . . *Geometry—*my God, man, this is a . . . skillet! It *heaved,* it moved up and down underneath his feet, it pitched up, it pitched down, it rolled to port (this great beast *rolled!*) and it rolled to starboard, as the ship moved into the wind and, therefore, into the waves,

and the wind kept sweeping across, sixty feet up in the air out in the open sea, and there were no railings whatsoever. This was a *skillet!*—a frying pan!—a short-order grill!—not gray but black, smeared with skid marks from one end to the other and glistening with pools of hydraulic fluid and the occasional jet-fuel slick, all of it still hot, sticky, greasy, runny, virulent from God knows what traumas—still ablaze!—consumed in detonations, explosions, flames, combustion, roars, shrieks, whines, blasts, horrible shudders, fracturing impacts, as little men in screaming red and yellow and purple and green shirts with black Mickey Mouse helmets over their ears skittered about on the surface as if for their very lives (you've said it now!), hooking fighter planes onto the catapult shuttles so that they can explode their afterburners and be slung off the deck in a red-mad fury with a *kaboom*! that pounds through the entire deck—a procedure that seems absolutely controlled, orderly, sublime, however, compared to what he is about to watch as aircraft return to the ship for what is known in the engineering stoicisms of the military as "recovery and arrest." To say that an F-4 was coming back onto this heaving barbecue from out of the sky at a speed of 135 knots . . . that might have been the truth in the training lecture, but it did not begin to get across the idea of what the newcomer saw from the deck itself, because it created the notion that perhaps the plane was gliding in. On the deck one knew differently! As the aircraft came closer and the carrier heaved on into the waves and the plane's speed did not diminish and the deck did not grow steady—indeed, it pitched up and down five or ten feet per greasy heave—one experienced a neural alarm that no lecture could have prepared him for: This is not an *airplane* coming toward me, it is a brick with some poor sonofabitch riding it (*someone much like myself!*), and it is not *gliding,* it is *falling,* a thirty-thousand-pound brick, headed not for a stripe on the deck but for *me*—and with a horrible *smash*! it hits the skillet, and with a blur of momentum as big as a freight train's it hurtles toward the far end of the deck—another blinding storm!—another roar as the pilot pushes the throttle up to full military power and another smear of rubber screams out over the skillet—and this is nominal!—quite okay!—for a wire stretched across the deck has grabbed the hook on the end of the plane as it hit the deck tail down, and the smash was the rest of the fifteen-ton brute slamming onto the deck, as it tripped up, so that it is now straining against the wire at full throttle, in case it hadn't held and the plane had "boltered" off the end of the deck and had to struggle up into the air again. And already the Mickey Mouse helmets are running toward the fiery monster. . . .

And the candidate, looking on, begins to *feel* that great heaving sun-blazing deathboard of a deck wallowing in his own vestibular system—and suddenly he finds himself backed up against his own limits. He ends up going to the flight surgeon with so-called conversion symptoms. Overnight he develops blurred vision or numbness in his hands and feet or sinusitis so severe that he cannot tolerate changes in altitude. On one level the symptom is real. He really cannot see too well or use his fingers or stand the pain. But somewhere in his subconscious he knows it is a plea and a beg-off; he shows not the slightest concern (the flight surgeon notes) that the condition might be permanent and affect him in whatever life awaits him outside the arena of the right stuff.

Those who remained, those who qualified for carrier duty—and even more so those who later on qualified for *night* carrier duty—began to feel a bit like Gideon's warriors. *So many have been left behind!* The young warriors were now treated to a deathly sweet and quite unmentionable sight. They could gaze at length upon the crushed and wilted pariahs who had washed out. They could inspect those who did not have that righteous stuff.

The military did not have very merciful instincts. Rather than packing up these poor souls and sending them home, the Navy, like the Air Force and the Marines, would try to make use of them in some other role such as flight controller. So the washout has to keep taking classes with the rest of his group, even though he can no longer touch an airplane. He sits there in the classes staring at sheets of paper with cataracts of sheer human mortification over his eyes while the rest steal looks at him . . . this man reduced to an ant, this untouchable, this poor sonofabitch. And in what test had he been found wanting? Why, it seemed to be nothing less than *manhood* itself. Naturally, this was never mentioned, either. Yet there it was. *Manliness, manhood, manly courage* . . . there was something ancient, primordial, irresistible about the challenge of this stuff, no matter what a sophisticated and rational age one might think he lived in.

Questions on Meaning

1. If the "right stuff" is as important to these men as the essay claims, why do they never talk about it?
2. Is having the right stuff completely admirable? Explain and defend your answer using examples from the essay.
3. Although the right stuff is a characteristic of an individual, Wolfe makes much of the social context. The "fraternity" of those with the right stuff is emphasized at the beginning, and the ending note includes those with it feeling superior to those without it. Why is the right stuff, in the context of military flight training, necessarily both an individual and a communal characteristic?

Questions on Rhetorical Strategy and Style

1. The essay uses the rhetorical strategy of definition, attempting to show what the quality the right stuff is. In the beginning Wolfe says the quality is "ineffable"—beyond simple definition with words. As the essay explores this quality, however, it does use many different words to describe those who have the right stuff. Find as many of these descriptive words as you can and explain how they help define this quality.
2. Another rhetorical strategy closely linked to definition is example. What are examples of the right stuff Wolfe describes in detail?
3. Paragraphs 5 and 6, which make up almost half the essay, use narration to tell how these pilots first experience aircraft carrier flight training. Reread these paragraphs. What does Wolfe do stylistically in this narration to make the story enjoyable reading and to define further the characteristic of the right stuff?

Writing Assignments

1. Think of other endeavors in life, outside the military, in which a concept of the right stuff applies. Write an essay in which you define this quality in terms of another profession or avocation, as Wolfe does with flight training.
2. The world described in this essay is entirely male, as military flight training once was. With more women now entering the military, would you speculate the quality of the "right stuff" would change when applied to women? Why or why not? Write an essay in

which you explore what personal characteristics are important in any career situation in which men and women work closely together.

The Struggle to Be an All-American Girl

Elizabeth Wong

Elizabeth Wong, a playwright and television writer, grew up in Chinatown in Los Angeles. Although she resisted, her mother insisted that she learn the Chinese language and culture when she was in grade school. Educated at the University of Southern California (1980) and New York University (1991), Wong has worked as a reporter and taught in the theater department at Bowdoin College. In this essay, which was first published in the Los Angeles Times, *Wong recounts her childhood rebellion against learning Chinese and her adult regret of her assimilation into American culture.*

1   It's still there, the Chinese school on Yale Street where my brother   1
and I used to go. Despite the new coat of paint and the high wire
fence, the school I knew 10 years ago remains remarkably, stoically
the same.

Every day at 5 P.M., instead of playing with our fourth- and fifth-grade friends or sneaking out to the empty lot to hunt ghosts and animal bones, my brother and I had to go to Chinese school. No amount of kicking, screaming, or pleading could dissuade my mother, who was solidly determined to have us learn the language of our heritage.

Forcibly, she walked us the seven long, hilly blocks from our home to school, depositing our defiant tearful faces before the stern principal. My only memory of him is that he swayed on his heels like a palm tree, and he always clasped his impatient twitching hands behind his back. I recognized him as a repressed maniacal child killer, and knew that if we ever saw his hands we'd be in big trouble.

Originally appeared in the *Los Angeles Times.*

365

We all sat in little chairs in an empty auditorium. The room smelled like Chinese medicine, an imported faraway mustiness. Like ancient mothballs or dirty closets. I hated that smell. I favored crisp new scents. Like the soft French perfume that my American teacher wore in public school.

5 There was a stage far to the right, flanked by an American flag and the flag of the Nationalist Republic of China, which was also red, white and blue but not as pretty.

Although the emphasis at the school was mainly language—speaking, reading, writing—the lessons always began with an exercise in politeness. With the entrance of the teacher, the best student would tap a bell and everyone would get up, kowtow, and chant, "Sing san ho," the phonetic for "How are you, teacher?"

Being ten years old, I had better things to learn than ideographs copied painstakingly in lines that ran right to left from the tip of a *moc but,* a real ink pen that had to be held in an awkward way if blotches were to be avoided. After all, I could do the multiplication tables, name the satellites of Mars, and write reports on *Little Women* and *Black Beauty.* Nancy Drew, my favorite book heroine, never spoke Chinese.

The language was a source of embarrassment. More times than not, I had tried to disassociate myself from the nagging loud voice that followed me wherever I wandered in the nearby American supermarket outside Chinatown. The voice belonged to my grandmother, a fragile woman in her seventies who could outshout the best of the street vendors. Her humor was raunchy, her Chinese rhythmless, patternless. It was quick, it was loud, it was unbeautiful. It was not like the quiet, lilting romance of French or the gentle refinement of the American South. Chinese sounded pedestrian. Public.

In Chinatown, the comings and goings of hundreds of Chinese on their daily tasks sounded chaotic and frenzied. I did not want to be thought of as mad, as talking gibberish. When I spoke English, people nodded at me, smiled sweetly, said encouraging words. Even the people in my culture would cluck and say that I'd do well in life. "My, doesn't she move her lips fast," they would say, meaning that I'd be able to keep up with the world outside Chinatown.

10 My brother was even more fanatical than I about speaking English. He was especially hard on my mother, criticizing her, often cruelly, for her pidgin speech—smatterings of Chinese scattered like chop

suey in her conversation. "It's not 'What it is,' Mom," he'd say in exasperation. "It's 'What *is* it, what *is* it, what *is* it!' " Sometimes Mom might leave out an occasional "the" or "a," or perhaps a verb of being. He would stop her in mid-sentence: "Say it again, Mom. Say it right." When he tripped over his own tongue, he'd blame it on her: "See, Mom, it's all your fault. You set a bad example."

What infuriated my mother most was when my brother cornered her on her consonants, especially "r." My father had played a cruel joke on Mom by assigning her an American name that her tongue wouldn't allow her to say. No matter how hard she tried, "Ruth" always ended up "Luth" or "Roof."

After two years of writing with a *moc but* and reciting words with multiples of meanings, I finally was granted a cultural divorce. I was permitted to stop Chinese school.

I thought of myself as multicultural. I preferred tacos to egg rolls; I enjoyed Cinco de Mayo[1] more than Chinese New Year.

At last, I was one of you; I wasn't one of them.

15   Sadly, I still am.   15

---

[1]Fifth of May, Mexican national holiday marking Mexico's victory over France at Puebla in 1862.

Questions on Meaning

1. Why did Wong's mother want her to go to Chinese school? What does she know about Chinese school now that she didn't realize when she was in grade school?
2. Why was the Chinese language a source of embarrassment for Wong?
3. What was the "cruel joke" Wong's father had played on her mother?

Questions on Rhetorical Strategy and Style

1. How does Wong compare and contrast her Chinese school with her American school? Why did she prefer the American school?
2. Sound plays a major role in many of Wong's descriptions. Identify the various sounds that have become part of her memory of Chinese school, her grandmother, and Chinatown. Explain why she remembers these sounds as being pleasurable or discordant.
3. How does Wong's final sentence change the tone of the entire essay? What is the irony of her title as revealed by this statement?

Writing Assignments

1. Describe some objectionable activity you were forced to do as a child because some adult authority figure knew it was good for you. Why did you resist? What was the long-term impact of the activity? What would you do now in the same circumstance with your own children?
2. Write an essay on assimilation. How important do you think it is for immigrants to become imbued in American culture? How much of their own culture should newcomers to this country retain? What conflicts between the past and the future does assimilation create?